The Economic Development of Nations

Consulting Editor
Donald Dewey
Columbia University

THE ECONOMIC DEVELOPMENT
OF NATIONS

JOSEPH A. RAFFAELE
Drexel Institute of Technology

Random House   New York

Copyright © 1971 by Random House, Inc.

All rights reserved under International and Pan-American Copyright Conventions. Published in the United States by Random House, Inc., New York, and simultaneously in Canada by Random House of Canada Limited, Toronto.

ISBN: 0–394–30456–X
Library of Congress Catalog Card Number: 79–126897

Manufactured in the United States of America by Kingsport Press, Inc., Kingsport, Tennessee

First Edition
987654321

Grateful acknowledgment is made to the United Nations Statistical Office and UNESCO for permission to incorporate data for use in tables from the following publications: *Demographic Yearbook, Monthly Bulletin of Statistics, National Accounts Questionnaire,* and *Statistical Yearbook.*

To Pia: For the key to new friends in different cultures

FOREWORD

Among the many consequences of World War II has been a greatly increased concern with the problems of economic development. The liberation of the many colonial countries of Asia and Africa, the spread of revolutionary movements throughout the underdeveloped world, including Latin America, and the heightened awareness by many in the developed countries that a world divided between rich and poor nations is inherently unstable have resulted in widespread efforts to determine the most appropriate policies for economic growth. Many of the specialized agencies of the United Nations have devoted themselves to this topic. The major former colonial countries have continued their economic and cultural involvement with the new nations born out of their empires and have accepted some degree of responsibility for helping them advance. The United States, as the wealthiest country in the world and the leader of an alliance of the affluent noncommunist states, has recognized that much of its overseas concerns must be with the third world of underdeveloped nations. The Soviet Union, as the oldest and most powerful of the communist countries, has also devoted some of its resources to development problems, both within the communist orbit and in the third world. To a considerable extent, the conflict between the communist and noncommunist power blocs, as well as the cleavage between Russia and China for communist hegemony, has involved struggles for influence in the underdeveloped countries.

The interest in the future of the third world has led the developed countries to foster investments, loans, and outright financial contributions manifestly designed to increase the productivity of the poor countries. The more affluent societies have also developed programs to increase the available skills in these nations by contributing to their educational systems, through monetary donations, technical assistance, or the sending of teaching personnel to work in local schools and universities. The need for expertise has also led to many programs that send industrial staffs, government officials, and scholars to work overseas in development programs. On a less savory level, a number of countries have also sought to affect the politics of the third-world countries through direct and indirect intervention in their internal conflicts. Both the United States and the Soviet Union, for example, support large research efforts and political organizations that seek to find the best ways to retain or recruit groups to their "side" in the international struggle.

This partial shift in the political concerns of the powerful nations from their own domestic problems to those of the underdeveloped countries has had a natural effect on the world of scholarship as well. Before World War II, relatively few American academics devoted much attention to the colonial nations or to Latin America. The needs of the government for expert knowledge of foreign areas during the war resulted in language training programs that sharply increased the number of Americans who had fluency in foreign languages. Many of those who have become leading academic authorities on various foreign countries first learned the necessary language skills in military-supported programs during the war. Recognition that the post-bellum United States would be involved in the world resulted also in a sharp increase in funds for overseas research as well as a considerable expansion of academic teaching programs designed to increase the national competency for such work. Both the large foundations and the federal government have made extensive grants to universities for area centers and international institutes. Similar developments have occurred within the Soviet Union, which has also established many area centers within the research academies. To a lesser extent, Britain, France, Germany, and other countries have done the same.

The expansion of academic interest and resources for work on the third world has literally resulted in the emergence of new fields of study within the social sciences. Economics, political science, and sociology have concerned themselves with problems of development. The economic problem has been fairly easy to define: how to mobilize scarce internal and external resources to bring about increased productivity and rising real per capita income. For sociologists, analysis of development has come to mean the study of the ways in which societies change from traditional to modern in terms of values and institutions. This has meant analysis of changing caste-class relationships, attitudes toward work and leisure, shifts in the structure of the family, and the like. Definition of the politics of development has been more difficult because developed countries themselves vary greatly in their political structures. But beyond this, there is no way of defining or measuring what progress in political development means. Scholars thus differ widely as to whether competitive party systems are viable or necessary for developing countries. Although political stability may be better for economic growth than instability, stabilizing regimes that retain social and economic structures that inhibit economic development are clearly retrogressive. Both the Western and communist countries are committed to high expenditures for social welfare purposes. Whether or not such commitments on the part of very poor nations are possible is not clear, however. Some suggest that the welfare obligations inherent in Western welfare state or socialist doctrines, which are generally accepted in the developed countries, have a negative effect on economic growth and value change in the underdeveloped and traditional societies. The rapid diffusion of modern means of communication and literacy in underdeveloped countries, subjects of study in themselves, has contributed both to breaking the value supports for traditional customs in many third-world nations and to raising levels of expectations among their citizenry to a point that cannot be met in any foreseeable length of time.

The heightened interest in problems of development among social scientists has resulted in the emergence of social science as distinct from the social sciences. The fact has become obvious that economists can explain only a part of the factors involved in economic growth. Their favorite variable, capital formation, explains considerably less than half of the variance in comparative statistical analyses. As a result, some economists are trying to incorporate sociological and political factors into their analyses. They are concerned with the social and political requisites of economic growth. Similarly, political scientists who are interested in learning the conditions that affect the ability of the polity to respond effectively to rapidly changing demands on it, in understanding how new political entities attain legitimacy, or in studying the sources of democratic politics recognize that they must concern themselves with topics that were previously of prime interest to economics or sociology. Sociologists, in turn, who are interested in understanding how societies modernize, change their basic values and institutions, and respond to newly emerging class structures, must analyze the factors that affect changing economic systems as well as the conditions that determine political stability, responsiveness to change, and the like.

Although many social scientists recognize and pay lip service to the need to become conversant with the frontier work in development in neighboring disciplines, few have, in fact, done so. Moreover, many of the efforts in this direction are published in the more technical academic journals and monographs, which are unavailable, or unintelligible, to those in other fields. The great merit of *The Economic Development of Nations* is that though written by a competent economist, Joseph A. Raffaele, it is a sophisticated treatment of the political and social problems of development as well. Professor Raffaele undertook an extremely ambitious task, to analyze the factors affecting economic growth, in the communist and noncommunist worlds, as well as in the less-developed parts of the Western world. In so doing, he obviously found it necessary to become a social scientist in order to gain familiarity with the problems of change that concern sociologists and political scientists. He has succeeded admirably in this effort. Clearly, this is as much a work in political science as it is a work in economics. And it will be of great interest to sociologists, anthropologists, and psychologists concerned with the emerging nations. Although written, in part, for use as a text, it is much more than that. The synthesis of information on the various countries of the third world is a creative piece of scholarship. I can only hope that more sociologists and political scientists will show themselves as capable of incorporating the work of the economists into their analyses as Professor Raffaele has done with our fields.

Seymour Martin Lipset

Harvard University
Center for International Affairs

ACKNOWLEDGMENTS

An interdisciplinary approach to economic development of necessity is a product of the assistance of many individuals who are specialists in areas other than one's own. Without listing a catalog of names of these persons, I want to state that without their aid this book would have been impossible.

My particular gratitude goes to two individuals: Russell McLaughlin, professor of economics at Drexel Institute of Technology, for his criticism of the manuscript, and, among the helpful editors at Random House, Mrs. Gloria Klopman, for her meticulous editing of the entire manuscript.

J. A. Raffaele

CONTENTS

PART FOUR THE UNITED STATES AND ECONOMIC DEVELOPMENT

LIST OF TABLES AND FIGURE

part one
SCOPE OF THE BOOK

INTRODUCTION

After more than two decades of immense expenditure of money and talent, the world of economic development is in crisis. Considerable investment outlays have not produced a significant rise in human capacities and in their employment. Instead, developing nations face starvation or semistarvation, rising unemployment, and recurring political crises. Nor is it clear that Americans see the implication of this outcome or the pertinence of the result to poverty in the United States. The issue is no longer whether there will be revolutions, but who will be their managers.

The annual per capita income of most of the world's nations is less than $500. Therefore, the preponderant number of families in most countries live in abject poverty. This means living under the following conditions: a one room dwelling without electricity, water, or toilet facilities or, in some places, living in the streets; one set of clothes per member; a diet of potatoes, rice, or beans that provides fewer than the 2,000 calories necessary to replenish energy consumed; illness as the normal course of events; little or no public services; a normal cash hoard of a dollar or two; and intermittent and unpredictable employment. The children do not attend school, even if one exists, and the parents can neither read nor write. These living standards prevail in a world that spends hundreds of billions of dollars annually on preparation for war.

The failures in developing nations can usually be traced to human deterrents to growth. These deterrents include populations that increase at a faster rate than the increase in productivity; failure to provide them with an educational system that responds to the needs of economic growth; inundation of the cities by an unskilled rural population that is more responsive to Roman circus government than to the dictates of growth; incompetent public administrators; failure to modernize rural areas and the consequent rise of an intractable urban subproletariat; use of international relations by government officials as a power game to obtain the resources of others, which deflects from the central problem of developing on one's own momentum; emergence of the military as a major force with its own needs, which often prevent a broad commitment of the population to growth; and failure to generate a movement that would cause the real wages of the laboring classes to rise faster than the earnings of the wealthier groups in the population.

These events confirm the insight of such men as Frederick Harbison and Gunnar Myrdal that economic development is a process in which an economy triggers a rise in both human capacities and incomes by putting these capacities to a productive use that will generate growth. According to this view, economic development is the evolution of labor utilization in a favorable institutional setting. Economic development is for the poor; its purpose is not just to make the rich richer.

Since the successes of the Western European nations and of those of British origin, only two countries have succeeded in creating a semiautomatic mechanism for economic growth: Japan with an essentially market economy, and the Soviet Union with a socialist system that has been marked by periods of enormous human sacrifice. Both have made considerable investments in human resources. No other development effort in the last half-century has produced similar results in the ascent from poverty.

These two nations have not only enjoyed the premium placed on the creation of human capital but have also benefited from a sense of national identity and social obligation, characteristics that were also shown by the modernized nations of the West in their critical periods of growth. Although the puritan ethic is now obsolete in the West, it is a vital characteristic of early growth. To state the obvious, a rise in the quality of men is crucial to economic development.

Therefore, a human resources approach to economic development is needed. Such an approach takes into account both the requisites and the end purposes of development and focuses on the bottlenecks to building quality producers. It places in perspective studies that seem to be mere statistical exercises rather than analyses of the particular problems facing developing nations.

A developing nation may be defined as one in which a preponderant number of the people are poor and possess low capacities, but where the application of modern technology in industry, agriculture, public administration, education, and institutions is creating a rise in living standards. The poverty is spread throughout most of the territory of the country outside its capital. As a practical reference, the per capita real income of a developing nation is approximately $500 or less.[1]

The line between developing and advanced nations is obscure. As T. W. Schultz states, even portions of advanced countries like the United States show characteristics of underdevelopment. Moreover, considerable variety exists among the developing countries. To place Spain and Upper Volta, for example, in the same category is a strain on credulity. Nevertheless, a broad initial separation between the developing and advanced nations is useful. Therefore, for the purposes of this volume, the following nations and regions are classified as developing: the nations of Asia, with the exception of Japan; of Latin America; of Africa, with the exception of South Africa; of Eastern Europe; and the Mediterranean basin region; that is to say, most of the world.

Although drawing a line at $500 per capita income excludes some countries that appear to be impoverished, a figure of about that amount is reasonable. The estimate should not be interpreted in terms of the purchasing power of the dollar in the United States. A per capita income of $500 does not mean a consumption equivalent to what that sum can purchase in the United States. The fact that the majority of the people in a developing country are working in the agricultural sector indicates that national income figures for these nations tend to underestimate the actual consumption of their people. The dollar figures are more valid in making comparisons between the developing countries themselves. For example, the living standard in Argentina is about twice that of Mexico, as reflected in their per capita income differences.

The difficulties these countries face in modernizing their institutions are attributable in part to the practitioners whose counsel they heed. Those who provide funds for economic development often equate progress with the number of bridges, dams, showpiece airlines, and highly capitalized plants—a view that is shared by politicians in developing countries and by those who control international purse strings. In addition, in their concern for quantitative measures of economic growth, planners may devote too few of their resources to the search for human obstacles to growth.

As a result, the order of precedence goes awry. Attempts are made to measure growth before a determination has been made as to what the indicators of growth actually are. The indexes that are used are those of Western-oriented economics, which are often based on assumptions not applicable to developing nations, and may obscure the search for the real obstacles to growth.

For example, statistics on the national income and the gross national product, from which the national income is derived, can be misleading.

---

[1] For this work, I assumed that a developing nation or region is one with a per capita income of $500 or less in constant prices as of 1964, plus Argentina, Mexico, Spain, Venezuela, and Uruguay.

These concepts were originally developed for mature economies and were later transplanted to the developing areas. Differences in the income of nations are in part a reflection of dissimilarities in the relative importance of the money sector of their economies. As development occurs, the shift in production activity toward sales in the marketplace has an exaggerated effect on growth rates that differs in degree from one nation to the next. When rural persons leave their family groups to become subsistence wage earners in the urban center, the apparent rise in income is an overstatement. Moreover, international comparisons between advanced and evolving economies through the medium of a dollar standard generally understate the actual value of the money of poor countries. This distortion arises from pegging dollar values to foreign currencies based on goods entering international trade rather than on the overall value of the currency in the issuing country. In addition, a good portion of the income of an advanced nation such as the United States should be discounted because of the costs of making that income or of recovering from its side effects. In some countries, the gross national product (GNP) is a political game where the problem of a low rate of growth is solved by recalculating the rate upward.

Consequently, the relationship between the national product and progress in creating human capital is not clear. At a low level of growth, the national product can rise dramatically with large capital projects that do not create long-term employment. As it increases, however, the level of nourishment and employment may fall. Moreover, GNP per capita may be misleading because distortions due to fluctuating rates of exchange are often combined with population figures that have been manipulated for political purposes at home and abroad.

How can actual progress in economic development be assessed? A better measure would be disposable income per household if such a figure were available. Kuwait, for example, has a higher per capita income than the United States, but the income is not spent by the people. On the other hand, statistics on household income for the Soviet Union type of economy take into account multiple job opportunities in the family but not the country's social and health services or the educational opportunities it provides for low-income groups. Consequently, one has to look to the earnings, the job opportunities, and the human capital formation processes in which a population is involved within a particular institutional setting. No single indicator measures the development of nations. If a single available figure has to be chosen, either national income or the more available statistic, national product, is appropriate. The figure should not, however, blind us to the complex facts of development.

Another Western-oriented measure used in assessing the progress of developing nations is capital formation. An estimate of the accumulated stock of physical equipment is important because the rise of such stock in relation to population reflects an increase in the capacity to produce more. Its calculation is subjective, however, and estimates for different nations reflect this fact. In addition, as economies become more sophisticated, additions to capital stock are the means of avoiding net disinvestment. Furthermore, some capital formation does not show up at all in national accounts. Human capital formation is at times underestimated, and many farm improvements do not appear in the official records.

Therefore, neither income nor capital stock formation measures the growth of nations precisely. Doubtlessly, developing nations are poor. But the Western-oriented calculus probably makes them poorer than they actually are.

Because of the shortcomings of income figures, some specialists rely on a composite index that includes food consumption, education, health, clothing, housing, and social insurance. Some of these criteria are difficult to translate into numbers, however. Other specialists use such indicators of industrialization as the amount of cement and electricity consumed, industrial employment, and the ratio of a country's developed regions to its underdeveloped regions. The criteria are important in making an objective judgment as to whether a nation is failing or succeeding in development policy. A balance has to be struck between the sound criteria and the availability of data. Because this book is oriented toward the human factor, judgments in the nation case histories are based on an overall view of employment, wages, education, productivity, the extent of the rise of a new managerial class, the degree of popular support of government, the efficiency of government officials, and the rise of institutions generally conducive to economic development. Because of differences in the criteria employed, different evaluations can be made of the same country. Another writer on economic development thus rates Pakistan as "succeeding," whereas the present writer rates the same country as "failing."

Why are most people in developing nations poor? Each nation presents a special combination of causes that are mutually reinforcing and that are transmitted down through the generations. The presence of one factor brings about the appearance or acceleration of another. These factors are physiological and socioeconomic. The latter factors, it is asserted, include a dearth of resources; a history of exploitation; insufficient tangible capital and technology; a fault in the traditional package of economic policies to bring about an economic takeoff including savings, investment, money supply, taxes, foreign exchange and trade, and marketing; and the characteristics of the poor themselves, including subjective judgments that they do not wish to improve themselves or do not have the ability to do so.

This interpretation throws together causes, symptoms, effects, and shibboleths. Poverty may exist in a nation regardless of whether any one of these factors is present or absent. Poverty may exist in an economy with abundant resources and may be nonexistent in one with scarce resources. The explanation of this paradox is of crucial importance.

The poor do, nevertheless, share some common characteristics. They generally have little faith in human relationships outside their circle of family and friends. They are alienated, not from themselves, as are the affluent in an advanced society, but from those who are successful. They rarely share in decision-making processes beyond the family. If they do, the decisions are often based on trivia. They do not respond to the exhortations of the power structure. A low investment has been made in them. For different reasons, they have little incentive to become more productive. They may spend endless hours trying to grow beans out of a stony soil. The poor are not lazy but trapped.

The implication of these diversities and similarities in world poverty is that no universal remedies exist for it. Although the basic objective in all cases is to raise the quality of human resources, each society is unique. Therefore, practical policies must be tailored to fit its particular exigencies.

The possibilities for self-sustaining growth vary. Some areas resemble a rock pile; some a heap of sand; others convey the feeling of life in a steam bath. Some leaders are trying to develop hide-outs from fifteenth-century barbarians. If some indigenous resource cannot be found and developed economically, a better idea may be to set aside these areas as a preserve or as a tourist attraction.

Economic development is a dynamic process of raising political, economic, and social capacities from the resources that are available to the nation in the long run. Its goal is a rise in the status and living standards of the poor. One cause of rising tensions in the world is that leaders tend to engage in economic and political showmanship rather than pursue this objective.

By such a process of human capitalization, the income of the poor is raised, and institutions and power relations are spawned that create a rise in the number of skilled and influential individuals. A developing nation has to plan the production of goods and services necessary to develop such human capacities. A country training a surgeon in plastic surgery instead of a physician in the cure of amoebic dysentery is not promoting its own development. Indeed much of the resources in developing nations are used for middle-class consumption. Furthermore, the cultural and political institutions that emerge from growth may not be British-American in character. This does not mean that they are necessarily undemocratic, however. In sum, the end result of economic policy is to be appraised according to the overriding purpose of maximizing human potential and putting it to use at a minimum of human cost.

Privileged castes in a society are a deterrent to economic development. A relationship exists between the opportunity for advancement and the extent to which a society is comprised of open and functionally related groups. In a closed system, the interrelation between groups is slight, as is the degree of common values. Leaders hold their positions because of their connections and their social origins perpetuate traditional values to the detriment of change. Young dissidents cannot rise in the society, and conformists cannot be dislodged.

Such a society can grow only if a large segment of the population is given the opportunity to increase its productivity and earn social and economic rewards for doing so. From this group, innovators are likely to emerge with ideas that will receive wide popular support. As more and more people become involved in the growth process, the will to innovate and the capacity to produce with rising efficiency will permeate the society. The increasing productivity will lead to the end product of economic development, the growth of man.

Accordingly, a requisite for economic growth is the will of people to improve their capabilities. They require a sense of self-worth and confidence of their importance in an environment that provides job possibilities for improving skills. To excite such a frame of mind, a widely accepted philosophy is required that holds together the emerging institutions of the society. Without these motives and persuasions, a basis does not exist for the productive use of tangible capital. Nor can it be assumed that oases of industrialization will spread automatically to engulf all of the people.

The components of a developing social system are men, culture, society, and the leader elites that link them. The term "culture" refers to the values that exist within the social system; "society" refers to the various institutional subsystems such as religion, family, polity, economy, and community. The changes the social system undergoes are caused by an imperfect fit of the four ingredients, by competition for influence, and by the rejection of succeeding generations of the ways of their predecessors. The goal of planners is to induce change in the four ingredients consistent with development objectives.

If a nation is to rise from poverty, its development must be viewed in the context of its cultural, social, political, demographic, educational, and institutional setting. The successes and failures of economic development cannot be understood in the absence of such a setting. The task is to relate these segments of the total reality in a manner that can be called a human resources approach to economic development.

A comprehensive strategy is indispensable. If the basic goal is raising the capacities of the people and giving them jobs and status, this strategy must provide for a total effort toward both rural and urban growth. The consequences of treating these interrelated phenomena separately can be disastrous. A free-market economy cannot achieve these transformations. As T. W. Schultz indicates, where contemporary development is based on a market system, one finds a record of inflation, income distortion, and social chaos. Economic and manpower planning is needed because the social structure will not undergo its own reformation automatically.

Economic and manpower planning should be coordinated. A plan with no manpower projection may give only an illusion of progress. The measure of planning success can be gauged by such indicators as labor efficiency in agriculture, industry, public administration, as well as rising educational achievements, participatory democracy, employment, and earned income. In such measures of change, human processes are at least as important as end results.

Raising the level of human capital, modifying obsolete institutions to achieve that objective, and creating new catalysts for change are not the needs of developing nations alone. The poor in American cities have attributes in common with the poor in the Mafia region of Sicily, in Mexico, and in Spain. In the final analysis, an economic system is no better than the men it produces. Developing countries can be laboratories for observing change, the findings of which are applicable to advanced nations. Economic growth is a pervasive force that provides a tool to study emerging currents of change on a cross-country basis.

An enormous amount of resources goes into forced economic growth. India alone can count on about $1 billion annually in its development planning. The funds come from various sources. The United Nations contributes through its specialized agencies including among others UNESCO, the International Labor Organization, and the Food and Agriculture Organization. Advanced nations have their own programs. The International Bank for Reconstruction and Development, commonly called the International Bank, provides government and private loans and grants. Technical assistance also comes from private foundations, such as the Ford Foundation. These organizations have not succeeded, however, in developing institutions to stop the ever-widening gap between the rich and poor nations.

The view of economic development presented in this book can be summarized as follows: The rise in tangible and human capital is the means of obtaining the production with which to achieve a better life. The aim of development is not just more production but the kind of production that provides the possibility of a better life. What constitutes the better life varies among nations and is not measurable by present economic calculus. In any case, development is an unending process and a problem that is not confined to developing nations alone.

The book includes material on the attitudes of people in foreign nations. We must understand how people think before we can understand how they can develop. Yet we have little of such insight. The United States' commitment in developing nations reflects this shortcoming.

The task of this book is to present a survey of world economic development since World War II within the context described. Its premise, influenced by Frederick Harbison, T. W. Schultz, and Gunnar Myrdal, is that contemporary economic development is a concomitant growth of economic and human resources in an environment of political stability, efficient government, and institutions conducive to such ends, a statement that represents no special revelation. The premise is there to see in the successes and the failures of economic development.

No effective institution exists that presents the complex ideas of contemporary economic development in terms understandable to a layman. New ideas are often recorded as dialogues among specialists and, as such, do not have the necessary impact. In an attempt to obtain a wider diffusion, solving the problem of communicating undiluted ideas is at times subordinated to achieving a marketable literary style. There is many a slip between discerning facts behind complex phenomena and transposing them into meaningful and understandable terms.

The pages that follow try to keep the various considerations expressed in this Introduction in balance.

1

TO THE STUDENT AND INSTRUCTOR

The material in this book was originally intended for use in a one-semester course in economic development. The notes that the work derives from went through a series of revisions intended to increase the student's interest, to encourage him to develop his own set of analytical tools, which he can apply to facts collected on his own initiative, and, in conclusion, to present him for his own evaluation a simplified general interpretation of economic development.

Much of the material is derived from on-the-spot investigations made in the Soviet Union, Spain, Argentina, Mexico, and southern Italy, for I agree with the view of analysts at the Economic Growth Center of Yale University that to expect meaningful results by sitting back in the United States and studying statistics of developing nations is to be naïve. Also incorporated in these pages are the findings of such innovators as Frederick Harbison, T. W. Schultz, and Gunnar Myrdal. Some of these pages may seem undiplomatically frank. It seems to me, however, that Gunnar Myrdal is right in his assessment that not speaking frankly about developing nations is tantamount to condescension. The overall purpose is to present in one volume a basic framework of economic development that fits today's realities.

Economic development is the emergence of nations from the vicious circle of poverty. It is not statistics and principles—constructs of the human intellect—*but something that is going on.* To understand economic development, therefore, students must grasp the meaning of events as they evolve. Accordingly, a theoretical base is presented in the first eight chapters followed by national case histories that are representative of different areas in the world. Each chapter is an independent unit.

There is sufficient material in this book for a two-semester course, particularly if the selected bibliographies are used. They contain readings on both advanced and developing nations in order that the similarities and differences between these two types of nations may be compared. There is much to be gained from such comparisons. A limited number of useful and easily available readings are indicated by an asterisk. My teaching experience in Argentina, Mexico, and the United States suggests the advisability of concentrating on general economic development problems in the first semester and on problems and policies of particular nations in the next.

In writing a work on contemporary economic development, one must make difficult choices and decisions. Sources are meager, and improvisation is necessary. Evaluations may not meet the test of time. Because events alter their courses swiftly and unexpectedly, there is an urge to delay writing the last word, but to do so postpones filling a pressing need.

A textbook is a summary of the state of knowledge in a particular field. Yet the choice and synthesis of ideas on economic development are an enormous labor because of the vastness of the subject. The field is claimed not only by economists but by political scientists, sociologists, anthropologists, and psychologists. The scope of a presentation in economics alone—foreign trade, capital formation, investment, and manpower—is enough to fill four volumes. I have thus had to limit myself to factors that substantially explain the modest record of economic development.

The field of labor economics is in a strategic position to make such a synthesis. It borrows such useful concepts from economic theory as supply and demand analysis, allocation of scarce resources, marginal analysis, and relations between labor and capital as factors of production. The most important concept, utilization of labor, gets to the crux of the economic development problem. By "labor utilization" is meant the number of people working in relation to the total population, the duration of their work, and the efficiency with which they work. Economic development strategy comprises a series of coordinated policies in human, tangible, and institutional investments to raise the utilization of labor by increasing the rate of actual hours worked to the theoretical maximum and by raising the efficiency with which such work is performed.

Labor economics does not inherit the weaknesses that are demonstrated when economic theory is used as a tool for studying developing economies. These deficiencies stem from the complacency with which theory treats institutional differences, from the stress that it places on tangible capital formation, and from the emphasis on differences in magnitude instead of differences in kind. Labor economics does not take institutional variations for granted. It focuses on human characteristics.

Because of its eclectic nature, the insights of disciplines other than economics can be incorporated into the analysis. Consequently, this approach furnishes a framework for grasping relationships among tangible capital, human characteristics, and institutions.

The standard works in labor economics are oriented toward economies of the British-American type, however. They are studies of nations with sophisticated methods of organizing labor and capital that made the transition from subsistence to abundance a long time ago. Moreover, they are pertinent to the study of only one-fifth of the world's population. Accordingly, to transfer indiscriminately the concepts and policies of such books to the problems of emerging nations would be misleading. Nor can institutional relationships that influence the utilization of labor in developing nations be inferred from those of modern ones.

It is useful, nevertheless, to adapt the approach of labor economics to the study of emerging nations. By so doing, the student makes the transition from developing to developed societies and back with less difficulty. Perspective is added to his knowledge of both. In this sense, the student who terminates the study of labor with a standard work has traveled only part of the journey. I try, in the chapters that follow, to provide a link between these two worlds.

Some subjects in the typical labor book are de-emphasized. An extended survey of collective bargaining in developing countries, for example, is a waste of scarce pages. A real question exists as to whether an institution such as collective bargaining meets the evolving imperatives of modernizing nations. Where the institution does exist in these countries, it is often a parody of the genuine commodity. In addition, the type of detailed statistical analyses that are made of the wages of highly industrialized nations are too sophisticated for the more simple wage structure of developing nations. Labor organization, however, is given substantial treatment in order that the reader will gain some idea of the political, social, cultural, and economic characteristics of the laboring classes, the power relationships that exist within the respective societies, and the way events are unfolding.

Some topics assume greater importance than others. A discussion of both the population question and the education problem is indispensable. Yet these topics are not discussed in the standard labor works. Of similar importance is the question of how to modify attitudes and institutions that obstruct the development process. This book is heavily weighted with descriptions of cultural characteristics because as developing nations pursue economic development, they undergo cultural change. This is a further reason why one has to be careful in comparing the Western experience of economic growth with the growth that is occurring in these countries in order to determine which facts are relevant. Such an important cultural consideration as the degree of schism existing in their societies is to be found in the discussion of labor organization. To some extent, the differences in subject matter and relative emphasis are shortcomings of British-American labor economics books.

In making these choices, problems of economic development become centered on the human being. With such a focal point, the parameters of economic growth fit more easily into position, and loss of perspective is avoided. The requisites of economic growth appear in the form of individuals with a spirit of inquiry and optimism who translate rising skills and insights into innovation, who take risks, and who shape a society that encourages the appearance of these attributes through monetary and nonmonetary rewards. The framework of the book thus comprises an inquiry into the characteristics of men and their institutions and the relationship of both to economic growth.

Because economic development is a dynamic social process, it is better understood when looked at in historical perspective. Consequently, the scheme of presentation does not employ the abstract economic models based on hypothetical assumptions that are characteristic of deductive economics. To interpret economic development and the human problems that are likely to accompany it, one cannot be detached; it is necessary to feel an intimate participation in the life of those caught in the swirl of change. Such immersion does not mean, however, that one should base his observations on his own needs and values or impute to the poor a sublime mission to perform. It is the means, rather, of controlling the bias that an observer from an advanced society brings to his observation of developing nations.

Two easily made generalizations must be guarded against in maintaining such a historical perspective and sense of affinity. One generalization is to view contemporary development as a repetition of Western economic history. As we shall see later, such a relationship does not exist. A second false generalization is to consider the development of each nation as unique and therefore incomparable. A middle ground must be found between these two extremes.

A book on developing economies that is filled with sophisticated economic principles at too early a stage serves little educational purpose. Rather, a student should be presented with problems, facts, and tentative generalizations as he moves along in his inquiry so that he will be stimulated to test the validity of the author's thesis. In the process, he will have the opportunity to think objectively and creatively and, finally, to reach general conclusions regarding economic development.

To sort out differences and similarities in growth, a geographical classification of developing countries is used, with subclasses within each classification. The general classifications include Asia, the new Black African nations, Latin America, the Mediterranean basin countries, and the nations for which the Soviet Union serves as a model. These areas add up to most of the developing world.

A geographical classification isolates and groups together particular political, economic, and cultural characteristics. This approach reveals the broad differences in cultural systems that produce dissimilarities in problems and outcomes. For example, although similar per capita incomes are found in Brazil and Yugoslavia, these similarities reveal nothing of the differences in the setting of these nations. Moreover, the study of the social cohesion existing within nations is facilitated by separating those that have a colonial history from those that do not. Geographical classification achieves such a sorting.

Within these classifications, the developing countries have political, social, and environmental problems that differ in degree. Rates of progress should be assessed in terms of the relative difficulty of such problems. When applying the same economic calculus to all, differences in rates of progress manifest dissimilarities in the complexity of these problems. The economic calculus available provides the opportunity to make subclasses within the broad geographical classifications and draw comparisons among the five general geographical headings. Accordingly, it is convenient to distinguish among some four or five stages of national development. As assessments of progress are made, one should keep in mind whether a country's problems are on the order of an Ivory Coast, a Colombia, a Mexico, or a Spain.

It was decided not to include a chapter on China in this book because no official data have been coming out of that troubled nation since 1959. Moreover, official information prior to that time is not reliable. The Asian bibliography contains useful works on China, the authors of which have labored well under extreme difficulties. Despite the feuding between China and the U.S.S.R., the problems and emerging institutions of China are reminiscent of those of the Soviet Union in its early period of growth.

A variety of concepts are used in this work and many of them are from the studies of Harbison and Schultz. The term "human resources" refers to the quantity of laborers or potential laborers and to the quality of their skills. The development of human resources is a process of improving economic, social, and political capabilities as they are needed to perform the work of the society in industrial enterprises, agriculture, social and political organizations, educational institutions, and households at a particular level of growth. The "human resource level" is the total accumulation of capacities in relation to the population and represents the production potential of an economy at a particular point in time. It can also be called "human capital." The human resource level of a society is a function of environment, age, education, enterprise, attitudes, and institutions. This may be expressed in the form of the following equation: $HRL = (EN, A, ED, EP, AT, I)$. Inherited capacity is assumed to fall in a normal distribution. "Manpower" is a more restricted concept and refers to individuals who are actually in the development pipeline of education and training, placement, and utilization in an economy.

"Human resource investment" or "human capital investment" refers to any planned activity, including some activities regarded as consumption, that results in a change in skills, attitudes, and well-being and thereby a rise in the total accumulation of human capital. Such planned activity may be in the form of education, health and nutrition programs, or participation in the affairs of society. For a particular human being, the desired effect of such investment is a sustained increase in his physical and mental capabilities and a change in his customary horizon. In terms of human resources, economic growth becomes autonomous when the education and social accommodation mechanisms are so structured that a new human resource problem induces an adjustment without external institutional changes.

"Institutional investment" refers to the restructuring of organizational relationships in agriculture, industry, government, and education, the result of which is a rise in labor efficiency and equality of opportunity as well as attitude changes that are favorable to such outcomes. Free agricultural extension services, worker councils, democratic community planning, and modernization of administrative procedures are examples of institutional investment.

Lastly, by "industrial relations system" is meant the relations, processes, and accommodations between employees, employers, government, and labor organizations, arising from human resources as producers and income recipients.

Out of necessity, material and sources have been used that would be questionable in an investigation of an economy such as that of the United States. These choices were based on whether they test the following theme: that economic development is a process of interaction between rising economic and human capacities spurred by a surge in demand, stable and efficient government, a unifying social philosophy, and institutions that create a network of effective relationships among these factors.

The author of a book on economic development should make explicit the values from which his analysis issues not because they are sacrosanct but because they alert the reader to the manner in which he amasses facts and evaluates policies. If the purpose of economic development is to raise the living standards and status of the poor, then certain goals are "good." These include equality of opportunity in education and employment, democratic participation in society, and modernization of institutions to achieve such ends.

A developing nation is caught in a vicious circle: Its low income produces low savings and investment and low productivity, and the small investment and productivity yield low income. The country is caught in an equilibrium of poverty that perpetuates itself. Attempts to break this cycle tend to be overwhelmed by forces that keep the system in balance. The discussion deals with how a developing nation seeks to break away from this cycle so as to pursue the values stated above.

The major policy areas in economic development include employment,

education, health, population control, community development, land reform, public administration, sources of capital, allocation of capital, and
foreign trade. Economics books generally emphasize the last three
areas.[1] This work stresses the others because they are the principal
reasons for failures in economic development. Nevertheless, comprehensive treatment is given to countries that are models of economic development in different political contexts. The book's crossing of professional
lines arises not from immodesty but because of the difficulty in explaining
to a student what economic development is when confining oneself to
"economic" factors alone.[2]

Statistical data from developing nations should be interpreted with
caution, for they often derive from crude statistical techniques and from
political motives. Nevertheless, the tables in this work are important
because the data from which they are drawn play a part in decision
making. Moreover, the relative magnitudes and changes between countries bear some relationship to reality and are therefore significant.[3]

---

[1] For suggestions on the economic data needed for an analysis of developing nations, see Lloyd
G. Reynolds, "The Content of Development Economies," American Economic Association, Papers
and Proceedings 81st Annual Meeting, Chicago, December 28–30, 1968. Professor Reynolds
suggests (1) growth models, such as factor characteristics of land, labor, capital; (2) sector analysis including the public sector, the modern private sector, the traditional urban activities of trade,
services, and handicrafts, and agriculture; (3) analysis of trade and capital movements; (4) analysis
of growth over time of the agricultural sector, export-import trade, the public sector,
manufacturing, and the interactions among these; (5) comparisons between countries.

[2] The evidence continues to accumulate that the forces that determine a country's capacity for
economic growth are more noneconomic than economic in character. In a study published in
1968, a model was presented based on the economic, social, and political characteristics of
seventy-four underdeveloped noncommunist nations during the period 1957–1962. When the multi-
pliers were ranked in order of importance, the majority of the ones above the median were noneconomic in nature. Important noneconomic factors include social attitudes toward modernization, literacy, secondary and higher education, social mobility, and the extent of the political
leadership's commitment to economic development. The implication is that concentrating investment on these factors would produce a high payoff. See I. Adelman and C. T. Morris, "An
Econometric Model of Socio-Economic and Political Change in Underdeveloped Countries,"
American Economic Review, Vol. 58 (December 1968).

[3] For the areas of capital sources, allocation of capital, and foreign trade, the following reading
is recommended: Antonin Basch, Financing Economic Development (New York: Macmillan, 1964);
Albert O. Hirschman, The Strategy of Economic Development (New Haven, Conn.: Yale University
Press, 1958); Ignacy Sachs, Foreign Trade and Economic Development of Underdeveloped Countries (New York: Asia Publishing House, 1965). The last work is a non-Western point of view and
recommended for this reason.

part two
GENERAL ANALYSIS

2

HOW DOES ECONOMIC DEVELOPMENT TAKE PLACE?

In this chapter, attention is given to representative viewpoints in the social and behavioral sciences on how economic development takes place and to a discussion of the policies that are presently needed to set it off.

Despite differences regarding the best means for energizing a traditional economy, there is a consensus in one respect: A rise in per capita output is an indispensable requisite to economic development. Nobody really believes anymore in the Robin Hood solution to the poverty problem. Nor do economists deny that, in citing as a primary objective a rise in the rate of capital formation, their expectation is an upward surge in per capita income. Without successfully grappling with the question of how to raise human capabilities so as to achieve this goal, modernizing nations do not go too far in their development. Their alternative is to persuade the world to subsidize their living standards permanently.

Observe what this problem of productivity implies. It forces us to ask why these areas are characterized by low productivity and what can be done about it. Our study of economic development should begin, then, with the processes by which a population becomes more productive. Economic development is by and for man, and difficulties in development stem from his nature and from his relations with other men.

Analyzing the nature of these human processes, however, poses a complex problem. Historical data describing the growth of Western nations have limited usefulness as a clue to contemporary development, for the conditions that led to economic growth in the West do not lend themselves to precise intercountry measurement. Although the causes have been subjected to the aggregate analysis of great European minds beginning with Adam Smith, it is difficult to discern from their studies the relative importance of the variables that affected Western development. Even if precise information were available it would not be particularly useful because conditions are different today. A need still exists for a precise weighting of the factors that produce growth and the effects of particular development policies.

A marked difference exists between the quantity and quality of labor during the early stages of Western growth and that in presently moderniz-ing countries. Although they are faced with increasing surpluses of unskilled labor, these newer nations are under pressures from planners to use a technology that is more sophisticated than the technology of early Western development. Therefore, the economic history of a country such as the United States does not suggest a universal strategy for contempo-rary development. The idea of economic growth as a single continuum with countries in line like geese is fascinating but of limited usefulness in selecting the policy that will meet a particular contingency, for progress is not merely a series of stages through which all countries will pass.

The social obstacles to growth in developing countries today did not exist in Western Europe, where labor was more emancipated and enlight-ened. The dominant spirit in the urban manufacturing centers was a demand for equality and achievement and a belief in the right to material acquisition. The emphasis was on cooperation, rather than extreme individualism. These attitudes are important factors in growth.

Within the framework of an acquisitive culture, the West proceeded from subsistence to improved diets, control of family size, better housing, and participation in power by the working class. These changes evolved in successive stages, from the mechanical replacement of human muscle, to mass production techniques that committed unskilled labor, to the sophisticated technology of today. The emerging nations, on the other hand, appear to want to shift overnight from a human muscle economy to automation and from a starvation diet to a television set. The availability of high levels of capital and technology in the West inclines these nations to borrow such factors, with someone else's savings, and to use them inefficiently.

This rush to affluence causes a distortion in perspective. On the first day of development, the miracle of the new steel plant is wrought. On the second and third days are issued the modernized army and the fashiona-ble textile plant. On the fourth, the national airline is trotted out, and on the fifth some agricultural miracle is put together. Consistent with mod-ern times, the sixth and seventh are days of rest. Next week, it will be necessary to shop for more funds. If instant progress does not occur, the blame may be placed on the remnants of colonialism.

SOME CURRENT INTERPRETATIONS

The great classical theories on the economic development of nations were created by such outstanding political economists as Adam Smith, Thomas Robert Malthus, and John Stuart Mill. Their contributions were followed in the first half of the twentieth century by those of men such as Joseph Schumpeter and R. F. Harrod of Oxford.

Our study of theories of economic development is confined to contributions since the beginning of the 1960s because by this time sufficient experience had been accumulated to determine what differences, if any, exist between contemporary economic development and that of the first modernizing nations that the early great political economists wrote about. We shall observe that classical theories and contemporary interpretations are not adequate in several respects: First, the early theories ignored or played down technological change. Second, neither the early nor the current theories account for the problems of changes in attitudes and the modernization of institutions. Third, they do not take into consideration the effect of climate on economic development. Almost all the developing nations are in hot climates where low stamina and debilitating diseases are common and the soil is frequently poor.

Berthold F. Hoselitz

Berthold F. Hoselitz, a distinguished contemporary student of economic development, draws a distinction between autonomous and intrinsic economic growth. Autonomous development is expansionist, in his view, with open social systems and diffused decision making. Intrinsic development is intensive, with a closed social system and centralized management. Hoselitz indicates that although there are exceptions, the growth of the West was on the whole that of the autonomous variety.

The economic evolution of the United States and Great Britain was expansionist in character, Hoselitz states. The United States expanded by extending its borders, and Great Britain by extending its foreign investment. Their experience contrasts with the intensive development of such Western countries as Switzerland and Denmark where economic growth was confined within fixed geographical borders. Therefore, there are not only differences in Western growth, but differences within the differences as well. As a group, the intensive-growth countries show cultural dissimilarities from economies of the British-American type. Moreover, they demonstrate an ingenuity in using export-import trade to compensate for deficiencies in geographical location and economic resources.

Professor Hoselitz suggests that the British-American experience in economic development offers the following insights. A requisite for growth is the introduction of industrialism, or the application of empirical knowledge to the problems of economic and social technology. This industrialism requires a cultural milieu that stresses material welfare and the possibility of solving problems through empirical inquiry. Industrialism also necessitates a political system like that of Western democracies and an economic organization based on private enterprise. In sum, these propositions suggest that an economy without the cultural and political institutions of the British-American system will not have the ability to achieve a sustained and appreciable gain in real income.[1]

Hoselitz's analysis suggests that the social systems of presently developing areas pose barriers to development and that no autonomous force will emerge to loosen these deterrents. Consequently, development in these areas has to be planned; it just does not happen. The history of Western growth is not an example of universal tendencies as much as it is evidence of the fact that certain social structures are conducive to growth. Accordingly, modernizing nations should find a theory of planned economic development more useful for policy making than a theory that interprets the factors that brought about economic growth in the West.

The Western growth took place in countries where the ethic of hard work, equal opportunity, and material acquisition was established in the society and was pursued with the expectation of success. But when these conditions are lacking, how can they be created? Hoselitz's judgment is that these noneconomic factors are important influences on growth and, where absent, have to be encouraged by planning.

It is useful to examine why the rich nations are rich. With the exception of Japan and the Soviet Union, the rich countries are either Western European or are populated by migrants from that part of the world. The economic concomitants of the development of these nations are readily distinguishable: the potential created by the discovery of mechanical energy, an abundance of fuels to provide such energy, a rise in agricultural productivity, an expansion of domestic and foreign markets, a rapid improvement in technology, and, what economists seem to ignore, a physical environment conducive to work. Two important ingredients that go along with these factors are managers of extraordinary abilities who combine economic resources with rising human capabilities to produce considerable wealth and a population possessing a strong incentive to raise its educational levels and well-being.

Man's spirit of critical inquiry of his environment is also important, for these countries with a dramatic history of accelerated economic growth opened up and utilized new resources. Man can take a cautious or indifferent attitude toward natural resources, or he can actually create resources by discovering new combinations of the material that nature provides.

The rich countries of today emerged with governments that were

---

[1] Theodore Morgan, George Betz, and N. K. Choudhry (eds.), "Social Implications of Economic Growth," *Readings in Economic Development* (Belmont, Calif.: Wadsworth, 1963).

relatively efficient. They also had the good fortune of having to deal with a less complex world. The governments of presently developing countries, on the other hand, are often newly established and must enter a competitive, efficient world with unskilled labor and high social costs.

A shift in values preceded the change in the economic structures of the rich nations. The British economist, Richard H. Tawney, notes that the Industrial Revolution was antedated by several centuries of intellectual speculation on the values of human life. Consequently, the economic history of these industrialized nations suggests the importance of cultural changes that stimulate economic growth. In sum, the thesis of Professor Hoselitz appears to be supported by contemporary experience in economic development and by the economic history of the advanced nations.

W. W. Rostow

W. W. Rostow treats brilliantly the time-honored question of the requisites for economic growth. Rostow suggests that a society passes through five stages of growth: the traditional stage of bare subsistence, the stage of preconditions for a takeoff, the takeoff itself, the drive for maturity, and the stage of high mass consumption. In the traditional stage of a society, a high proportion of its resources is in agriculture, little or no upward social movement exists, and its value system is a fatalistic one. In the precondition phase, there is a diffusion of the idea that economic progress is good and possible, accompanied by a broadening of the education effort, a rise in investment (especially in social overhead capital[2]), and a modest beginning in manufacturing. These preconditions are rather fluid in Rostow's analysis and cannot be used in anticipating trends in economic development.

In the takeoff period, the resistance to growth is finally overcome, and economic growth becomes a normal condition of life. According to Rostow's thesis, three conditions are necessary. There has to be a significant rise in the rate of investment to something in the magnitude of 10 percent of the national product. Manufacturing has to become the leading growth sector, with one or two industries showing substantial growth rates. Lastly, a political structure favorable to growth must emerge. The key industries in manufacturing, which one cannot predict, stimulate the growth of lesser industries by providing them with capital goods and materials or by filling the needs of the lesser industries with their products. A successful takeoff requires some three decades.

The drive for maturity is characterized by rising levels of technological sophistication in which the economy can produce almost anything that is desired. The only limitations on production are with regard to choices of product and availability of resources. In the subsequent stage of mass

2 By "social overhead capital" is meant services required for the development of industry such as power, transportation, communications, and other technical services.

consumption, durable consumer goods and services gain primacy in production. The society may now choose between pursuing international power, developing a welfare state, or increasing its consumption further.[3] As Professor E. E. Hagen states, the concept is analogous to an airplane that labors to leave the ground but once aloft continues mechanically thereafter. Rostow estimates that developing countries will require approximately eight decades to reach the point of high mass consumption.

The different economic stages that Rostow describes are logical. The description suggests a faith in an orderly transformation from a bare subsistence economy to one of high consumption in less than a century of effort. It also indicates abrupt transitions in which deterrents to growth dissipate and the next stage erupts. He does not indicate, however, how nations actually experience precondition and takeoff stages.

Rostow shows a laissez-faire bias in attributing specific outcomes to "historical forces" rather than to men operating within the mechanism of government. He does not take into account the fact that pressure groups wanting power may bring about changes in government institutions or that the government itself may anticipate those changes before such pressures occur. Moreover, growth may begin in spite of the presence of an arbitrary government.

A question also arises as to whether increases in social overhead capital and agricultural output precede other advances. In fact, the events of economic growth do not occur in neat linear progression but take place in an irregular and unpredictable locomotion similar to the movement of an amoeba under a microscope.

The significance of Rostow's investment rate of 10 percent is that it exceeds the rate of population growth and thus means a per capita increase in capital investment. In the light of the experience of presently developing countries, this rate of investment is a consummation devoutly to be wished; few countries have such a record. Data for nations suggest a rather disparate rate of growth, accelerating and decelerating in a dissimilar pattern. In general, the acceleration, if it occurs, is slow and uneven.

Obviously, growth is likely to be initiated in one sector of the economy. But where does this sector obtain its self-generating impulse? In a dynamic economy, industries grow and decline at different rates. Growth is interwoven with the state of technological art in a particular industry and does not automatically occur in an industry linked to the expanding industry. Of course, there are differences in the total technological advance of countries within a time period. Making such comparisons of technological change, however, involves an extremely difficult problem of measurement.

[3] W. W. Rostow, *The Stages of Economic Growth: A Non-Communist Manifesto* (Cambridge: Cambridge University Press, 1961).

To criticize aspects of Rostow's interpretation of economic development is not to dismiss it summarily, for it is a substantially accurate description of historical events. It recognizes that economic development is a process and that bottlenecks change over time. Being more taxonomical than analytical, however, it is of limited usefulness as an aid in formulating policies for particular developing nations.

Everett E. Hagen

Professor Everett E. Hagen gives primary importance to psychological factors as causes of economic development. His basic assumption is that the study of societies, being actually an analysis of human behavior, must include a theory of personality. The catalysts of economic growth, Hagen states, are groups that lost status in society several generations earlier and are seeking to regain it as new opportunities arise for upward social movement and as new personality types are molded. Because feelings of inferiority had been transmitted from one generation to the next, the younger generations channel their consequent aggression toward the use of technology and the accumulation of wealth, thereby assuming roles of creative leadership and acquiring some degree of acceptance. The creative individual with the burning desire to perform is not characteristic of the traditional society.

The impetus for economic development thus comes from the children of families without status in the community, and by implication, the pursuit of new technology is not initiated by individuals whose status in the community is already established. Hagen also implies that growth is not blocked by such economic obstacles as a lack of markets for products but by the reluctance of the community as a whole to change its behavior to permit the growth of innovation. Applying this interpretation to former colonial territories, Hagen attributes their developmental failures to the continuance of the same personality disorganization among the indigenous populations that existed when they were under the dominance of colonial powers.

Hagen, in substance, places the chief blame on faulty methods of child rearing. Echoing the pessimism of Freud, he says that little can be done to change the human personality once it has been structured in childhood.[4]

Professor Hagen makes a notable contribution by emphasizing the fact that the personality can act as a deterrent or stimulus in economic growth. Societies have experienced growth, however, without a loss of status by their elite groups and without being hindered by their personality disorganization.

4 Everett E. Hagen, *On the Theory of Social Change: How Economic Growth Begins* (Homewood, Ill.: Dorsey Press, 1962).

David C. McClelland

Professor David C. McClelland also seeks to isolate psychological factors that provide the impetus to economic development. Societies differ, he states, in the extent to which their members possess certain personality traits that stimulate economic growth. Two such important attributes are what he calls the achievement motive, or the characteristic that induces a person to seek solutions to problems, and what sociologists refer to as "other-directedness," or the extent to which individuals respond to their environment.

By tracing the history of twenty-three countries from the time of ancient Greece to the present, McClelland finds a high association between the extent of their achievement motive and their level of per capita income. Furthermore, he discerns that a society characterized by sustained growth is one that has become responsive to public opinion. Social sensitivity is not a characteristic of traditional economies but appears rather early in the development process.[5]

Professor McClelland's analysis raises two central questions: Why does a high level of achievement motivation lead to economic growth, and how can such motivation be developed in individuals? In answer to the first question, McClelland indicates that persons attracted to risk-taking ventures, the outcomes of which can be clearly measured in terms of success or failure, are inevitably drawn to entrepreneurial activity that spurs economic growth. The theme of entrepreneurial drive is a time-honored one expounded by the Austrian-born economist Joseph Schumpeter before World War II. As to the second question, McClelland notes that male children have a high achievement motivation when their sense of initiative is not thwarted by a dominating father and when their mothers reward them for personal accomplishments. As in the case of Hagen, McClelland's explanation of a society of high economic growth is thus based on childhood experience and on culture.

McClelland stresses the introduction of industrialization and group activity as instruments for breaking down traditional thinking and encouraging other-directedness. He does not, however, suggest any methods for encouraging achievement motivation. Furthermore, he merely describes the classic entrepreneur of the economist in psychological terms. Thus each branch of the sciences tends to rediscover in its own terms the insights of another. McClelland's contribution is the technique that he has developed to measure the extent of the achievement motive in a society.

William F. Whyte

To state the obvious, the works of sociologists stress cultural deterrents to growth. Foremost among them are Professor William F. Whyte's

---

[5] David C. McClelland, *The Achieving Society* (Princeton, N.J.: Van Nostrand, 1961).

contributions. Whyte complains of the neglect of cultural problems by the economic development planners. His studies in Peru explore a fundamental question: Why is it that so few firms in that nation are founded and developed by Peruvians? Put another way, why is new entrepreneurship in that country in the hands of immigrants or the sons of immigrants?[6] His answer lies in the cultural characteristics of both native Peruvians and the immigrants.

By "culture" Whyte means the way people think and feel about the world around them, their values. Whyte measured these values in a lengthy questionnaire given to male high school students in their senior year at institutions representing different social levels of Peruvian society. He finds three factors that are significant deterrents to economic development: the low regard for manual work, the suspicious nature of the Peruvian, and, as a consequence of both, the motivational drag on development.

With regard to manual work, Professor Whyte reports that these students had a distaste for blue-collar jobs, even when earnings were comparable to those of white-collar occupations. When asked whether they preferred being a white-collar or blue-collar worker, the students gave the same response regardless of what their social level was or whether they were taking vocational courses.

Whyte also notes a high level of suspicion among Peruvians involved in organizational activity. In his view, this mistrust produces formidable obstacles to the creation of an efficient industrial relations system. Because subordinates cannot be trusted to do the things they have to do unless closely supervised, centralization of control results. Moreover, workers fear that doing something for a colleague may be interpreted as a sign of weakness. Organizations with similar interests find it difficult to develop a collaborating relationship.

In analyzing the motivational drag on development, Whyte found that some 50 percent of the industrial arts students aspired to be small businessmen; only 25 percent chose work in a factory. For those enrolled in other courses, the expressed preferences were government service and banking, with few, if any, choosing factory work or small business. He adds that these individuals, to the extent that they came from well-to-do families, did not feel any aversion to using influence to obtain positions.

Professor Whyte concludes that a country will progress economically if effort and ability are sufficiently rewarded. A deterrent effect occurs if such application is not rewarded or if rewards are distributed to the undeserving. Consequently, the problem lies in providing opportunities for advancement among the children of humble origins, where there is a greater reservoir of effort and ability. If such opportunities for upward social mobility do not exist, they will have to be found. It is not clear

---

[6] It is a universal fact that entrepreneurship derives from foreigners in developing nations: Italians and Spaniards in Latin America, Indians in Africa, Chinese in Southeast Asia, and so on.

what factor in the environment of the boys from elite schools makes them disinclined to exert independent effort. Eventually, Whyte states, by the exercise of influence they assume positions that are important to the economic life of the country.[7]

Do real differences exist between the characteristics of such countries and those of advanced nations? There are similarities in occupational and industrial preferences. The difference of real importance may lie in the degree of effectiveness of interorganizational cooperation. The more advanced countries have managed to construct an industrial relations system that reconciles values, technology, and power relationships. There is no highly industrialized society that does not have an effective system of interorganizational cooperation. Countries in which intense organizational rivalries exist have managed to achieve accelerated growth because the leaders in these countries display an ability to reach a consensus; thus, the anomaly of a proliferation of economic and political organizations and collaborative industrial relationships. The crucial factor often is the ability of production-minded employers to cope with these rivalries effectively.

These analyses of outstanding researchers demonstrate what has happened to the scope of studies of economic development over the years. The pioneering investigators were economists (and also moral philosophers) who analyzed the problem in terms of national economic aggregates. Their approach was impressionistic but remarkably accurate. Because there are no restrictions on entry, the field has been entered by psychologists, sociologists, and even political scientists, each of whom has an explanation of economic development that reflects his own occupational specialty. Sociologists are thus impressed with cultural barriers to development, and political scientists find a high correlation between the existence of competitive political systems such as the British-American variety and the rate of economic development.

In addition, the focus of these inquiries has shifted in 200 years from the study of nations to the study of the attitudes and the behavior of groups in a particular community. As the point of observation shifts downward, the insights of each particular occupational specialty are placed in separate compartments. The one notable exception is the work of Professor Hagen, which seeks to synthesize the contributions of different behavioral sciences. Despite their orientation toward a particular discipline, these ideas are highly useful to a comprehensive explanation of economic development.

As noneconomic explanations proliferate, the core of the economic interpretations continues to be the relation of capital to output. Points of view vary, however, as to what factors cause the evolution of both. For

---

[7] William F. Whyte, "Culture, Industrial Relations, and Economic Development: The Case of Peru," *Industrial and Labor Relations Review*, 16 (July 1963).

example, Hollis Chenery views the process as one that involves a rise in the independent variable capital stock that results from domestic saving or inflows of foreign capital. P. N. Rosenstein is concerned with the effective utilization of the additions to capital stock. T. W. Schultz indicates ways in which this effective utilization depends on the concomitant development of human capital. Arthur Lewis relates the emergence of capital to the condition of the labor supply. In a first stage, according to his view, an infinite supply of labor is available to a sector that starts to capitalize. Capital widening thereupon occurs. In the next stage, as real wages rise because of labor scarcity, capital deepening takes place.

The foreign trade approach also relates to the means of raising capital formation. The traditional exports of a developing nation are primary materials and agricultural products, and its imports are manufactured goods. To finance its rising imports, the country has to increase its exports, and manufactured products provide the greatest opportunity. In so doing, the country increases its tangible capital and its human capital by committing labor to industrial employment.

POLICY IMPLICATIONS

From the nature of economic development, the discussion now turns to present-day policies. Development policies in economies that are not based on the Soviet model focus generally on a prudent allocation of capital investment that is expected to launch a semi-independent mechanism of industrial expansion and rising agricultural productivity. Greater agricultural productivity is to be gained not only through rural investment but also through a reduction in the number of people supported by the produce of the land, principally through migration. Together, these investments are expected to raise the income of the population base faster than the income of others in the society. In furthering this objective, the need of the poor for more food must first be satisfied as quickly as possible. Beyond this goal, increases in consumption take the form of the acquisition of industrial products.

Thus viewed, the policy differences concentrate on investment and savings and on displacement of labor in rural communities. In planning investment, the central concerns are placement of capital and the timeliness of the investment. Differences of opinion occur as to whether or not savings are sufficient, the reasons for existing levels of savings, and why savings are not channeled into productive investment. Lastly, differences center around whether labor should be displaced to other economic sectors in the same community or to established urban centers outside the community and the extent of labor displacement that is desirable.

Such policies imply that (1) human capital growth will result from capital investment and rural migration to urban areas; (2) the necessary shift in employment patterns can be achieved through the market mechanism; (3) the depletion of the supply of talented youth in the rural community by emigration will not cause a stagnation of the rural area; and (4) the helter-skelter erosion of old cultural values in consequence of centralized treetop economic policies will be a stimulant rather than a deterrent to economic growth. These policies thus take certain man-oriented goals for granted by assuming that man will behave in a manner necessary for economic growth. One suspects also that politicians in developing nations feel that such a laissez-faire approach is more rewarding to themselves.

It is apparent, however, that such policies may not create the surge necessary for an economic takeoff. The reason may be a lack of investment in human resources, both productional skills and political and social relationships, as John P. Lewis points out in his book on the economic development of India. The failure of the Indian planner to take seriously this problem of raising and employing human capabilities has brought that country to the brink of disaster.[8]

If man is to behave in a manner necessary for economic growth, two sets of characteristics must be mutually reinforcing: those that inhere in the individual himself and those that derive from the man-to-man relationship. The first includes a man's education and training, his attitudes toward himself, the type and importance of his foremost preoccupations, and his estimate of what constitutes success. The second category includes the social structure of the community, its actual seats of power, the attitudes of men in the community toward one another, the amount of income they are receiving vis-à-vis their contributions to gross income, the intellectual demands being exacted by the community, the job opportunities, and the characteristics of the public and private leadership.

Inquiries are needed on particular sets of these factors to determine their relative importance and the impact that particular policies would have on them. Then some progress could be made in ascertaining the proper policy mix. Such an inquiry is difficult to pursue, however.

As the level of knowledge and discernment rises throughout the world, individuals shape their lives by selecting from an increasingly larger number of alternatives. Accordingly, development policy becomes subject to an increasing number of choices produced by the changes in outlook of the population, unexpected shifts in environment, and new discoveries. To complicate the problem more, it is affected by factors arising from the evolutionary process of change that are often remote from the policy itself. Although the poor are presumably the silent but willing partners of development planners, they can, by their energies or their inertia, bring to naught the policies of professionals.

Here again, economic development policy must be analyzed in terms of particular individuals and institutions, and the economic calculus of

---

[8] John P. Lewis, *Quiet Crisis in India* (Garden City, N.Y.: Anchor Books, 1964).

development—input-output analysis, optimum export-import trade, and optimum capital allocations—must be placed in perspective.

Policy has to address itself to human capital. The inputs needed to raise its quality include not only education and training but also the social, political, and cultural arrangements that contribute to the end result of more productive human beings who have a habit of technical inquiry, persons more capable of solving such problems as finding economic resources, capital placement, foreign trade combinations, and marketing arrangements.

Professor Edward Mason's statement on the requirements of growth provides a concise summary of what development policy should do. He observes that economic development requires a set of institutions, habits, incentives, and motivations of such a nature that the inputs necessary to a continuous increase in output are self-generating. The essential inputs are capital, trained manpower, and technology, and they are likely to be self-generating only in an environment in which the population seeks to improve its physical well-being and in which the rewards of effort are at least roughly proportional to the productivity of the effort.[9]

Economic development means drastic changes. Institutions must emerge whose interaction produces conditions favorable to a rise in human capital. Such change is induced by the rebellion of a new generation that revolts against the status quo and compares present values with what should be. A successful rebellion provides the climate for the new institutions, habits, incentives, and motivations necessary for capital growth.

CAPITAL FORMATION

The need for increasing capital formation raises three fundamental questions. What amount of funds is needed? Where are these funds to come from? Where are they to be invested? Up to a certain point, the answer to the first question depends on how much a developing nation wants to increase its national output annually. Economists develop capital-output ratios that determine the amount of investment necessary to obtain a given increase in output. Although readily computable, these ratios have limited practical usefulness in policy making. They assume the existence of an adequate supply of labor to use the capital. Furthermore, they are actually abstract averages of a wide series of investments. At one extreme, a nation can in theory produce all machines and no butter and, at the other end, all butter and no machines; the limit of investment is what the nation can absorb. For practical purposes, the amount of funds invested is simply the amount of funds that is available for investment.

The sources of these funds may be internal or external. Internal funds

9 Edward S. Mason, "The Planning of Development," in *Technology and Economic Development* (New York, Knopf, 1963), pp. 182–183.

come from private savings (consisting of funds lent privately to others, savings channeled through financial institutions to borrowers, or savings going directly into securities) and from government savings (excess of revenue over expenditures). Principal government revenue sources are taxes and, for some governments, such industrial income as oil exports (Iraq) and cocoa (Ghana). Some governments are reluctant to increase the flow of internal funds by imposing new taxes. A principal source of revenue, agriculture, is often operating at such low efficiency that additional taxation produces a low yield. Some governments, chiefly in Latin America, find it preferable to finance development through a more subtle form of taxation: inflation. But whether or not the use of deficits as a means of raising the rate of capital formation is effective is questionable, for inflation tends to destroy confidence in saving. If kept within bounds, however, it could conceivably produce incentives for employers to increase their production and investment.

External funding derives from donor nations, from lending institutions that offer loans and grants, and from private foreign investors. The flow of external funds is subject to the vagaries of international relations, and developing countries encounter difficulty in paying back their obligations. In some instances, they reach a point where the funds they acquire are consumed just in meeting their international obligations. Consequently, these nations favor soft loans, that is loans made on lenient terms or repayable in the receiving nation's own currency, and outright grants. In the long run, governments have to develop domestic institutions that generate savings and channel them into investment.

Investment is allocated between two categories: human capital and tangible capital. The former is investment affecting the quantity, quality, and distribution of human resources. Tangible capital comprises housing, public buildings, industrial plants, rural improvements, power production, and transportation and communication facilities. Resources should be apportioned to the class of input that promises the greatest increase in productivity. As a matter of policy, the developing nations tend to favor tangible capital over human capital and industrial investment over agricultural investment. But the actual amount of investment in human resources may be underestimated, and, as a result, the rise in output may be ascribed unduly to tangible capital formation.

Table 1 gives a picture of the capital formation situation in developing nations. Generally, countries with relatively low rates of inflation experience also rising capital formation per capita. Table 2 indicates the role of government in investment. Savings represent the surplus of income over expenditures. Investment represents the government portion of gross domestic capital formation combined with contributions from the private sector. A high proportion of government investment may be indicative of high inflation. A sustained galloping inflation dries up savings deposits, bond markets, and life insurance as a source of investment funds. Data

TABLE 1 □ Gross Domestic Capital Formation as a Percentage of Gross National Product, Changes in Gross Domestic Capital Formation, and Rise in Consumer Prices, for Selected Developing Nations and Japan

Country	Capital Stock*	Absolute Change†	Per Capita Change†	Prices‡
Argentina	17.3	steady	steady	1017
Bolivia	16.6	rising	steady	184
Brazil	14.3	rising	falling	3003
Burma	16.4	falling	falling	—
Chile	8.0	falling	falling	632
Colombia	17.4	rising	rising	245
Congo (Leopoldville)	14.4	falling	falling	152
Costa Rica	14.3	steady	falling	112
Dominican Republic	13.5	steady	steady	108
Ecuador	12.2	falling	falling	136
Ghana	13.8	falling	falling	203
India	12.8	rising	falling	161
Mexico	16.7	rising	steady	120
Pakistan	14.6	rising	rising	134
Spain	24.0	rising	rising	166
Taiwan	16.3	rising	rising	156
Japan	31.3	rising	rising	117

Source: *National Accounts Questionnaire,* United Nations Statistical Office, and *United Nations Monthly Bulletin of Statistics.* Data on capital formation for India from W. B. Reddaway, *The Development of the Indian Economy* (Homewood, Ill.: Irwin, 1962).

* Computed from the latest available year between 1964 and 1966.

† Calculated from 1958.

‡ For 1966, with 1958 as a base period.

TABLE 2 □ Government Savings of Developing Nations as a Percentage of Total Government Expenditures and Government Investment as a Percentage of Gross Domestic Capital Formation

Country	Savings		Investment	
	1958–60	1963–66	1958–60	1964–65
Bolivia	3.6	1.8	10.0	12.5
Brazil	—	—	47.4	33.5
Burma	—	—	21.7	49.2
Chile	15.2	8.1	—	—
Colombia	68.7	16.2	—	—
Costa Rica	10.4	8.6	28.1	32.0
Ecuador	26.8	24.6	—	—
India	21.5	12.6	—	—
Spain	54.1	55.9	—	—
Japan	35.9	46.3	31.6	33.3

Source: Computed from *National Accounts Questionnaire,* United Nations Statistical Office.

for Japan are listed in both tables for purposes of comparison.

These data, together with national income information (given in subsequent chapters), suggest the following economic differences between countries at different levels of economic development: Rate of capital formation is associated with level of economic growth. At the bottom of a ranking of countries by per capita income, the rate of capital formation rises with the level of economic growth. At a middle stage, the rate of increase slackens as the proportion of the GNP devoted to consumption rises. At a more advanced stage, the rate of increase rises again as net investment slackens. In addition, the higher the level of economic growth, the greater is the contribution of government to capital formation.

Nations can be classified usefully into five categories: underdeveloped, developing, semideveloped, developed, and advanced. Countries that are exemplary of the first four classes respectively are: Burma, Colombia, Mexico, and Japan. The United States would be an example of an advanced nation. These classifications, although they produce arbitrary results in some instances, allow an assessment of progress based on problems facing a country at a particular level of growth.

Not all developing nations are presented in these and other tables in this book because of the unavailability of data. For example, some countries do not present gross national product and capital formation data in their response to the United Nations questionnaire on national accounts. As these nations catch up with modern statistical techniques, economic development analysis also becomes more meaningful, and the point becomes clear that no single measure exists that indicates unequivocally the extent of a nation's progress. Without corroborative evidence from a variety of approaches, each single indicator, standing alone, can mislead.

An increase in the tangible capital of a developing country would seem to be solid evidence of growth, a manifestation not only of a physical capacity to produce more but also of an increase in the knowledge of the population and its capacity to use this knowledge. Data covering an increasing number of nations suggest, however, that a rise in tangible capital does not assure growth. This information indicates that liberal exchange rates and capital credits may in fact dampen the evolution of widening capital and labor structures. In a noteworthy study, Professor Henry J. Burton examined the growth of five Latin American nations (Argentina, Brazil, Chile, Colombia, and Mexico) in the period 1940–1964. During World War II, firms in these nations were forced to use their capital stock with increasing effectiveness because little capital came from abroad. Consequently, scarce capital was adapted to the existing labor supply, creating a springboard for a rise in labor productivity. After the war, foreign capital became easily available and firms switched to labor-intensive forms of production. Pure productivity growth fell. The emerging economy was based not on local factor endowments but on a rising flow of imports. Competition declined as business concentrated in the hands of politically favored employers. In short, there was a reversion to the colonial-type economy.[10]

---

[10] Henry J. Burton, "Productivity Growth In Latin America," *American Economic Review*, 57 (December 1967).

The experience of these countries suggests that to set off a spiral of rising productivity, the policy of developing nations should be based on growing on their own momentum. Liberal foreign capital movements to such nations may actually curtail their rate of growth.

Summation

The hard fact of economic development seems to be that a sustained rise in human and tangible capital per unit of population is a fundamental requisite. Therefore, the problem is to understand by what processes such an outcome is produced. Initially, foreign capital played little part in the development of the United States, Great Britain, and Japan. Yet the major energies and the most important source of capital of presently developing countries is focused on capital from abroad. In so doing, these countries tend to underestimate their internal human resources problems and ascribe their ensuing difficulties to the policies of wealthy nations and to what some of them call the remnants of colonialism.[11]

The seeming ease with which the West acquired sustained economic growth furnishes the developing world with only a limited example. Development in the absence of considerable government intervention is not possible for the new economies. Such government intervention can, however, be more a symptom of difficulty than a cure. The spread of modern mass communications media has produced a diffusion of knowledge that causes mass discontent. The mass pressures force the government to intervene by transplanting capital and technology that evolved in the West as a gradual process over some two centuries. The modernizing nations embark on a deliberate policy of trying to accelerate change and thereby create social changes that they must control or see their efforts frustrated.

The classical interpretations of economic development do not provide guidelines for policy making in such periods of change. Contemporary theoretical interpretations of economic growth, on the other hand, have biases that reflect the discipline from which they are drawn. Even the useful insights of anthropologists such as Ralph Linton and Clifford Geertz are geared to their discipline. Overall, these modern interpretations stress capital investment, foreign trade, culture, status frustration, achievement motivation, and political systems. Thus, they are partial explanations. Their merit, however, lies in the way they push thought in the direction of an interdisciplinary explanation of economic development, which has as its focal point the human factor in economic growth. The great contribution of Hagen lies in the case he makes that an interpretation that does not combine "economic" and "noneconomic" variables is not an interpretation at all.

[11] W. W. Rostow (ed.), *The Economics of Take-Off into Sustained Growth,* Proceedings of a Conference, International Economic Association (New York: St. Martin's Press, 1963).

Moreover, the development problems of emerging nations vary with the stages of growth. General explanations, therefore, do not address themselves to their problems or to the policies that would deal with them effectively. The policy maker in economic development has to pick and choose, assign relative values, and weave together the different parameters facing the growth of his particular nation.

In the absence of a general theory of planned economic development, growth planning suffers. No theory has been developed as an alternative to the approach of the communist economies. Economic liberalism is beset with many problems, and nations that practice it appear to flounder.

Difficulties occur in approaching development in terms of human evolution. Economists have demonstrated through prodigious efforts in research that human capitalization was a crucial factor in the economic growth of the United States. Yet, the analytical tools for human capital formation have not been developed to the same degree they have been for tangible capital formation. There is an aversion to viewing human beings as capital, even though this is not a demeaning idea and the classical economic notion of labor as an adjunct to machines is a better example of debasement. The economist who views a person as a potential is more idealistic than the lawmaker who treats human costs of production and human obsolescence with less concern than he does the costs and obsolescence of machines. The term "human capital" connotes potential, an ideal that implies the ability to create. Without such a vision of human excellence, the growth of the West might not have occurred. Man might have remained, in the lines of the poet Edwin Markham, a thing with "the emptiness of ages in his face and on his back the burden of the world."

A creative economy is a society of mutual help, mutual honesty, and mutual respect. Subsidies of international banks, foundations, and governments may provide a structural basis for such an economy, but they may also create a dependency and a psychological climate that stifle the growth of human capabilities. Therefore, a concept of human capital is useful for emerging countries. It keeps objectives in perspective and simplifies in some degree the difficult problem of assigning values to development inputs and outcomes. The ethic of efficient work and commensurate rewards may be old-fashioned in the West, but it is highly pertinent in the developing world.

A theory of economic development whose focal point is the human factor may, more than any other approach, remove theory out of its present disarray. In any case, it is clear that as the accumulating interdisciplinary knowledge is synthesized, economic development is likely to become not just a special branch but a very much needed restatement of economics.

3

THE POPULATION QUESTION

The population problem afflicts all nations. For the advanced, it forestalls a life of quality; and for the developing, it is an automatic mechanism for economic growth. An exploration of the population problem is vital.

SCOPE OF THE PROBLEM

There are some 3.5 billion human beings in the world. Every year this number increases by an amount in excess of the population of Great Britain. By the end of the century, the world's population will be more than 6 billion, at present rates of growth. Put another way, although a time interval extending from the beginning of civilization to the beginning of the present century was required to attain a world population of 1.5 billion, it took considerably less than a century to double that number. Should this trend continue, by the year 2500 there will be available for every individual approximately one square yard of the world's surface. Even if by an enormous effort the birth rate is reduced by half, the population will still rise 1.5 billion by the year 2000.

The population problem is not only one of absolute size, nor is it confined to developing countries alone. The progress of all nations is affected by the density, age composition, quality, and rate of acceleration of their populations. But in modernizing nations, these factors, if adverse, are more detrimental because these countries are trying to increase rapidly their rates of economic growth. These magnitudes are not the same for all nations undergoing development, nor would they have similar effects if they were the same. Nevertheless, unless modernizing nations control their populations, they are not likely to make much progress in economic growth.

This chapter is concerned with the factors responsible for the surge in population; the impact of population growth on the economies of developing nations; alternatives and prospects of population control; and the implications of population trends for the world economy.

A population growth rate of only 2 percent can have enormous results. If such a rate of growth were to occur in Latin America, its population, now 200 million, would be 600 million by the end of the century. If the population of the United States were to increase at the same rate as that of Costa Rica, Americans would double in number to some 400 million in the short time of twenty years.

TABLE 3 ☐ Population, Rate of Population Increase, Birth Rate, and Death Rate for Japan, United States, U.S.S.R., and Major Developing World Areas, 1966

Area	Population (millions)	Population Increase	Birth Rate	Death Rate
Western Africa	100	2.3	50	27
Eastern Africa	88	2.4	45	21
Middle Africa	33	1.9	42	23
Tropical South America	135	2.9	43	14
Middle South America	59	3.5	45	10
Temperate South America	36	1.8	28	10
Caribbean	23	2.4	38	14
Japan	99	1.0	17	7
Other Eastern Asia	55	2.8	40	12
Southeast Asia	255	2.6	43	17
Southwest Asia	68	2.4	42	18
Middle South Asia	681	2.5	43	18
U.S.S.R.	233	1.4	22	7
United States	197	1.5	18	9.5

Source: United Nations, *Demographic Yearbook,* 1966.

The highest rate of population growth occurs in areas of deepest poverty, where food production does not keep pace with the population rise. Eight out of every ten of the world's children live in these areas. In Asia's Indus valley, for example, there are ten more mouths to feed every five minutes, at the same time that an acre of ragged agricultural land is lost. The rate of population growth in these areas is much higher than it ever was in the West. To shrug off the problem by thinking that it will eventually decline as it fell in the Western nations is a risky business for developing nations. After prodigious efforts to raise their incomes, the poor nations may find per capita income rising by an imperceptible amount should they manage to keep down the population increase to 2 percent. Because of population pressure, these countries may backslide into increasing human misery (see Table 3).

Population growth estimates are usually intelligent but conservative guesses; the actual percentages may actually be greater. Accordingly, the inability of the world to support its population lies within the realm of possibility. An outstanding student of the problem, Professor Kingsley Davis, notes that "the human population is now growing at a rate that is impossible to sustain for more than a moment of geological time." [1]

The population explosion is only a relatively recent phenomenon in human history. For many years, the population of the world was sparsely distributed and was subject to sharp declines because of warfare, pestilence, and hunger. Not until the beginning of the seventeenth century did the world's population begin to increase.

Like the first economic takeoff of modern times, this population expansion first took place in the countries of Western Europe and was caused primarily by a marked decline in the death rates of these nations, as is the case today in the developing nations. One result of this sharp numerical increase was a series of mass migrations to other parts of the world. In addition, births began to be controlled effectively, in no small way by the postponement of marriage. In rural areas, the procedure of selective inheritance of property that was followed in order to maintain units large enough to maintain a family forced the disinherited either to postpone marriage or to emigrate.

Subsequently, a restraint on population growth was imposed by people's rising expectations of better living standards and their ability to fulfill these expectations. Industrialization and urbanization imposed serious inconveniences on large families. A strong desire to avoid the dissipation of increasing economic opportunities thus acted as a restraint on population growth. With rising living standards, people learned to place a limit on family size in accordance with available economic resources. In this manner, the economic growth of Western European countries, unlike the development of the presently modernizing nations, forged ahead of the rise in population.

A similarly fortuitous experience is not likely to occur in presently developing nations. In the first place, population growth rates of the new nations are considerably greater than the rates experienced by the West. Moreover, the population surge in new nations takes place at a much earlier stage in the industrialization process. Although the death rate in developing countries often falls precipitously, birth rates tend to remain high. The rapid descent in death rates derives substantially from the importation of advanced methods in medicine, public health, and sanitation. The ability to keep a greater number of children alive through prenatal and postnatal care becomes the undoing of development goals. In addition, strong political pressures to provide the poor with food and housing create a potential for an even greater rate of population rise without a concomitant increase in productivity. The technology these

[1] Kingsley Davis, *Technology and Economic Development* (New York: Knopf, 1963), p. 20.

countries borrow from advanced nations thus creates new problems out of the solutions it affords.

Although the drop in death rates is associated with rising economic opportunities in some developing countries, the decline occurs even in nations where no such increase takes place. People in developing nations seem to be twice as fertile as those in advanced economies. In Latin America, as the rate of population increase edges toward 3 percent, the rise in per capita income increases only slightly. According to United Nations sources, during the period from 1950 to 1960, the Latin American population went up 29 percent, compared with a world population rise of 19 percent. Latin Americans seem to prefer to take their productivity rise in babies.

IMPACT ON DEVELOPING NATIONS

Population increase appears to have a depressant effect on economic growth. The argument that the population surge in the West served as a stimulant to economic expansion does not appear to be tenable for the presently modernizing nations. Heads of families in these nations do not command the resources necessary to develop the skills of their children. Developing nations are introduced to a level of technology much greater than the level that existed at the time of the initial surge of industrialization in the West. They have neither the urban opportunities for work nor the chances of mass migration beyond their national borders that existed during the early growth of the West. Urban centers are burdened not only with their own population increase but with the increase resulting from the mass rural exodus as well. The result is a rapid growth of a subsidized mass of unemployed.[2] The population problem thus becomes acute because it inhibits a fundamental requisite for an economic breakthrough: highly utilized, efficient labor.

The population problem can be viewed from two aspects: absolute size and rate of growth. Professor W. B. Reddaway indicates that a large population in itself aggravates problems of growth by the demands that it makes on capital and on consumer goods. A relatively large grant thus becomes infinitesimal when donated to a nation with a large population. For example, of the 3 million tons of food grains furnished annually to India by the United States, the daily per capita allocation amounted to three quarters of an ounce. On the other hand, the purchase by India of such a quantity abroad would have caused a serious burden on her balance of payments.[3]

A significant increase in the rate of population growth increases the demand for capital just to cope with the increment in population. In India, savings must be obtained merely to grapple with the problems

[2] Kingsley Davis estimates that by the year 2000, India's largest city will be inhabited by 50 million people, if present trends there continue.
[3] W. B. Reddaway, *The Development of the Indian Economy* (Homewood, Ill.: Irwin, 1962).

raised by a population increase of 8 million every year before any thought can be given to using savings to increase capitalization per capita. Increased growth rates thus raise not only industrial and agricultural problems but also problems of social overhead capital, including transportation, communication, utilities, schools, and medical facilities.

Populations can be not only excessive but also uneconomically distributed. As was the case in England in the 1740s, big concentrations of the population in one or two urban centers are common in Latin America. Its cities increase at an average rate of 5 percent annually, doubling every fifteen years. The massing of population in the cities localizes capital at the expense of the remainder of the nation and raises the costs of taking care of the unemployed and underemployed. In some of the world, the population rise concentrates in the rural area and becomes excessive in relation to agricultural production.

Developing countries that have high birth rates often have acute food production problems. Many such nations import up to one half of their food supply. The constant threat of hunger does not seem to persuade heads of families to control births, however. The United Nations Food and Agricultural Organization estimates that to provide a minimal diet necessary for productive lives, world food production has to treble by the end of this century.

A surge in population is self-reinforcing. Once the ground swell has begun, a policy designed to restrain it may take many decades to become effective, just as the time required to come to a full stop in an automobile depends upon its rate of speed. The surge creates a younger nation and thus causes a relative increase in the number of individuals with longer periods of fertility. The necessity for restraint becomes evident when a setback occurs in living standards as the increase in the percentage of the younger segment of the population outpaces resources and job opportunities. Because of undernourishment, labor productivity declines. Returns on educational investment decrease. The diversion of income to expanding food requirements siphons off purchasing power that could be used to expand the demand for industrial goods.

Figures on the populations of developing countries in Table 4 indicate that the percentage of the population 19 years of age and younger ranges from 57 for Costa Rica and Mexico to 36 for Japan. The data suggest that the percentage declines as a nation reaches a higher level of economic growth.

In the past a population increase automatically brought about a rise in per capita output; if more mouths had to be fed, more young production hands were available. Today's world, however, does not want unskilled youth as producers. Developing countries, especially, are faced with a rising number of nonproducers relative to producers. Many children of poor countries are consumer nondurables, performing a consumption function during their short time on earth.

The argument can be readily advanced that the relative increase in the youth of rural areas is a growth depressant because per capita income declines. However, to some extent, the young manage to earn their keep, thus forestalling a drop in per capita income. Still, the result is a thinning of education budgets and a decline in parental effort per child.

Population impact can also be determined by analyzing the relationship between population size and total number of hours worked in the whole economy. Up to a point, the hours worked by the rural individual

TABLE 4 □ Total Population of Developing Nations and Percentage of Their Population Under 20 Years of Age, 1962–1965

Country	Population	Percentage
Africa		
Botswana	528,995	53
Central African Republic	1,016,910	45
Congo Republic	12,733,590	46
Gabon	462,000	44
Ghana	6,727,000	53
Kenya	8,636,300	56
Latin America		
Argentina	22,352,000	39
Brazil	70,119,071	53
Chile	7,374,115	49
Costa Rica	1,336,274	57
Dominican Republic	7,630,700	46
Haiti	4,485,000	49
Mexico	44,145,000	57
Asia		
Burma	25,246,000	50
India	438,774,729	49
Pakistan	90,282,674	53
Japan	99,056,000	36

Source: Computed from data in United Nations, *Demographic Yearbook*, 1966.

are limited by such physical factors as endurance or by environmental factors such as the number of daytime hours. A second limitation might be the absence of goods to exchange for his work. Another factor that may restrict work below potential is that the rural worker requires more food as he extends his hours of work. The peasant knows intuitively the truth of this relationship. He does not work harder or longer if the cost of the required additional food exceeds the return gained from the additional work. A fourth limiting factor is the lack of a market for the added output.

A rise in population may not increase the total number of hours worked. In the rural area, although there may be an increase in the total number of persons available for work, the decline in food per capita probably will serve as a brake on any possible increase in hours worked.

In sum, disguised unemployment, rather than additional employment, occurs. As the rural labor market becomes glutted, the possibility of urban employment becomes attractive; furthermore, a day's work in the city, when available, is more remunerative than a day's employment in the countryside. The urban labor market thus becomes glutted, and a rise in urban unemployment occurs. Moreover, the rural worker may view the social services provided in the urban center as an incentive to become part of the urban unemployed. This tendency is strengthened by the fact that rural persons have fewer wants than persons with a long period of urban life. After fundamental needs are met, the opportunity to make more money loses its attraction. The low level of demand is strengthened if a laborer lives in an area that is not exposed to advertising pressures to consume more. The so-called demonstration effect does not occur. The worker's preference for leisure rather than additional employment also means that he is less likely to expose himself to training that would raise his potential. In sum, a population rise may not increase total labor hours, and may actually cause a decline in productivity as urban job opportunities and wages increase.

There is a difficult ethical aspect to the problem of providing incentives to increase labor hours. Shops with consumer goods and high-pressure advertising for consumer goods can be used to whet the appetite of a laborer. Food can be offered at prices lower than the wages received for the extra work. But a point may be reached where providing incentives is a euphemism for manipulation of workers.

In sum, the population question compounds further the already difficult problems of developing nations. Jobs have to be found for an increasing number of unskilled laborers. Decisions must be made as to whether such employment should be developed in rural areas or urban centers. The latter choice faces the hard fact that because of the availability of advanced technology, industry does not readily hire these new members of the labor force, despite the demand for additional output. Employers may supply the additional output by raising productivity rather than by creating new jobs. Therefore, the government may feel forced to subsidize industrial plants to hire laborers of low efficiency in the hope of raising their potential and to avoid being confronted with a rising army of unemployed. The government may thus be compelled to become more paternalistic. An increase in government subsidies may, however, be self-defeating because such assistance neutralizes the restraint that low labor productivity has on the size of the population. In the past, the inability of a people to raise their productivity served as a brake on their numbers. Such is less the case today.

The poverty of a large rural family is self-perpetuating. Each addition to the family increases the possibility of a life of illiteracy and poverty for all. The family head is constrained to exploit the children as soon as possible in order to stop the accumulation of debt and the deterioration of his credit standing in the community. This early exploitation of the children assures their coming to adulthood as unskilled producers who will also have families living in poverty. Patrimony and parent time per child are split into an increasing number of shares. The volume of savings per individual family declines. In fear of poverty, the poor beget as many children as possible only to make their poverty irrevocable and hereditary.

The vicious cycle may be broken when a family member, through an unexpected rise in income, succeeds in accumulating savings. The claims of his family may succeed in dissipating these savings, however. Moreover, the windfall is likely to occur when the more intelligent and more motivated of the family emigrate from the rural area, thereby leaving the community to stagnate further.

Improved living standards often set the basis for future backsliding. A famous publicity photograph in a Latin American country shows a rural family with six small children who are approximately a year apart. The family has been given new housing under the Alliance for Progress program. The mother seems capable of bearing children for at least another ten years, and the enlarged family would probably be accommodated by the new housing. Hence, a cycle from subsistence to higher living standards and back to subsistence in two generations.

EXPERIENCE WITH POPULATION CONTROL

In dealing with population problems, policy makers are faced with two alternatives. They can elect to do nothing and grapple with the attendant problems through a patchwork of relief services and more social overhead costs or they can try to prevent the population increase from occurring. The latter objective is accepted in some areas but meets little receptivity where Muslims and Roman Catholic populations predominate.[4]

The number of births in the rural areas of developing nations tends to reach a biological maximum for a variety of reasons. Women marry soon after puberty, if only to escape the confinement that has been imposed on them since the beginning of this period. These early marriages prolong the child-bearing years and thereby increase the probability of large families. The lack of job opportunities for women further increases the chance of reaching the biological maximum, because jobs postpone marriage and increase incentives for intermittent employment after marriage. Aside from body chemistry, the only real checks on population increase in these areas are stillbirths, infant mortality, and the limited life expectancy of the female, which, however, increases as health and social services improve.

[4] Tunisia is the first Arab country to commit itself to family planning. Its annual population growth rate is 2.5 percent. At family planning clinics, women are given information on how conception occurs and are then informed of possible birth control methods and the advantages of family planning. If they so request, they are supplied with birth control material gratis. *The New York Times,* December 17, 1964.

Because the population is scattered over a wide area, it is more difficult to control births in rural areas than in urban centers, and the control program is costly. Adding to the difficulty is the people's resistance to the efforts of the urban-educated class to control the size of rural families. Attempts to enforce programs on a widely dispersed, suspicious, and illiterate population can become a comical exercise in futility.

The necessity for control can be demonstrated by figures showing the relationship between economic growth and the population explosion. Suppose that a country has an annual growth rate of 4 percent. If the population increases by 2 percent annually, the yearly increase in per capita income is also 2 percent. If the annual per capita income is $300, at the end of 10 years of considerable development effort, per capita income will have increased to approximately $400. If the increase in population is underestimated, however, the rise in per capita income may be nil.

Of the countries where birth control has been tried and where no religious barrier exists, only Japan has had notable success. The point should be made, however, that the Japanese economy was already at a high level of growth when the policy was established and its people were enjoying higher living standards than those of presently developing nations. Therefore, success in the control of births may be attributed more to a change in attitudes as a result of high living standards than to government policy. Some students of the problem, accordingly, take the view that government should forget birth control and seek to improve the productivity of the population despite the obstacles, allowing the resulting change in attitudes to have an effect on births. Other students compare this view to a game of Russian roulette.

In other quarters, the encouragement of emigration from the rural area rather than birth control is proposed as a means of easing population pressure. But the migrant who leaves the rural area because of population pressure is generally the more talented. Resources invested in the depressed area to raise the capacities of the talented are wasted if he does not return, and his savings may also be invested elsewhere. Southern Italy, for example, has experienced an enormous emigration since the beginning of this century; entrepreneurial talent has thereby been provided for northern Italy, Western Europe, and the Americas. But if migration were the answer to the population question, southern Italy would be an economic paradise rather than one of the most depressed areas in the world.

The demands that population control programs make on developing nations are unique. In effect, the governments of these countries are asked to develop attitudes in such a sensitive area as birth control before rising living standards and education make their people more responsive to such an outlook. The Western nations, which did not have to face such a problem, are now in the position of advising developing countries to pursue a course of action not previously expected of them. Modernizing nations are apt to view this counsel of advanced countries with mixed feelings. In addition to the aversion based on religious belief, they may think that a larger population is a source of greater strength and may be suspicious of the advice of powerful nations to limit population growth. These developing nations face an enormous problem of communication between the educated individual and the illiterate rural person on whom the program is focused, especially the rural male, who holds the key to the success of population control programs.

In population planning, as a general guideline, if the social costs of maintaining births exceed their eventual contribution to production, the government can economically devote expenditure to birth control. This production gap looms large in countries where from one-third to one-half of the children die before reaching a productive age and where at any given time about half of the population is living on the other half. The success of the government effort depends largely upon ascertainment of the reasons for large families. An important question is whether the population is increasing because of ignorance of birth control methods or because of indifference to these methods. A government may thus expend resources on techniques that are not used. The suggestion of a prominent economist that developing areas be subjected to a barrage of birth control devices dispersed by airplanes may prove uneconomical. The people below may not use them or may use them mistakenly for ornaments.

There is no substantial information on the extent to which ignorance of birth control methods is a cause of large families. One would suspect that ignorance and choice of control among different methods intertwine. The lack of precise knowledge as to methods probably results in a disinclination to use them. In some cases, incentives to have as many children as possible override any consideration of control. The strong desire of men to perpetuate themselves and the fear of not having a surviving male child for security in old age render meaningless such an abstraction as per capita income. Although control is sound from an economic point of view, it is irrational from the point of view of the family head.

The measures used in government birth control programs may include legalized abortion, education in planned parenthood, a higher minimum age for marriage, birth control clinics, vasectomy operations on males, and taxation of large families. These measures demonstrate differences in effectiveness. Postponement of marriage by raising the age limit may not prevent premarital cohabitation and conception. In some countries, legalized abortion is politically unfeasible. The use of taxation as a method of control is not feasible on social, economic, or political grounds. Such a tax is difficult to impose and difficult to collect; it could even lead to bootleg babies. Similar objections exist to the opposite approach of paying a bonus for practicing birth control. Generally, birth control methods are more easily employed in the middle-class environment of large cities than in rural areas where the problem is more acute.

Vasectomy is an extreme form of birth control consisting of voluntary sterilization of the male. Professor S. Enke reports that some states in India offer a bonus to any married man who has two living children and who, with the consent of his wife, submits to such an operation. As Professor Enke indicates, the strongest objection to vasectomy is that, for practical purposes, such surgery is irreversible. Repugnance against such a method has to be overcome by some reward redounding to the children of the individual undergoing a vasectomy, such as investment in their education.[5]

Where the problem is of massive proportion, as in India, voluntary vasectomy operations are ineffective, so the Indian government has been pressing the use of the intrauterine device as a method of birth control. To a considerable degree, the success of the program depends upon the attitudes of the male.

The regard for human dignity with which some religions approach the question of birth control is understandable. But the argument seems to ignore both the dignity of the women in question and the lack of dignity with which the children of depressed areas live. Perhaps the prime consideration is not that some methods of birth control are more offensive to human dignity than others but rather that the dignity of the women and children of the poor is paramount and is being offended because an effective form of birth control has not been recognized.

The views of the American government have changed with regard to its efforts in support of population control. The government is now disposed to support research and to participate in the development of population strategies and the dissemination of information. The Agency for International Development responds to requests for information on population control methods and on the relationship of population to economic development. Efforts to increase knowledge concerning the factors that affect childbearing are supported, as is the creation of family health and social welfare services in the communities of developing areas. Countries having family planning programs can obtain information on them; the guiding principles are freedom of access to knowledge and freedom of choice. Most governments, however (especially those of Latin America), appear hesitant to go beyond the fact-collection stage of population control. Breakthroughs have occurred in Islamic nations, as in the case of Tunisia mentioned above.[6]

Shifts in attitudes are taking place in the communist nations. Originally, the ideological view was that population problems in the West were a result of neo-Malthusian fallacies. The official view was that no

---

5 Stephen Enke, *Economics for Development* (Englewood Cliffs, N.J.: Prentice-Hall, 1963), p. 379.
6 The United States government has a new Center for Population Research under the Public Health Service.

population problem existed under communism; such problems occur only in capitalist societies because of deficiencies in production and distribution. But the two colossi of the communist world no longer make such statements. Where population pressure exists, communist countries have gone ahead with measures to reduce the rate of increase. Poland, for example, has liberalized abortion laws. Even communist China is finding that investment in birth control programs is a profitable use of resources and has set a target of reducing the population increase to 1 percent. The Chinese also use a Western-inspired term: planned parenthood.

A critical world area for population control is Latin America, where Roman Catholicism is the dominating religion. Some breakthroughs are apparent in the thinking of Roman Catholic theologians on birth control, and prominent Catholic laymen have made contributions in research on birth control methods. The possibility of a significant breakthrough was diminished, however, by Pope Paul VI in 1968 when he ruled out birth control by means other than the rhythm method. Catholic and non-Catholic countries with high living standards tend to have similar low birth rates. The encyclical may aggravate the population problems in Latin American countries where living standards and the level of education are low.[7]

There are many variables affecting birth rates whose interrelationships are not precisely known. They divide between such external factors as employment and such internal factors as attitudes. The econometric models fixing these relationships are useful as an academic tool of analysis in speculations on policy. Even if factors causing behavior of the poor were precisely known, policy has to consider the political situation. The essence of family planning is reconciliation of the social goals of the state with the capacities and proclivities of copulating young adults. The critical decision makers are government administrators and male heads of rural households. It is a combination guaranteed to prevent communication.

Population control does not appear to be obtained by making effective birth control devices easily obtainable. Economic incentives have to be provided to use them. Large families have to be made undesirable through changes in the tax structure and reduction of child-bearing years by prohibition of early marriages.

Summation

The experience of Japan provides clues as to possible outcomes in the population problem of presently modernizing nations. The same marked

---

[7] For an econometric approach to population planning, see Arnold Packer and R. Scott Moreland, "An Adaptive Role-Playing Model for Population Planning," and Marc Nerlove and T. Paul Schultz, "A Demographic-Economic Model of Family Decision-Making," Papers presented at the Annual Meeting of the Econometric Society, December 30, 1969.

fall in death rates was experienced by that country at the turn of the century as industrialization gained momentum. Soon thereafter Japan's birth rate began to decline also, in the same manner as the rate had declined in Western Europe. After World War II, the decline was so sharp that Japan would have found difficulty in reproducing its own population had the drop continued indefinitely. To ascribe the fall in the birth rate to government policy does not appear to be warranted. Nor was legalized abortion the dominant factor. More important was a marked increase in the postponement of marriage and in the use of methods to prevent conception. Japanese families thus reacted similarly to Western Europeans, limiting births in their personal interest rather than for any concern with the question as a national problem. Accordingly, government policy may succeed when the viewpoint of individuals assures the success of such policy. Providing people with educational opportunities and jobs may be the most effective method of birth control.

The idea that the threat of hunger serves as a limit on births appears unwarranted. The poor in a subsistence-level economy do not seem to restrict their numbers out of fear that they will be unable to feed more children. In fact, insecurity impels them to produce more. If such a fear should enter their mind, the feeling is that God or the government will rescue them from their plight. Moreover, the prospect of increased government intervention in the form of a subsidy appears more likely as living standards increase. In effect, the subsidy given to alleviate the problem then assures its continuance.

The idea that developing nations, their populations growing twice as fast as those of advanced nations, are only experiencing an age-old problem that eventually resolves itself may appear to offer some hope. But the facts seem to indicate the contrary. The populations of emerging countries are increasing at an earlier stage of economic development than was the case in Western Europe. A further difference is that in the newer nations neither job opportunities nor real wages rise in proportion to the increase in the labor supply and the workers in these countries have no place to emigrate to.

The issue becomes a question of which event will occur first: a reduction in births or serious conflicts between countries of high population density that share borders with countries of low population density. Moreover, government intervention in economic development creates forces that compel the necessity of further intervention to forestall deterrents to growth such as a population explosion, thereby increasing the potential for international conflict.

The growth potential of a society depends not on the absolute size of its population but on the level of capacity possessed by that population. If the fundamental objective of a society is to raise the quality of men, such a goal cannot be accomplished with a disregard of quantity.

The population increase raises problems for advanced nations also.

For a country such as the United States, additional millions of individuals will compete not for food but for fresh air, space, water, and good schools. As populations of advanced nations jam themselves into metropolitan areas, the right of privacy is at a premium. In a way, the problem for advanced nations is more insidious. Thinking that they can afford large families, the affluent contribute more than their share to the problems raised by population increase.

For the developing countries, population control, in itself, will not result in development miracles. Together with human resources policies, the control of populations assists in generating an industrial revolution. To the extent that population control raises the living standards of individual families, productivity will be increased.

For these areas, the present consequences of overpopulation are clear. Yet one wonders whether the population problem may suddenly vanish, as did the dire prediction of population decline that was made by respectable economists in the 1930s.[8] The economist can afford such speculations either way, but the policy maker cannot. Population policy has become part of the total package of economic development strategy. Its inclusion recognizes the fact that population growth frustrates the major objective of raising per capita income.

Most of the countries that concern us in this book have population growth rates that are considerably higher than those of advanced nations. The initial decline of the death rate in the Western countries came as a *consequence of economic growth* and not because of public health services. In Black Africa and many parts of Asia and Latin America, the trigger of the population rise—public health services—has not yet fully materialized. Furthermore, unlike the advanced countries, the population rise in the developing nations triggers a rise in effective demand that is not matched by an increase in productive power. These are the factors that make the population rise in developing nations so alarming.

[8] For a view of the tapering effect of rising living standards on population growth, see Everett E. Hagen, "Population and Economic Growth," *American Economic Review* (June 1959).

4

DEVELOPING HUMAN CAPITAL

Human capital problems vary with stages of economic growth. In the subsistence stage, the economy is based on agriculture; workers are, in the main, self-employed and generally receive goods rather than wages for their labor when working for someone else. Where no land reform has taken place, many of those who work the land are renting it. The few industrial workers are mostly in construction jobs, small artisanry, and retail trades, or in big industrial enterprises that stand out sharply in the midst of low-scale, inefficient production. The spectrum of occupational specialization is narrow and stable. In short, the labor force is oriented toward a rural economy of low efficiency.

In the first stage of economic growth, a system of money earnings emerges. The poor enter the labor market to work for wages in order to buy goods ranging from textiles to bicycles and shotgun shells. The confines of labor markets broaden beyond native villages, and a classical feature of the labor market in a developing economy appears: a surplus of unskilled labor. In the next stage, a dual economy emerges with a modern industrial sector and the nucleus of an established labor force. The circle of low motivation to work, low productivity, and low wages is partially broken. Labor mobility increases as workers seek higher wages to satisfy their expanding wants and as they become disposed to perfect their skills. Workers are confronted with an increasing number of work alternatives from which to choose. The stock of human capital increases.

This rise in human capital is accompanied by an accumulation of tangible capital. The task of the policy maker is to allocate resources in a manner that assures a harmonious growth of both. Because the gestation period of each of them tends to differ, the policy maker must decide how to make varying investment allocations so as to achieve outcomes desired at different periods of time.

CHARACTERISTICS OF UNDERDEVELOPED HUMAN RESOURCES

The characteristics of the labor force at the start of development are important because inherent in them are the deterrents and catalysts to growth. Economic growth is hindered if workers are illiterate, possess little incentive to raise their productivity, and lack the critical skills needed for modernizing the economy. The general picture of workers in the traditional economy is one of low nutritional levels, inadequate housing, and lack of services to make life easier. The typical laborer in many developing nations is of slight stature and low stamina, possessing little energy or incentive. His labor organization, if it exists, is more an instrument of social and political identification than a means of bargaining over employment terms. Somehow, a spiral of économic growth has to come out of the extensive use of this labor. It is not surprising, therefore, that large enterprises find the provision of substantial hot meals and housing for their employees an economical investment, for these services increase not only the incentives but the quality of the labor force.

The developing economy has to make the transition from agriculture to industry and commit its laborers to an industrial work force (see Table 5). The dilemma that this goal raises is that, to avoid unemployment, the surplus of unskilled and underemployed rural labor must be reconciled with the compulsion of modern enterprises to adopt the highly capitalistic methods of advanced economies. Unemployment raises more difficulties for developing nations than for advanced ones, where the problem is more receptive to monetary and fiscal policies. In modernizing nations, technology and low literacy tend more to shut out individuals from employment. The problem is more acute when one adds to its dimension the small number of days the laborers work each year and the low efficiency with which they work. If they are to make any substantial economic progress, developing nations must commit a rising proportion of their populations to efficient forms of work.[1]

To formulate employment policy, reliable statistical information is needed. Data are required on the number and characteristics of the employed and underemployed, the age and sex of persons in the labor force, and their education, experience, and geographical location. Because of the expense, few nations make this effort.[2] When they do, the enumeration is sometimes made with an eye to political ends.

[1] See W. Arthur Lewis, "Economic Development with Unlimited Supplies of Labour," *The Manchester School of Economic and Social Studies* (May 1954).
[2] As far as can be determined, Iran, in the early 1960s, was one of the first developing nations to take such an inventory.

TABLE 5 ☐ **Index* of Industrial Employment and Production of Developing Nations and Industrial Production as a Percentage of Gross Domestic Product (1958 = 100)**

Country	Employment	Production	Percentage†
Africa			
Cameroon	62	—	—
Gabon	182	—	—
Ghana	152	119	—
Kenya	109	—	—
Nigeria	154	—	11.9
Sierra Leone	193	—	—
Tanzania	101	—	—
Uganda	103	—	—
Zambia	106	115	13.9
Latin America			
Argentina	74	—	38.2
Chile	108	146‡	—
Colombia	113	—	45.5
Ecuador	112	—	19.5
El Salvador	115	184‡	17.8
Guatemala	102	133	10.2
Honduras	78	—	—
Mexico	117	168	35.2
Panama	157	—	31.4
Peru	139	—	38.4
Asia			
China (Taiwan)	153	229	53.9
India	128	162	32.7
Pakistan	135	224	13.0
Philippines	116	145‡	33.4
Other			
Spain	123	169	67.7

Source: United Nations, *Statistical Yearbook,* 1965, and *Monthly Bulletin of Statistics* (December 1967).

* For 1964, except Nigeria (1962) and Peru (1962).

† For latest available year, 1960–1965.

‡ Index of manufacturing.

Labor inefficiency is not necessarily due to a lack of innate capacity. More likely, the low efficiency can be ascribed to a lack of education and work opportunities. The literature on development contains many reports of the successful conversion of illiterate rural individuals into skilled workers after a relatively short training period. The problem is not the incapacity to learn but rather the desire to learn; the best techniques must be found to stimulate this desire, and healthy bodies, capable of making the learning effort, must be developed.

The manager who has been trained in an industrially advanced society may be first perplexed and then irritated when the worker in a developing area fails to take the logical next step in production. The obvious answer —that the worker is lazy—does not take into consideration the fact that the worker may not see the next move, or if he does, may see no reason why he should take it. The worker may not see the consequences of an evolving work situation until a point of crisis is reached. This form of critical, long-range inquiry does not come about readily, especially if one has lived in an atmosphere of servitude and has no zest for learning.

Consequently, the worker in a developing economy must be more closely supervised as part of a well-planned policy to stimulate incentives for raising capabilities. Such training can be more effectively performed by the employer. The necessary increased outlays in capital and personnel may, however, require government incentives to encourage such training.

Men may have an aversion to work. In some countries, the existence of a substantial female work force is considered a mark of male astuteness. The absence of work incentives for men may derive from a power structure that they do not identify with or from cultural values that have been reinforced by a long history of foreign exploitation. (The ethic of the virtue of hard work is confined generally to Western nations and to countries that became heir to that value by migration.) In addition, workers may be forced to live in the hovels of urban centers as the price of staying alive, all the while dreaming of the day when they can escape from their sordid surroundings and return to the rural village. In regions where a strong individualist tradition exists in the culture, incentives are also decreased by an aversion to mass production methods.

Social, political, and ideological cleavages, as well as racial differences, often assert themselves in the employment relationship and reduce work incentives. The resulting inefficiency is indicated by such factors as high absenteeism and turnover, high accident rates, and low-quality output. When the boss belongs to another race, it is silly to work hard and diligently for him and then find oneself out of a job for the effort.

In some areas of the developing world, for example Burma, people may resist industrialization because the society is already doing a creditable job of satisfying human wants. In such instances, discontent may be fostered by making the people aware of the superior living standards of others. To increase the incentive to work, people would have to be persuaded that they really need what they did not want before. Such manipulation, however, raises a moral question of consent.

Social immobility in these areas is a principal deterrent to development. Income above subsistence, educational opportunities, and status in the community are reserved for the few, and the poor, no matter how great their abilities and their motivation for work, may be unable to rise out of their group. The society may be one in which a small group of adults, together with their children, have an inherited right to these returns, to the exclusion of the remainder of the population. With this immobility, and an ensuing sense of injustice, a country finds it difficult to unleash the stream of energies required for its progress. The way to obtain the assistance of the poor in development is to provide new opportunities for them or for their talented children; otherwise, little basis exists for their cooperation.

Responsibilities to the family clan may also impede the increase of human capital. The worker who succeeds in breaking away from the circle of poverty in his community finds an increasing number of relatives feeding at his table. His developing business tends to stay within the family at the expense of efficiency, and his mobility is stifled by these attachments. Paternalism may also spill over into the political arena, where elected politicians often push the interests of certain families at the expense of others. Although the extended family may provide a rational answer in a hostile environment where resources and opportunities are scarce, it must be readapted in an atmosphere of opportunity. A family business usually shows resistance to techniques for increasing productivity, but this type of association can be used as a basis of cooperative factory relationships. The problem of development generally is how best to employ traditional institutions in the service of desired change.

A major feature of a subsistence economy is the deceptive appearance of a labor surplus. There seem to be too many people at work on a particular chore, too many others idling about. In this situation, the economist asks himself how the surplus can be shifted elsewhere and why the wage does not fall until the labor supply is fully employed.

Actually, the unemployment is more apparent than real; almost everyone is needed at some time during the year. During the peak of production, the work that has to be done requires more workers than the number of people available to do it. Nor does the reserve of underemployed act as a depressant on wages. Theoretically, lowering the wage below the level needed for subsistence could reduce the labor supply to zero.

Social and political restraints on the employer force him to pay a wage that is considered an irreducible minimum rather than one reflecting individual productivity. If he is in a monopsonistic position, rather than force wages down to the limits of his power, he is more likely to seek social respectability by setting rates higher than the prevailing wage level. The wage of the laborer may also reflect his social standing rather than his productivity. Yet a developing nation can least afford such a system of wage payment. In brief, factors on the demand and supply side of labor in a developing economy do not behave in the manner they do in advanced economies.

Koji Taira has drawn some conclusions about wage differentials in developing countries, although he notes the difficulties of international comparisons due to a lack of standardization of data. First, the differences in wages between the skilled and unskilled blue-collar workers are greater in developing countries, reflecting, in Taira's judgment, a greater scarcity of skills in those countries. Second, differences between manual and nonmanual occupations are also wider. Third, unlike manual skill differentials, white-collar occupational differentials seem to be widening in developing nations. Lastly, this change is a product of the evolution of a labor force commitment to a modern economy as nations shift from underdevelopment to industrialization.[3]

A rise in education in developing nations affects wage differentials in some occupations by affecting job attitudes. For example, the rubber worker in Africa who becomes literate begins to disdain work on the plantation and, by so doing, creates upward pressures on plantation wages.

An impressive characteristic of the economic activity of laborers in a subsistence economy is trading. An extraordinary number of individuals are involved in the selling of goods, mostly on a part-time basis. These goods range from food to imported merchandise, from empty beer bottles to clandestine imports of clothing. The returns may range from a few pennies for a day's work to a windfall for individuals who use their ingenuity not to create production facilities but to consummate a sharp trade.[4] This large volume of trade activity is found everywhere: Africa, Asia, and Latin America. Yet it does not enter into the statistics on the occupational distribution of the labor force and is not considered adequately in theories of economic development.[5]

These part-time activities are proof of the difficulty of measuring the actual amount of work performed in these economies. The enumeration of laborers by regular occupation underestimates the amount of work actually performed. Every able-bodied person from preschool age upward is working at some time or another during the year, but not necessarily for wages. Moreover, the intermittent employment shifts between agriculture, industry, and trade, depending upon the rhythm of agriculture. Under these conditions, statistics on the number of employed and unemployed or the occupational distribution of the labor force should be treated warily, for they do not reflect the extent of the job shifting done by the population. The poor are masters of daily improvisation, and the low level of skill content in jobs makes their shifting among occupations easier.

In addition, the economic activity peculiar to traditional economies creates jobs that do not exist in highly industrialized economies. *The Occupational Handbook of the United States,* for example, does not list

[3] Koji Taira, "Wage Differentials in Developing Countries," *International Labour Review,* Vol. 93 (March 1966).
[4] In Rio de Janeiro, vendors of candy-coated peanuts at 2 cents a bag are lined up one behind the other. In another Latin American country, women returning by plane from the United States sell imports they have worn en route at a price covering the cost of the plane trip.
[5] See P. T. Bauer and B. S. Yamey, "Economic Progress and Occupational Distribution," *Economic Journal,* Vol. 61 (December 1951).

agricultural mediator, job broker, letter writer, town crier, or specialist in thatched roofs.

The data on wages paid in developing nations should also be treated warily. They often show wages as low as 3 or 4 percent of the wage level in the United States. The low wage is supplemented in some way, however; it may be by a variety of menial tasks performed by the family in return for goods and services, by supplies of goods and services where employment is with a large firm, or by family allowances. Laborers can manage to consume more than they earn by obtaining credit from money lenders and storekeepers, credit that becomes so heavy that liquidating it is impossible even in a lifetime of work. Under these conditions, a wage increase means a faster reduction of debt rather than a rise in investment or a further rise in consumption.

Some doubt exists as to whether the narrowing of the wage structure of blue-collar workers in these economies acts as a depressant to growth. One can argue that paying workers of low skills more than the value of their product destroys incentives to prepare for skilled occupations. On the other hand, one can also contend that subsidizing unskilled workers is an investment for the industrial commitment of rural workers and that economic growth would lag without such a commitment.

These characteristics of labor in developing economies weigh more heavily in some countries than they do in others. They are more representative of Colombia, for example, than they are of Nigeria. The impact of an economic takeoff on the labor force produces the reverse of these conditions. For instance, the population becomes more mobile and begins to shift location to a greater extent. There is an increase in literacy rates, training levels, social mobility, and participation in labor organizations. Rates of female participation in the labor force also increase. Laborers become a changed statistic—from underemployed in the rural area to unemployed or employed in the urban labor force. The occupational distribution changes. Job classifications, ranging from unskilled to skilled, broaden as a modern industrial structure emerges. In some nations where a strategic and profitable corporation exists side by side with small manufacturing shops, the wages paid laborers in the corporation may be three or four times as great as those paid in the shops. In Spain, for example, a large foreign-owned corporation may be on the same street as a hole-in-the-wall *taller* (workshop) whose Spanish owner hires the same skills at considerably less pay. But not all labor changes at this point in economic development are favorable to the desired end result of an efficient and fully employed population. Of this more will be said later.

PLANNING HUMAN CAPITAL GROWTH

Given the labor characteristics of the developing economy, the task of planning is to set off a spiral of rising capabilities and work opportunities. The objective is a productive job for everyone who can work and capital investments that raise skill levels and provide earnings commensurate with those skills. With growth, the range of skills expands to include a greater number of technical and craft categories. The amount of labor available at the start of the planning period is not the total number of persons but is rather the existing level of human capital stock in the economy.

Manpower planning maintains a balance between the development of human resources and the evolution of the economic plan. Therefore, marginal computations are involved. That is to say, estimates are made of the increments in occupational skills necessary above those existing at the start of the planning period. To such existing amounts are added vacancies created by anticipated retirements from the labor force and deaths. These increments are calculated for each phase of the economic plan.

As was done in Algeria in 1967, the initial step in such planning is to take a labor inventory as a prelude to the setting of skill targets. The available manpower is ascertained, together with its present capabilities. In addition, the total stock of skills needed at different target dates in the future must also be estimated. Approximations are made for each sector, including government, agriculture, industry, education, transportation, and communication. These approximations for the future can be cross-checked against the labor force distributions of nations at an advanced but proximate stage of industrialization. Thereupon, a reconciliation process takes place between the actual labor force distribution, the estimates of future manpower needs extracted from targets set in the economic plan and from international comparisons, and the amount of funds available for manpower investment.

Individual preferences tend to make the manpower plan go awry. Persons in training for a particular occupation may choose another one upon graduation. At any point in time, a particular individual who can perform a range of jobs may not select the one anticipated by manpower planners. Nor can planners control deaths or the extent to which individuals move in and out of the work force.

Other factors affect the manpower plan. Individuals who are rising from the bottom of the social scale may be blocked from entering a particular profession by members of that profession through means such as exaggerating the requisite qualifications. The structure of jobs may also shift beyond that anticipated by the plan. Furthermore, the population can evolve in an unforeseen manner, both as to size and location. Knowledge accumulation is also so rapid in some occupations that to maintain the planned framework of occupational specializations, more resources have to be devoted to education than anticipated. These factors are difficult to control because a developing nation lacks detailed and timely statistics.

Generating the forces needed to carry out the manpower plan within a democratic framework is not easy. Manpower planning and freedom of choice may prove incompatible. The people may not accept the idea of capitalizing themselves by forgoing consumption. In addition, planning becomes more complex with economic growth because as the alternative targets widen, the population makes selections from a widening range of choices.

Fortunately for the planner, offsetting factors tend to neutralize these tendencies. Planners can count on the malaise stirred up among the population by mass communications media to create a desire to raise skills and earnings. If economic planning creates new jobs, the resulting labor shortages may create a demand that exceeds planned targets to a considerable degree. The personality of an educated person can create its own labor demand. Moreover, as previously stated, an estimate of required skills can be made more reliable by checking the labor force distributions of countries at a somewhat higher level of economic growth. Caution is necessary in making these comparisons, however, because there are probably differences in job content and because there are no universal standards applicable to job qualifications.

The next stage in planning consists of the execution, control, and evaluation of the manpower plan. Instruments have to be devised that maintain a balanced evolution of manpower and enterprise at the national, regional, and local levels. At the national level, the manpower organization should receive data on the allocations of investment funds and foreign aid and should have some degree of control over capital planning. As the plan evolves, capital projections should be revised periodically to reflect changes in manpower needs so that distortions, including possible unemployment effects, can be kept to a minimum. As this evolution occurs, regional and local instruments must be devised to feed back the necessary information to the national organization. Jobs have to be found for skills as they proliferate, for a lack of job opportunities may cause social tensions.

Labor techniques and institutions must emerge to achieve the end result of raising the level of skills and earnings. Large-scale production provides opportunities for occupational specialization, efficiency, and enlightened employer wage policies. In addition, employers and employees must find ways of settling among themselves any political and ideological conflicts instead of turning to the government. Conflicts over income distribution that end in the political arena may deter economic growth. Yet the rise of institutions favorable to conflict resolution cannot be taken for granted.[6]

The planner must make choices of strategy in order to achieve man-

---

6 Argentina provides an example of how evolving institutions such as labor unions can stifle economic growth. The emergence of a powerful labor organization and a ruling oligarchy backed by the army has created an impasse.

power goals. For example, should rising labor efficiency be sought by encouraging urban migration or by developing the rural area? How should the social structure be changed? Should cultural patterns be attacked directly or should they be left to the impact of the industrialization process? For economic growth to occur, the attitudes of labor have to be changed. This problem raises one of the great ethical issues of the age. Should developing countries and their donors seek the full knowledge and consent of the poor? Or should economic forces be unleashed in the prospect of changing their attitudes? Put another way, what rights sanction the indirect manipulation of the poor without their knowledge and consent?

ECONOMIC DEVELOPMENT AS COMPREHENSIVE COMMUNITY DEVELOPMENT

If one accepts the principle of consensus among different groups, some deferment to the values of the poor has to take place. The objectives of the rural person cannot be explained solely in terms of maximizing his economic opportunities; in fact, he may consider a person guided by such motives as irrational. The rural worker thus does not respond in the manner hoped for by the use of incentives based solely on an economic calculus. Furthermore, when rural labor is concentrated in modern cities, the political power of these workers is accelerated more rapidly than their rate of productivity. Therefore, allowing this reorientation of values to take place in urban centers may be an error of far-reaching consequences.

Obtaining a consensus in rural areas means that manpower development should be based on a system that would permit the poor to participate in decision making in order to diminish their distrust of the proposed changes. But this involvement may or may not be conducive to development. The participation of the poor must be sufficient to bring about a rise in their productivity concomitant with a growth of enterprise that they believe to be of their own creation. Before this happens, however, their participation may bring about a rise in their political power and a demand that the consumption of the poor be subsidized rather than based on their productivity.

The necessary concomitant growth of skills and earnings can be facilitated by the creation of model communities where change can be planned rather than left to the chance effect of public expenditures.[7] Labor investments in these communities include social and health centers, agricultural extension services, libraries, such socioeconomic organizations as cooperatives and education and training centers, discussion groups examining such questions as production, birth control, family

[7] The model community concept is extensively developed in the chapter on Sicily.

health care, and occupational training to participate in community projects that are consistent with the capital formation plan.

To be a motivating force, growth has to be visible; hence, the value of the model community. The poor require an opportunity to display the evidence of their contribution to increased productivity. Failing individual responsibility for growth and rewards commensurate with contribution, the rural effort may collapse, as has frequently happened in the history of cooperative plans.

Therefore, the model community will have to seek maximum involvement. Its evolution will, however, be subject to pressures of competing interests. Different groups, both indigenous and foreign to the developing area, are likely to pursue their interests in the name of the general welfare. The formerly poor may style themselves as experts in economic development and demand participation in the program. Yet if they take over the program without the counsel of technicians and a cadre from the modern sector of the economy, they may cause the program to collapse. Local politicians and administrators may see new outlets for their ambitions. These pressures may promote the interest of the population, albeit in a rather oblique way.

The model community should be strategically placed. The choice of location should take into consideration both the need for efficiency and the goal of maximum social impact. Although proximate to a subsistence area, it should nevertheless be a distinct entity in which men shape their own destinies. A basic objective of the community should be to shift the economic and social structure away from traditional seats of power. The aspirations and fulfillments the communities embody can provide an élan to growth not otherwise obtainable, for the traditional rural value of assistance based on reciprocity can be a potent source of the needed esprit de corps.

A handsome school building in the center of the model community assists in bolstering such a spirit. The school should be staffed with the ablest instructors available and stimulate a zest for learning. It can be the focal point of a variety of community projects including the planning of housing, health and sanitation programs, agronomy, credit alliances, home economics, and business projects. Here, too, an overall plan can be drawn up incorporating fixed tangible objectives that are realizable in the short run. The ability of illiterates to become deeply involved in such projects can be easily underestimated.

Social objectives are attained in the model community by a rise in the influence, capability, and employment of the population. By capability is meant the individual's awareness of the opportunity to make choices among a stock of realistic possibilities that are available to him. The processes involved in democratic participation are no less significant than the outcomes, which may be tangible in the form of goods or intangible in the form of community policy making and control. Out of the pursuit of this social optimum emerge new institutions that affect the utilization and efficiency of labor.

The importance of jobs in the strategy of a model community cannot be overstated. A technology that excludes the rural population from involvement in production is a deterrent and not a catalyst to economic development. Economic planners have a bias against employment-producing investment in rural areas, however; they criticize such investment as being too costly. But the social costs incurred by the cities through migration from the rural area and the stagnation of the rural area in the absence of employment-producing investment are not considered in this criticism. The erection of a modern industrial plant in a city may have little to do with the development of an economy.

Building a new plant in the model community makes long-run economic sense. If the manager of such a plant is an enlightened paternalist, all the better. He may provide his employees with hot meals, bathing facilities, nurseries, social clubs, medical care, training, housing, and opportunities to purchase goods at discount prices. A manager who cannot afford these indirect labor costs may have to be subsidized. Thinking has changed about such paternalism, which was formerly considered a means of ensuring employee subservience. Used in a developing economy, a paternalistic policy represents a first step in the development of independent and enterprising workers. A mark of the policy's success is when workers become disgruntled with their above-average employment terms and join a labor organization. This ingratitude is a sign of human capital development.

A skilled cadre of workers from the modern sector of the economy should be used in this initial involvement of the rural population in modern employment. These workers are the means of creating a new industrial elite from the unskilled and should be hired on short-term contracts stipulating that the cadres will eventually return to established industrial areas. The experience of the Olivetti-Underwood Corporation in southern Italy suggests that a low level of technology designed deliberately to involve laborers of low skills is not prohibitive in costs. In a sense, labor efficiency is raised by tolerating a certain degree of inefficiency in the short term. Unskilled workers of high aptitude react favorably to the challenge of increasing mechanical complexity. The task of managers is to ensure that such a disposition is not changed into hostility toward modern technology by managerial malpractices.

In sum, the rural population is uplifted not by exporting the most enterprising and talented workers but by providing employment opportunities within the rural area. But such an alternative to urbanization is risky. The long period necessary to raise the capabilities of the rural population means that a quick payoff from such investment cannot be expected. Because the Olivettis are few in the developing world, such an approach means government subsidization.

MEASURING HUMAN CAPITAL GROWTH

A major problem in human capital investment is one of input-output analysis. Should human costs be considered an input? The criticism has been made of some developing economies that although the capacities of the people have been increased, the task was accomplished at considerable human cost. Moreover, how does one determine how much human growth he is getting for his money? How does one aggregate such returns as greater opportunity for social movement and more possibilities for creativity? The Social Sciences Department of UNESCO is performing useful work in this area. The problems of input-output analysis are formidable and attract competent economic investigators. Few efforts in the field of the social sciences to surmount considerable obstacles have been as heroic.

Several approaches have been used to measure changes in the capacities of an economy. Change can be estimated through the medium of money, either in the form of total expenditures for education or in the form of earnings resulting from the rise in human capitalization. An alternative approach, perhaps more suitable for comparing developing economies, is to analyze the changing enrollments in education. In their study of human resources development, Professors Frederick Harbison and Charles Myers sought a measure of the highly skilled human resources of foreign countries including managerial, administrative, professional, and technical manpower.[8] Their efforts were not successful until they resorted to using figures on the number of enrollments in secondary schools and colleges. From such data, they devised a composite ratio of the proportion of each age group enrolled in secondary and higher education, weighting the latter by five so that more emphasis would be given to college enrollment. By so doing, they found a high correlation between their composite index of human resource development and the gross national product per capita of the particular country.

As the authors suggest, the correlation does not indicate that an x percent increase in high school and college enrollments would produce a y percent increase in product. They do indicate, however, that for a certain amount of tangible capital investment, a country has to calculate a certain amount of human capital investment. On the question of which is cause and which is effect in the association between education and economic growth, more will be said in the subsequent chapter.

Implicit in measures of human capital is a subjective judgment as to what a nation wants out of economic development. Is the objective international power, showmanship, a rise in living standards, immortalization of a leader, or such a nebulous but important human value as

---

[8] For a succinct statement of their position, see Charles A. Myers, "Human Resources and World Economic Development, Frontiers for Research and Action," *International Labour Review*, Vol. 94 (November 1966).

creativity and dignity? Comparisons of developing countries are more meaningful if made between countries that pursue similar goals. If human ends are paramount, capital formation is a means to an end. To stop at capital formation is to ignore the human side effects of cost and opportunities. Economists do so at times not because of the unimportance of these side effects but because they are not particularly susceptible to economic calculus.

ROLE OF LABOR ORGANIZATIONS

In the development of human capital, labor organizations must find a useful function for themselves or else see their influence diminish. The trade unions of developing areas generally have not experienced a growth concomitant with the rise of industry. Rather they are a political, precariously existing transplant from older industrial societies that becomes a rallying point for class consciousness and social protest. Trade unions are symbols of frustration rather than of human resources development. In some areas of the world, they are tools of industrialists, the government, or foreign powers.

After the process of development is under way and the protest movement has dissipated, unions require new functions in order to sustain their momentum. Performing the role assumed by their counterparts in mature economies of protecting the managed against the managers gives them no substantial function when the employer is a pacesetter and pays wages that are considerably higher than the average for the nation. If they do not seek to involve themselves in human capital development in the name of some ideology, their future is likely to be bleak.

Such is not to say that unions should give up their role in politics; rather, their problem is the degree and manner of such involvement. If labor organizations in developing countries were to remove themselves from politics, they would isolate themselves from the changes that unfold with development. By remaining neutral, they are likely to find themselves eventually with little influence. Their problem is to shift successfully from obstructionism to some form of critical collaboration.

What functions can these labor unions perform? Together with employers and government, they can assume some responsibilities in training. Generally, however, they appear to fail to see this opportunity. They can collaborate with national and regional manpower planners. They can serve as a mediating influence between managers of enterprises and the new labor force in gaining acquiescence or agreement of workers to industrial discipline. These organizations can provide assistance in raising productivity and in providing social services; they can assist in a reorientation of values. In assuming such tasks, a labor leader must acquire an education like everybody else in the developing nation. Table thumping is insufficient.

Is it in the interest of these labor organizations to join the drive to raise labor productivity? The answer to this question depends on whether the employer uses modern technology as a means of curtailing his labor force and whether the labor leaders identify with the political leaders of the nation. In the former colonial territories, this identification is more likely than in Latin America, for example.

Summation

The developing nations operate under an economic assumption that does not always prove workable—that tangible capital investment generates employment. Despite the rising proportion of the national income that is devoted to capital investment, unemployment continues to mount. Developing countries do not have the machinery industries that might partially absorb this unemployment. The rising army of unemployed is an ill omen, because the key to human capital growth is industrial jobs. Economists generally assume that urban unemployment declines with development. There is contrary evidence that economic development actually creates unemployment, however.[9]

What accounts for this paradox? Workers flow into the cities in unprecedented numbers, spurred by inflation, increased educational opportunities, more sophisticated job attitudes, and the breakdown of rural equilibrium caused by the population explosion. The rising disproportion between urban and rural wages adds to the migration incentive. The more the urban wage rises because of political rather than productivity reasons, the more the rural person is willing to take whatever partial employment he can obtain in the cities.

Accordingly, most of the capital investment is concentrated in existing urban centers and is wasted to a considerable degree on prestige projects. Automation in the home and industry worsens the problem by excluding the unskilled from a job commitment. The application of these methods to industrial record keeping, for example, excludes the lower middle class from this occupation. Automated techniques in materials handling eliminate the unskilled blue-collar workers. Consequently, the initial entry of workers into the labor force is seriously curtailed.

What are the implications of this situation? Capital must be invested in rural areas to place restraints on urban migration. Import duties may have to be placed on mechanical equipment in order to retard mechanization. Tax incentives may have to be provided to encourage employers to use unskilled and semiskilled labor more extensively.

Karl Marx predicted that the Western nations would be faced with a

---

[9] For the unemployment effect of modern technology in developing areas, see the works of Arthur Lewis and the research findings of Professor Lloyd Reynolds, who observes that in Puerto Rico, after a decade of considerable capital investment, employment has remained stable.

rising army of unemployed. He was wrong. But it would be ironic if the self-styled socialist nations of the developing world today were to demonstrate that for them Marx was right.

The evidence is impressive that, in striving for basic economic development goals, a general strategy for human capital growth is necessary. The economic development planner has two fundamental goals: to raise the level of human capital and to create job opportunities for its use. Whenever he plans a capital project, the political authority should inquire as to the number of long-term jobs the project will create. This strategy stems from the assumption that the essence of the productivity of labor and capital is the usable knowledge and habits of mind that become an integral part of man. The real wealth of nations is the sum total of the curriculum vitae of the people. If the stock of this wealth is to be increased, the efficiency and utilization of labor must rise. Investment must be made to provide the skills, incentives, and employment opportunities needed for the involvement of the population in a widening range of activities.

To a considerable degree, the efficacy of such involvement requires local planning. Manpower and capital investments have to be closely coordinated, and shifts in problems anticipated at different stages of growth. New job opportunities have to rise faster than the rise in human capital. Disappointments are to be expected, however, in democratic participation on the local level. Such participation may result in the establishment of a talking society controlled by vocal mediocrities more concerned with palliatives than cures. These outcomes appear to be endemic in social work. The qualifications of practitioners and the criterion of measuring their productivity are sufficiently nebulous to make entrance into the profession easy.

Concentrating the human capital program on the children of the well-to-do is a mistake. Such a concentration of effort and funds tends to perpetuate inequities and to sharpen the instruments of exploitation that are available to the privileged groups in developing areas. To create a mass engine of growth that brings forth new ideas and that facilitates the implementation of such ideas, the talented sons of the poor have to be given priority. In exchange, they commit themselves to community development.

Should the developing nation succeed in fomenting a harmonious development of tangible and human capital, its continuance must be assured according to a quasi-mechanical process. Institutions have to be developed, however, that reduce the likelihood of a reversal.

In this development of human resources, labor organizations can perform a useful function at both local and national levels. The leaders of these organizations also need to develop their own skills, however. Should they not do so, they are likely to perform a diminishing role in economic development as soon as the protest phase is over.

To conclude, the goal of human capital development is to raise economic, political, and social capabilities and to put these capabilities to use in rewarded activity. Moreover, this is the ultimate objective of the broader goal of economic development. The following chapter discusses the role of education in attaining this goal.

5

EDUCATION AND ECONOMIC DEVELOPMENT

Half the world's population lives in developing countries, and half of this number cannot read or write. To state the obvious, in no prosperous nation in the world are substantial numbers of the people illiterate. Argentina, for example, has the highest level of education and the highest living standard in Latin America.

The economist's view of education is colored by the concepts of his own discipline. He asks certain questions that are fundamental to educational planning: What kind of output is desired from education? What are alternative methods for obtaining such production? How much does each method cost? How are the returns on educational investment to be measured? Given the available resources, how can investment returns from different allocations be maximized? How should the education be financed? In ascertaining the manpower needs of an economy and the educational system geared to fill such needs, economists talk about manpower and education planning. In short, the economist believes that education has a production function that must be at least considered if not treated as a basic constraint in decision making.

A not-so-obvious question in this discussion is whether education is made possible because of economic growth or whether economic growth depends upon education. A forceful argument can be made that the level of education in a developing nation has a profound influence on the efficiency with which that country uses capital. Productive use of capital implies a well-trained labor force. Therefore, the argument of whether to begin an educational drive before or after the creation of a broad tangible capital base is too puristic. To postpone such an investment is a risky business for developing nations.

"Education" is intended here to mean a planned activity between teacher and learner, aided by equipment, materials, and administration, to produce a rise in the capabilities of the learner. Education can occur anywhere and through a variety of media. Commonly, however, it takes place in schools, enterprises, and, in haphazard but vital fashion, in the family.

Developing nations labor under imprecise information as to what activities constitute education and the effect of education on early stages of growth. For example, what are the different inputs that comprise an education experience? How can they be isolated and measured in order to determine their relative contribution to learning output? How should the output of investment be measured? Is the higher income of the educated person really a measure of his contribution to the economy or is it a measure rather of the status his society accords him? The answers to these questions have an important bearing on policy. For instance, just because a college education pays off in increased earnings, such a payoff is not necessarily a mandate to use scarce resources of government for such education.

Advanced nations allocate considerable resources to education and training. The Soviet Union, the United States, and Denmark are outstanding examples. Countries such as Argentina, however, with similar expenditures in relation to their income, do not experience similar rates of growth. What does such an outcome suggest? Are the differences due to dissimilarities in the types of education offered? Or do similar programs differ as to the quality of their inputs?

To study the association between education and stage of economic growth, one has to make an inquiry into the experience of different nations. For South Asia, Gunnar Myrdal's judgment is that expenditures do not indicate the quality of education offered and that the sudden increase in enrollments in the Asian nations has brought about a deterioration of quality. In the pioneering study of Frederick Harbison and Charles Myers mentioned in the preceding chapter, countries are classified as underdeveloped, partially developed, semiadvanced, or advanced. Using quantitative indicators of the level of education, these authors found a significant correlation between the amount of education and the per capita gross national product of each country. These relationships do not indicate why similar educational levels in two countries do not pay off in similar rates of growth, even where their resource endowment is approximately the same. Argentina, for example, ranks with Sweden in educational level but is far below that country in economic growth. Therefore, the Harbison and Myers study suggests the importance of probing into such questions as: What individuals are getting the education? What quality of education are they obtaining? What are they doing with their education? Where are they applying it? Two countries with the same number of people possessing diplomas may not have the same amount of education.

Motivation of students as well as educational quality are the primary factors that condition the economic progress of nations. The number of individuals with high school and university diplomas is only an approximate estimate of these factors. Individuals may seek advanced education to avoid economic activity rather than contribute to it. Educational programs differ in the extent to which they develop the skills and motivation necessary at a particular phase of growth. Therefore, a developing country must take an inventory of prevailing attitudes and programs, ascertain available resources for education, and utilize these resources in a manner that maximizes growth. Economic development in a sense entails a deliberate breakdown of manpower characteristics in an economy. Education is its principal weapon.

STATISTICS ON EDUCATION

Statistics on education in developing nations tend to overestimate the amount of education being obtained. Census takers tend to take a rather liberal view of what constitutes a literate person. School enrollments do not indicate the low attendance. The enrollments of high schools and institutions of higher learning do not indicate the low quality of instruction. Functional literacy, the ability to use reading, writing, and arithmetic in problem solving, is more important to a developing country than literacy. Yet the literacy rates do not indicate the extent to which the population comprises functional illiterates.

Gunnar Myrdal concludes that, with the exception of Ceylon and Malaya, radical changes must be made in the educational systems throughout South Asia. He quotes from the report of an Indian education commission as follows: "Indian education needs a drastic reconstruction, almost a revolution. We need to bring about major improvement in the effectiveness of primary education; to introduce work-experience as an integral element of general education; to vocationalize secondary education; to improve the quality of teachers at all levels and to provide teachers in sufficient strength; to liquidate illiteracy; to strengthen centers of advanced study and strive to attain, in our universities at least, higher international standards; to lay special emphasis on the combination of teaching and research; and to pay particular attention to education and research and allied sciences." [1] The quotation applies to developing nations generally and should be kept in mind when studying the following statistics.

Table 6 indicates illiteracy rates and stages of economic growth. A

[1] Gunnar Myrdal, *Asian Drama: An Inquiry into the Poverty of Nations* (New York: Pantheon, 1968), p. 1811.

TABLE 6 ☐ **Percentage of Illiteracy and Stage of Economic Growth for Selected Developing Nations, the United States, and Western Europe**

Country	Illiteracy Rate	Stage of Growth
Africa		
Basutoland	65.1	underdeveloped
Congo Republic	84.6	underdeveloped
Gabon	87.6	underdeveloped
Malawi	93.5	underdeveloped
Niger	99.1	underdeveloped
Senegal	94.4	underdeveloped
Uganda	74.9	underdeveloped
Asia		
Burma	42.3	underdeveloped
Cambodia	69.2	underdeveloped
India	72.2	underdeveloped
Indonesia	57.1	underdeveloped
Iran	87.2	developing
Japan	2.2	developed
Latin America		
Argentina	8.6	developed
Bolivia	67.9	underdeveloped
Brazil	39.3	developing
Chile	16.4	semideveloped
Costa Rica	15.7	developing
Cuba	22.1	semideveloped
Dominican Republic	40.0	developing
Ecuador	32.7	developing
El Salvador	51.0	developing
Honduras	55.0	developing
Mexico	34.6	semideveloped
Nicaragua	50.4	developing
Paraguay	25.7	developing
Peru	39.4	developing
Other		
Spain	13.3	semideveloped
United States	2.2	advanced
Western Europe	1.7	advanced

Source: UNESCO, *Statistical Yearbook,* 1965.

rise in literacy manifests a nation's growing capacity to draw from other countries, to develop on its own, and to use knowledge for the solving of problems. Although the precise effect of literacy has not been fully determined, economists generally agree as to its favorable effect on economic growth.[2]

For the convenience of the reader, the nations are classified into one

[2] See Howard Schuman *et al.,* "Some Social Psychological Effects and Non-Effects of Literacy in a New Nation," *Economic Development and Cultural Change,* 16 (October 1967).

of five stages of economic growth on the basis of per capita gross domestic product at factor cost (in dollars) as follows:

Underdeveloped	0–200
Developing	201–500
Semideveloped	501–650
Developed	651–1500
Advanced	above 1500

Generally, illiteracy rates decline with stages of economic growth. For underdeveloped nations, the range is 42 to 93 and for the advanced, 1.7 to 2.2. For countries in Africa and Latin America, illiteracy rates are affected by the percentage of nonwhites in the population. Thus the nonwhite population in Argentina and Costa Rica is small; it is important for Ecuador, Peru, El Salvador, and Bolivia, in that order.

Table 7 lists pupil-teacher ratios in primary schools and educational budgets for developing countries, the U.S.S.R., and the United States. As

TABLE 7 □ **Pupil-Teacher Ratios in Primary Schools, Educational Budgets as Percentage of National Income, and Trends for Selected Nations, 1961–1965**

Country	Ratio	Percentage	Budget Trend
Argentina	20.2	3.2	Steady
Bolivia	29.8	2.2	Rising
Brazil	29.6	2.2	—
Burma	31.8	2.7	Falling
Burundi	57.9	—	—
Chile	50.0	3.2	—
Colombia	41.5	3.3	Rising
Congo (Dem. Rep.)	36.6	—	—
Costa Rica	29.2	4.6	—
Cuba	33.6	5.0	Falling
Dahomey	40.9	—	—
Dominican Republic	51.5	3.9	Rising
Ecuador	37.3	2.5	Rising
El Salvador	48.7	2.7	Falling
Gambia	54.8	—	—
Ghana	33.0	4.1	Rising
Guatemala	33.7	1.6	Steady
Haiti	45.5	1.1	—
India	48.9	2.8	Rising
Indonesia	39.9	1.2	—
Japan	21.8	7.1	Rising
Mexico	46.6	3.0	Rising
Pakistan	33.4	1.9	Rising
Paraguay	27.6	2.5	—
Spain	34.9	1.5	Rising
United States	28.9	6.3	Rising
U.S.S.R.	26.5	8.1	Rising
Venezuela	34.2	4.0	—

Source: United Nations, *Statistical Yearbook,* 1966, and UNESCO, *Statistical Yearbook,* 1965.

a group, developing countries have higher pupil-teacher ratios than developed nations and use a smaller percentage of their income for education. To a considerable degree, the high ratios reflect a population explosion.

Table 8 indicates the number of persons in school relative to the school-age population. The unadjusted enrollment for the first level of education is based on the estimated population from five to fourteen years of age. For secondary enrollment, the ratio is computed from the estimated population fifteen to nineteen years of age. The adjusted figure is an adjustment of population size to reflect the actual duration of schooling. For international comparisons, unadjusted figures are considerably less reliable than adjusted data.

Because the data from which the percentages derive are not precise or strictly comparable, Table 9 presents an approximate relative distribution of college students in developing nations. Generally, countries in a "successful" developing stage have a more even distribution of students. Others show a considerable concentration in law, humanities, and social science. Correspondingly, the relative number in natural science, engineering, and agriculture is low.

EDUCATIONAL PLANNING

Developing nations have no choice but to plan; hard choices have to be made regarding the use of their scarce resources. A new method of thinking has to be developed through science and mathematics. The social sciences have to be employed to break down fixed positions. Difficult decisions have to be made as to where the emphasis should be placed: urban or rural areas, men or women, primary or higher education, youth or adults. Such questions have to be resolved as: Should available resources be used to acquire needed skills in the shortest possible time or to correct social injustices? Should training concentrate on broad occupational categories or specialized skills?

These choices are made in an atmosphere of competing demands; the cost of meeting those demands would exceed available funds. The visible evidences of investment that capital equipment provides attract scarce resources more easily. Nor do these choices offer solutions that can be applied uniformly throughout a developing country. An adult education program thus may command a low priority generally but may be urgent in a particular area. In making these decisions, the economist can assist by indicating outputs that would accrue under a different allocation of resources and by proposing methods of minimizing educational demands on the government budget.

Educational costs of developing countries can easily get out of hand. The target in the United Nations Declaration of Human Rights of universal primary education means that an extraordinary amount of funds will be needed by most developing nations and that other possibly more pressing

TABLE 8 □ School Enrollment Ratios for Japan and Developing Countries, 1955 and 1963

Country	Unadjusted Primary		Unadjusted Secondary		Adjusted Primary and Secondary Combined	
	1955	1963	1955	1963	1955	1963
Africa						
Basutoland	63	89[a]	3	5[a]	53	76[a]
Becuanaland	25	67[a]	9	4[a]	23	61[a]
Cameroon	37	79	2	8	31	67
Central Republic	12	34	1	3	10	28
Chad	3	19	.2	1	3	16
Congo (Rep.)	37	54	2	6	34	49
Congo (Brazza.)	32	74	3	13	27	64
Gabon	29	55	2	10	24	48
Gambia	7	14	2	9	6	15
Ghana	28	54	20	37	28	52
Guinea	5	23	.8	3	5	22
Ivory Coast	11	38	1	6	9	33
Kenya	29	53	2	5	24	45
Malawi	39	48	.9	3	33	40
Mali	4	10	.5	3	4	10
Mauritania	3	9	.4	2	3	8
Nigeria	27	31	2	6	22	27
Tanzania	16	25	1	3	13	21
Latin America						
Argentina	71	68	28	37	72	73
Bolivia	34	49	12	19	35	50
Brazil	33	50	12	25	37	58
Chile	69	69	26	46	69	78
Colombia	37	51	10	24	41	60
Costa Rica	64[b]	73	20[b]	32	70[b]	84
Cuba	53	70	14	31	51	74
Dom. Republic	65[c]	59[d]	7[c]	20[d]	61[c]	65[d]
Ecuador	48	56	12	20	47	57
El Salvador	37	49	9	15	40	54

Source: UNESCO, *Statistical Yearbook,* 1966.

[a] 1964 data.

[b] 1956 data.

[c] 1952 data.

educational needs will have to be curtailed. The construction of new schools to take care of the greater number of primary school children is not as burdensome as the sustained costs that accrue afterward, including the costs of teacher training and teacher salaries that, for some nations, have quadrupled since the beginning of school construction. Moreover, because teacher salaries often reflect inferior social scales rather than the demand for quality instructors, further increases are needed to attract competent personnel. For these reasons, ambitious

Country	Unadjusted Primary		Unadjusted Secondary		Adjusted Primary and Secondary Combined	
	1955	1963	1955	1963	1955	1963
Guatemala	26	36	5	9	27	38
Haiti	26	27^d	5	6^d	23	24^d
Honduras	32	47	6	8	33	49
Mexico	45	61	6	18	47	68
Nicaragua	36	46	6	11	37	49
Panama	59	64	27	38	62	70
Paraguay	63	67	10	16	60	65
Peru	42	59^a	11	26^a	46	68^a
Uruguay	63	59	31	50	66	71
Asia						
Afghanistan	4	9	.7	3	4	9
Burma	24	34^a	9	23^a	33	51^a
Cambodia	32	45	2	14	26	42
China (Mainland)	58^e	—	17^e	—	58^e	—
India	27	38^d	18	31^d	25	38^d
Indonesia	39	45^f	7	10^f	37	44^f
Iran	18	37^a	8	19^a	19	40^a
Japan	64	50	94	110	92	86
Jordan	49	60	27	43	54	68
Malaya	49	54	18	33	47	57
Pakistan	19	25	15	22	23	30
Philippines	54	60^d	25	26^d	70	76^d
Saudi Arabia	4	11	.4	4	4	11
Thailand	51	60	14	15	46	55
Turkey	35	48^a	10	20^a	36	55^a
Vietnam Rep.	16	61	4	19	20	57
Other						
Spain	67	67^d	20	31^d	59	67^d

^{d} 1962 data.

^{e} 1958 data.

^{f} 1961 data.

educational programs can easily reach 25 percent of the government expenditures of a developing nation.

As a result, policy makers have to discriminate against particular groups and locations. One age group may be given educational preference over another. Administrators may have a bias against rural areas because of the greater efficiency of instruction in urban concentrations and the difficulty of recruiting teachers to work in the countryside. One is again confronted with the necessity of planning in order to place these choices on a rational basis.

TABLE 9 □ Relative Distribution of College Students of Developing Nations by Field of Study* for Latest Years, 1960–1964

Country	Humanities	Education	Fine Arts	Law	Social Science	Natural Science	Engineering	Medical Science	Agriculture
Africa									
Basutoland	.52	.08	—	.09	.02	.29	—	—	—
Burundi	.30	—	—	.15	.52	—	—	—	—
Cameroon	.15	.05	—	.45	.35	—	—	—	—
Congo (Brazza.)	.19	.27	—	.21	.01	.03	.22	.07	—
Ghana	.50†	—	.14†	.08†	.24†	.01†	—	.02†	.01
Guinea	.26	—	—	.02	.11	.05	—	.56	—
Ivory Coast	.16	—	—	.63	—	.18	—	.03	—
Kenya	.12†	—	.19†	—	.15†	.16†	.28†	.10†	—
Nigeria	.20	.10	.03	.05	.23	.16	.06	.08	.09
Uganda	.19†	.18†	.04†	—	.18†	.16†	—	.19†	.06†
Latin America									
Argentina	.12	—	.05	.13	.16	.08	.09	.35	.02
Bolivia	—	—	.05†	.16†	.23†	.06†	.22†	.28†	—
Brazil	.11	.06	.03	.21	.19	.04	.14	.16	.06
Chile	.04	.27	.05	.11	.10	.05	.20	.12	.06
Colombia	.08	.07	.09	.13	.14	.08	.21	.13	.07
Costa Rica	.54	.11	.06	.05	.12	.01	.04	.04	.03
Cuba	.04	.15	.02	.02	.24	.07	.16	.25	.05
Dominican Rep.	.06	—	—	.19	.22	.21	—	.31	.01
Ecuador	.04	.08	.05	.16	.13	.05	.21	.24	.07
El Salvador	.14	—	—	.19	—	.17	.28	.22	—
Guatemala	.15	—	.06	.42	.33	.01	.01	.01	.01

Source: UNESCO, *Statistical Yearbook,* 1965.

* As a percentage of total enrollment.

† Incomplete tabulation.

The general purpose of planning is to develop links between the educational system, on the one hand, and particular national economic development objectives, on the other. Increases in human capacities must be correlated with development goals so that the squandering of scarce funds is minimized. Two assumptions should be made in such planning: (1) the existence of a direct relationship between the amount and quality of education and per capita output, and (2) the necessity of stimulating motivation for the acquisition of education. These relationships vary among countries. Furthermore, in order to plan properly, education must be conceived as a stream of processes in which the level of accomplishment at a particular point in terms of numbers and quality is dependent on processes at prior points in the educational flow.

The sequence of planning entails *preplanning* to assess the present situation, *drawing up the educational plan* after a determination of goals in economic growth and manpower needs over different points in time,

Country	Human- ities	Ed- uca- tion	Fine Arts	Law	Social Sci- ence	Nat- ural Sci- ence	Engi- neer- ing	Medi- cal Sci- ence	Agri- cul- ture
Haiti	.07	—	—	.42	.03	.06	.10	.27	.03
Honduras	.06	.04	—	.34	.43	.02	.01	.10	—
Mexico	.12	.01	.05	.13	.25	.08	.17	.15	.04
Nicaragua	—	.17	—	.17	.26	—	.13	.21	.06
Panama	.28	.10	.04	.05	.22	.21	.07	.02	.01
Paraguay	.08	.03	.10	.22	.20	.11	.03	.15	.08
Peru	.18	.20	.01	.08	.19	.06	.09	.10	.09
Uruguay	.05	—	.11	.27	.14	—‡	.06	.32	.06
Venezuela	.08	.08	.03	.15	.21	.02	.18	.20	.05
Asia									
Afghanistan	.15	.07	—	.16	.11	.15	.08	.22	.06
Burma	.43	.04	—	.02	.04	.33	.04	.09	.01
Cambodia	.20	.47	.03	.11	.01	.04	.02	.11	.01
China	.05§	.21§	—	.02§	.03§	.06§	.41§	.13§	.09§
India	.45	.02	—	.02	.09	.30	.05	.04	.04
Indonesia	.02	.05	—	.29	.21	.06	.14	.20	.03
Iran	.32	.05	.04	.09	.03	.09	.09	.24	.05
Japan	.15	.10	.02	.13	.34	.03	.21	.01	.01
Pakistan	.46	.04	.01	.05	.14	.16	.04	.05	.05
Philippines	.14	.31	.02	.01	.29	.02	.14	.05	.02
Thailand	.02	.12	.02	.22	.42	.04	.04	.08	.04
Other									
Spain	.11	.01	.03	.13	.10	.18	.17	.23	.04

‡ Included In humanities.
§ 1957 data.

and *executing the plan.* The range of this planning includes a considera- tion of student enrollment projections (which can be derived from man- power projections) at different points of the pipeline, because they affect the remainder of planning decisions, including capital expenditures to be made at different points, teachers and staff, and subjects to be taught at different levels.

In assessing the situation, the planners must weigh the possibility that compulsory education laws may be disregarded in some countries. In former African colonies, for example, no more than an estimated 25 percent of the children have ever been to school. Furthermore, there are likely to be serious distortions in educational attainments. At the bottom of the scale, the great majority has little or no schooling. At the top, college enrollments comprise the offspring of the wealthy who take courses that offer prestige value and care little about making a contribu- tion to economic growth.

Education may also be casual and unproductive. In the national university of a developing country, for example, professors lecture three hours weekly. Classes are suspended a month or two before examinations and do not meet for a month or two thereafter. Numerous holidays, both scheduled and improvised, are honored. In addition, further cancellations occur because of visits by distinguished visitors and special celebrations. In Latin America, strikes by students, professors, or staff may be the order of the day. In some areas, whether or not the professor will show up at all for class is problematical. This kind of casualness makes a qualitative study of education imperative.

Another characteristic of these educational systems is inefficient administration. A conservative estimate is that the educational output of developing countries can be increased by a fifth merely by an efficient use of existing resources. In such a climate, the returns to economic growth of a given educational outlay cannot be predicted as easily as returns from investment in capital equipment. Consequently, advantages are likely to be exaggerated both by the exponents of a heavy dose of educational investment and by those critical of diverting capital funds to education.

Attitudes also differ regarding the purpose of education. Some persons look upon additional programs as a means of eradicating social injustices. This goal means a universal schooling minimum. Others view the objective as the rapid production of a small number of qualified personnel for government and industry. Still others, although not stating so for the record, see in education a means of attaining social distinction for their children.

These attitudes create stresses at different points in the educational stream. The children of the affluent tend to be pulled out of the public system at the primary level as the goal of universal free education becomes widespread. This trend toward segregation defeats the national objective of social cohesion. Unless sound elementary instruction is maintained at close to universal levels, future generations that would provide a broad base for rapid growth are not likely to be forthcoming. Stresses at the primary level affect high school and college education. Because of inadequate preparation, a considerable number of talented individuals may not succeed in entering secondary and higher education. The social distinctions that appear during the years of primary education are consequently perpetuated and strengthened.

Successful planning requires that the goal of using education as a tool for correcting social injustice be reconciled with that of maximizing the output resulting from expenditure for education. The concentration of scarce resources among the poor may not be immediately as productive as the placement of these resources among more privileged groups. Poor children have special problems that require more expensive programs. They are also likely to live in rural areas where education is more costly.

Educational policy must necessarily deal with social cleavages, which may be aggravated by not providing subsidies to allow poor children to remain in school and by inadequate birth control policies that decrease family educational effort per child. Communities with little sense of responsibility for their own welfare also contribute to a delay in visible results. If these problems are not taken seriously, a goal of human resources development, the right of the individual to achieve his full potential, is thwarted. In addition, there is the danger that taking care of immediate needs in economic growth may crystallize into permanent objectives.

The universal problem in education is to reconcile the long-run goal of producing educated persons with the more immediate objective of creating the needed complement of competent producers to fill the governmental and industrial positions of society. These goals can be mutually reinforcing. Individuals should not be viewed as instruments rather than ends of development. The individual who understands who he is, is more apt to be a better producer than the one who does not. Concentrating on the preparation of a small technical elite makes economic sense on the surface. But the surge in the aspirations of the population can create political problems that, if ignored, may result in peril for the government concerned. Mexico furnishes an example of a possible compromise. In that country, although secondary and higher education expenditures rise sharply, elementary education outlays expand at a higher rate.

Certain practical guidelines that are useful in developing a balanced educational plan include an evaluation of the character of the people and a consideration of how the plan can be made consistent with such character, as well as with the particular needs of each stage of development.

Preplanning

In some nations, such basic information as the number of children in the population is unknown. Preplanning activity should therefore include the collection of information, a function that is performed most efficiently by a statistical bureau. The bureau should be staffed with economists and sociologists working closely with the organizations that are responsible for the national economic plan and manpower projections. From these organizations, information can be obtained on the extent of expansion in the priority fields of business, public administration, education, medicine, science, and technology. With this information, the statistical bureau can make projections on the number of enrollments needed for specific occupations.

Another aspect of preplanning is an internal audit of the existing educational situation, including course content, teaching methods, educational materials, the supply and training of teachers, organization of the school system, extent of educational planning, and equipment and buildings. Such an inventory is likely to disclose that the teaching method emphasizes memorization rather than empirical inquiry and a method of inquiry that is based on outmoded ideological premises. Courses also are not likely to reflect the environment that is affecting the economic growth of the country. Courses tend to focus on the cultures and economy of advanced nations rather than the hard realities confronting the nation and may be slavish imitations of courses taught in highly industrialized societies. Universities in developing countries that seek American professors to teach courses in operations research are not putting first things first. An appropriately oriented course does not, in the end, cost more than a poorly oriented one.

On the other hand, the educational system in developing nations may have advantages over that of advanced countries where courses may tend to proliferate as a consequence of shifting academic fashions sensitive to the immediate demands of business and government. Although in modernizing nations, the course content appears divorced to some degree from the environment, subjects are often taught thoroughly and in depth. If these countries were to adopt the courses and methods of advanced nations, this in-depth teaching might be sacrificed.

A nation's educational attainments can be inventoried by analyzing the average number of years of schooling of the population; the percentage of youth enrolled at each educational level and the total potential within each level; the relative distribution of college students in the humanities, the physical sciences, social and behavioral sciences, law, engineering, medicine, agronomy, and teaching; the ratio of teachers to students at different levels of education; the number of classrooms per density of population in different areas of the country; and the extent and type of vocational training. To a considerable degree, the choice of method depends upon the reliability of data available.

An inventory of existing vocational instruction is crucial. The various educational levels and geographical locations at which such instruction is given must be determined; the course content and the qualifications of the instructors must also be analyzed. The overall costs of an educational program can be reduced by salvaging as many of the courses as possible and building on existing outlays. These vocational programs are generally wasteful of resources because they are not attuned to actual occupational needs. Moreover, whatever skills are imparted in them are often lost because of the interval between the time the skills are learned and the time they are utilized in production. The inventory should also cover private educational institutions with the intention of using them to reduce costs.

Drawing Up the Educational Plan

The essential step in educational planning is to determine the amount of additional funds that should be allocated to education in preference to other policy areas, especially production. Given existing funds for education, an analysis must be made of the relative benefits accruing from noneducational expenditures and from alternative distributions of educational outlays. The choices depend on returns that are expected to obtain from both over a series of future periods at various distributions of investment. At any particular point, the return on capital invested in production depends on the quality and amount of training in production methods that has been undergone in order to utilize such investment efficiently. Consequently, the growth of the developing country is linked to the ability of its educational outlays to produce human capabilities that are a pace ahead of capital formation. Educational planning must be tied to overall planning to ensure that the increase in these capabilities does not precede an increase in job opportunities.

In making these allocations, planners can err in the direction of too much and too soon as well as too little and too late. However, because an increase in human capabilities is not tangible evidence of economic development, the tendency in the early stages of growth is to underestimate the amount of educational investment that can be profitably employed. At an early stage, the provision of jobs to improve transportation, communications, public power, and land takes priority over a massive increase in educational expenditures. The government that gives equal weight to both job creation and education may cause an adverse political reaction, and political stability is an important requisite in development planning.

Can modernizing countries solve their education problems by copying the methods of advanced nations? The answer is yes and no: Those methods are not entirely exportable. Furthermore, they are expensive. Poor nations cannot afford to be as lackadaisical as the affluent ones in raising educational productivity.

An educational plan has to fix the overall amount and allocation of expenditure in education vis-à-vis noneducational forms of investment. To expend their resources rationally, developing nations have to forecast the benefits to be derived from additional educational expenditures compared to benefits derivable by placing such investment elsewhere. Such a cost-benefit approach is beset with difficulties. Allocations reflect the political power of government officials competing for funds. Benefits reflect the values of a society. If these nations are serious about economic development, however, they have to convince their people that the overriding benefit to be sought from education is a rise in output. Therefore, they need refined tools to ascertain which allocation of total available education funds produces the greatest rise in output.

The techniques and data available to measure output returns to education are not sufficient to make such measurement with precision. Approximations of returns, however, can be made through a variety of approaches. The income approach, of which T. W. Schultz is a foremost exponent, assumes that an association exists between differences in the life income of individuals and education inputs. However, income differences are also a measure of privilege and intelligence. Specialists are working at refining the income approach by taking these two factors into account.[3] If precise relationships can be established between output and education, the size of the educational budget on a particular program can be increased so long as the returns are greater than those that would accrue if the investment were placed elsewhere. These benefits may be in terms of skilled manpower needed at a particular stage of economic growth.

Highly sophisticated methods have been developed associating education with output. Professor Jan Tinbergen has developed a model relating the stock of educated persons with the output of goods and services. Another method is isolating the so-called residual factor—that factor accounting for the rise in GNP that is neither labor nor capital inputs. The pioneering work in this approach done by Robert Solow and Edward F. Denison leaves little doubt as to the importance of education in accounting for economic growth in the United States.[4]

The manpower approach, tied to economic planning, provides the most practical method available for making a decision on the amount and allocation of education funds. It has weaknesses, however. First, projections of manpower needs are not particularly reliable beyond five years whereas a shift in manpower education policy often takes some nine years to materialize. Second, the skills that should be developed for a particular occupation are affected by technological change. Third, no guarantee exists that the skills developed will emerge in the right places at the right time. Fourth, the intensive development of a compensable skill can often be developed more economically by the organization that employs the worker. Despite these shortcomings, planners have to look at education in terms of manpower needs. In many developing countries, cabinet ministers are easier to find than secretaries to assist them. The planners must decide to develop fewer Latin scholars and more technicians, managers, economists, and engineers. By so doing, they make the pattern of education in their country more suitable to the occupational needs of economic development.

Accordingly, the types and numbers of needed skills previously determined by manpower analysis are translated into educational policy. The policy maker must somehow measure the potential of human resources and relate it to equally vague educational concepts and processes. He

[3] See C. Arnold Anderson and Mary Jean Bowman, "Theoretical Considerations In Educational Planning," in Don Adams (ed.), *Educational Planning* (Syracuse, N.Y.: Syracuse University Press, 1964).
[4] Robert Solow, "Technical Change and the Aggregate Production Function," *The Review of Economics and Statistics,* Vol. 29 (August 1957), and Edward F. Denison, "Measuring the Contribution of Education to Economic Growth," in John Vaizey and Edward A. Robinson (eds.), *The Economics of Education: Proceedings of a Conference Held by the International Economic Association* (New York: St. Martin's Press, 1966).

has to consider manpower demand, which depends on the total volume of production planned and the level of the technology that will be employed in production. Technological level is associated to a considerable degree with the increase in per capita income. The volume of production is a measure of available resources, which can also be a determinant of income. Therefore, manpower needs can be predicted roughly from per capita income projections.

Once these manpower requirements are set, the number of students needed at various points in the educational stream can be ascertained also. The planned expansion of education at any one level creates pressures on other levels, particularly above the point where such expansion takes place. Thus, increased outlays at the primary level soon exert pressure on resources at secondary and eventually tertiary levels. A major educational decision creates a problem of logistics at various points in the educational stream.[5]

Coordinating the educational and manpower plans is crucial. The drawing up of an educational plan requires a precise comprehension of the manpower projection; the latter, in turn, is derived from economic targets. Tentative improvisations of the educational plan may indicate that political pressure should be exerted to change manpower and economic goals. Here, the need for the chief political administrator to assume the role of mediator among specialists in education, manpower, and economics is paramount.

The decision faced by planners regarding the extent to which the goal of universal primary education is to be curtailed may be difficult in view of the probability that the chief of state has been making extravagant promises of a free education for all. Quality universal primary education is a long-term solution to the demands of accelerated growth because many modernizing nations do not have the resources for such an objective in the first years of planning. A restricted number of years of universal primary schooling followed by selective training has to suffice.

The extent of preprimary school instruction, if any, is another difficult choice to make. A year of such education may be more productive than a fourth year of primary education because the initial schooling increases the efficiency of instruction at subsequent levels. In many areas, such instruction may be the child's first exposure to the national language. The children of the poor especially enter primary school without adequate preparation for learning and thus are more likely to become dropouts. Their education can be made more economical by curtailing parental influence on learning habits during the preprimary school years. Preprimary schooling also assists in attacking attitudes prejudicial to the climate necessary for economic growth. The evidence mounts that the costs of creating an efficient work force are determined to a considerable

---

[5] See the pioneering work of John Vaizey, *The Economics of Education* (London: Faber and Faber, 1963).

degree by learning habits and motivations acquired in the years before primary school.

At the secondary school level, education usually forks out into two branches. The poor child is usually shunted into vocational training that often has little bearing on developmental objectives. Because of pressing family needs for more income, the child who undergoes such training may terminate it before he has fully acquired the skills he might have put to use in remunerative employment. The less indigent child may be given a classical education that is of not much more utility in reaching developmental goals. The criterion in this form of segregation is, more likely than not, social status. The rich man's son, no matter how modest his abilities, goes to the classical school, whereas the son of the poor man, no matter how talented, enters the vocational school.

Using public funds to perpetuate social discrimination is questionable. The policy of separation tends to decrease the rate of return on educational investment. A developing nation cannot afford to provide students beyond the primary level with an education that is based on social distinctions and political influence rather than on aptitude. Nor does a nation furnishing education on such a basis easily gain a commitment from the poor to support development efforts.

A case can be made in support of a school-work program in which everyone up to college entrance level would be expected to work part time in the development effort. Beyond that point, a choice would be made between full-time employment or college entrance. This program would increase the likelihood of training that is geared to developmental needs. In terms of real output, keeping students in school up to the age of sixteen or seventeen would become less costly. Such a program might also assist in breaking down social and attitudinal barriers to growth. Students in private secondary schools might take courses jointly with students in public secondary schools, thus promoting further the goal of social and attitudinal change.

Restricted educational resources mean that urgent economic objectives must be reconciled with pressures for social justice. Where the school population is scattered, secondary education funds for rural areas may have to be curtailed. Girls may have to be discriminated against in preference to male enrollments. Classical education may have to receive less financial aid than technical education. The discrimination in secondary education can be implemented partially on the basis of competitive examinations for available openings, thus permitting those with the greatest potential to continue with their education. Those rejected can continue on a pay-as-you-go basis. The alternative policy of charging tuition for all students discriminates against the poor. Any charges necessary should be employed so as to favor the bright poor.

Educational charges incurred by government can be partially recaptured by requiring graduates to work for a stipulated period on priority development projects. A moral and economic justification exists for such policy. An individual whose education has been financed with public funds incurs a responsibility to contribute to society's production. Such a commitment is not only a Soviet custom; it is common business practice in Western societies. The difficulty of this alternative is that in developing nations, the principal industrial employer often is the government. Even though such a policy excites ideological controversy, some system of occupational choice can usually be worked out that reduces coercion to a minimum.

Thus it is evident that because of the scarcity of available resources, drawing up the plan necessarily involves the ascertainment of educational priorities. Time goals are set for a graduated array of educational attainments, and the most immediate occupational requirements are translated into the enrollments that are necessary in each of the educational programs. Thereupon, determinations are made as to the source of recruitment of these individuals and the location of facilities to ensure that a necessary number of graduates will be available when needed.

When priorities have been fixed, estimates can be made with regard to the teaching staff and their expenses, as well as capital equipment costs. If both labor cost as a percentage of total educational cost and total cost per student are known, total costs can be projected with fair accuracy. The problem thereafter is to bargain with the comptroller of the government budget on the specific allotment for education.

Executing the Plan

A cumbersome centralized bureaucracy can impede the efficient execution of educational goals, but this inefficiency can be minimized in a variety of ways. Good private schools, where available, can be employed in executing the plan, their costs subsidized according to the number of students they enroll under the plan. This procedure reduces participation of the bureaucracy in capital outlays. In addition, the widest form of local autonomy should be exercised so as to involve the population in its own educational problem and to evolve a program sensitive to local needs. As soon as the central government has established a system of educational standards and enforcement, the system should allow local areas some flexibility in the choice of teachers, courses above a basic minimum, and the utilization of teaching skills. The efforts of many countries are unnecessarily hampered by excessive centralization of decision making. In these nations, the minister of education can look at his watch and know what is being taught at that moment in any school in the country.

To the maximum extent feasible, new educational facilities should be placed in developing areas in such a way as to provide the best possibilities for achieving goals and evaluating the results of the strategies. The manner in which these areas are chosen is discussed in Chapter 13.

Dramatic results in a few well-chosen sites have more of an impact on the population than modest and widely scattered results. In addition, the close association of such investment with industrial development provides opportunities for a harmonious growth overall. A display of rewards for education provides the poor with a sense of meaningful participation in development.

The greatest resistance to education is likely to be found in the rural areas where it is needed most. People who have been living at a subsistence level for generations dare not innovate; they believe the risk is too great. Therefore, adult education programs in these areas are apt to suffer from high dropout rates. Consequently, incentives have to be provided to stimulate interest in such education so that the programs can be economical.

The educational program for rural areas should include such ways of improving the quantity and quality of food production as improving the soil; shifting to the production of more favorable crops as determined by soil conditions and marketing opportunities; and diversifying crops to remove some of the uncertainties of single cash crops. Training should also be offered in food processing, including food preparation, and in the preservation and utilization of water to raise agricultural yields and to make industrialization feasible in the area. The program should also include general farm management, the overall objective of which is to shift rural energies and resources into production that gives higher yields. Resource management is one of the most important skills needed in rural areas. It is a vital link in the drive to raise the general productivity of the rural community. Competent agricultural technicians are needed for such training.

A variety of possibilities is available with regard to the financing of the educational plan. Charges may be imposed on those who use the new skilled manpower, or private schools and the armed forces may assume part of the costs of the educational program. There is a danger, however, that the army may elect to take over the government. New taxes for educational outlays are inevitable and may be placed either on the general economy or specifically on the developing area. An additional source of funds is foreign aid in the form of either materials or personnel. Donor countries can furnish experts, instructors, and teacher training personnel, or they can donate manpower by taking on a limited number of students in their own country. Depending upon circumstances in the recipient nation, the greater return from such foreign aid may result from contributions in kind or foreign exchange to be used for school construction or for the purchase of materials. Another means of financing is to raise the fees placed on classical education—especially if the more wealthy students are enrolling in such education. Poor students finding themselves thereby at a disadvantage could be offered scholarships on the basis of ability.

Various other avenues are open to control spiraling education costs. Developing nations can cooperate in specialized educational programs by sharing facilities. Courses may be accelerated or integrated. Teacher costs can be reduced by hiring young instructors or instructors from donor nations. Costs can also be lowered by placing schools within population centers or areas that are expected to attract manpower, by establishing pay-as-you-go school programs, by shifting the responsibility for training to employers to the degree that such a shift facilitates the economical use of resources, and by investing employers with responsibility for training in particular applications and restricting formal education to a theoretical base for subsequent applied studies.

Once the plan is in the execution stage, certain criteria are used to ascertain the extent of its impact and direction. These criteria include measurement of percentage increases in enrollments at the primary, secondary, and higher education levels above increases due to population growth, relative shifts of enrollments in different curricula, changes in teacher-pupil ratios, teacher salary increases relative to increases in other occupations, dropout rates, and employment after termination of school, with due consideration given to changing market conditions.

In summary, the following principles apply to the formulation of an educational plan:

1. The plan has to be worked out in collaboration with the manpower authority and the economic planners.

2. A main objective of the plan is not only to expose students to a learning sequence but to rescue them from accumulated errors and, if feasible, to retrain particular individuals with a view to correcting current occupational imbalances.

3. In the initial stages of growth, mass literacy programs, either for children or adults, must be highly selective; choices should be based on individual ability and on the critical needs of particular developing areas.

4. Each short-term objective must be consistent with the resources that are available with the planning period.[6]

EDUCATION IN THE SOVIET UNION

The Soviet Union offers a primary example of the use of education as an instrument of rapid economic growth. The services of teachers in that nation are accorded a high relative value. For example, a college professor earns more than a physician. The results of the Soviet experience have broad implications not only for communist nations but also for Western societies and developing nations generally.

[6] The International Institute for Educational Planning, sponsored by UNESCO, is a source of educational assistance for developing nations. Its stated purpose is to provide aid in adapting educational systems to the needs of economic development.

The Soviet educational system is integrated with capital investment and employment and serves as an underpinning for economic development. Over 8 percent of the national income, the highest percentage in the world, is spent on education. Since the early days of the communist regime, the goal of Soviet society has been a literate and highly educated people. At the end of World War II, the educational effort was stepped up further. Thus, between 1950 and 1961 expenditures per pupil in constant rubles rose 79 percent. In 1964 teacher salaries were increased by 25 percent. In 1969 a major shift took place from a seven-year to an eight-year mandatory school system.

A primary purpose of Soviet education is to prepare individuals for employment and to train them to participate in collective activity to promote the public good. According to this policy, students must teach one another the necessity of self-improvement based on enlightened self-interest. Each student has to assist and evaluate the performance of others and is encouraged to mete out rewards and punishments.

The school system begins in the nursery schools and ends in the universities, from which men and women graduate at about 23 years of age. At the age of seven, a child enters an eight-year primary school, where emphasis is placed on the sciences and technical subjects. Of the basic subjects, mathematics is taught for the entire eight-year period; physics and a foreign language are taught for five years; and chemistry is taught for four years.

The observer of a primary school class in the U.S.S.R. is impressed by the family atmosphere and the teacher's lavish display of affection for the children. A concerted attempt is apparently made to encourage formation of a bond among members of the learning group. Dr. Fred M. Hechinger, Education Editor of *The New York Times,* describes this atmosphere as one that inspires a strong desire for knowledge and study.

After a student completes primary school, a choice is made among three alternatives. The young person who becomes a factory or farm worker can attend secondary evening school for three years. The other options are secondary polytechnical schools that prepare students for skilled jobs or general secondary schools that lead to matriculation at higher institutions or enrollment in vocational schools related to enterprises. The social science subjects in the secondary schools are infiltrated with highly doctrinaire points of view, but students seem to approach such courses with the same zeal that students in the Commonwealth of Pennsylvania react to mandatory courses on the history of Pennsylvania. The educational target is at least two years of secondary education for everyone. Total primary and secondary enrollment in the U.S.S.R. runs ahead of that of the United States.

Khrushchev, the deposed leader of the Soviet Union, proposed changes in the school system before his overthrow. He advocated transferring more responsibility for child rearing to the school system. Every three-month old child would be enrolled in a nursery school and would progress from there to kindergarten and boarding school. His plan envisaged that by 1980, every Soviet child would enter such a nursery school. At the secondary level, Khrushchev proposed that all students in the senior grades would be required to spend approximately one-third of school time at work in a factory or farm.

Khrushchev's proposals were set aside after his dismissal. Aside from the rhetoric leveled against him, convincing arguments were made that his recommendations would be costly and wasteful. A Soviet economist specializing in education reported that only about 11 percent of secondary school graduates with training in the methods of production actually entered such work upon graduation.[7]

The preponderant number of students in the institutions of higher learning come from the general secondary schools. The total enrollment, which is about evenly divided between men and women, is approximately 3 million and is expected to climb to 8 million by 1980. Courses may be taken on a full-time basis, in the evening, or through correspondence. The colleges are essentially technical schools specializing in such fields as engineering, agriculture, and economics. The more qualified students are accepted by the universities, whose basic specialities include humanities, law, economics, agriculture, medicine, and education. Both types of institutions are also heavily involved in basic and applied research. Students are encouraged to write theses on problems faced by industry. Each course runs five to five and a half years. The academic year, including the examination period, is ten months long for most institutions, and lecture attendance is obligatory. Universities are administered by a governing board composed of the rector, the deans and chief administrators, faculty members, and public representatives of organizations that employ graduates.

At the universities of Moscow and Leningrad, the academic year comprises two semesters of seventeen weeks each. Courses require more class hours than those in the United States—about thirty a week. The degree of training is high, and the student choice of courses is low. In other words, the degree of human capitalization in Soviet university education is high.

Supplementing this regular education program are substantial adult education programs that give the workers an opportunity to continue their education either through correspondence courses or in plant training programs. Estimated enrollment in the former is over 1 million; in the latter, approximately 100,000. Labor organizations are a prime source of propaganda encouraging enrollment in the plant training programs, and

7 Harold J. Noah, "The Economics of Education," in *Problems of Communism* (Washington, D.C.: United States Information Agency, 1967). The article is useful reading on the economics of Soviet education. Noah points out that as far back as 1924, Soviet economist S. G. Strumilin made an analysis of inputs and returns to education.

they also have their own schools for the training of trade union leaders. In addition, unions operate some 14,000 "palaces of culture" that offer films, library services, concerts, lectures, art displays, and amateur productions. The Soviet trade union federation has its own publishing house, *Profizdat*.

Under Soviet law, all education is tuition-free. Special vacations, living allowances, and other benefits are provided for students in higher learning institutions. To prevent discrimination, the law also stipulates that firms must establish a quota of persons under the age of eighteen who are to be accepted for their training programs and subsequent employment. In addition, these firms have to commit a certain number of jobs to secondary school graduates.

The underlying philosophy of the educational system is apparently equal opportunity for everyone regardless of their social position. By "education," the Soviets imply the maximum development of producers consistent with individual abilities. The adult emerging from the system is supposed to be cooperative and self-assured—a person who seeks work and strives for efficiency in order to promote the social good. Group activity is fun and, perchance, is more efficient than individual activity.

The system seems to be highly regarded by the people. In an economy where some 65 percent of the workers' wages is spent on food and where quarters are crowded, a boarding school for children is an advantage to mothers who want to work. In these schools, children obtain opportunities that they might not receive otherwise, such as good food and artistic training. Soviet parents are keenly aware of the educational advantages existing now that were not commonly available before the revolution of October 1917.

The educational program is influenced by the shifting problems of labor supply and demand, which determine both the quality and quantity of students that will be needed. As an example, in the mid 1960s, an excessive number of college aspirants were created by the educational program and could not be absorbed by institutions of higher learning. This situation brought about an increase in the number of unskilled youths, many of whom manifested a dislike for manual work. As a result of the increased unemployment among this age group, job training in the primary and secondary schools was given added emphasis. But this shift, in turn, brought about new problems. Some school children began to learn trades for which they had no special interest. Management, on the other hand, became disinclined to take on young trainees, necessitating still another series of adjustments.

Educational planning is more efficient when labor is scarce and jobs have broad specifications. Despite inadequacies in their educational preparation, workers are more readily absorbed. In contrast, as jobs become more scarce and more specialized, educational planning becomes correspondingly more difficult. Because of greater specialization, detailed educational planning becomes difficult as the economy reaches an advanced stage of economic growth.

What assessment can be made of a system that seeks to control education from infancy and that focuses sharply on economic growth? Professor Urie Brofenbrenner notes that Soviet children of preschool age are less aggressive toward each other and toward adults than are children of the same age in the United States. He observes the emotional blandness of Soviet children and misses the "smiles, the spontaneity and interest in other persons." [8] Speculating on the effects of the system, Brofenbrenner notes the strong, almost unrealistic Soviet tendency to avoid deviant behavior. He feels that although education may perpetuate this conformity, its deleterious side effects will eventually cause the system to be modified along more humanistic lines.[9]

Whatever the outcome, the Soviet experiment in education has important implications.[10] For the first time in history, millions of children are being raised outside the family from the first months of their lives until late adolescence. In the West, family control over children yields haphazardly to powerful forces of the market place and mass communications. By juxtaposing both experiences, interesting lessons can be learned regarding the imparting of values and social responsibilities by instruments other than the family.

THE RETURN ON THE INVESTMENT IN EDUCATION

Real results from educational planning cannot be expected for at least a generation, at the end of which the individuals born at the beginning of the program will have been fully exposed to it. That a revolutionary change in the education of a people can be achieved in a generation is attested by the Soviet experience. Moreover, a generation of investment in education is the least coercive approach to the removal of social and institutional barriers to growth.

We can assume that an increase in human capabilities is the main objective of education, that incentives exist to seek higher incomes out of the increase in those capabilities, and that jobs exist to utilize the higher level of capabilities. Although these assumptions may not be warranted for all groups in a society, a society dominated by such values succeeds readily in transmitting them to minorities.

Nevertheless, developing nations can begin with the same amount of resources, the same level of existing capacities, and the same economic structures—and achieve different results. Identical expenditures on education do not always bring identical rates of return.

[8] Urie Brofenbrenner, "The Making of the New Soviet Man: A Report of Institutional Methods of Education in the U.S.S.R." (unpublished paper).
[9] *Ibid.*
[10] The methods are also applied in other communist countries.

The ability of a country to make profitable educational investments is related to its rate of population growth. If the population rises precipitously, the individuals of educable age outnumber the producers, thus dissipating educational outlay and threatening educational objectives. Furthermore, the more technologically advanced the developing nation, the greater is its return on educational expenditures. In a nation with an already high level of technology, education serves to accelerate the rate of technological change to the detriment of employment objectives. A developing nation can thus actually overspend on education.

In addition, differences in family and culture patterns can produce different rates of return on the same investment in nations with similar rates of illiteracy. If a nation such as Spain provides a clue, a country that transmits a wealth of culture from one generation to the next and possesses family relationships based on strong ties of affection often provides a zest for learning that increases the returns from educational investment. There are exceptionally motivated poverty-stricken families that respond favorably to educational efforts. In some developing areas, however, the family environment lowers returns on investment. Accordingly, society has a legitimate concern for the family life patterns of the poor on whom public resources are concentrated. Whole societies exhibit these family differences. In one sector, the poor may have a sound relationship; in another, the relationship may border on the pathological. These differences have a profound effect on returns to education.[11]

Education input includes instruction, administration, courses, and capital as well as the incentive and intelligence of the learners multiplied by the total years of instruction. The amount of payoff varies with the amount and quality of these inputs, each of which may have a depressing or an elevating effect on the others. The amount of capital invested and its distribution among the other inputs depend on returns that accrue at different input combinations, and these in comparison with returns that would accrue by placing investment in industry, agriculture, and social overhead.

As a general rule, the rate of return from a given amount of education should exceed the costs of such an education, which include teachers' salaries, costs of erecting and maintaining buildings, costs of books and other materials, and administrative overhead. The net addition to output varies with quality of instruction,[12] course content, materials, administra-

---

[11] The impact of disorganized family life on educational investment is reported in the findings of Dr. Charles A. Malone, Associate Professor of Clinical Psychology at the University of Pennsylvania. Malone points out that the ability to play with ideas, a requisite to learning, is damaged in homes where children witness drunkenness, sexual promiscuity, violence, and abuse. *The New York Times,* January 16, 1966.

[12] By "quality instruction" is meant a thorough grounding in the most current knowledge of the particular subject taught, the ability of the student to apply such knowledge, and, in the case of future teachers and scientists, the ability also to increase such knowledge.

tion, number of years of education, demand for the newly acquired skills, ability of the learner and amount of time spent in the labor force, which in developing areas is affected by the risks of day-to-day living.   The allocation of funds to the support of a mass drive for adult literacy is defensible for sentimental reasons but wasteful because returns from such investment are necessarily short term.   The motivation of learners is affected by such characteristics as economizing spirit, cooperative spirit, political and social knowledge, extent of participation in decision making, and physical and mental health.   Institutions that encourage these qualities increase the rates of return.   Consequently, income from investment is also increased through investments in such areas as public health and housing.   An allocation of funds should thus be made in these areas so long as marginal returns are greater.   Furthermore, the relationship between these two categories is reciprocal.

Generally, the higher the level of the skill demanded, the higher the educational investment cost, but the greater the uncertainty that the skill will be used.   This uncertainty is mitigated to the degree a scarcity of skills exists in the market in relation to the demand for such skills.

Demand and supply factors have reciprocating effects on each other that may be generated by external forces.   Thus, a rise in labor demand may induce an increase in educational investment.   The higher-level capabilities that result from this investment may cause the labor supply to swing to political radicalism, which may in turn reduce collective labor efficiency and cause a decline in available investment funds.

Strategy that concentrates expenditures on the education of children defers a payoff further into the future, increases the possibility of dissipating the investment because of delay in its use, and consumes scarce funds more readily by spreading them among a greater number of individuals.   This is not to say, however, that a position of semiautonomous growth can be reached without the mass education of children. Generally, returns are maximized by concentrating investment in the young, the most able, and the most motivated.   The longer a developing country can prolong the productive life of such a person, the greater the return is going to be.   This generalization assumes that excessive lulls do not occur in the training or employment of the young person.   If there is a substantial breach and it is not filled by refresher training, much of the educational investment is lost.   Moreover, educational investment is wasted to the extent that work opportunities are not provided to put it to use.

Investment may be made steadily or intermittently, depending on the type of skill being developed and the changing demand for it.   In any case, in order to sustain incentive, a relatively quick and visible payoff should accrue to students or trainees who undergo sacrifices.

As an overall rule, the payoff of income spent on education does not rise perceptibly during the initial stages of educational investment but increases significantly thereafter and then begins to decline. The fall is associated with a decline in investment per capita as the educational program is extended and as the recipients of the investment advance in age.

At early stages of economic development, a close association exists between individual capability and individual earnings; however, as the economy matures, the relationship becomes blurred. The formal evidence of education, the diploma, becomes a social claim on output rather than evidence of an individual contribution thereto. Wealth becomes a symbol of political bargaining power. The level of individual income is based on rights of inheritance, rights to the earnings of commercial enterprises, and political influence. At the same time, education as consumption rather than as human capital formation rises. In brief, the traditional society in many of its aspects reappears.

The returns on investment costs incurred by a particular user of new skills may accrue to subsequent users. For example, the return on an investment in military training may accrue to subsequent employers of the acquired skills.

The more specific the training, the less it is transferable. Therefore, the more does labor turnover make the cost of such training a loss, both for the training organization and for the individual with the specialized training. Conversely, the more general the training, the more widely diffuse or wasted is the productivity that arises from it.

There are a number of ways in which the investment in education may be wasted. For example, it may be used to develop skills for which a demand does not exist during the planned period, or it may be expended on individuals whose resulting productivity is lower than that of others to whom the education could have been given. Qualified persons may leave a country or an area once they have acquired their education. In addition, the educated may move toward employment that is traditionally low in productivity, such as services and government.

Nations differ in the pressures they exert on people of low productivity to improve their skills. A developing country that has a modern sector and a land surplus paradoxically may have more economic difficulties than one less endowed because workers tend to move either toward new land areas, where they produce inefficiently, or to cities, where highly efficient methods of production reduce industrial opportunities to raise their capabilities.

Educational investment refers to any planned activity that increases human capabilities. Research can conceivably affect the capabilities of the investigator and may be worth the expenditure for that reason alone. Until more is known of the educational process, a method of deriving the greatest returns per given outlay cannot be effectively determined.

Summation

Writing before Christ, a philosopher made the following recommendation: Sow corn if planning for a year; if planning for a decade, plant trees; if planning for life, educate. The idea he expressed is not without some pertinency to the problem of expecting from education a payoff in economic growth.

Education constitutes a process of *creation* of a body of knowledge by a teacher-student interchange, of *absorption* of the creation by the learner, and of *use.* The knowledge imparted in education is *generalized* and *specialized.* The learner in a modernizing society is faced with a rising generalized and specialized fund of knowledge. The problem is how to impart these funds of knowledge in the most economical way.

That a complete man, rather than merely an efficient producer, should be the product of education is a commendable goal. But unless developing nations view their educational resources primarily as an instrument for achieving economic growth, they are likely to fail to acquire the economic structures necessary to attain the goal of a complete man.

To conclude, developing nations face difficult choices with regard to their educational policy. Five are foremost. First, how should resources be divided among the different levels of education? Second, what should be the distribution of college enrollments among the different faculties? Third, should the emphasis be on quality or quantity? Fourth, how much of the educational load should be shifted to employers and private organizations? Fifth, what incentives should be provided to get individuals into the right education and into the right jobs? For these hard choices, the principles of education cited here provide practical guidelines.

6

LABOR ORGANIZATION DIFFERENCES BETWEEN DEVELOPED AND DEVELOPING NATIONS

Central to any discussion of the relationship between labor organizations and economic development is the question of how the structure and policies of labor organizations emerge as a nation pursues its economic development—that is, as the country forms a labor force of rising productivity, as its agriculture becomes more efficient, and as the spectrum of its industrial activity widens. Furthermore, is this evolutionary experience similar for all developing nations? Lastly, as the economies of these countries approximate the industrial input-output patterns of mature economies, are more sophisticated forms of labor organization also approximated?

Such an inquiry must deal with two significant related issues. The first is the role, if any, that these evolving organizations play in the developmental process. Do they facilitate or hinder this process? The second issue to be considered is whether the ideological basis for their structure and conduct is Western democracy or Marxist authoritarianism. Both of these issues are difficult to analyze because of the brief history of trade unionism in developing countries.

An analysis of labor unions apart from the economic and cultural environment in which they are found is not too meaningful. In addition to the stresses created by its own rank-and-file members, the union is subject to the pushes and pulls of different interest groups within society including management, unorganized workers, and other organizations claiming worker loyalties. The multiple relationships among these groups, as well as the cultural context in which they occur, vary among nations. So many variables are at play in an industrial relations system, especially in a democratic society, that analyzing them is vastly complicated. To be meaningful, however, the role of the labor organization has to be placed in such a setting.

In both developing and advanced nations, there are organizations that refer to themselves as the representatives of labor. These organizations vary in form, function, influence, and degree of involvement with the government. For some countries, whether "labor organization" is the proper term for these entities is a question of semantics. The debate with regard to what a labor organization is and what it is not is confused by the manner in which the question is posed. American trade unionists and students of industrial relations tend to simplify the problem. Organized labor as it exists in the United States is viewed as a prototype of goodness in labor organization. Departure from this model represents less than goodness. The reasoning behind this argument is that American trade unions are influential and free, and democracy exists in the United States. Therefore, only where trade unions are free and powerful (that is to say, are like American labor organizations) can there be freedom and democracy. There are variations on this theme, but all are based on the same set of premises.

These arguments do not appear to consider the manner in which the American economy evolved and the way its labor organizations have subordinated themselves to government. The assumptions also exist that collective bargaining, as it is practiced by American trade unions, is exportable, regardless of the cultural context and economic growth level of the recipient nation, and that collective bargaining is the sole means of guaranteeing industrial democracy. Both assumptions merit critical examination.

In developing countries, democracy is neither guaranteed by the existence of powerful unions (as evidenced by Argentina) nor precluded by the existence of weak unions (as evidenced by India). Moreover, American students of trade unionism lack objectivity regarding what American labor is now and, because of the rapidity and uncertainty of change, what unions in developing economies are likely to become. Will the mounting pressures and ebbing influences to which these movements are presently subject ultimately push them toward some common ground? To speculate on this hypothesis, the origins and historical evolution of the different labor movements have to be studied in detail.

The environment in which these movements originate and the history that they inherit shape their initial characteristics and control their subsequent evolution. The milieu of a labor movement includes the range and complexity of the economic structure at the time that the movement emerges, the prevailing political system and its historical origins, the extent of social mobility and class consciousness, the degree of difference in education and training among the various social classes, the diversity and degree of compatibility of cultural values, the value standards of the laboring classes (for example, the relative importance of such concepts as individualism and pragmatism), and what the society in general and the working class in particular believe to be success in life.

Of similar importance are factors that influence the character of labor organizations and condition their evolution. These elements include relative claims to leadership of the working classes, the individuals and institutions in the country that exert a coercive influence on labor leaders, the degree of worker protest, and the intelligence and technical training of the leaders. The successful labor union official has to control and reconcile both the imperatives of economic development and the environmental forces in a manner that will enable his organization to survive and prosper.

Conceivably, the dissimilarity of labor organizations among countries may not be ascribable to different stages of economic development and may not be expected to disappear at advanced stages of growth. Indeed, to speak of "stages" may be premature at this point. Different institutional forms and processes may ultimately result from the confrontation between the universal imperative of industrialization and the preemptive rights of the particular cultural system.

CONTRASTS WITH UNIONS OF THE WEST

The history of American organized labor is a record of its response to the industrial revolution that took place in the United States in the nineteenth century. The aftermath of this period of economic development was the evolution of a diversified mass production economy and an efficient labor force whose expectations had, for the most part, been realized. Despite adversity, crisis, and conflict, the singular consistent feature of the American economy has been the success achieved by both employers and employees in the pursuit of the values of their society. For most, economic achievement was the reward for hard work and perseverance. Unlike workers in most nations, American workers have optimistically faced the prospect of a lifetime of work as a means of improving their living standards and those of their children. They have rebelled only when these standards were threatened by other groups.

Labor organization in the United States is an outgrowth of the westward movement of the country's human and economic resources and the vastness of its markets. The accelerated westward expansion that followed the financial crisis of 1857 was made possible by an abundance of land, timber, coal and other mineral resources, and enterprising individuals. New modes of transportation facilitated more efficient production and distribution, and by 1869 both the rail system and the economy spanned the continent.

The evolution of American labor organizations was a reaction to this economic expansion. With some dramatic exceptions, the confrontation between employers and trade unions generally focused on the necessities of particular plants and firms, each of which represented a varying combination of resources, technology, philosophy, and consumer tastes that the union sought to control in its own interest. The geographical location and the scale of production affected employer costs, which, in turn, influenced each firm's rate of capitalization, efficiency of production, and competitive position. With substantial success, American labor organizations responded to this diversity with variety in their own policies.

American trade unionism is thus a product of pragmatic optimism rather than despair. Segments of the population that experienced frustration either did not become part of the labor movement or were absorbed in such manner as not to change its general outlook. The absence of feudalism in the United States has also meant that neither employer nor employee has found labor demeaning. The line of distinction between employer and employee in the United States is more blurred than is the case in developing nations and is more functional than social. If the American employer has had feelings of superiority, the rule of the game has been not to assert them but to talk to his employees in a common language. The existence of rural slave labor and an urban subproletariat were aberrations, but they too have had to conform to the mainstream of economic growth based on optimism and egalitarianism.

Consequently, American labor unions do not have a precise parallel, even in Western Europe. The high degree of centralization of European labor organizations is reflected in their national bargaining patterns and in the contracts that they stand ready to negotiate with the national government. The labor unions of Western Europe are the product of the feudal and guild systems. In these countries, capitalism was an opprobrious term and class consciousness was the rule rather than the exception. Out of this milieu, the European labor unions emerged as national working-class movements that became closely allied with political parties and began to play an influential role in the governing process. That some unions should abandon hope for obtaining wage increases that are too high for the nation as a whole to support is conceivable in Europe but improbable in the United States.

In other words, European unions have a greater national identity. In the United States, the union began not as a national protest movement but as a particular craft in a local area. A national outlook has had to evolve slowly and, at times, painfully. American unions placed their emphasis on collective bargaining with particular employers. European unions sought broader objectives through collective bargaining, affiliation with political parties, and cooperative movements in industry.

The unions of France and Italy deviate from the European labor union tradition in political and ideological orientation. These differences are due principally to the greater distinctions that exist in these nations between rich and poor. Added to these greater social differences are the divisive effects of the influence of the Catholic Church, the absence of a craft orientation, and the greater individualism.

The evolution of American trade unionism was unparalleled in that trade unionists, favored with a labor scarcity, found it more beneficial to establish a commitment to the employer who hired the workers they represented rather than to political parties. The trade-union federation in the United States was averse to the use of legislation to raise labor standards and departed from such a policy only three decades ago. European labor unions, on the other hand, bargain for fringe benefits in their parliaments. American labor unions have looked upon the employer less as an abstraction and more as a source of economic opportunity.

In the developing countries, the unions may be in control of a political party and, with different degrees of success, may seek to govern in order to achieve specific economic and social goals. Union leadership at various levels is expected to conform to the political image set by the top echelon. At the plant level, employer-trade union agreements are negotiated only when a labor dispute erupts. The employer may pursue his business without ever talking to a trade-union official.

Consequently, the unions are also less a response to the industrialization process than a means of social and political identification, and therefore, they easily become instruments for promoting the ambitions of politically minded union leaders. Nor are these organizations a means of craft identity or exclusion or a means of protest against industrialization. The workers in these organizations do not want to smash the machine; indeed they may be enthralled by it. They do not even appear to be particularly interested in a method of stipulating conditions of employment with a particular employer.

The labor organizations of developing countries are not the product of the successful rise of capitalism. The economies of these countries are state-operated. The biggest source of ferment is the drive for self-respect. Unions in these nations are more likely than not highly fragmented. Their incidence is severely limited by the paucity of large-scale industry and by the employment of the dominant part of the labor force in agriculture. In the industrial relationship that does exist, they are dominated by the employer and live by his sufferance. Moreover, their leaders generally do not rise from the workshops but are rather professional and white-collar employees using labor organizations to promote their political ambitions and ideologies. The unions are more competent in generating mass protest than in improving work standards by projecting a series of goals bargainable with an employer over the long run. In fact, as mentioned previously, employer bargaining often is not a pressing concern.

The principal propellants of the growth of these unions are nationalism and anticolonialism. Politically minded union leaders in Asian and African countries view labor organizations initially as instruments of national independence. The unions are expected to mobilize the masses in support of national objectives as soon as they have been decided upon. Having begun as a political force, these unions try to maintain that role after the acquisition of national independence, but they thereupon are considered to be a possible obstruction to economic development. In Latin America, where national independence is not an issue, the labor organizations protest against the power structure of the society in which they operate.

Alliances of these labor organizations with political groupings may be in the form of either a variety of labor federations, each allied with a particular political party (as in Chile and India), or a single federation dominated by a particular political persuasion (Argentina). Where strong pluralistic forces are present before the beginning of the development process, the labor organization–political party pluralism tends to survive. Where totalitarian forces are strong, the authoritarian ruler may succeed in consolidating and dominating the labor organizations.

The labor organizations are concentrated mostly in the government service, in a key industry of the developing country (banking, services, communications, and transportation), or in the characteristic industry of the country (oil refining in Venezuela, extractive industries in Africa, and fruit plantations in Central America). Geographically, these unions are located mostly in the capitals of their respective countries, a situation that hinders the growth of an efficient national organization and curtails their influence in fixing labor standards.

Because labor organizations have evolved in this way in developing nations, the servility of union members may be perpetuated even though union leaders acquire status. The laboring classes may continue to view the government rather than the individual employer as the focal point of concessions to improve their standards and may not view self-improvement as a product of individual effort acting through their organizations. In return for government concessions, the working classes may be expected to stand ready as the political prop of the chief of state. Such a tendency toward Roman circus economies is a threat to economic development in these countries and may forestall the rise of an efficient labor force.

New influences may eventually produce more favorable results. The governments of developing countries may ultimately recognize the importance of an enterprising labor force. The cycle of mass protest and government assuagement may be broken; reliance on government as the provider of bounty may decline. The unions can provide leadership by encouraging their constituents to remove grievances from the streets and channel them into institutions that do not hinder the rise of efficiency.

CHARACTERISTICS OF LABOR IN DEVELOPING NATIONS

Labor organizations of developing countries are similar in a number of respects. In each country, for example, the unions evince a generally strong egalitarian spirit. Also prevalent is the reluctance of the rank-and-file members to provide financial support for the unions.

The union leaders are restricted by the same factors that hinder the growth of powerful industrial organizations—mass illiteracy, the migratory character of labor, and the periodic shifting of labor in and out of the work force. Obviously, it is difficult for a labor leader to operate an organization when the rank-and-file members cannot read the bulletin board.

In some countries, labor organization is inspired and directed by the government. The government official is given time off to pursue his activities as a labor official. Where the development program is controlled by an authoritarian government, the unions either are neutralized as a source of influence or are made a part of planning and strategy. The greater the degree of such planning, the greater the degree of control imposed on organized labor consistent with such planning. In brief, some modernizing nations try to make organized labor impotent or to subordinate it to national objectives in return for participation in the government.

An enterprise in the developing country that hires workers in considerable numbers provides a strategic foothold for labor organizations. Several factors account for this situation. The higher level of education and training among these employees compared with other work forces provides a base for the growth of competent trade unionism and industrial efficiency. The efficiency provides the economic wherewithal to improve employment terms and to give credit to the union for so doing. Furthermore, the frictions that are often the result of the intimate relationship that exists between a union and small enterprise are not present in the large firm, where the management is generally more enlightened, more affluent, and even at times more inclined to assist the union in becoming a functioning institution. This assistance, in turn, may induce the rank and file to support their labor organization morally and financially. A trade union that thus thrives may establish a base for expansion to other industrial and geographical sectors.

The diversities that exist among developing countries with respect to their labor organizations are based on the countries' historical origins and on their levels of industrialization. Generally, the lower the level of industrial development, the more the power of the labor organization is dependent on the willingness of the government to encourage its growth by legislation. In the new countries of Africa, the growth of labor organizations has taken place within the context of the national movement. The people who come into political power are associates of, if not the same persons as, those who lead the labor movement. Barring any ensuing struggle for power, political and labor leaders consider themselves collaborators. No such association exists in the older developing nations, such as those of Latin America where these leaders may have an arm's-length relationship or may even be hostile toward each other. An industrial relations system can thus be seen as a useful vehicle for measuring the degree of alienation among different segments in the economy. The greater the alienation, the greater can be the deterrent to growth.

Labor organizations in these countries differ in the extent of their claims to working-class loyalty. In Argentina, for example, the claim is strong; in India and Pakistan, it is weak. To some extent, this loyalty is a measure of the effectiveness with which unions succeed in obtaining concessions from employers. It is also a measure of the ideological bond between labor official and the rank-and-file member.

The influence of intellectuals within the labor organization may also have a different effect in different countries. In India, for example, intellectuals have tended to weaken the organization's effectiveness, but such leaders have not had this effect in Mexico. The dissimilarity may be a reflection of the level of skill of these individuals and of the amount of time they devote to the union. So long as the educational level of the worker is low, the so-called intellectual (meaning a person with a college degree or high school diploma) fills a need. If the rank-and-file union member cannot obtain assistance through an articulate union leader, he is likely to acquiesce to the domination of his organization by an individual with political ambitions.

Dissimilarities also exist in the degree of political orientation. Some organizations (Indonesia, Chile) are adjuncts of political parties. Others (Argentina, Mexico), although related to particular political parties, have some degree of independence. The political orientation, where considerable, may be due to labor's sense of alienation from society (Latin American nations generally, with the exception of Mexico and Cuba). The orientation may arise from the initial creation of labor organizations as an arm of political parties at a low level stage of economic growth. In some authoritarian countries that are undergoing economic development, labor organizations may shun political alliances out of a desire for self-preservation.

The labor-management relationship in these economies is generally characterized by feelings of class consciousness. Managers may belong to an unapproachable social class or to a separate race. In the extreme, as in some Latin American countries, the working class may view management as the enemy whose members would be among the first to be liquidated with a change in the political order. This feeling is often exacerbated by the supervisor-employee relationship, particularly if the supervisor has recruited the workers from rural areas with the intention of deriving a maximum of work at a minimum of wages.

As mentioned earlier, a paternalistic philosophy on the part of employers may be in the interest of the long-term growth of human resources.

The worker is susceptible to exploitation by his industrial environment in a manner that only the paternalistic employer can effectively do something about. Moreover, some managers pursue a deliberate policy of paternalism to gradually wean the employee of dependence. In the short term, such a policy weakens labor organization. Management can, however, assist the union in evolving into a militant and skilled organization, but such a variety of paternalism is rare.

Unions differ also in their degree of effectiveness at the company level. The negotiating advantage at the bargaining table is, by far, on the employer's side. The future of the unions is frequently dependent on employer attitudes, and if the unions are effective, it is often the employer who has elected to make them so. An employer can create differences within labor organizations by giving the union a positive role to perform and assisting the union in doing so.

In the main, an authentic bargaining relationship between employers and organized labor does not exist in these economies. Some employers would rather do without the institution, and employees often are indifferent to the idea. To the extent that a bargaining relationship does exist, it is subject to limits imposed by the employer. The establishment of any degree of collective bargaining arises from a variety of such mutually reinforcing factors as a high level of economic growth, employer choice, sympathetic government support, and absence of a sense of alienation from society among the laboring classes. Therefore, in some countries collective bargaining is extensive (Mexico, Argentina), in others it exists to a limited degree (India, Chile), and in still others (Pakistan, Peru), it is only a glimmer.

A lively dispute rages among students of economic development as to whether labor organizations hinder the developmental process by diverting scarce capital to consumption and whether they should therefore be restrained by the government. The argument is advanced that because the urgent problem in developing nations is economic growth, the unions must subordinate their drive for wage gains to this end. Further, no basis exists for sharing profits of industrial enterprises. The argument is an exaggeration. At initial stages of economic growth, unions are so weak that they need prodding. Those that exert some influence are usually found in large enterprises, where bargaining power rests with the employer and their demands can be blown over with a stern grimace.

Workers are not likely to accept the primary need of developing nations to raise labor efficiency without giving them a share in the returns. To achieve economic development, a rise in consumption is as necessary as savings are necessary for investment in order to improve the physiological-psychological states of workers. To the people of developing areas, consumption is not some theoretical goal achievable through first increasing savings but rather it is having something today that they lacked yesterday. They have to consume more before they can be more productive. Prudent saving habits may be desirable in order that a saving spiral may ultimately be set in motion, but the rural person is already frugal. The problem lies more in opening up productive channels of investment for such savings and in convincing the rural person that he will not be cheated as in the past. If labor organizations are hostile to economic planners, it is often because of the abstract manner in which planners treat the problem of savings and consumption.

Suppressing trade unions is not a requisite for economic development, even though authoritarian regimes have done so. The suppression serves more the quest for monolithic power. Governments can actually accelerate growth by seeking the consensus of trade unions, because these organizations have the opportunity to convince their rank-and-file members of their responsibilities with regard to savings and productivity. The alternative is to try to seek these objectives at considerable human cost. The idea that labor organizations hinder economic development appears to be an abdication of leadership.

EXTERNAL INFLUENCES

Organized labor of developing countries is the attraction of self-serving groups throughout the world who claim to save their workers from the ideological perils of the present world and those of the next. The proselytizing forces are without historical parallel, surpassing the efforts of Marxists to influence the European and American labor movements in the last century. Beginning with the end of World War II, when the Allied governments established a policy of wooing labor, resources in money and talent have steadily increased. Foreign governments, their labor organizations, church organizations, and sundry other groups have sought to affect the thinking of the workers in developing nations. They have provided financial assistance, guided tours in the donor country, so-called education and training programs, and even furniture. Some governments that preach against communist subversion have used their espionage agencies for subversion of labor organizations in the name of promoting democracy in developing nations. In Asia, Africa, and Latin America, Eastern- and Western-oriented groups work side by side.

These proselytizing organizations are of 4 principal types: internationally federated labor organizations, national labor organizations with direct relationships in other countries, the organizations of foreign governments, and international agencies of the United Nations. In the first group, the International Confederation of Free Trade Unions (ICFTU), together with its regional bodies in developing areas, holds a prominent position. Allied with it are the international trade secretariats, which consist of trade unions that represent the same industry and craft in different countries. The counterpart of the ICFTU in the communist world is the World Federation of Trade Unions, an organization comprised of unions in the communist countries and communist-dominated federations of other nations.

The ICFTU seems to have difficulty in gaining new adherents and in keeping old friends. In the developing countries of Africa, it tends to be associated with foreign nations who have acquired a tarnished image in these countries. Because of alleged inaction and misuse of funds, the organization also incurs the displeasure of the AFL-CIO in the United States.

Other intercountry organizations include the Confederation of Arab Trade Unionists, which promotes regional interests in Arab countries; the All-Africa Trade Union Federation, which has ties with the East; and the African Trade Union Confederation, which has a Western orientation.

Among the proselytizing national labor organizations, the American AFL-CIO holds a prominent position. Through the American Institute for Free Labor Development (AIFLD), a quasi-public agency supported by the American government, the American labor federation already has a heavy commitment in Latin America and may even seek to extend its influence in Africa and Asia, especially in areas where the ICFTU is not influential. The British Trades Union Congress, the AFL-CIO counterpart, is influential in Commonwealth countries that are in the process of development, whereas the West German Federation of Labor allocates its resources throughout Africa, the Middle East, and (to some extent) Latin America. France also manifests an interest in becoming influential in Latin American countries.

Several other national organizations are worth mentioning. The Yugoslav Confederation of Trade Unions manages to remain unaffiliated with international labor organizations of either East or West. Cuban and Chilean trade union organizations seek to create a hegemony in Latin American countries. The ORIT (Organización Regional Interamericana de Trabajadores) in Mexico is a regional organization of Latin American federations that belong to the ICFTU. Lastly, the All-China Confederation of Trade Unions seeks to exert influence in that area of the world.

The extent of the influence of foreign governments over labor organizations in developing countries is difficult to weigh because governments often wield influence indirectly through other organizations. For example, the United States government uses the AFL-CIO as an instrument of policy. Although the AFL-CIO asserts in its public statements that its organizations operate freely, the extent of the interrelationship and mutual influence that exist between government and federation are apparently not fully revealed to the public. The American government also plays a role through foundations supported by the Central Intelligence Agency (CIA). For instance, the Asia Foundation seeks to exert influence on the power structure of fourteen Asian countries, but it was ordered by the Indian government to close shop in that country as a result of its acknowledgment that it had accepted funds from the CIA.

The United Nations and such UN member organizations as the International Labor Organization (ILO) and the United Nations Educational, Social, and Cultural Organization (UNESCO) are included in the category of international agencies. The ILO exerts pressure on labor unions (with some success, even in the Soviet Union) to conform to general trade union standards, but it has a greater influence with the organized labor of developing countries than with that of mature economies. The ILO labor training program is located at the International Institute for Labor Studies in Geneva.

Overall, these organizations seek to wield influence in several areas. They attempt to export their own structures and industrial relationships, although the exported model and the organization established in the recipient country often diverge. This situation is inevitably caused by such factors as occupational and industrial differences in the respective labor forces of donor and recipient nations and dissimilarities in their ties with other indigenous organizations, such as political parties and governmental and community agencies.

Competitive attempts are also made by these organizations to transfer their ideologies, as the AIFLD does in Latin America. In such a pursuit, the labor spokesmen of the United States and the Soviet Union are both guilty of expounding an ideology that is at variance with actual domestic situations and events. At the same time, the recipients are inclined to think of these individuals as spokesmen of the foreign policy of their respective nations.

Lastly, exporting organizations seek to develop a proficiency in the skills deemed necessary for the functioning of labor unions in the developing economy. Of the technical assistance that emanates from the United States, something will be said in a later chapter. Obviously, what is considered technical competence by a Western exporter may not be so regarded by a Marxist proselytizer.

The United States has placed great emphasis on influencing organized labor in developing countries. The government has brought over some 6,000 labor officials from developing nations since the end of World War II. The annual budget of the AIFLD amounts to over $1 million. In addition to Latin America, the United States has commitments in Puerto Rico, India, Uganda, Manila, and Tel-Aviv. The effects of these efforts and resources are not precisely known because this information is difficult to obtain from either the exporting or receiving organizations.

Labor officials trained with American funds are not averse to articulating words their benefactors like to hear. But whether the subsequent behavior of these officials in their own country differs materially from what it would have been without such training is doubtful. Their actions appear to be influenced more by their socioeconomic background, their education, the elites and workers with whom they deal, and the enterprise in which they operate.

American trade unionists are not especially prepared to assist labor organizations in developing nations, primarily because their training in trade unionism is inappropriate to the conditions in those nations and is becoming inappropriate to some degree even in the United States. These unionists are proven masters in obtaining wage increases for their members. Experience in gaining such increases in the American environment, however, is not sufficient preparation for the different contingencies that arise in developing nations.

American and foreign trade union officials belabor each other with false conceptions. Industrial relations personnel in developing countries visiting the United States frequently comment on the extraordinary degree of government control of the American industrial relations system that was not evident from their long-distance observations or their conversations with American trade union officials. Contributing to this distortion is literature lamenting the greater degree of government control in developing economies. Furthermore, American trade unionists speak of "free" American labor without due consideration of the changes that have occurred in the United States since the end of World War II.

With regard to their role in economic development abroad, American trade unionists assert that fostering trade unionism and anticommunism promotes development. Such an approach presents the possibility that the developing unions will be committed to a course of action that may be damaging to their growth as an institution. Developing nations can ask some pertinent questions: Why should their unions agree to be molded in the American image? What ideas do American labor officials have to offer about mechanisms and processes that would be useful to the recipient nations? Why should foreign labor leaders be accepted as leaders in a country where they are not citizens and where they might subvert local institutions?

The pressing requirement of unions in developing countries is not to learn highly sophisticated techniques of old industrial economies but to wage a cooperative effort to develop the human resources of their country and to teach their following that the quid pro quo for a higher standard of living is higher productivity. If these trade unionists do not become involved in these problems, they may find themselves isolated from the institutions that evolve in the course of national development.

FACTORS ACCOUNTING FOR INTERCOUNTRY DIFFERENCES

When labor organizations of developing countries are placed in the broader context of their industrial relations environment, a number of major factors emerge that account for intercountry differences. These factors include:

1. *Degree of competition allowed by the political system.* In a democ-

racy, there will be a proliferation of rival labor organizations. An authoritarian regime tends to absorb all existing labor organizations.

2. *Diversity of group values.* These values may be due to a quirk of history or a summation of a past that no longer exists. They affect group objectives by determining what is just, who is loyal to what group, and what constitutes the good life on the basis of the experience of past generations. Values fix the groups and institutions whose coercive influence leaders in the industrial relations system resist or voluntarily yield to as it fits their preferences.

3. *Differences in objectives of labor leaders.* The objectives of labor leaders may range from reforming society to finding a comfortable niche in an organization and avoiding leadership altogether. Their goals may be either technically or ideologically oriented. They may mirror the aspirations and points of view of the rank-and-file members, or the masses may be used as instruments of personal gain.

4. *Differences arising out of structural relationships.* The outlook of the labor official is affected by his place in both the labor organization and the industrial relations system. The size of the organization, the characteristics of coworkers at his level of organization, and the complexity of pressures at a particular organizational level influence his outlook and behavior.

5. *Extent of competition for leadership of labor.* In many countries, labor organizations are not the sole organizers of labor; a variety of rival organizations may exist in the economic, political, religious, and social spheres.

6. *Differences in worker success.* In each developing country, the working classes experience different degrees of success. Such experience has an impact on the tone of labor organization.

7. *Characteristics of the employer-employee relationship.* Disparities may exist in education and training, as well as in relative perceptions of individual success, values, and degree of community integration. The extent to which the employer is viewed as a hero by society and as a master by his employees also colors the relationship.

8. *Differences in characteristics of the laboring classes.* The working classes may vary with regard to the pressure that they exert on the land, their political power, community involvement, social mobility, acceptance of social institutions, homogeneity of outlook toward the future, responsiveness to organizational necessities, attitude toward social conflict, and the status value that they place on their own skills. These factors affect the degree of conservatism of the labor organization, including the inclination to defer to employer leadership.

The difficulty of analyzing these complex factors increases with the relative diversity of economic structures. Such comparisons may be rendered meaningless as a result of differences in terminology. Moreover, what appear to be contrasts among emerging labor organizations may disappear with evolutionary growth, and combinations of government, employer, and labor union policies may change over the years.

Summation

Labor organizations in developing countries operate in dissimilar cultural environments to which no superior-inferior scale of any scientific merit can be applied. However, these environments must be considered if the methods and returns of these organizations are to be measured accurately. The convergence of cultural values according to some law of increasing international similarity has not been proven.

Labor officials have to consider the realities they face in their own country. If, because of their political ambitions, they continue to clash with the government, they may be excluded from the formulation and control of policy. If labor officials in developing countries are trained to emulate labor officials of mature economies, they must be prepared to work in a vacuum.

As an instrument of expressing and fulfilling worker aspirations, the labor organization in the developing country is not an inexorable threat to the economic planner. The provision of a useful role for the labor organization may be in the interest of the developing government, although such a course of action may eventually be painful as the organization becomes an influential body. A stronger base may thus be provided for the progressive and stable society that is required for the governing process.

If the labor organization really represents the workers of the developing country, it is a force that has to be reckoned with. The hopeful expectancy of planners is that organized labor will learn that, without a rise in human capabilities, there will be no rise in living standards. The labor organization that holds the loyalty of the population also retains the key as to whether such an expectancy can be effectively sold to the people.

As frustrations in economic development mount, an authoritarian ruler is likely to assume control, and labor movements may be expected to submerge their interests for a long period of time. In such an eventuality, the economic growth pattern of the developing country may be modeled after that of the Soviet Union or Mexico rather than that of the United States or Great Britain.

Labor movements of this type, once willing creatures of authoritarian governments, have passed to another stage of development and have become functional members of the industrial relations system with influences of their own. The perception of this evolution by ideological adversaries, however, may require a painful three or four decades.

7

POLITICAL SYSTEMS IN DEVELOPING COUNTRIES

This chapter is concerned with the characteristics of developing governments, their role in planning, and the question of whether economic development and democracy are compatible in today's world.

CHARACTERISTICS OF DEVELOPING GOVERNMENTS

Governments of developing countries are subject to pressures that people in donor nations have difficulty comprehending. Among the most significant of these is the strong anticapitalist attitude, for capitalism is regarded in former colonial countries not as a promise of fulfillment but as a symbol of injustice. In many countries of Latin America, for example, capitalism is an opprobrious term. If Americans can conjure up a historical personage representing the worst type of American employer, they may succeed in grasping the image of the capitalist in many emerging nations. Their governments express this anticapitalism by confiscating the businesses of foreigners—a reaction that assists them psychologically but hurts them in the pocketbook.

Moreover, these governments are expected to provide strong central direction to economic growth.[1] The term "government intervention" is not anathema to their people, who see government as a symbol of the highest aspiration in society and expect substantial governmental accomplishments.

[1] Successful contemporary economic development often means successful government intervention. Japan and Mexico have achieved it under an alliance of government and business.

Some of the statements made by governments of emerging nations cannot be taken literally; they may have been made merely for the record or for purposes of domestic consumption. Often, too, these pronouncements represent statements of long-term aspirations that are put aside from day to day. In addition, a government may make a commitment because of a desire to accommodate, as is done in Latin America, but without an intent to follow through. Whether or not these expressions can be taken at face value is a continuing puzzle.

The pressures of economic development make it easy for donor nations to strike a hard bargain. Consequently, developing governments are often under strong pressures to make concessions in bargaining with donor nations that they may eventually find difficult to live with. Moreover, if the agreement is not consistent with the national ethic of the emerging nation, the bargain may eventually produce repercussions against the negotiators and the country that extracted it.

Business of any consequence with governments of emerging nations must be conducted at the highest levels for several reasons. First, the developing country is likely to have a scarcity of competent administrators in the middle ranks of its bureaucracy. Second, highly centralized authority is common at such levels of economic growth; the government of a subsistence economy may consist of hardly more than a police force and an organization for foreign representation. Third, new governments have had little time to develop a subdivision of labor and decentralized decision making. With economic growth, the development of public administration, and time, decision making becomes more diffused.

These very characteristics may, however, create a sense of responsibility. In the highly sophisticated governments of advanced nations, decisions are bland and difficult to trace; the prudent bureaucrat avoids making an imaginative decision for which he may be personally held accountable. In developing countries, on the other hand, the government official who makes the decisions cannot as easily indulge in buck passing; he may be swept out of office. Officials of developing nations are thus more likely to operate on the basis of personal relationships with their constituents. Moreover, the rural character of their societies produces less of the detachment that exists between the civil servant and the public in a nation such as the United States. If the government official in a country such as India does not know the person with whom he is dealing, he is more apt to be suspicious of him. Doing business with a voice on the telephone is a product of high levels of economic growth.

Typically, these government officials have a classical education in law or economics, which makes them receptive to a theoretical interpretation of developmental problems offered by economists of advanced countries. Correspondingly, they are either disinclined or not technically prepared to come to grips with problems as they exist at the base of the population.

Industries in emerging nations are generally comprised of a small number of big enterprises and many small shops. The large firms, often of foreign ownership, may be so influential as to shape government policies. In some countries, this relationship may produce distrust among the people of both large industry and government.

Emerging governments have difficulty in developing and placing indigenous managers. At the beginning of the modernization drive, the individuals at the top of the social structure have small interest in industrial productivity. To achieve economic growth, those toward the bottom have to be encouraged to move upward in the social structure and become a new class of innovators. The governments thus have to develop their own industrial managerial talent against the widely held view that the pinnacle of success in the society is a secure government post.

In addition, these governments may have heavy social commitments that have a deterrent effect on the expansion of production and employment. For example, they may have systems of social welfare that they cannot afford and that are poorly administered by huge bureaucracies. In addition, considerable controls may exist in the relationship between employer and employees, which, taken collectively, are usually a symptom of poor labor relations rather than a cure.

New governments that have inherited established traditions of governing can depart little from customary procedures. Once a government has developed a style of policy making and policy implementation, a vested interest in these procedures is created that makes radical changes unlikely. Postrevolutionary governments, on the other hand, possess the advantage of being able to develop a finesse that is more in keeping with the imperatives of economic growth than with the needs of bureaucracy. Some nations waste this opportunity, however.

The political system of a developing country is not an independent variable so much as an expression of pressures that shaped the course of its history. Each country has a tradition of the manner in which ideological differences were first formed, the way the population base has acquired political power, and the process by which historic social cleavages have been reconciled. These historical differences create institutions that survive the forces that initially created them. Although the originating factors cause persisting diversity among these nations, the common pressures that they are exposed to in seeking rapid economic growth may, however, reduce these dissimilarities.

The political systems in these nations manifest different degrees of radicalism at their population base. Mass radicalism is generally greater in Latin America and Asia than in Black Africa. This radicalism is an expression of the socially alienated, who do not feel part of the society. Some alienation of the people from their European-educated leaders does exist in Africa, and these radical tendencies may increase as urbanization increases, causing a period of rising discontent. There is substance to the generalization that the conservative rural person swings to the political left after he settles in the city. The sharper the contrast between urban groups, the more extreme the radicalism is likely to be. Furthermore, this extremism is strengthened by the reluctance of the privileged upper classes to share political power with the population base.[2]

The proliferation of political parties in Asia and Latin America is due partly to intense social cleavages and individualistic tendencies. Another factor is the system of proportional representation, under which parties can manage to stay alive despite the small electorates they represent. This is not to say that a multiparty system is less efficient than a two-party system in reflecting the national consensus. Proportional representation permits diverse ideological judgments to be reflected, and the various groups can bargain out their differences on particular issues. In Black Africa, single-party systems are more prevalent. This tendency evolved in these countries during the drive for national independence, when group aspirations were welded together into a single political force. Such unity, however, seems to break down once national independence is achieved. If the existence of many political parties does not necessarily indicate an incapacity to achieve a broad national consensus, a dominating single political party does not mean the lack of a democratic process. In such cases, it may occur within the party itself.

The differences in the political cleavages within these nations may be attributed to their different origins. Those of Latin America originated in Spain, Italy, and Portugal and were influenced by cultural and religious differences. Asian political divisions resulted from a mixture of social caste differences and the residue of colonial rule. Those of Black Africa arose out of tribal animosities that were locked into the nations by the manner in which they were originally carved out during colonial rule.

The chief of state in the modernizing nation is often either an authoritarian ruler or a figure under the control of the conservative elements in his nation. In former colonial countries (the notable exception being India) or in those countries that underwent a drastic political change as a consequence of World War II, the individual wielding power is likely to be an authoritarian. The style of each man varies, but his general type is found in all three continents. The other prototype, the man controlled by an oligarchy that seeks to restrain economic development in its own interest, is typical of Latin American leaders. The authoritarian ruler in Latin America is a conservative compared to the same type of ruler in other continents, where he more commonly identifies with the population and is fomenting change. The rulers of some African nations, such as Liberia, show this type of authoritarianism.

The success of the authoritarian ruler in generating rapid growth is

---

2 See S. M. Lipset, *Political Cleavages in Developed and Emerging Polities*, Reprint No. 244, Institute of Industrial Relations and Institute of International Studies (Berkeley: University of California Press, 1964).

influenced by his ability to recognize his need for competent technical assistance in matters of policy and strategy. Ironically, his authoritarian position is weakened as economic development progresses. He cannot expect the population to feed indefinitely on his flair for verbiage, nor can he expect to provide them with a sense of well-being by juggling state finances and indulging in international intrigue. Eventually, he must come to grips with the reality that living standards rise through a massive effort to raise the utilization and efficiency of labor. If he ignores this dictum and does not seek the assistance of technicians to bring about such a result, the demagogy on which he leans may be his undoing. Without the support of the military, the authoritarian may have to yield to another politician.

What are the characteristics of the legislatures of these governments? Where the parliament has a long tradition of decision making and where it has not been discredited, it continues to be an influential force (as in India). In former colonial territories where no such tradition exists, the legislature tends to be overshadowed by the chief of state. As in Egypt, the ruler may prescribe the rules under which the parliament is to be elected and determine which political parties are legitimate and which are not. The effect of these rules is to create legislatures that rubber stamp the policies of the chief of state.

In Latin America, legislatures are frequently an exercise in futility, and with the notable exception of Mexico, consensus is difficult to obtain. An effective piece of legislation that does manage to issue from the legislature runs the gauntlet of mediocre bureaucracies whose orientation may be unsympathetic with the intent of the law and of powerful oligarchies who do not wish to see the law successfully administered. In some Latin American nations, the parliaments are weak because of a lack of tradition. The void that results from their ineffectiveness is exploited by the chief executive to enhance his own power. Countries with many political parties in their legislatures that are not capable of negotiating their differences and parliaments with no tradition in the exercise of power are generally ruled by a strong chief executive.

The bureaucracies in these countries occupy a strategic position because of their ability to affect economic development. The bureaucracy comprises individuals who are on the government payroll at each level of its administrative, legislative, and judicial branches less a nucleus that proposes and initiates major changes or that is elected into office. Not all bureaucrats have a significant effect on the developmental process, however. Those who do are either at the top involved in planning decisions or at the bottom with contacts at the population base. With the exception of key personnel, the level of skills of the bureaucrats is generally low.

The government bureaucracy provides an opportunity for unaggressive, educated individuals to acquire status and a haven from the mundane business of production, where social mobility is less attainable. In a sense, it is a mark of astuteness in developmental planning to avoid serious obstructions that can be raised by the bureaucratic mentality. The universal characteristics of the bureaucrat—caution and unimaginativeness—are likely to bring the revolutionary ideas that issue from top planners to naught.

To give the established bureaucracy a significant role in the planning and execution of the new development effort may be a mistake. As soon as such power is given, an irrevocable series of events may occur. The developing area may spawn a huge expansion not of production but of the traditional bureaucracy that stifles the rise of local leadership. As has been frequently demonstrated, an established bureaucracy is less efficient than a new quasi-independent organization that recruits special skills for the development effort. In short, in a program aimed at increasing human capabilities, the problem is how to avoid having that program led by individuals who are themselves incompetent. This dilemma is not solely that of developing nations; it also afflicts programs of mature economies, such as the antipoverty program. Each country must deal with its bureaucracy in its own way.

The best attack on bureaucracy is not a frontal one. A direct attempt to alter visibly the functions, composition, and quality of a bureaucracy leads to a struggle in which the bureaucracy can win by sheer inertia. To exclude the bureaucrat from the process of economic development is difficult, and thus the wise planner makes his meddling as innocuous as possible. Somehow, bureaucrats must be given a feeling of being kept fairly busy while necessary goals are pursued without their knowledge and without the possibility that their contribution may have a significant effect. The problem is how to neutralize their flair for mediocrity and at the same time to derive advantage from their resources and their power to institute change.

GOVERNMENT ROLE IN ECONOMIC PLANNING

Governments of developing countries are intervening in the economic growth process in a manner that has no precedent in the early history of the older economies. They are heavily involved in the development and placement of human and tangible capital in an attempt to accelerate economic growth. The commitment to sustained economic growth is a universal one and has been adopted as their major function. In addition to the urgent need for social overhead capital, emerging nations have other impelling needs that cannot be filled by private initiative. Comprehensive industrial programs have to be started so that a balanced economic structure may be created. The social structure must be broken up in a manner that brings about the rise of an innovating middle class.

Price and labor market distortions that arise in the early stages of forced growth have to be controlled. Rates of investment in the private sector must be limited to avoid an outcome that is inconsistent with the overall economic plan. Young industries that are spawned have to be protected from foreign competition.

The danger of rural stagnation is another considerable problem that these governments must eventually face, for private initiative cannot cope with it. Yet the governments generally do not take the problem seriously and shy away from it by allowing urbanization of the rural poor in order to reduce the magnitude of the problem and by ineffective rural development programs. It is clear, however, that the retarded growth of the countryside affects overall efforts at industrialization and modernization. Without a successful solution to the rural problem, a government is not likely to realize its aspiration of becoming a modern nation.

In laying the basis for a sound economic structure, these governments face problems of internal organization. The work of managers and technicians is not adequately integrated, for managers appear less inclined to leave technical questions to professionals, either because of the manager's inability to recognize and attract technically competent individuals or because of his need to appear omniscient, when, in fact, he is not. If he has some doubts about his omniscience, he may be more inclined to consult with peers similarly ignorant of such matters than with a younger man eager to show off his newly acquired Ph.D.

The central planning unit of these governments is often a new agency without the status and power of established ministries and bureaucracies. The new unit has a multiple set of relationships within and outside governments that makes older organizations jealous of their prerogatives. The planners, generally younger men conscious of their modern education, are often cautious and hesitant, so that planning tends to become a difficult search for a common denominator between the new and the old.

Bottlenecks may result when trained personnel are forced to work with individuals who do not understand the scope of what they are doing, and who were appointed because of their political connections. (In a typical instance, the top administrator of the development agency in one Latin American country was coached on what to say on broad policy matters by a young graduate from an American university who was one of the statisticians in the organization.) Developing nations are thus caught in a bind. They have to institute structural changes by legislative and administrative means, even though policy makers do not see the issues in all their ramifications.

Corruption may also have an inhibiting effect, but corrupt practices are not an exclusive characteristic of developing nations. (They may be more prevalent in older countries because they have been working at it longer.) Corruption may range from extortion at ministerial levels down to petty bribe-taking by minor government clerks. In Latin America and Asia, the amount of corruption appears high; in Africa, it is less a matter of public record.

The actual extent and effects of corruption in developing nations are difficult to determine because the available facts are not substantial enough for a meaningful inquiry. Doubtlessly, nations whose government officials do not accept bribes for speeding up administrative matters would not be easy to find. Some nations in which corruption appears to be prevalent do well in economic development, whereas others do not.[3]

Unless the problem has reached a point where there is a considerable loss of faith in government efforts and a disinclination to pay taxes, the economic problem of corruption can be overstated. More serious to the economic development effort is the inefficiency of government offices. Government employees develop a flair for doing little skillfully. They loiter around as in the waiting room of a railroad station performing paper work, the rationale of which seems to be to provide an appearance of work. It is difficult to infuse a psychology of efficiency, of the importance of productive work and time, in a society so long as government officials set such a model for the population.

To some extent in Latin America, more so in Asia, and even more so in Africa, feelings of inferiority to the West weaken the government officials' sense of self-respect. In Asia and Africa, this sense of inferiority is tied to white dominance, the effects of which are slow in dissipating. There is considerable pressure, however, to forestall an evolution of normalizing relationships between modern and developing countries. Africans and Asians, grappling with rising expectations that exceed income, can find race consciousness rewarding and thus may perpetuate it. Only such an extraordinary individual as the President of Senegal, Leopold Senghor, could be indifferent to these temptations and rise above the emotions of racism. Moreover, the disbursement of foreign aid by whites to nonwhites serves also to prevent a normalization. Such aid makes the encounter between donor and recipient an awkward one, and when races confront each other at the bargaining table, the situation is worsened.

The sense of insecurity and inferiority frustrates a genuine meeting of minds, either because the receiving government may not be inclined to disagree with the donor or because it may be sensitive to demands for concessions. Genuine bargaining based on give and take is difficult. Intense anti-American sentiment exists in some countries because of hostility to particular Americans and to particular American policies. Critical attitudes may also arise because of the presence of American business in the developing country. Even when the criticism is no longer justified, it may persist to serve domestic political purposes.

[3] Gunnar Myrdal takes a dim view of the payment of bribes (baksheesh) in India. One would suspect that a real difference between nations is that in a country such as Mexico, for example, a *propina* brings prompt and efficient action, whereas in India, baksheesh produces somewhat less than the usual lethargy.

The developing government is at times a government in a hurry, seeking to generate or accelerate economic processes that might have evolved eventually from private initiative. It does not wish to go through the technological evolution that occurred in the West. Instead, it is inclined to skim off the best of Western technology and to move instantly from an economy of human muscle to an economy based on the computer. These technological transplants may have unintended and opposite results. The urge to borrow is strong, however, and the functions of these governments increase rapidly because they facilitate such a process of borrowing.

Private capital flows to developing nations are not sufficient to fill their demands. The precipitous termination of colonialism, with its ensuing instability and uncertainties, has reduced these flows. Moreover, new private capital tends to go to nations at already high levels of economic growth where investment outcomes are more predictable. Growing disparities in living standards between donor and recipient nations limit the number of corporations whose products can find mass markets abroad. Furthermore, the increasing number of public loan agencies tends to create its own demand. The combination of these factors increases the relative importance of nonprivate capital and widens the scope of these governments in economic development.

Government involvement has also increased because the predominant ideologies are sympathetic to such an increase. Managers of contemporary development are educated in concepts of the welfare state and Marxism. Roman Catholic ideologists advocate a socialism of their own variety. This inclination toward strong government involvement is further strengthened by the masses who view their poverty as caused by the absence of the proper degree of government intervention. To them, the private entrepreneur is more an exploiter than a hero. It is difficult to state convincingly, under such conditions, that social and economic objectives in development can be attained by means other than heavy government involvement.

Another cause of deep government commitment to development efforts is the fact that a rise in production creates problems of distributive justice. As human capabilities are improved through education, jobs that are required in the growth process become less desirable, and thus changes are created in the labor supply that is available for industry. These dislocations are reflected in wage demands and production costs. The rising income that then occurs upsets traditional income relationships and leads to charges of inequity. These changes assure further government involvement in the search for a rational approach to the proper distribution of income.

Such governments are besieged with rival demands. Requests are made for expenditures for social overhead, education, and tangible capital investment. As a result, scarce resources, including skilled human resources, must be allocated among competing interests. These rivalries tax the abilities of these governments to structure efficient internal relationships among their component organizations and to carry on effective relationships with foreign governments.

An association does not necessarily exist, however, between increasing government involvement and effectiveness in the developmental process. Developing countries often invest heavily in state enterprises and suffer considerable losses. They may also impose irrational bureaucratic controls on the expansion of private industry. Yet governments with no tradition of governing appear anxious to assert their authority, although in an ineffective way.

The degree of government control of the economy may range from mere stimulation of private enterprise by means of government tax and credit policies, to so-called mixed economies, such as India, to a comprehensive form of planning. The popular hybrid of the mixed economy presents the government with the delicate problem of balance between state and private enterprises. It has to decide at what point to take the initiative when private entrepreneurs are not being as effective as deemed necessary in a particular area or industry. There is also the matter of whether to control the rate of growth of private enterprises and under what conditions state enterprises should be turned over to the private sector. The dilemma raised by state enterprises is that if they do well, the government is inclined to increase its investment in them so as to obtain more income; if they do badly, private enterprise is reluctant to buy them.

The effectiveness of government intervention is measurable in terms of the particular objective being sought, the alternative means by which it can be reached, and the relative costs involved. Viewed in this context, government intervention can be too little or too much, depending on its effectiveness. For one thing, the ability of a government to impose a dead hand on the upward surge of ideas from the population should not be underestimated; an increase in the quality of human resources can be inhibited. No alternative exists, however, but for government to provide the wherewithal for a ground swell of innovation and then to seek to play an unobtrusive role in its evolution. A government faced with serious deterrents to the improvement of human capabilities cannot rely on the market mechanism to eliminate such obstructions.

A last point that should be made regarding the role of government in economic affairs is the difficulty of defining what this role actually is. Two levels of reality may exist—what people say the role is and what the role really is. In the United States, for example, the government discharges a considerable responsibility, but popular opinion refers to the economic system as private enterprise. In India, people speak of democratic socialism, but the economic function of the government seems to be less extensive than that of the United States.

ECONOMIC DEVELOPMENT AND DEMOCRACY

Why do some presently developing countries abandon political systems that are considered instruments of democracy in the West, whereas others adhere to them precariously? Why do these countries show little sign of developing stable democratic systems? Are the demands of an economic takeoff in these times incompatible with democracy? Are differences between the Western nations and the modernizing ones due rather to an inability on the part of Western observers to discern processes of democracy in forms different from those of the West?

We are concerned with these questions for political scientists suggest an association between the rate of economic development and the prevalence of competitive political systems of the Western type. The problem is thus posed in terms of whether developing countries can succeed in evolving political systems similar to those of the West. Presumably, countries that do, will accelerate their economic development. Since they apparently move in an opposite direction, the question of economic development and democracy is an appropriate one.

There may be a flaw in these comparisons. Historically different factors contributed to the present-day political systems of the West. Moreover, it is difficult to speak of a Western political system; but even if the Western nations are treated as a single group, the schisms out of which their systems emerged differed from those of developing nations. These cleavages produced a series of political and economic concessions made by the privileged classes to their fellow nationals at the population base. The forces of protest and change in developing countries are not arrayed in the traditional Western manner. Rather, the confrontation may be between nationals and foreigners, nationals supporting foreigners against those who do not, or between religions, tribes, and castes. The protesters may be comprised of an alliance of the sons of the poor, the middle class, and the military caste. In short, to detect signs of democracy through evidence of Western political systems is of little usefulness. It is more fruitful to study in depth the process by which consensus takes place in these developing nations.

Clarity is brought to this fundamental question if the focus is directed to tasks of government that have existed from time immemorial: to promote the well-being of the people as interpreted by a consensus of these people; to protect and promote the interests of its citizens in their relationships with the citizens of other countries and their governments; and to promulgate and maintain rules that preserve the public order consistent with individual liberty.

If it is agreed that these are basic governmental tasks and that democratic processes are a valued means of achieving them, the next problem is to define democracy. To keep to the basic issue, the definition should not merely answer the question of what instruments may be used to achieve democracy. Therefore, democracy may be defined as a process of achieving maximum consent with regard to the policies that the government employs to discharge these fundamental responsibilities.

Some implications follow from this view of the democratic process. If the position is valid, everyone in the body politic who desires to express an opinion can do so with impunity. Furthermore, the government responds to this opinion on the basis of reason rather than power, and the reasonableness of a person's view is not based on the amount of power behind it. In addition, if the judgment of the individual is a minority one, he has the right not only to express his views but also to try to persuade the majority to adopt his outlook. The government not only cannot purge him from the body politic but has the duty to protect his person. The government thus does not seek to promote only the interests of the powerful but actively attempts to help minorities to assert themselves effectively.

Moreover, the government in a democracy takes an active role in the discharge of these basic responsibilities. It assists citizens in clarifying issues by pursuing a policy of maximum disclosure of the facts. It seeks to encourage a sense of common interest among the people in situations where strong sentiments exist to the contrary. It provides opportunities for the people to develop their lives to their full potential and to prevent particular groups from exploiting others. Lastly, the government allows the people, in an atmosphere of noncoercion through the right of the secret ballot, to continue the incumbents in office or to choose their successors. By these assumptions, such a Western nation as the United States falls short of democracy in some respects just as developing countries do.

What are examples of democracies and nondemocracies? If one were to look beyond North America, for instance, Sweden and Great Britain come to mind. Their instruments of democracy are not identical, but it is difficult to find nations that are more democratic. Examples of nondemocracies in Latin America, Asia, and Africa should not be difficult to find either. The countries on these continents, however, are in the throes of resolving immense problems. In discharging their responsibilities, they have to reconcile strong social conflict. In pursuing national interests, they frequently adopt courses of action without the confidence that would be characteristic of a people at a higher level of economic growth. Some of these governments, nevertheless, are willing to take the risks of sacrificing some efficiency in allowing greater participation and consent of the people.

The history of many democratic governments suggests that democracy comes to a nation as a consequence of difficult and, at times, violent struggles; few nations have pursued a tranquil march to democracy. Moreover, their institutions, once gained, can be lost if the body politic is unable successfully to overcome deep economic and political crises. The road leading toward or moving away from democracy is characterized by the degree to which different groups in a social system are inclined to bargain and abide by a consensus.

If history provides any example, Western-style democracy cannot be expected to evolve inexorably from economic development, as evidenced by the experiences of Latin America, Africa, and Asia. Mexico is modernizing rapidly and is developing a democracy *sui generis.* Western-style democracy, where it exists, had a long and stable history before the beginning of modernization. The example of the Soviet Union looms large as a demonstration of high rates of growth achieved under authoritarianism followed by a painful transition to more democratic forms. In some countries, however, as in those of Latin America, attempts to increase democratization may be thwarted by the installation of authoritarian regimes.

Where the modernization drive is set off under an authoritarian leader, democratic processes may not develop until after his death. The more common evolution is for the authoritarian to entrench himself further during his lifetime. Even at his death, however, instability may ensue and other authoritarian rulers may take over.

The reason why the first stages of modernization have such antidemocratic tendencies is that the authoritarian ruler is usually motivated more by a desire to gain international prestige than a desire to encourage a democratic base. In fact, the stimulation of democratic processes in his country may, in his judgment, hinder his international ambitions.

Moreover, the inevitable shifting of power at the beginning of development mitigates the growth of democracy. This problem is not unique for modernizing countries, but because they foment rapid change, the transition becomes telescoped into a narrow period of time and thus becomes more readily apparent. Some turmoil is to be expected until the shift takes place from an agricultural to a diversified economy and as the quality of human resources is improved.

Paradoxically, genuine consensus must wait for a rise in conflict. The absence of conflict in the developing economy indicates acquiescence to felt inequities rather than a genuine meeting of minds. In other words, it means resignation and not agreement. Change produces a rise in the belief that inequities can be adjusted. A government that creates effective mechanisms for resolving conflict brings felt inequities to the surface and initiates the indispensable prelude to consensus. Accordingly, the rise in conflict can be an indicator of progress. Unfortunately, the encampment of rural labor in urban centers side by side with an emerging middle class that does not assume a mission of innovation discourages this mechanism from emerging.

One of the many difficult problems of modernizing governments is to mobilize   the   population   base   behind   an   effort   at   consensus.

Noncommunist governments confronting a laboring class with powerful left-wing affiliations are faced with a delicate problem. They can seek to isolate the leaders of such groups and run the risk of thereby discouraging a collective effort in behalf of growth; or they can try to mobilize this force and run the risk of generating a counterreaction by conservative elements in the nation. The task of the government comes down to this: It must, on the one hand, persuade different groups that everyone is going to benefit by the developmental effort and then, on the other, proceed to discriminate in behalf of particular groups. In such an instance, the best way to achieve consensus is not to reveal the facts fully. The problem of mass mobilization is made even more difficult by the fact that any significant change in the economic position of the population base may take generations.

The question of political development returns the discussion to the central theme that a prerequisite to growth is the improvement of human resources. A strategy for economic development that ignores the importance of arousing individual effort is incomplete. Moreover, a basis for the growth of a democratic process cannot be laid without this realization.

Everywhere in the developing world, democratic structures seem to be faltering. The trend seems to be not toward democracy but toward authoritarianism. Despite these tendencies, the future favors the growth of democratic processes. If modernization succeeds, it also brings a rise in human capital. An educated, technically competent population with habits of inquiry and responsibility living under authoritarian rule indefinitely is unlikely. An authoritarian government generating the forces of modernization thus lays the groundwork for its own demise. Such an evolution, however, makes it unlikely that the emerging democratic institutions will be like those of the West. Democracy may issue from a dominant single political party in which conflicts are resolved within the party organization. In any case, the evolution of democracy in developing countries may take many decades of uncertainty and instability if such nations as Mexico provide any clue.

Summation

In economic development, government serves as an instrument for changing the rules on the use of human and economic resources; a development program is inconceivable without such a change. With the exception of the first industrializing nations in the West, no economic growth of any consequence has taken place without deep government involvement. Changes are made in the rules regarding the use of land, capital, and labor. Existing property rights are modified in the process, and the real issue is the degree of coercion necessary on the part of government. In altering these rules of the game, the governing process may be frustrated by conservative forces in the economy, a frustration that further increases the ruler's penchant for authoritarianism. In times of crisis in changing structures, these forces may seek to seize the government, but at best, they can only assure postponement of the day of reckoning. Eventually, they have to accept some strategy of change or lose their privileges entirely.

A policy of rapidly urbanizing the rural population without modernizing the rural area aggravates the problems of developing governments. This subproletariat represents a potentially explosive mass. A basis is laid thereby for the type of government that is sensitive to immediate pressures but not able to pursue an efficient long-term course.

Countries beginning their modernization at low levels of human capital are not likely to be democratic for a long time to come. The government of these nations can be likened to a holding company, with the chief of state as chairman of the board. The chairman stipulates and interprets the major rules of the political and economic game of the various corporate affiliates. Organized countervailing power is likely to be repugnant to the board chairman; nor is it likely that the population would find his system intolerable until an appreciable rise in human capabilities occurs.

Massive government involvement can be expected to have some deleterious effects. Management interest in efficiency may slacken if the government nurses enterprises and protects them from foreign competition or if it interferes in managerial appointments.

The traditional bureaucracy adds to obstacles in the way of economic development goals. Neither an inefficient nor a corrupt bureaucracy raises insurmountable barriers; rather, such a bureaucracy poses a challenge of strategy. Eventually, steps must be taken to make the bureaucracy more effective. The problem is a vicious circle with bureaucracy and population acting on each other to the detriment of efficiency, but the situation will be ameliorated as the general level of education and training rises.

The conserving and changing forces in developing nations are not identical with those out of which Western growth evolved. Consequently, observations made from Western-oriented assumptions are misleading. College-educated youth represent a force for change. The radicals are not necessarily the poor; their ranks are filled also by the children of the wealthy and the military caste. These young persons have a common interest: rapid modernization. They cross lines in unorthodox fashion, resulting in alliances alien to Western experience. Working agreements are hammered out between such odd combinations as Christians, communists, and anarchists.

Where developing economies cannot achieve a political consensus, the end result is often a takeover by a military regime. A military regime in a developing environment is inherently unstable; it is an expression of chaos in the body politic that is suppressed rather than eliminated by the succession. The spit-and-polish training that military men bring to power does not prepare them for the complexities of economic development. Moreover, the neat pecking order they establish encourages animosities in their ranks. Consequently, pressures are placed on them as soon as they take over the government to defer to civilian rule; if they are successful in resisting those pressures, they must govern in an atmosphere of confusion, dissension, and instability. In general, a military that exerts influence indirectly can be a force for change as well as consolidation, but one that takes over and retains power seems to be inept at generating economic growth.[4]

Lastly, in many developing nations what the government says it will accomplish in economic development provides few clues at times as to what the government is likely to do. Gunnar Myrdal uses the term "softness" to describe the statements of government officials and the actual steps taken to make the transformations necessary to produce economic development. However, what may appear as "softness" to Western eyes may be rational behavior to Asians, given the complexities in which their government officials say and do things.

It is difficult to construct a series of successive benchmarks that indicate whether or not a country is developing politically. Emerging differences in forms do not imply inferiority in substance. As will become evident in some of the nation case histories, however, political stability is a requisite of economic development, but politically stable regimes do not automatically produce economic growth. Moreover, authoritarian regimes can generate economic growth, but whether they can remain authoritarian and continue to grow economically is doubtful.

[4] See Morris Janowitz, *The Military in the Development of New States* (Chicago: University of Chicago Press, 1964).

8

SOCIAL STRUCTURE AND ECONOMIC DEVELOPMENT

CHARACTERISTICS OF A SOCIAL SYSTEM

Economic development takes place within the framework of a particular social system. What social relationships exist in that system before the start of the developmental process, and how do they change afterward? How do economic and social changes affect each other? These questions are dealt with in this chapter. Its thesis, based on writings of Latin Americans, is that a free market type of economic development stimulates a change in social relationships that may have deterrent effects on further growth.

Two major characteristics of any social system are causally related: the *attitudes* toward life and the *institutions* within which men pursue their lives. In a developing area, attitudes are often negative: a contempt for manual work, submissiveness to authority and exploitation, and a low degree of aspiration. The institutions characteristically reflect social stratification, the noninvolvement of the poor in the power structure, and their low representation in the educational system. These attitudes and institutions are mutually reinforcing.

Their net effect is low productivity and little inclination to do anything about it, for low productivity is not a transitory phenomenon but a way of life manifesting a balanced set of social habits with which the people have learned to live with a minimum of conflict.

In the static rural society that is characterized by a scarcity of resources, social relationships are based on reciprocal duties and obligations within stratified groups, the members of which cooperate rather than compete with one another. So long as there are no income inequities within a group, there is little conflict but also little, if any, change.

A sudden rise in economic growth alters this stable social structure. As new differences in income appear, the stability of the relationships within and between groups becomes upset. Therefore, the question arises as to how society can anticipate this loss of equilibrium and control these social changes in a manner that facilitates economic growth. It cannot be accomplished through legislation. The law, if it is arrived at by democratic means, mirrors the social structure; it is a ceremonious acknowledgment of changes that have already taken place. Legislation thus reflects rather than produces social change.

ALTERING THE SOCIAL STRUCTURE

Modernizing nations are therefore faced with a difficult choice. To bring about desired economic change, a radical alteration of the social structure is necessary. This social change can be accomplished in any of three ways: through a violent revolution that successfully liquidates the power structure; through a peaceful revolution brought about by educating the talented poor who can then challenge those who control the traditional seats of power; or through the random workings of an emerging free-enterprise economy.

At the time of economic takeoff, each person belongs to a group that is ranked anywhere from inferior to superior by the collective estimate of the society. In such a society, the amount of land one owns and the fact that one does not have to work in order to live are usually evidence of superiority. There is little or no social mobility, and, in fact, little aspiration to move from one group to another. Each group has its own ideological orientation. In some societies, ideological differences are small and a high degree of harmony exists; poverty then poses a threat to society as a whole. In other societies, greater ideological differences exist, and they increase the degree of stress in the social system.

Ultimately, however, the society devises generally acceptable rules that keep conflict between these groups to a minimum. Men seem to prefer to be resigned to inequities rather than to exist in perpetual turmoil. Because of this resigned attitude, there is little interest in raising efficiency in the society. In fact, most people probably would not know what efficiency means.[1]

The occupations in a rural community reflect the culture of the people and are geared to serve the needs of subsistence farming. For example, the occupations of a traditional Mexican community would be priest,

[1] In asking Sicilian peasants questions on efficiency and waste the first difficulty was in finding the proper dialect word and the second dealing with the ensuing bafflement.

teacher, storekeeper, shoemaker, carpenter, mason, butcher, agricultural surplus buyer, baker, barber, ironworker, silversmith, midwife, herb doctor, and fireworks maker.[2] These occupations, aside from the last, which reflects the Mexican fondness for fireworks, are typical of traditionally rural areas in the world.

Such a community is highly interdependent. The men may be called upon from time to time to pool their labor for community projects. They communicate not through reading and writing but through dialogue and ritual and ceremony, including dance and music. Education and medicine are influenced by superstition.

A breakdown of this social structure begins soon after the beginning of economic growth. Industrialization brings modern plants, rising income, retail shops with diversified goods, and men from the modern sector of the nation. The affluent at the top of the social structure, unless they have attained their position as a result of revolution, oppose this breakdown and lament the passing of old times. The key to overcoming their opposition and achieving a successful social transformation is to be found in the upward mobility of the sons of the poor, who have less of a vested interest in the traditional social order and who, with the new opportunities that are brought about by economic expansion, can rise in the power structure. By staging a violent revolution, this group can achieve more rapid upward mobility. Such revolutions, however, often substitute new injustices for old, disrupt the production mechanism, and delay the developmental process. The sudden political shifts in power that attend these revolutions contribute to the hiatus.

A more peaceful and efficient revolutionary change can be brought about by providing education and job opportunities for the talented poor. This initial step often gains the acquiescence if not the support of the managerial class—those in private and public positions whose decisions shape political, economic, and social events and whom Latin Americans refer to as the *clase dirigente*. In the broad meaning of the term, they are the politicians of the society. By accepting the newly trained young people, the established managers weaken the general acceptance of their own values without fully realizing what they are doing and thus become vulnerable to a challenge to their own power. As a result of this change in the rules governing the employment of economic and human resources, the society moves a step closer to its goal of economic development.

For the change to be appreciable, substantial numbers of these youths have to be moved into positions of influence in industry, the trade unions, the government, and the teaching profession. This infiltration may result in an increase in technical competence, a spirit of objective inquiry, and a sense of dominance over the environment. Labor organizations are in a favorable position to ferret out such individuals and to support their

[2] Robert Redfield, *Tepoztlan: A Mexican Village* (Chicago: University of Chicago Press, 1930).

upward movement in the economy. In Latin America, many of these young men are the sons of European immigrants.

A social reorientation may also come about as a backwash of tangible capital investment. This is essentially a laissez-faire course of action in which desired outcomes are expected to ensue as a consequence of an expansion of the economy.

THE MASS-MARKET MAN

The change in earnings, jobs, and attitudes, and the new hostilities that result from such investment alter traditional values and produce a new type of industrial being—the hastily hatched mass-market man who is the offspring of aggregate economics. He attempts to transfer overnight from subsistence to affluence. If one were to enter his one-room dwelling, one might find a mule in one corner and a television set in the other (as in Sicily). Liberated from the constraints of a traditional social structure, he becomes subject to the control of mass markets and communications.[3] Proliferating consumer goods are symbols of soft living rather than suggestions of industrial complexity and human skills. He acquires political power before he acquires power as a producer. His ideas are listened to soberly by the leadership elite, and he readily learns that quicker returns are available in the political arena. The new man learns that success is achieved by making fast deals.

Therefore, the precipitous, uncontrolled breakdown of traditional values may usher in a period of expediency. A breakdown in family values occurs. The sense of personal ethics of the rural area diminishes in the new environment of the rule of mass-market exploitation. Personal behavior becomes less controlled than in the system of mutual obligations that existed in the undeveloped society. The individual is faced with favorable or unfavorable situations that he must manipulate to achieve his own objectives. Whether the spirit of expediency can evolve into the values necessary for economic growth is a real question.

Developing market economies are more susceptible to the evolution of this mass-market man than were older industrial nations. In an unprecedented manner, they subject themselves to the effects of a massive introduction of modern technology that precedes a significant improvement in human capacities. Their rural populations are moving in considerable numbers to urban centers where the middle classes are conspicuously consuming sophisticated goods. It is as though the 200-year evolution of production, savings, and consumption of the West were telescoped into one decade.

A characteristic of urban populations that migrate from the country-

---

[3] The pronounced rise in literacy in Mexico has made comic books the most dynamic sector of the publishing business. One Mexican firm has annual sales of over a million, with extensive sales throughout Latin America.

side is insecurity. Caught in an incomprehensible swirl of change, they seek to stabilize themselves by submitting to authoritarian leadership. Their frustrations are relieved by a leader's appeals for "social justice" and "equality" and his promise of bountiful goods. Without jobs, skills, or social influence, the newcomers have no status in the urban center. With a leader supplicating in their behalf, however, they become part of a crusade.

Such insecurity among the population does little to ensure the rise of new social relationships favorable to economic development and responsible political leadership. In fact, in some developing areas, the leadership feeds on envy, hatred, and violence. Even when such leaders are cast off by forces of their own making, they leave a legacy of a need for authoritarian guidance and a conviction that the inevitable fumbling of a young democracy is proof of such a need.

In the urban center, there is a deterioration of the family as the creator of values. Contrary to the family ethic of personal responsibility, exploitation in direct human relationships is acceptable behavior. To be sure, the loss of family control is a universal phenomenon that affects even affluent societies. There are differences, however. In the United States, the deterioration was preceded by the acceptance of high productivity and self-improvement as values. Communist countries attempt to meet this problem through a systematic inculcation of values in the educational system. In noncommunist nations, this inculcation may be considered objectionable.

Developing countries may find that this deterioration of family control through urbanization is a serious threat to their growth. At an early stage in development, the values of the family are replaced by those of the movies, mass-market literature, and the television screen. One gains the impression that these media do not stimulate an interest in creativity and development but rather promote self-indulgence and self-pity. By contriving "needs," the media impose demands on an unsophisticated population more pressing than those of the developmental process. Because they have not institutionalized efficient production processes, underdeveloped nations can least afford such unrealistic enticements to their people.

Consequently, to expect from uncontrolled urbanization in developing nations an orderly progress toward modernization may be unwarranted. The United States did not experience an exodus of untrained rural illiterates to its cities before the industrialization process took a firm hold. Rural migration was a later phenomenon. Moreover, it was cushioned by a high level of production sophistication and a high value for efficiency. The problems this migration create would have to be multiplied manyfold for one to grasp those being created in developing nations. There the unskilled have a significant effect on the economic structures of the cities; they are not inclined to accept middle-class values as in the United States. With their acquisition of political power comes a sense of contempt on the part of the discerning, and this can become the basis for serious social ruptures.

The new mass-market man may view personal responsibility as lunacy. What the mass believes is good is so by that fact. He is aware of his newly acquired power. His ideas, no matter how questionable, and his tastes, no matter how extraordinary, are taken soberly by the functionaries wielding economic and political power. A child of hothouse economic growth, this urban prototype is a major force in contemporary economic development, particularly in Latin America. Industrialization is not the prime mover in his ascension but an instrument of it. What he is disposed to do and not to do is a guideline to leaders in developing areas. The behavior of such leaders does not appear rational outside the context of this relationship.

Such factors make a consensus among the population on the responsibilities of growth difficult to obtain. The installation of the rural poor in the cities side by side with social groups that seem to enjoy high levels of consumption but that feel participation in industry a mark of inferiority is not propitious to such a consensus. The new middle classes are not the innovators one had expected to arise from modernization but, rather, a new source of irritation.

Most elites have a healthy respect for their populations. Circumstances of history cause varying configurations as to who the elites are and their relationship to the population. Their changing style mirrors the characteristics of their constituents. The price the elite pays for ignoring the predilections of the population is a loss of influence through evolutionary change or upheaval. In developing areas, such leadership often obstructs the development of human resources. Constrained to promise more than they can produce, the managers of the mass-market man create new problems for themselves.[4] The worker acquires a taste for consumption that is greater than his willingness or ability to pay. This has been a universal problem as people have been beguiled by leaders pursuing power in the name of their welfare. It has been a universal tendency of leadership at different stages of economic growth, whether the subjects are called the masses or the public, whether the manipulators are called leaders or decision makers, and whether their methods are called demagogy or public relations. An important difference exists in these times, however; the conditions under which the rising aspirations of people assert themselves are unprecedented.

The mass-market man is not as powerful as he thinks, for his decisions are controlled by two types of manipulators: innovators who seek to modify his behavior, claiming it in his interest to do so; and conservatives who try to exclude him from change. Although pleading in the name of

4 One is reminded of the reaction of the Argentine population during the Perón regime. In the first years of his power, Perón told the people that the material bounty of the country was theirs. Later, having learned some lessons in economics, he began to tell them of the importance of raising their productivity. The people were indignant.

freedom, both types are hostile to its premises of full disclosure of possible choices and the wherewithal to choose rationally. The new manipulators, who may be employers, labor organizers, or government officials, encroach upon the traditional predevelopment spheres of influence—the landed gentry, local politicians, and charitable organizations. An important difference exists between this configuration of influence in a developing area and the power structure of countries at a higher level of economic growth. The latter emerge slowly in the course of development, whereas the leadership in developing areas superimposes itself, at times forcibly, on the population at the beginning of development. The leaders control rather than lead and do so often without full consent.

This is not to say that we should expect the same outcome in all social changes. There are always some creative individuals who are more inclined to reconstruct than to accommodate to prevailing forces in their society. They have ideas for radical change and, seizing on a favorable turn of events, proceed to transform their ideas into reality despite bureaucratic resistance. There is no reason to believe that innovators will cease to exist, and therefore, no telling what new forms may emerge from developing nations.

Nevertheless, development in its initial phases appears to have universal characteristics. Even after incumbents are replaced, occasionally by violence, the leadership continues to be paternalistic and opportunistic, for the style of the new managers does not usually change radically from that of the deposed. Depersonalization of the human relationship follows, as individual responsibility declines and man is appraised according to his worth in goods and the labor markets.[5]

Development managers are therefore in a race against time. Because spreading knowledge is generally accompanied by spreading discontent, they are confronted with marked changes in social attitudes that are not conducive to development. In the face of the depersonalization that provides a climate in which demagogues can operate, development managers have to forge an engine of growth based on individual responsibility.

Mature economies may have lost their puritan ethic, but developing nations (if they succeed in creating such a force in the first place) cannot afford to lose it for long. They must stave off the evolution of the new mass man despite strong forces acting to the contrary. Historical precedent is against them; the greater likelihood is an era of opportunistic government. Politicians are not inclined to teach their people the sober facts of development; instead, they are more disposed to blame failures not on their own policies but on the imperialism of advanced nations.

---

[5] Sicily is an example of the opportunism and decline in traditional values that industrialization brings. After twenty years of development, the billion dollars in investment was dissipated because of political patronage. The president of Sicily's largest bank went to jail for making illegal loans totaling millions of dollars to members of the ruling political party. In a study of Sicily's legislature, Roberto Couni notes the change from professional men to village politicians whose qualification is astute manipulation of emotions. From Robert C. Doty in *The New York Times,* April 24, 1967.

The personal responsibility implicit in a program of human capitalization requires a continuous program in education not only for the managerial elite but for everyone. But resources for such an effort are usually scarce, and the population may be disinclined to undergo the sacrifices necessary to improve its capabilities.

Markets have neither moral principles nor social values. The long-term consequences of the emergence of the new mass man are not precisely foreseeable; but one can observe his own behavior as new products and processes burst into his life. His ingestion is indiscriminate and perplexing. Whether the same commercialization of human relation-ships will occur in the developing nations as happened in old industrial societies is not clear. The issue is whether to allow this social evolution to occur willy-nilly or to steer change toward desired social goals.

PROBLEMS FACING DEVELOPMENTAL PLANNERS

The pressures against planned social change are considerable. As con-servatives work to prevent it, opposing forces arise that cause upheaval. A libertarian society is likely to pursue a policy of economic growth by increasing the money supply but taking no action to control the ensuing social dislocations. A totalitarian society is inclined to impose social controls, often at considerable human costs, and to curtail consumption by concentrating on broadening its industrial base.

Economists are prodigious performers in measuring the output of a society such as the Soviet Union. Their efforts, however, often neglect to measure the human costs of economic development. In their indexes, the type of man that emerges in a controlled society and the costs of his evolution are hazy, for economic inputs and outputs do not include these factors. It is for this reason that comparative studies of industrial rela-tions systems are important. In such inquiries, one can observe human processes and results that are as significant as the output of goods.

The United States has a formidable record in human outputs. There is no example in economic history of any country raising its population's capacities so rapidly, to such high levels, at such a minimum of human cost and with so little loss of individual responsibility. This is not to imply that an index of economic development in the U.S.S.R. that was oriented toward people would result only in debits. As Professor Simon Kuznets observes, it is less than honest to ignore the opportunities that exist for the people of that country that were not available under the former regime. The opportunities for jobs, education, and upward movement are there, and the capabilities of the people of the Soviet Union have risen considerably. These objectives were attained without sacrificing the people's sense of social obligation.

In libertarian societies, the development policy may strive to control the depersonalization process that comes with the rising demand for goods by preserving rural values, which are based on participation, consent, and good faith in personal relationships, and thereby build the new society on existing cultural patterns. The preservation of rural values does not lend itself, however, to the economic measurements of planners and for that reason is not taken seriously by them.

The stability of rural life often provides a climate for humanism in development that does not exist in the urban center. If the forces unleashed by development do not allow humanism to survive, there is, as Latin American social scientists point out, a question as to what *will* be developed. Indeed, this is a basic issue for all economies—whether humanism can be reconciled with technology and whether the technological process itself can be humanistic. The price that may have to be paid for not proliferating rural values is the postponement for decades of attitudes necessary for human development. Opportunism will dictate points of view; individual responsibility will not be taken seriously. Nor will politicians be inclined to stem the tide. Rather, they will be more likely to accelerate the movement by courting the favor of the mass man in order to remain in power.

The rural youth are the key to humanistic development. If their capabilities were used in their own community, they could become the vanguard of the socially controlled industrialization of the rural area. Incentives must be provided to keep talented poor children in school. To persuade these youths not to emigrate, they must be assured jobs and rising income. A nation that tolerates such losses in its rural areas entails social costs in the urban centers into which the migrants move.

Moreover, drawing manpower away from rural areas to established urban centers may serve as a depressant rather than a catalyst to growth. The migrant tends to gravitate toward the city before he is ready to cope with its sophisticated levels of technology and consumption. He wants his consumption before his diploma. A fundamental lesson drawn from the economic history of the United States is the need for highly productive rural areas as a base for economic growth.

Modernizing a rural area raises considerable problems. It is easier to expand existing industry in urban centers. Rural development requires a thorough reconstruction of the social, economic, cultural, and political order. As John P. Lewis stated, new functions have to be introduced, old ones must be changed, and the sociopolitical substructures in which these activities are housed must be revamped "while all the time the tenants continue to occupy the premises." [6]

The problems of rural development are related not only to agriculture but to all social institutions and activities that impede the full employment

[6] John P. Lewis, *Quiet Crisis in India* (Garden City, N.Y.: Anchor Books, 1964), pp. 148–149.

of human resources. The rural mind is both a hope for humanistic development and a principal stumbling block to progress. The social structure of the society is such that advancement is denied the sons of the poor. The yield of the land is low because of obsolete techniques and lack of capital. Credit rates are harsh. The grower may be exploited by middlemen who reward his increased productivity by cutting his prices. In short, the society may punish rather than reward ingenuity. The social order operates on the psychology of pessimism.

In a climate of surging demand, there are two compatible approaches to a partial breakdown of this rural system: by education and training and by provision of immediate rewards for rising productivity. Because existing rural divisions obstruct the pursuit of these objectives, some areas have to be abandoned entirely, and others must be consolidated, a reshuffling that may be opposed by the traditional elite. Many rural development efforts fail because they attempt a piecemeal approach rather than one within the context of a total system. Some amount to bland sociological exercises in do-goodism.

In such modern nations as the United States, the rural exodus began after modern roots were established in both rural and urban areas. In presently modernizing countries, the exodus occurs long before this base of industrialization takes hold. Unless the resulting forces can be controlled, economic development for developing nations may comprise a politically unstable capital city surrounded by a land of backwardness and stagnation.[7]

Latin America, Black Africa, and Southern Asia comprise three major cultural areas of the developing world. Because each represents a different cultural orientation, they experience dissimilar confrontations with modern technology. Out of this confrontation may issue social structures that differ from those of the two ideological adversaries: the United States and the Soviet Union. In each of the three regions is likely to emerge a nation model of the most successful marriage of social structure and economic growth and a nation model of the least successful. A continuing study of countries within these regions would provide clues as to the validity of the thesis of this short chapter.

Summation

In speaking of social structure, one refers to the individuality of man and his relationships with other men. In economic development, this social structure changes. From the point of view of growth, something is gained thereby and something is lost. There are three possible policies for

[7] For an intensive analysis of this problem, see Philip M. Raup, "The Contribution of Land Reforms to Agricultural Development: An Analytical Framework," *Economic Development and Cultural Change*, Vol. 11 (October 1963).

dealing with this change. The first is really no policy at all, but consists of high-level economic policies without a conscious attempt at controlling or heading off the excesses that follow in course. The second is a mixed type, consisting of attempts to guide social attitudes and institutions by voluntary methods, either by government or private organizations. The third is a totalitarian system that imposes social control and exacts human sacrifices, often with a minimum of dissemination of free knowledge and without soliciting consent. Pertinent ethical questions arise from each of these three choices.

Change inevitably produces conflict. The sudden alteration of traditional income patterns that comes with development generates a conflict of interests. In a traditional economy, warring groups learn to keep at arm's length so as not to make the situation worse. Economic development disorganizes this stand-off policy and brings conflict to the surface. Pressures are created to forge new means of cooperation and new institutions to channel conflict into instruments of decision making. The new institutions must simultaneously encourage individual restraint and creation; they are not developed overnight. In developing nations, there are few examples of successful institution building. Their mass communications media do not appear to encourage restraint and creation. The building of effective institutional mechanisms does not appear to be the inevitable consequence of economic policy. If the United States is an example, several decades often are required to build effective industrial institutions; once they are established, they soon become obsolete.

The allocation of political and social power in the West was a fairly orderly process tied to successive stages of industrial growth. Producer power came before political power. People earned the concessions they obtained. The difficulties in developing countries in achieving this harmony curtail the rise of social maturity. The unleashing of forces for generating growth may lead instead to its undermining.[8]

This chapter discussed the adverse impact of both urbanization and the emergence of a free market. Some urbanization is required for industrialization. But it does not always help economic growth; especially when it transfers underemployment and low productivity to big cities. In addition, free-market choices do not inevitably produce the attitudes and institutions necessary for economic development. Laborers must want not only what the market stands ready to offer; they must want also to work harder and more efficiently, to save, to keep their families small, and to sacrifice. The free market inhibits the growth of such attitudes. Investment policies do not automatically produce such a result. The government must plan for the emergence of frugal, efficient laborers.

[8] See Gino Germani, *Política y Sociedad en una época de transición* (Buenos Aires: Editorial Paidos, 1962).

To conclude, economic development is not merely a matter of economic facts, figures, principles, and models but is something that is *going on*. What goes on is social. This chapter presented a point of view of social evolution that is inimical to economic development.[9]

[9] Having now read the issues on political and cultural factors in economic development, the economics student would find it useful to read Irma Adelman and Cynthia Taft Morris, "An Econometric Model of Socio-Economic and Political Change in Underdeveloped Countries," *American Economic Review*, 58 (December 1968), and the comments of Sara S. Berry and Peter Eckstein and reply, in the *American Economic Review* (March 1970).

The debate raises the issue as to whether a priori models or empirical research is more useful in understanding contemporary economic development.

part three
THE CASES

9

THE SOVIET UNION

There is no one economy that is typical of the economic development of all communist countries. These nations entered into communism at different levels of economic growth and with different strengths and weaknesses in their agricultural and industrial sectors. Yet the model of the Soviet Union can serve all communist countries because all of these systems generally are based on the Stalinist policy of emphasizing the quick build-up of heavy industry and imposing controls on the labor force in the initial stages of planning.

The differences among these systems arise from dissimilarities in culture and quirks of history as well as differences in economic structures and in the amount of sacrifice that these nations extract from their people. But similarities exist that are obscured by differences in the periods during which the systems emerge. Therefore, this chapter presents the model of the U.S.S.R. to indicate the mainsprings of communist economic growth generally and the attraction of noncommunist developing nations to Soviet expansion.

SOVIET INDUSTRIAL RELATIONS

To do so, it is useful to look at the economic growth of the Soviet Union through its industrial relations system so as to understand its national character and power distribution. With varying degrees of influence, the agents of Soviet industrial relations set employment terms within a particular cultural context. The industrial relations network has characteristics that reveal processes of change. For example, the movement of power flows in a direction opposite from that occurring in the United States. Through the encouragement of institutions at the base of the society, the power that resides at the top is being pushed downward by the policies of the monopolistic political party. The political and economic power held at the beginning of forced industrialization under authoritarian rule is shifting, with party acquiescence, to a new professional elite.

The present industrial relations system of the United States originated in the relationships within small employer-employee groups, which were based on property rights. As time went on and the economy changed, these relationships were transformed by the rise of organized labor and by the intervention of the three branches of government through their interpretation of the public interest. In the U.S.S.R., the Bolshevik revolution made everyone in a production enterprise a government employee. Thus, both the legal basis of the labor-management relationship and the worker's image of his employer differ from the situation prevailing in the United States.

The rate of change in the Soviet Union is faster than those of Western economies. Having begun from a peasant society not far removed from servitude, the U.S.S.R., through accelerated industrialization, produced a diversified economy after four decades. Accordingly, the Russian worker is willing to accept the close guidance of a political elite over a wide area of his affairs under a system of leadership by patriarchal exhortation. A clue to party efficacy in using the thrust of a collective conscience behind its policies is its inheritance not of a highly industrialized society but rather of a feudalistic patriarchal village system in which people were not strangers to each other and were willing to accept the political image of a stern but benevolent father. This system has grown in a cultural climate of Eastern dogmatism rather than Western pluralism.

The methods and policies of the Soviet system have their roots in the application of law. Adjudicators are not concerned with the conciliation of diverging viewpoints. Violations are assumed to be committed in ignorance of the law or are viewed as antisocial acts that are committed despite cognizance of the law.

The ultimate arbiters of the system are the high councils of the party. It would be misleading, however, to interpret this control as sheer unilateral exercise of power, for the party organization is expected to perform a role of persuasion and mediation, acting as a fixer, catalyst, and instiller of pride in efficient performance.

CULTURAL OVERVIEW

In the Soviet mind, the term "culture" is colored by the impact that rapid industrialization has had on the population. A person of culture is not simply one who understands and appreciates the arts but one whose tastes and behavior are *au courant.* The individual who enjoys bronze-plated door knobs, tassels, and plush decorations and who behaves in public places like a clumsy peasant is not *kulturni.* On the other hand, both the man who buys books but may not read them and the man who basks in the reflected glory of a great artist but may not understand his technique can both be men of culture. The Russians watch each other for cultural signs and report about them in their press. They thereby project the standards of a new middle class that is rooted in industry. For example, occupations have status in proportion to the amount of education they require. The intrinsic nature of the occupation seems less important than the particular diploma it represents.

The Soviet worker appears to have a zest for learning. One is impressed by the way he lines up to buy books. He seems to be a mixture of submissiveness and defiance. He has a more collective sense than the American worker. To American eyes, his society is a goldfish bowl in which each fish is a vigilant overseer of whether the others behave exemplarily; it is a state technocracy whose monopolistic leadership rules by constant exhortation; it is a society whose exhortation is increased productivity. He complains about wages and the pace of work, but he does not appear to question the basic philosophy behind the industrial relations system.

Russians are the Texans of the Slavic world. By their own calculations, they have the largest hydroelectric power plant, the world's lowest temperatures, and the biggest industrial plants. They lead the world in housing construction and electrified railroad lines. The escalators in the Moscow subway are probably the fastest in the world. What the United States has, the Soviet Union has too, but bigger. This giantism at times extends to the number of individuals employed per task. In Moscow, one sees four women cultivating the soil around a single shrub; what is more, they manage not to get into one another's way. There is a dualism in the Russian character—a zeal for modern technology and a tolerance for human qualities.

The Russians seem to have escaped the depersonalizing effect of industrialization. They maintain intense personal relationships and move freely day and night without fear of assault. There may be no other industrial society where a stranger on a bus will tell another that his tie is not straight and where paying the fare is based on the honor system.

The relative influence of decision makers in the Soviet Union is a puzzle. The traditional method of deciphering it would be through economic, historical, and legal analysis. A more effective way in that country, however, is by a field investigation using attitude survey techniques. Nevertheless, when an American attempts to conduct such research in the Soviet Union, he is confronted with an almost pathological dislike of such probing. The Russians feel vulnerable, fearing that the purpose of the investigator is to undermine the beliefs that provide meaning to their lives. They may view criticism of their society as a sign of weakness. Still conscious of the cultural lag that existed before the Bolshevik revolution, they feel obliged to present a solid front to Americans. Some Russians may see such an inquiry as an inquisition, some as an opportunity to become loquacious, and some as a chance to display their patriotism.

Three levels of Soviet reality exist. There is the official written record of events that has been transcribed since the revolution in a manner consonant with the Marxist-Leninist ethic. There are the restive, critical spokesmen of Soviet life who run the risk of condemnation by the power structure. Finally, there is the muted voice of the people, whose behavior may or may not be in keeping with official party truths.

By not succumbing to the temptation to be critical, by maintaining a professional mien, and by cultivating empathy, the American investigator in the Soviet Union may make some progress. It is only through such an approach that insights into the way in which Soviet institutions operate can be gained. Such an investigation may reveal that the differences between American and Soviet labor are less than believed.

Another stumbling block to understanding is the unrelenting hammering home of official truths in the U.S.S.R. The scholar may view conformity to dogma with suspicion and disaffection. To him, individualism may be a sign of strength and integrity, but to those he observes it may represent weakness and falsity. The American may use candor as an instrument of rapport; and the Russian may react with confusion and suspicion. Even if an American acknowledges some of the objectives of Soviet propaganda as laudable, it is difficult for him to accept as valid responses that lack individuality. In answer to his sympathetic inquiries, he is given a series of stereotyped images that make him wonder what in the Soviet Union is real and what is not. Moreover, if he is able to elicit the responses he is looking for, the interviewee, annoyed with himself for having deviated from the official line, is likely to become hostile.

Besides getting interviewees to say what they really think and not what they think their colleagues and managers want them to say, the investigator must determine reasons for both the similarities and the differences in the responses obtained. The responses will reflect the Russian's estimate of the investigator and his methods. If interpreters are employed, an already difficult situation is further complicated because they may inject biases that impair the investigation's validity. The practice of alternating interpreters may convert a study of Soviet industrial relations into a comparative study of interpreters. If the inquiry has moved from English to Russian and back to English, its findings may be in serious question.

The investigator must be especially wary of ideological barriers that may distort the findings. One of them is the official image of the Soviet citizen as portrayed constantly in the Russian press. In this official portrait, Soviet man is pictured as a cultural hero who is uncontaminated by the false values of individualism and religion of the West (particularly of the United States). Persons who are interviewed may be anxious to conform to this image, thus making it difficult for the investigator to obtain meaningful responses. For this reason, a field inquiry has to steer clear of matters obviously ideological and appear factual on the surface.

Consequently, understanding Soviet industrial relations is a laborious task of fitting together a complex mosaic. After having painstakingly accumulated data, the researcher nears completion of the investigation only to find a new event or clue that may force him to discard a vital part. It is difficult to know when to stop the search for "facts," and it is also difficult to present an integrated description with assurance. Rather, a series of loosely fitted pieces of partially substantiated information has to suffice. There are few experts on Soviet industrial relations, and the differences in their expertness lie in the degree of ignorance and the type of bias they bring to their task.

Experts studying the same data can draw opposite conclusions. For example, the rising influence of plant union committees in the Soviet Union is viewed by one interpreter as a device to make authoritarian management palatable and by another as increasing industrial democracy. In describing the labor legislation passed in the U.S.S.R. since 1956, one author concludes that the concern of trade unions for the welfare of workers seems to be vanishing altogether and that the labor-management productivity committees, the so-called permanent production conferences, are a failure. Another author presents precisely the opposite view.

Professor Gregory Grossman arrives at the following conclusions in using the published statistics on production in the Soviet Union. The figures on industrial output make some sense, upward distortion being more common than downward. The bias is consistent from year to year, however, and therefore calculable. Falsification is probably not practiced so much as selectivity to reflect a favorable point of view.

The communications media of the Soviet Union are part of the political monopoly. They range from highly propagandistic to fairly objective. Newspapers rarely fail to exhort their readers to increase their productivity and to report on phenomenal increases in production. Complaints against the bureaucracy's handling of production matters appear frequently, but such criticism rarely is leveled against members of the central committee of the party. Accounts of the Soviet institutions of samokritika and kritika, of exposing one's own errors and those of others, make good press copy.

ECONOMIC OVERVIEW

The Soviet Union has a planned economy—planned in the sense that a goal is set for a desired future state of the economy and the use of resources is directed toward achieving that goal. The model is a five-year plan consisting of a series of phases described in terms of output targets and input limits that specify the amount of different products to be produced and the resources that should go into them. In addition, the government has the complex task of determining the more than 8 million prices in the economy.

Students of Russian economic development trace its beginnings to the 1880s, when the government began assisting key industries. A slackening took place after the 1905 revolution, but the decline was stopped by private efforts, principally by bankers. World War I and the ensuing civil war curtailed output drastically, and it fell to 25 percent of the peak level before the Bolshevik revolution.

Appreciable growth took place during the first five-year plan that began in 1928. Factors of production were there ready to be used; capital equipment needed repairing, and labor was available. The subsequent period up to World War II witnessed an accelerated growth that was carried along on the backs of peasants who gave up their surplus to the industrial sector without receiving consumer goods in return. The high growth rate of the 1950s is explainable on the grounds of an appreciable rise in human capital investment during that decade.

Simply stated, the fundamental aim of Soviet planning is rapid growth. This goal is different from traditional socialist planning, which is designed primarily to remove disproportions in production that arise out of individual decision making so as to bring about an increase in social welfare. Should bottlenecks appear in rapid growth, the Soviet policy is to shift resources until they are eliminated.

The same policy of centralized direction and planning exists in foreign trade, which the Soviets estimate to be in the area of $18 billion annually. Of this amount, $5 billion represents trade with developing nations. Principal exports include industrial machinery, equipment, and materials. The trade is managed by a state monopoly whose overall objective is to achieve national economic and political goals. These goals can be achieved, according to the planners, by taking advantage of international specialization of labor.[1] The Soviet government aspires to get away from its emphasis on raw materials and fuel in its overall export trade and to play an increasingly international role in the sale of industrial products. As individual enterprises exercise initiative to stimulate their own exports, the structure of the state monopoly is likely to change.

The Soviet Union's aid to developing nations includes both technical assistance and loans at an annual rate of interest ranging from 2 percent to 2.5 percent. The low rate of interest may actually be compensated for by the prices that are pegged on the goods sold. Soviet aid is concentrated in Asia, Africa, and the Middle East. The Soviet Union is also making significant penetrations in Latin America.

---

[1] There is much controversy as to what the Soviets mean by international specialization of labor. Some critics believe that they intend by such policy a colonial relationship involving the sale of manufactured goods and purchase of raw materials.

Soviet planning methods produced psychological as well as economic effects. Government planners were in a contest for power with enterprise managers, and their interests were not the same. There was uncertainty as to the pressures planners should apply. For example, Khrushchev was notorious for unexpectedly putting pressure on managers of the economy.[2] As the goods produced and consumer tastes became more diverse, however, there was an increasing demand that quantity and quality output decisions be given to the enterprise managers. In addition, the arbitrary setting of prices by planners had the effect of producing distortions in resource allocation. Decisions were made not on the basis of the best allocation of resources but on what output was desired and what resources were needed to obtain that output.

As the central government became overwhelmed by decision making, Khrushchev decided to turn over many economic decisions to some one hundred regional councils. The solution of his successor Kosygin was embodied in the so-called economic reform.[3] The following functions were handed over to enterprise managers: determination of the extent of product differentiation and sales volume; allocation of the wage fund; determination of the level of profits; budget allocation; utilization of productive capacity; and determination of the volume of capital investment. Central planners retained the following functions: price fixing; major allocation of investment in the economy; determination of the product mix of the economy as a whole; fixing of the wage fund; and major allocation of materials and equipment.

In addition, the economic reform introduced a new meaning of profits.[4] The planned profit, in which the central planners fix the profit from each enterprise, is retained to provide an incentive for efficiency. The enterprise is allowed to retain some of the profits accruing from efficient use of its resources for use as capital and for distribution to its employees in the form of increased earnings and fringe benefits. The first changeover of enterprises under the economic reform was made on January 1, 1966. By the first quarter of 1967, some 2,500 enterprises had been converted.

Prior to the reform, the yardstick for measuring the success of the economy was volume of production. The change introduced eight success indicators: volume of goods sold; assortment of goods sold; level of profits; amount of money paid in wages; amount reverting back to the state budget; volume of capital investment; extent of new technology introduced; and allocation of material. The answers these success criteria give may be contradictory. In accomplishing his mission of obtain-

---

[2] The ouster of Khrushchev confounded political scientists on two counts: that it happened and that no struggle for power ensued. Political models do not account for the rise in living standards and occupational skills. A theory of political power per se appears sterile.
[3] The economic reform movement was initiated by E. Liberman, economics professor at the Kharkov Engineering and Economics Institute.
[4] For a detailed article on the reform, see Keith Bush, "The Reforms: A Balance Sheet," *Problems of Communism*, July–August 1967 (Washington, D.C.: United States Information Agency).

ing the highest bonus possible, an imaginative accountant may be the manager's best friend.

What have been the results? The annual per capita income in the Soviet Union is approximately $1,000. About half the current total output is in the form of either industrial products or construction, compared to about 28 percent for the first five-year plan. The output rise during the first planning periods up to World War II was achieved by the forced urbanization of the rural population and the recruitment of women and not by drawing away labor from existing production; moreover, it was accomplished without any significant rise in urban overhead for the new recruits. Soviet estimates show an average annual growth rate of about 11 percent between 1950 and 1958. Thereafter, according to estimates of American economists, the rate declined progressively to about 5 percent (or more if one accepts CIA figures) and then rose somewhat. Estimates of the volume of Soviet gross national product (GNP) vary, but informed sources place it at about one-half the United States figure. While this growth has taken place, the labor force has increased faster than the population. The Soviet government reports that since the economic reform, gross production rose over 8 percent in the converted enterprises after the first year of operation.[5]

Whether Soviet economic development can be considered a success depends on the criteria one uses to measure it. An assessment on the basis of resource use is difficult to make, for planning is not based on optimum returns. Because the production rise from the preceding year is used to determine quotas, and because it is prudent not to plan production beyond a small percentage increase, planning may actually have a deterrent effect on output. This caution places management in the position of discouraging suggestions to improve productivity and of hoarding inputs for future use. On the basis of agricultural efficiency, the proportion of the population in agriculture declined from 80 percent at the beginning of the first five-year plan to less than 40 percent at present. On the basis of productive efficiency, output per unit of input is rising at approximately 3 percent a year, faster than in the United States; but that does not mean that the Russians are more efficient. On the criterion of personal income, the five-year plan for 1966–1970 calls for a rise in industrial wages of 20 percent and an increase in the income of collective farmers of at least 35 percent during the period.

POPULATION AND LABOR FORCE CHARACTERISTICS

According to the Russian press, the model Soviet worker feels a moral obligation to work for the good of the collective. Labor is a duty and a

[5] The Joint Economic Committee of the U.S. Congress reports a 6 percent rise in Soviet GNP for 1966–67, including 7.6 percent for industry and 3.7 percent for agriculture. From *Soviet Economic Performance, 1966–67* (Washington, D.C., 1968).

question of honor with him, and he is eager to make personal sacrifices to increase the wealth of this society. He who works not, neither shall he eat. He observes labor disciplinary rules and eagerly takes courses at night in order to raise his productivity. He does not fear automation because he knows it will help make his work lighter, reduce his work-week, and eliminate differences between white- and blue-collar workers.

The Soviet worker is convinced that the one-party system in his country is natural and logical and that a multiparty system is obsolete. Because there are no class antagonisms in his country, there are no grounds for the existence of many political parties. He believes that the Communist party is a superior institution that expresses the interests and will of all the Soviet people.

Moreover, each worker seeks status by helping his colleagues to improve their performance and by helping the leader to perform his job. If the leader sets high production goals and forces others to increase their production, he is not a threat but a hero who should be emulated rather than despised. The worker exhibits this zeal not only at work but in school, in the party ranks, and in the multiple dwelling units in which he lives. He is outside the mores of the collective only when he is asleep.

A firm believer in Marxism-Leninism, the worker hero is neither a revisionist nor a dogmatist. He accepts communism as a science that expresses the laws of life and social development. Thus Marx was the first sociologist and everything since Marx has been an interpretation from the original book of Genesis. As a good Marxist-Leninist, he is also an atheist who believes that religion is a reactionary ideology run by para-sites who are drugging men's minds. He is deeply grateful for what the party has done for him and feels that his life improves every day, thanks to the unstinting efforts of the party.

The typical industrial employee works a five-day, forty-one-hour week. His leisure time on Saturday and Sunday may be spent at a sports event, an amusement park, or the movies, or shopping or engaging in some activity at the local palace of culture.

He may have recently moved his family of four into one of the much publicized two-room apartments at a rental of about 10 percent of his income. His previous housing may have been one room, with kitchen and toilet facilities shared with other families. If he is a factory worker, the amount of his earnings depends upon a combination of several factors. His basic hourly rate depends upon his job classification, which is fixed according to a government manual, but this basic rate is not generally guaranteed. He must produce to get it. (If he feels improperly classified, he can file a grievance with the union factory committee.) In addition, he may receive a premium for "hot" or "harmful" work, for "heavy" work, or for work performed under adverse climatic conditions. He may also pick up additional earnings for length of service and individual incentive as well as group bonuses for overfulfillment of the production plan. If he is a skilled worker, he can make as much as fifteen times more than an unskilled worker, including bonuses.

The wage rates for job classifications are set by state planning bodies, the State Committee on Labor and Wages, the trade-union federation, and the particular union to which the worker belongs. The relative influence of these organizations is a matter of conjecture. In the heavy metals industry, each worker is slotted into one of six classifications and paid accordingly.

Planners preplan the wage cost per unit of product. In addition, there is a planned annual increase in productivity of 7 percent. Because total industrial production and the expected rise in productivity are known, the wage cost can be estimated. In recent years, average earnings have been rising in the area of 3.5 percent annually. An unanticipated rise in productivity does not bother planners. The increased production can be used, and the additional wage costs can come out of increased profits.

If the Soviet press is an indication, the Soviet worker's wage complaints have a familiar ring. He apparently finds differences in gross earnings unfair, wage systems of payment complicated, and job classifications inequitable. The incentive systems also create many grievances.

Under Soviet law, the worker is required to bring his labor record book when looking for a job. A prospective employer may ask him for letters of reference, job résumés, prior wage record, and certificates from his apartment house management or rural soviet attesting to his conduct. Formal employment exchanges do not exist.[6] The worker finds a job through the press, the radio, his friends, or through government placement after finishing his education. He may also apply at a plant on his own volition, pursue notices on company bulletin boards, or sign up in the special recruitment campaigns for developing areas. Notices of job openings are posted in public places, but they are mostly for service and unskilled jobs. If he loses his job, he receives two weeks' severance pay.

In December 1966, by a joint decree of the party central committee and the U.S.S.R. Council of Ministers, labor resource utilization committees were organized in all of the Soviet republics. They are designed to take over the old recruitment administration that came out of World War II (*Orgnabor*).

The population of the U.S.S.R. is 233 million, some three-fourths of which lives in one-fifth of the country, European Russia. The rate of population increase, 1.4 percent, is about the same as that of the United States; the male deficit caused by World War II is declining. Approximately 46 percent of the population is in the labor force (Table

6 There is a move in the direction of employment exchanges. In December 1966 the party central committee and the Council of Ministers authorized the organization of State Committees on the Utilization of Labor Resources. The committee set up in the Russian republic has local offices and apparently is performing some placement of labor in addition to labor supply and demand analysis. In 1969, a Soviet labor economist suggested unemployment compensation for workers laid off to increase productivity. (E. Manevich, *Voprosy Ekonomiki,* Akademia Nauk S.S.S.R., Institut Ekonomiki, No. 10, 1969.)

TABLE 10 □ **Estimates and Projections of Population and Labor Force in the U.S.S.R.**

(In Thousands)

Population	1950	1960	1970	1980
Total	——	212.3	——	267.1
Population aged 14 and over	129,708	151,234	179,706	——
Male	53,633	64,825	80,220	——
Female	76,075	86,409	99,486	——
Labor force	97,005	108,621	129,422	——
Armed forces	4,600	3,300	3,000	——
Civilian labor force	92,405	105,321	126,422	——

Source: Joint Economic Committee, U. S. Congress, *Soviet Economic Performance, 1966–67,* Washington, D.C., 1968.

10), a participation rate that is the highest in the world.[7] About three-fourths of the labor force is in European Russia. Patterns of rapid urbanization began in the Soviet Union at the time of the first five-year plan. By 1960 some 70 percent of the population was already living in urban centers.[8]

Table 11 indicates the pattern of the wage structure in the Soviet Union. Employees in scientific services receive the highest wages, and those in state farms the lowest. The rates of increase manifest political pressures (state farms) and economic pressures of demand and supply (construction). The wages of blue-collar workers are rising faster than the salaries of white-collar employees. With 1950 as a base, the wage index rose from 127 to 146 during the period 1960–1966.

TABLE 11 □ **Average Annual Money Wages by Selected Sector in the U.S.S.R. and Percentage Increase, 1940–1966**

(In Current Rubles)

Sector	1940	1966	Percentage Increase
Scientific services	560.4	1,423.2	153.9
Government	465.4	1,324.8	184.6
Transport	416.4	1,315.2	215.8
Industry	408.2	1,281.6	213.9
Construction	406.8	1,357.2	233.6
Education	387.6	1,146.0	195.7
Communications	337.2	904.8	168.3
Trade	300.0	951.6	217.2
State farms	262.8	957.6	264.5
Average of all sectors	396.0	1,190.4	200.7

Source: Joint Economic Committee, U. S. Congress, *Soviet Economic Performance, 1966–67,* Washington, D.C., 1968.

[7] The figure compares with 40 percent for the United States, 35.8 for Africa, and 35.2 for Latin America. *Demographic Aspects of Manpower, Sex, and Age Patterns of Participation in Activities* (New York: United Nations, 1962).
[8] The data are from Emily Clark Brown, *The Soviet Manpower System,* January 1963, a limited circulation document of the U. S. Bureau of Labor Statistics.

Overall, the relative number of white-collar to blue-collar workers is rising but has not reached the same level as in the United States. With this transition has come a decline in the relative number of unskilled workers. Soviet women make up some 54 percent of the labor force, ranging from 47 percent of the industrial workers to 91 percent of those on the private farms. The percentage is declining as the male deficit falls.[9]

The annual increase in workers comes from the following sources: primary and secondary school students terminating their full-time education, specialists from vocational schools, higher education graduates and dropouts, former rural workers, and women shifting away from full-time household management.

Manpower is allocated by a combination of planning and reliance on market forces in the economy. The government has become less arbitrary in resolving the conflict between manpower planning and the worker's right to choose his occupation and place of work. Wages are used as a principal instrument in allocating labor. Manpower planning is restricted to determining how many more or fewer workers are needed, where they are needed, and from what source they can be recruited.

In this planning, the number of workers seeking employment for the first time is estimated by republic, region, and district. Employers are given quotas as to the number of school graduates and dropouts they must hire. Thus the planning group has to make two estimates. It has to determine the future size of the population and extrapolate from that figure estimated increases in the labor force. Second, on the basis of estimates of future production, it has to determine the number of additional employees that will be needed in the various industries and public services. Soviet experts say that the difference between the two sets of data is reduced through incentives that move workers where needed. As in the case of planned production, labor planning works better during manpower shortages than during manpower surpluses.[10]

Soviet economists complain that precise data are limited to total employment and do not indicate the total manpower available or the skills of such manpower—a complaint of manpower specialists generally. An increasing Soviet problem is short-term labor surpluses due to such factors as population shifts, workers displaced by improved technology, seasonal employment, individuals leaving farms, women entering the labor force, and individuals released from the armed forces. The policy problem raised by these short-term surpluses is compounded by the party dogma that unemployment does not exist in the Soviet Union. It appar-

[9] John B. Parrish In *Soviet Womenpower as a Professional Resource* reports that Soviet women In the early 1950s comprised 50 percent of enrollments in higher education. They represented 38 percent of university faculties, compared to 9 percent in the leading American universities. He reports, however, that few professional women succeed In advancing toward the top.
[10] There are many complaints in Russian periodicals over Soviet manpower planning. Soviet economists assert it is Ineffective and call for a state organization with responsibility for manpower planning and placement.

ently does, and Soviet manpower specialists state that the problem is not automatically resolved.

The Young Communist League in the Soviet Union is the guardian of the morals of young workers. It provides, by its own behavior, models of excellence in work, flushes out parasites, and publicizes relapses to decadent capitalism. In an issue of the Young Communist League (YCL) newspaper, *Kommsomolskaya Pravda,* a member describes some moments of troubled conscience. He is considering quitting his job at a new blast furnace because of the prospect of having to perform menial rather than heroic tasks.

> I asked to be released. After getting past all the barriers—the senior foremen, the Young Communist League staff, the construction chief—I held my release slip in my hands. One more day and I would never see my blast furnace again, which had become the most important thing in my life. The gates would close behind me as upon any outsider. I went up to the fellows on the brigade. I had met them back in Moscow, at the YCL city committee, and in nine months they had become my close friends. They were digging away at the frozen soil and it seemed to me that each of them was saying with his glance: Turned coward, eh? Running away? I had never felt so alone in all my life. It seemed to me that each of them viewed me as a deserter. You are going in the wrong direction, my conscience whispered, in the wrong direction. The wind caught the torn bits of the release slip and I felt so good and light of heart. I had a sense of rebirth. With horror I thought about how I might have lost my friends and never again have seen our Kuznetsk Young Communist blast furnace, and labeled myself a coward.[11]

In 1959 the party central committee decreed that workers should participate in maintaining public order. The Soviet press estimates that in the Russian republic alone there are some 1,300 people in volunteer detachments. Their principal tasks are making night patrols and detaining troublemakers, holding discussion groups and other forms of indoctrination, and sending letters to places where misbehaving individuals live or work. They also organize agitation teams, prepare "windows of satire," in which the unseemly actions of disorderly workers are ridiculed, visit the places where the troublemakers work and live, maintain contacts with the courts, and find jobs for persons without regular employment.

A satirical newspaper published by a Moscow detachment carried a caricature of a drunkard named Ogaezov. The issue was posted on a wall at the place of residence of this violator of community morality. The next day, all the residents knew of Ogaezov's drunken orgies. His conduct drew universal censure and contempt, and so great was the force of this public opinion that Ogaezov went to YCL headquarters several times to request that the caricature be taken down, pleading that his neighbors would not let him alone.[12]

---

11 *Current Digest of the Soviet Press,* Vol. 13, No. 22.
12 *Ibid.,* Vol. 12, No. 46.

MANAGERIAL ELITES

Our next concern is with the managerial elites. We discuss the Soviet employer, trade-union officials, and party officials, in that order.

The Soviet Employer

In the official view, the Soviet employer is a person who heads an enterprise, institution, or public agency by virtue of the will and authorization of the workers, and can be removed at their will. His relationship with them is based on mutual trust and comradely cooperation. In contrast, the employer in a capitalist society represents the ruling class of exploiters.

According to this view, the Soviet employer has lofty ideals, a capacity to subordinate personal interests to the common good, and persistence in accomplishing tasks. He has a broad political and cultural horizon, deep scientific knowledge of his work, initiative on the job, and organizing skill. The art of human relations apparently has come to the Soviet Union also, for the official view describes employers as benevolent figures deeply understanding of the workers' feelings and moods. In brief, the outstanding employer is a man with Leninist style. He is the embodiment of those qualities found in Khrushchev before his ouster—boundless energy, great organizational ability, closeness to the masses, and readiness to propagate communist ideas.

By official Soviet standards, the bad employer is one with no initiative. His decisions are weak, for he fears risks. He does not make a move without a directive from above. He barks too many commands at workers, looks for chances to be critical of them, and blows up at every mistake they make.

To get away from myth, the typical Soviet employer appears to be self-made. He often comes from humble social origins and has come up through the occupational ranks or from a technical institute or engineering school. Although not a worker in the party organization, he is usually a party member, if only out of convenience. He is more production-oriented than his American counterpart, who may be a lawyer or specialist in finance and marketing. But he does share the capitalist motivations of prestige and material acquisition. He has learned to reconcile pressures so as to get to the top and stay there. He thus recommends to planners only those production goals that he is sure he can meet successfully. If a material shortage exists, he must know where to find a supplier: perhaps someone whom he helped once and who is disposed to return the favor, or a fixer who can be of assistance for a fee. In short, he learns how to improvise within the strictures of the system. The success of the system, therefore, is as much a measure of his ingenuity as it is a measure of efficient planning.

Trade Unions

A second branch of the leadership structure is the trade unions, to which, according to the Russians, some 90 percent of the labor force belongs. The nature of their role is viewed with skepticism in the United States. Although some national unions in the United States are inclined to talk to them at least, the executive council of the AFL-CIO maintains a quarantine policy toward Russian trade unions and views them as instruments for driving workers to higher levels of productivity.   Soviet trade-union officials are sensitive to this criticism and take the position that the rise in productivity and living standards of the workers are tied together and are not conflicting.

At the time of the communist takeover in 1917, there were an estimated 2 million trade-union members.   Membership had grown rapidly by the acceleration of industrialization at the turn of the century and soon thereafter had become the tool of contending political interests.   Drastic shortages following the civil war engulfed the unions in a struggle for survival.   They quickly became instruments for increasing production.   In the ensuing dictatorship, trade-union prerogatives were progressively reduced, and no convention was held for seventeen years.   Union officials became the servants of the central committee of the party.

A period of liberalization began in 1957 with a resolution of the party central committee detailing tasks allotted to the trade unions.   So began a process of change in which the party deliberately attempted to make the unions more independent and more responsive to the interests of workers. Under the reform, unions were organized into two lines of authority: vertically, by placing virtually every wage and salary earner into one of twenty-two industrial unions, and horizontally, by the trade-union federation, which has republic, territorial, regional and city councils.   With the exception of new entrants into the labor force and occasional workers, almost every Soviet employee thereby became a member of the trade unions.

The principal unions are the metallurgical, maritime, communications, education, railways, government employees, engineering, food, textiles, coal mining, power, performing artists, and health.   Membership is supposed to be voluntary.   The extraordinarily high percentage of membership probably comes from the social pressures in the plant to become affiliated and the privileges that membership brings.

The supreme body of the Soviet trade unions is the interunion convention, which, according to its bylaws, must meet at least once every four years.   The convention elects the federation council, comprising some 200 members, and a smaller presidium, which becomes the executive council.   In addition, a secretariat is selected: a chairman, six secretaries, and a staff to discharge the day-to-day business of the federation.

In the national unions, the highest body is the biennial convention.

Delegates are selected in rank-and-file meetings according to rules fixed by the central committee of the national union. The convention elects the members of this central committee, the auditing commission, and delegates to the federation convention. In turn, the central committee elects among its members a presidium of nine to eleven members and two principal officers, a president and secretary. Similarly, each union has its own staff secretariat.

Depending on its strength in a particular region, each national union may be organized vertically within the different republics of the U.S.S.R. and thus may have representation at the republic, regional, district, and city levels. In addition, in conventions held every two years, the union selects representatives to the national federation. These national unions also organize themselves into area councils and, because of the decentralization of industry, acquire such functions as planning and meeting production goals.

This trade-union structure terminates at the plant level in the trade-union committee, called the *zavkom,* which has the overall function of negotiating and enforcing collective agreements. A decision of the central committee of the party in 1957 recognized the right of these committees to take part in financial and production planning in determining output standards and systems of remuneration, ensuring compliance with labor laws and collective agreements, making judgments on candidates for managerial posts, and preventing the dismissal of workers without the committee's consent.

Membership dues are reported to be on a sliding scale that ranges up to 1 percent of a worker's monthly pay. Dues are paid on a voluntary basis to a union collector, an automatic checkoff system being prohibited by law. The collector sells stamps to the member, who pastes them in his membership book. The major part of these funds are reportedly spent on cultural activities. Expenditures are controlled by auditing commissions at the plant level together with the auditing commission of the federation, which, in turn, submits reports to its convention.

The plant union committee sets up special commissions on wages, production, and other important matters. Shop committees are also elected, as are the union organizer, insurance delegate, safety inspector, and others in each shop. In 1958 a law was passed authorizing unions to take part in management through production conferences in plants. The purpose, in the words of the party central committee, is to reconcile the principle that management must remain in the hands of a single chief with the necessity that employees exercise effective supervision over management.

The production conference acts under the direction of the union committee. Members are elected by a general meeting of employees, the trade-union committee, management, the party organization, the Young Communist League, and local technical and scientific societies.

Conferences are organized in enterprises of one hundred employees or more, and smaller organizations hold informal meetings of their personnel. They meet at least once every three months and make a biannual report of their work at a general meeting of the enterprise. The purpose of these production conferences appears to be to ensure fulfillment of production plans and to increase productivity.

Under the 1958 law, other functions of plant trade-union committees include representing workers in all matters pertaining to their labor, living conditions, and cultural activities; assisting in the drafting of plans for the production and capital investment of the enterprise; receiving reports from management on the progress of production plans and on conditions of employment and demanding elimination of shortcomings; advancing proposals to management and the government for improving the operation of the enterprise; presenting views on candidates for managerial posts and placing before the appropriate agency the matter of replacement or punishment of management personnel who fail to meet their obligations; participating in the setting of production standards; ensuring that workers receive proper benefits under social insurance programs, including the determination of the size of their pension; and checking the operation of the plant cafeteria. By law, all government agencies are expected to render every possible assistance to trade unions in discharging these functions.

Complaints of top trade-union officials in the Russian press furnish clues as to what the government expects of the trade unions. They complain of trade-union councils and committees not delving deeply enough into production matters, concerning themselves only superficially with encouraging competition among workers, and failing to assist workers in the production pledges they assume. They also pinpoint the failure to lower production costs; erect new housing for workers; increase worker skills; reduce labor turnover, absenteeism, and idle time; report on production to workers; support workers' suggestions for improved efficiency; and report to them the proposals submitted and those adopted. In addition, they complain about the lack of concern about recreation, sanatorium, and resort facilities for workers and summer recreation for children. These reports suggest union functions in industrial engineering, personnel administration, and worker welfare programs.

These reports also dwell on the international relations work of the union federation. Special mention is made of contacts with national unions in Asia, Africa, and Latin America. Contacts with the "progressive" unions are good. The development of ties with trade unions in capitalist countries demonstrates a growing interest in the life of the Soviet people and the activity of Soviet trade unions. The extraordinary statement is made at times that this interest is showing itself more and more among workers in the United States. There is increasing evidence of a desire for unity on the part of the working people of the world. Here, the consensus is that the World Federation of Trade Unions is a point of consolidation for all forces in the international trade-union movement who are seeking unity.

Following are typical responses of trade-union officials to questions posed in discussions. To an American, they may suggest an ambivalence in objectives that may not exist in the mind of the Russian.[13]

From a chairman of a union plant committee:

What do workers expect of you as their union leader? To do my best in improving their living and working conditions. And that we do. They also expect us to promote fulfillment of the plan and to raise their cultural conditions. We give an account of our work to the convention. If the workers find us inadequate, we can be recalled.

What is the most pressing problem of your union? Completing the transition to the forty-hour week while at the same time maintaining wages. Our other problems are producing high-quality equipment and raising productivity. We must constantly improve mechanization and reduce manual labor both in industry and agriculture. Another problem is to raise the skills and education of workers and to give them a sense of solidarity with other workers of the world. Only by friendship and peace can we achieve better conditions.

What is the most pressing problem you have had to face as a union leader? Constructing efficient machine tools. The problem differs every year. Now it is how to achieve automation.

What criteria would you use to measure trade-union achievements? Protecting the interests of workers, fulfilling the production plan, and raising the cultural level of workers.

Will you explain how a worker is discharged with the consent of the union? This is a severe limitation imposed on the plant management. The manager needs our concurrence. If he does get it, the worker can still appeal to the people's court. Discharge is rare anyway. We have cases, for instance, of habitual drunkenness or repeated leaving of one's place of work. Usually we try to talk to the man and straighten him out. But often the only way to do this is to discharge him. We do not want to resort to discharge. We need help badly. Sometimes the dismissal has a good effect and sometimes it does not. Sometimes we try to apply group pressure on the worker.

From another chairman of a union plant committee:

What are your most important responsibilities? Controlling the committeemen in their work, holding conferences, and making decisions. Calling in the chairmen of the separate departments. Every Tuesday I hold a seminar on the work that is to be done in the plant. I also check to see that the collective agreement is being maintained.

What do workers expect of you as their union leader? Workers go first to the department committee. They expect me to assist in fulfilling and over-fulfilling the plan. In that way the union receives money that it can use for leisure and cultural activities.

What is the most pressing problem of your union? Fulfilling the plan, promoting plant safety and health, providing good living quarters for worker families. If we overfulfill the plan, we use the money to build apartment houses, nurseries, and pioneer camps.

[13] These responses were obtained by the author during a visit to the Soviet Union.

People talk about success in life. What constitutes success for you? A larger plant, higher wages, better conditions for the workers. I feel better when the plan is fulfilled. Then I know I have success in life, like a draftsman who has designed a new machine and who eventually sees it operate.

What criteria would you use to measure trade-union achievements? The same as for my answer on success. A larger plant, higher wages, better conditions of life.

What do you feel are the most pressing needs of Soviet workers? Housing is a serious problem. In Leningrad about 7,000 houses were destroyed in the war. In my district there were only wooden homes; we used them for firewood. According to the plan each family will have its own apartment. The main problem is peace. And peace depends on the two great countries. We would like to visit your country. I would like to go.

From a trade-union chairman and party member:

What does the slogan "catching up with the United States" mean? We are behind in some production compared to your country. The reason is that we inherited a backward country and socialism has been in existence only about forty-five years. In some branches of industry we have gone ahead. Our pennant was the first on the moon. In one year, we built more apartments than the United States, Britain, and France together.

We do not have unemployment as in your country. If we can live in peace, we all can enjoy prosperity and help other countries. I began as a mechanic in the shop, and then the workers elected me as their chairman. The union has many rights in the Soviet Union. We take care of living conditions of workers, social insurance, the children of workers. The 1957 law gives us many rights and no restrictions as in your country. We have all the same task: to build communism.

What does communism mean to you? It means a society without class distinctions; everyone has equal rights, and the living and cultural standards are high. We now possess the material base for communism. Communism will come in my lifetime. But we need peace in order to get it. Your people want peaceful coexistence, but with your government it is another question.

People talk about success in life. What does success mean to you? You do not mean my private life? It means to satisfy material and spiritual demands; to bring up my children well. For every man on this planet it means work is a pleasure. I know in capitalist countries there are many labor-management conflicts; conditions are not good. It is not right that 10 percent live well and 90 percent badly. Marxism teaches that every man is equal.

We in the unions accept the leadership of the party because the members of the various organizations are intermingled. Policies are supported by everyone. Our government represents all occupational groups. All workers have the right to belong to the unions. Each worker submits an application to his group, which makes a decision after consultation with the plant committee. The members themselves decide; they look at his work record and morals. If a person is rejected and he improves, he will be accepted for membership later.

What do workers expect of you as their labor leader? The law says we must have close associations with workers. Sometimes we do not have time to do this; we accept many foreign delegations. Sometimes the workers criticize us too. We have many responsibilities. We control the dining rooms, and there is the social insurance which must be looked after. There are special problems too. Once they were stacking six high in the warehouse when the standard was five. [Reference here is to longshoremen storing goods in warehouses.]

Which aspects of American trade unionism do you like and which if any do you dislike? I am sorry. I have never been to the United States. It is too complicated, your country. I cannot understand why there are so many unions on board one ship.

What do you feel are the most important needs of the Soviet worker? Fulfilling the plan ahead of time; mechanizing; carrying cargoes ahead of time; housing; making his life easier; making suggestions on innovations; increasing his cultural life.

What is the most pressing problem of your union? The plan has to be fulfilled. Measures have to be taken to fill the plan, including the housing plan. Work standards such as the load a worker is required to lift must be controlled. Mechanization is another problem. The worker is not afraid of mechanization. A longshoreman who is displaced by technology can take a free course on mechanical loading and continue to draw his wages.

The case of the West against Soviet trade unionism is summarized in the following allegations brought against the Soviet government by the International Confederation of Free Trade Unions before the International Labor Organization of the United Nations from 1950 to 1954:

1. Collective bargaining agreements in the U.S.S.R. do not determine wages or conditions of employment but aim to assist the government in reaching production goals.

2. Union organization policy is determined by the party and not by the union.

3. Workers cannot leave their place of employment without employer consent, and if they do, they suffer extreme penalties.

4. Children can be deported to places of employment and be bound there by contracts.

5. Foremen exercise dictatorial rule over the workers, who have no voice in the setting of wages.

6. Incentive pay systems are devices to speed up workers.

7. Soviet trade unions are not genuine because workers do not have the right of free association, nor do the unions perform traditional functions of defending worker rights and improving living standards.

8. Soviet law makes no provision for the right to strike.

9. The constitution of the U.S.S.R. confirms the fact that the trade unions are a tool of the state.

10. The former president of the trade-union federation was appointed to his post by joint action of the party central committee, the Council of Ministers, and the presidium of the Supreme Soviet.

11. In 1933 the trade unions in effect became a state organ when the functions of the labor commissariat were transferred to them.

The Soviet government made a general denial of the allegations and called them slanderous. The government asserted that Soviet trade unions are in fact the freest organizations in the world and constitute a nonparty public organization of considerable influence; that they have many functions, including administering the social insurance program, maintaining a watch on the application of labor laws by employers, providing cultural and sports activities for workers, assisting in the drafting of legislation, and concluding collective agreements with employers. Compared to the capitalist countries, the response continues, where more than half of the national income is held by the exploiting classes, the entire national income of the Soviet Union belongs to the workers: they receive three-quarters of the national income and the rest goes toward socialist production and other national and community purposes.

The Soviet Union also answered the allegations in specific terms:

1. Collective agreements are based on demands made by workers themselves at open meetings. They include health and safety regulations, wage schedules, working conditions, training of manual workers, housing, cafeteria arrangements, and cultural activities.

2. The party does not interfere with the internal affairs of trade unions. Party rules apply only to its members, but the party has won the confidence of all the people. The trade unions accept the direction of the party of their own free will because such direction has contributed to their defense of the workers' interests, their fight for constant improvement of material and cultural conditions, and their task of building socialism. Furthermore, the guidance is channeled through party members who are also union members, and who thus would not work to the detriment of the union. Lastly, the relations between party and union exist in noncommunist countries also.

3. The decree of June 26, 1940, restricting labor mobility has been repealed. There are no laws dealing with forced labor in the Soviet Union because there is no forced labor. Every citizen has the right to work in accordance with the constitution and to choose any branch of activity according to his desires and abilities.

4. Young people receive free education, and the government provides them with food, clothing, and lodging. When their training is finished, they are offered work commensurate with their skills and training. This explains why young people enter these schools gladly. Industrial plants also offer courses for increasing their skills.

5. The interests of foremen and workers are identical. The foremen not only organize production but also assist workers in improving their skills and performing their work. In contrast with capitalist countries, where the foremen act for the capitalist class, in the Soviet Union they belong to the undivided community of workers.

6. Incentive systems are accepted by workers because they know their income increases as output and quality are improved and costs are reduced. Moreover, the rapid rise in productivity has come about not from increased physical effort but from improved technology.

Furthermore, Soviet trade unions have an important voice in setting piece rates in the plant.

7. The unions organize workers on a strictly voluntary basis. Their purpose is to ensure constant betterment of the material and cultural circumstances of the working population. The government at this juncture quotes a report of officials of the old American federation, the CIO, who visited the Soviet Union in 1945 and who, according to the government, were impressed by the magnificent and many-sided activities of the Soviet trade unions in securing worker interests in the economic sphere, cultural activities, and social welfare. The Soviet government also cites Article 126 of the national constitution, which reads in part:

> In conformity with the interests of the working people, and in order to develop the organizational initiative and political activity of the masses of the people, citizens of the U.S.S.R. are guaranteed the right to unite in public organizations, trade unions, cooperative societies, youth organizations. And the most active and politically conscious citizens in the ranks of the working class, working peasants, and working intelligentsia unite in the Communist Party of the Soviet Union, which is the vanguard of the working people in their struggle to build communist society and is the leading core of all organizations of the working people, both public and state.

8. On the right to strike, a collective stoppage is not and has never been regarded as absenteeism. Soviet law does not impose penalties for a stoppage called by workers in support of their demands. There is no reason for surprise at the absence of strikes. Workers can be heard in other ways, through production meetings or through governmental bodies whose membership consists of workers' representatives.

9. The constitution spells out the regulation of trade-union organization. Article 152 states that any trade union organized upon principles drawn up by a competent congress need not register with state institutions as prescribed for associations and unions in general but shall be registered with the central federation of unions to which it is affiliated in accordance with the conditions prescribed by the union congresses of trade unions. Article 153 provides that associations not registered with central federations of unions shall not be entitled to call themselves trade unions or to claim the rights of such organizations.[14]

10. The former president of the trade-union federation was not chosen but recommended to the post, and was subsequently elected at a general meeting of the federation. Furthermore, his successor was elected in 1956 in accordance with the statutes of the trade union.

11. On the abolition of the People's Commissariat of Labor in 1933, some of its responsibilities, such as the administration of social services and labor law, were taken over by the unions. In 1955, state responsibility

---

[14] In effect, what the government is saying circuitously is that although theoretically a worker organization can be created voluntarily, it must register with the existing union federation if it is to be called a union organization.

in the field of wages was given to the State Wages and Labor Committee.

What clues do these allegations and replies give on the Soviet system of industrial relations? Many of the allegations are now academic. In addition, although the possibility of Soviet workers' organizations outside the trade-union federation is not excluded, for all practical purposes the possibility is remote; the party does provide the leadership in formulating trade-union policy, but just who exerts influence on whom is a riddle; the determination of wage levels and basic terms of employment generally is not the prerogative of union leaders, but that is not to say they do not have a hand in policy formulation.

There is little question that trade-union officials have an increased influence in Soviet society. It is difficult, however, to distinguish between influences as a trade-union official and as a party member. The higher a man's level in the trade-union structure, the greater the likelihood he is a member. Lastly, in a rapidly developing economy, the assumption of a role in productivity on the part of a union official may be necessary for his survival.

Party Officials

The third branch of the leadership structure in the Soviet Union is the party officials. The ultimate arbiter in a dispute is the ranking party official within the lines of organization that surround the conflict. His arbitrament is not heavy-handed; rather, he is expected to play a role of persuader, mediator, and catalyst. One of the indictments against Khrushchev was his erratic and ponderous intervention in affairs once the party policy line had been drawn.

The International Labor Organization concludes that the party organization, by seeing to it that production plans are met, is unquestionably the guiding force of trade unions. This guidance may be based on a decision of one of the organs of the party, the government, the unions, or a combination of these three. The party organization contains members who have risen from the working class and are therefore aware of worker problems. The party seeks to protect their interests, within the context of national goals.

The party central committee itself has something to say about the role of the party in trade-union affairs. In a resolution passed in 1957, the central committees throughout the Soviet socialist republics were instructed to improve their guidance of trade-union organizations and to concern themselves above all with the training of trade-union personnel and recommending for union posts the workers who were the most highly trained and who enjoyed prestige with people. The central committees were reminded that trade unions are nonparty organizations, that their work is based on methods of persuasion, and that the use of administrative fiat and petty tutelage is inadmissible.

The role of the party as catalyst requires maintaining organizations at industrial enterprises, construction sites, transportation offices, and farms. In theory, the prominent production official who holds a party card is subordinate to the lesser light who holds a position in the local party structure. In fact, the party man is apt to defer to the production official, particularly if he is a prominent member of the party. These nuances in prestige between members and nonmembers, party officials and simple card carriers become less complex as one moves toward the top.

The plant director and the union committee chairman may be party members, but both are responsible to the district organization. The system apparently creates checks and balances of sorts. Each level of leadership is tolerant of the mistakes at subordinate levels because of possible repercussions on itself. To appear in the best possible light, each reports situations at variance with the facts. Each elects not to meet issues head on. In this fashion, an authoritarian system of increasing complexity in function becomes manageable and benign.

In an interview, a party member made the observation that the collective spirit of the system was inherited by the party. Capitalism existed in Russia for a few years only. The feudal patriarchal system never perished, and the party built on its foundations. He said he wanted to write an article on the idea, but he knew it would not be published. The party members, he continued, are respected either because of their competence in economic matters or at least because they are honest. He recalled once boarding a train filled with noisy party members going to a meeting. Commiserating with him, the stationmaster pointed out that at least they would not steal his bag. The party members, he added, have a role similar to that of clergymen in the old rural community: Their power is accepted because the people want to follow their leadership and because their decisions might be appealed up the party structure.

INSTITUTIONAL RELATIONSHIPS

The rules-making function in Soviet industrial relations is pyramidal. At the top, the central government sets the rules in broad outline that implement party policy. Next comes the authority of the Supreme Soviets of the federated republics, then the collective agreements of the plant directors and union committees, and last the labor contracts between employers and individual employees. Each layer is supposed to be consistent with the layer above, spelling out the rules in greater detail.

The Russians estimate that there are some 13,000 collective agreements in force in the U.S.S.R. The agreements set forth mutual obligations between managers and workers with respect to fulfillment of production plans, methods of improving productivity, systems of wage payment, disciplining of workers, ways of upgrading workers, safety regulations, and housing and cultural services for workers. By law, they are renegotiated each January and must be concluded by the end of the month. Recommendations for change come from plant meetings and from suggestions of the trade-union federation in Moscow. The agreements are seen as an important means of enlisting the working people to boost production, stimulating creative activities among workers, and promoting criticism of administrators and union functionaries.

In the labor contract between employer and employee, the worker agrees to perform a stipulated type of work and the plant manager commits himself to employment terms consistent with the collective agreement and the law. For example, management cannot require a worker to perform work outside his job description without the worker's approval. Temporary transfers can be made, however—generally a reassignment from one plant to another in the event of a plant shutdown—for a period not to exceed one month. In exceptional cases, the period can be extended with the approval of the plant committee, but in no case can it exceed three months.

Labor contracts are concluded either for an indefinite period, a definite period not to exceed three years, or the time required for completion of a particular project. The worker has the right to cancel an indefinite term contract after giving the employer twelve working days' notice. A fixed-term contract can be cancelled only for such compelling reasons as illness, incapacity to perform the work, or violation of labor laws by management. The employer can cancel for the following reasons: liquidation or reduction of the labor force; temporary disability of the worker exceeding four consecutive months; inefficiency or absenteeism without valid reason; commission of crimes; return to the job of a worker who held it previously. As previously mentioned, all dismissals must be approved by the union plant committee.

The government uses a heavy hand in specifying terms of employment. The workday and workweek are specified by law. Workers are guaranteed at least 2 weeks' paid vacation, lunch breaks of up to 2 hours depending on the nature of the work, and 6 paid holidays in celebration of the New Year, May Day, the October Revolution, and Constitution Day. The government sets limits on overtime work; provides pensions at age sixty, the amount depending on prior income; and pays for social benefits, including medical care and occupational training. It forbids refusal of employment because of pregnancy, fixes the scope of the collective agreement, and determines such particulars as mandatory rest periods in cold climates and the issuance of soap for dirty jobs. If a Soviet worker is injured on the job or his health is impaired by his work, a compensation claim can be brought against the enterprise with the backing of the plant committee. If settlement is not reached, the case is brought to court.

The handling of disputes over terms of employment provides clues to Soviet institutional relationships. The Labor Disputes Law of 1957 stipulates three procedural steps: the Labor Disputes Commission at the plant level, the union committee, and the people's courts, which are comparable to the courts of lowest jurisdiction in the United States. The system does not employ the third-party arbitration familiar in the United States. Arbitration is found in the Soviet Union in a board at the Council of Ministers level, and its function is the settlement of economic disputes between government organizations.

The Labor Disputes Commission (LDC) is comprised of an equal number of representatives from the union plant committee and from management. Its members are selected for a specified term of office. Where plant or service units are small, several of them in one locality may be combined under one LDC. This consolidation occurs especially in rural commissions in which the local trade-union committee brings together the union members of several independent organizations. In such instances, management representatives on the commission are appointed by the director of the organization or enterprise in which the aggrieved worker is employed.

The LDC deals basically with the protection of established rights and not with the establishment of new ones. Accordingly, it is authorized to consider disputes between worker and management arising out of the application of labor legislation, the collective agreement, the individual labor contract, plant work rules, and conditions of work determined by management and the union plant committee. Disputes arising as a result of an order issued by organizations above the plant level can also be heard by the LDC. Should it decide that the order was imposed unjustly, it has the power to annul. The most frequent disputes arise from job classifications of workers and work standards in incentive systems.

Certain types of disputes do not fall within the jurisdiction of the LDC; for example, disagreements between the trade-union committee and management; workers' complaints on employment terms fixed jointly by the committee and management; and appeals against a discharge that had been approved by the union committee.

The law is also specific in excluding the following employment terms from the jurisdiction of the LDC: transfers of employees holding positions covered by special regulations; workers covered by rules in particular industries such as railroads, marine transportation, and communications; changes in wage and salary scales; changes in managerial staffs; calculation of social insurance and pensions; and housing allotments.

According to an interpretation of the Soviet trade-union federation, management bonuses are not subject to appeal to the LDC but to the next higher managerial level. Management can, however, appeal to the LDC on such questions as vacations and holidays. As a general rule, managers can initiate a grievance only when they can prove that material loss has been caused by the worker.

The LDC cannot refuse to accept complaints by a worker, even one apparently out of its jurisdiction. In the absence of a union plant committee, complaints are submitted through a union organizer. Grievances rejected by the LDC can be appealed before the union committee. No time limit is set for filing complaints, but there is a statute of limitations on retroactivity of compensation. Hearings are open to the public, and the dispute can be heard only if the affected worker is present. He has the right to challenge any representative on the LDC, such challenge being accepted or denied by either the plant manager or union chairman, depending on whose representative is being accused. If the grievance is against the plant manager, he decides its validity.

Decisions of the LDC must be unanimous. If no agreement is reached, or if the worker is not satisfied, the next step is the union committee, whose decision is final. If the worker is still not satisfied, he can appeal to the courts. In a one-year study of the grievance system in the province of Moscow, out of 199 suits in the people's courts for reinstatement of discharged workers, 114 involved employees who were dismissed without the consent of the plant union committee. It is not clear from the record whether or not 199 was the total number of discharge cases that had gone to the courts.[15]

Soviet judges complain that workers are not dismissed for just cause and that trade-union committees concur too readily in dismissals. In one case, a dining-car worker went for a walk away from the train platform. The stop was unexpectedly cut short, and he was left behind, without money or documents. He managed to reach Moscow and returned to work immediately. What was so terrible about the whole incident, the court asked? A man was left behind. This can happen to anyone. Yet the worker was dismissed for absenteeism. The presumption is that the trade union had concurred in the dismissal.

Apparently, the Soviets also have a problem of legal advocacy in the settlement of worker grievances. One Soviet attorney confessed, "I sometimes feel ashamed for those legal consultants who exert themselves to the utmost in court to discredit a man simply to show that the director is right. After one such trial, I invited the representative of management —he was a man with a higher juridical education—to my office. When I asked him why, he, a jurist, defended an obviously wrong cause and distorted reality, the representative of management answered: 'What is wrong with this? I have to defend the honor of my enterprise.' The administrator has no right to dismiss a subordinate without the consent of the local trade-union committee. Unfortunately, not all trade-union organizations make use of their rights." [16]

Sovetskaya Yustitsia reports that in a two-year period labor disputes going to the courts dropped almost 50 percent below the prior two-year period. Many instances of improper dismissal still exist, however. Trade-union committees appear to give their consent because they do not

[15] *Sotsialisticheskaya Zaknonost,* in *Current Digest of the Soviet Press,* Vol. 12, No. 4.
[16] *Current Digest of the Soviet Press,* Vol. 12, No. 35.

wish to spoil their relations with management. The article suggests that the courts seek to recover from plant officials the damages paid to a worker for improper dismissal. Other newspapers complain that workers are discharged without the knowledge of the union plant committee. Trade-union representatives are reported to be dismissed despite a law that forbids such actions without the consent of the district or province union committee.

The method of settling disputes arising out of employment terms does not seem clear even to the Russians. Soviet students of labor legislation express the view that disputes arising at the plant level should be taken up by a higher trade-union headquarters or economic body. Although the Russians concede the possibility of disputes on interpreting employment terms, they express the conventional truth that since workers own the enterprises they would be indulging in a futile exercise to strike against themselves. If differences arise between labor and management, labor laws are there to be applied. If applied incorrectly, institutional arrangements exist to correct the situation.

A labor strike in the Soviet Union is viewed not as a means of achieving a meeting of minds, as it is in the United States, but as a vehicle of social and political protest of serious proportions. Even revolutionaries like job security. The party official or plant director faced with worker opposition is apt to roll with the punches rather than allow such a conflict to materialize. He does not have a property interest in resisting demands as much as a desire to avoid a difficult situation that may reflect on his competence or cost him his job.

In summary, what can be said of the trade-union role in Soviet institutional relationships? Without doubt, Soviet trade unionism is a big business. Unions spend several hundred million rubles annually. About 75 percent of the membership dues is spent at the local level at the unions' discretion. Added to this expenditure are the earnings from union social and cultural functions and government contributions for cultural and sport activities.

The official Soviet view is that the labor organizations have functions of greater scope than those in capitalist societies. Soviet labor unions, it is said, participate in such important functions as drawing up labor legislation and production plans, administering labor law, and organizing cultural activities, which are not the concern of unions in Western economies. There is similarity in one respect, however: the writing of collective agreements and the handling of grievances.

The differences between the two systems, the Soviets state, follow from the contrast between capitalist and communist societies. Dissimilarities in systems cause differences in functions. They concede that their trade unions are supervised by the party. They add, however, that so are all Soviet citizens, that party direction is accepted freely, and that the party was instrumental in fostering the growth of the trade unions.

They state, moreover, that major steps affecting workers must be taken by joint action of the State Labor and Wages Committee, the Council of Ministers, and the presidium of the trade-union federation. Finally, it is acknowledged that trade-union members have certain advantages in social insurance not available to nonmembers. The disparity between the two groups is being eliminated, however, with the consent of the trade unions, and in any event this type of advantage is common in capitalist countries.

There is apparently a policy of encouraging trade-union activity among workers and promoting union influence in the industrial relations system. The press exhorts labor officials to implement the rights of their organizations by criticizing those who do not. A clue to the success of this objective is in the long-term behavior of union committees. Many of their decisions are binding on management, and apparently this new prerogative is an instrument for introducing controls at the base of the system. Russian press reports indicate, however, that in a showdown the plant committees tend to defer to the plant director.

The party has decreed that the area of joint decision making by trade unions and management should be increased. Management is required to make decisions jointly with the union on the discharge of workers, the setting of production standards, job classification, the payment of production bonuses, and the appointment of management officials.

What do Soviet labor-union officials say are their responsibilities under this reorganization? In interpreting their responses, one has to recognize that the labor leader in any country is a political entity who develops an ability to make evasive responses. What he conceives as reality is whatever can enhance his position or deter his advancement. His responses are thus political, for the record, and a measure of the pressures he feels he must yield to. Therefore, they lack objectivity.

Union officials stress that the major function of the Soviet trade union is to promote labor productivity. It is difficult to assess whether or not workers share this view. Chambermaids, waiters, taxi drivers, and strangers in the street do not constitute a representative sample of workers, but these are individuals with whom rapport can be more easily established. Soviet grievance procedures pose similarly difficult analytical problems. An employee who resorts to the courts to contest the discharge that his own union has concurred in is in a difficult position. The law is not sensitive to the nuances of particular situations. If the trade-union decision falls within the broad scope of the law, it may be useless to him to push his case further. Moreover, what is his attitude toward his union thereafter?

A comprehensive breakdown of grievances by type of case and the level at which they are settled is not available.[17] The Russians state that most disputes are settled through mediation efforts by the LDC and that

[17] In her book *Soviet Trade Unions and Labor Relations* (Cambridge, Mass.: Harvard University Press, 1966), Emily Clark Brown furnishes some evidence in this respect.

for the three steps in the grievance procedure, the estimated percentage settled in each step is 85 percent, 10 percent, and 5 percent respectively. Furthermore, they advise that the number of cases going to the courts has decreased considerably through the efforts of labor disputes commissions and the increased prestige of the plant trade-union committees. When asked what the role of the party is in grievance settlements, the answer is to furnish broad ideological and political guidelines and not to engage in specific activities.

The ideological controversy over Soviet and American trade unions has been clouded to some extent by the revelations of CIA infiltration in American unions. The extent of government influence generally in American trade unions, not yet fully revealed, weakens the American position that Soviet labor organizations are stooges of the government.

LABOR PRODUCTIVITY

Labor productivity in the Soviet Union is important on ideological grounds, for it measures not only labor skill but also the degree of efficiency of the society generally to manage labor. The Soviets are sensitive to criticism of their capacity to utilize labor, technology, capital, and management and to comparisons with the United States. Such a comparison between a market and nonmarket economy is difficult, however. There are two basic methods of comparison: measuring the value in currency of the aggregate product per unit of labor and computing the physical output per unit of labor for as many equivalent products as possible.

A considerable difference exists in the U.S.S.R. between its performance records in industry and in agriculture. For a variety of reasons, its agricultural record is poor and tends to pull down total performance. First, the Soviet Union has a considerably shorter growing period than the United States and a more extensive dry season, with resultant erratic crop yields. The weather is not only colder and drier but more variable. Second, the American crop land of some 300 million acres is on the whole better land than the Soviet Union's 500 million acres. Third, there is less investment in Soviet farms and less modern technology, such as tractors, implements, fertilizers, herbicides, and fungicides. Fourth, not only is the amount of equipment low, but because of neglect and lack of parts, it is also poorly used. Fifth, despite the dryness, irrigation is not stressed. Finally, the Soviets have not effectively solved the problem of scarce quality seed stock. In brief, although modern technology is emphasized in the industrial sector, it is relatively neglected in agriculture, and adverse physical conditions tend to worsen the effect of this neglect.

The average collective farm in the Soviet Union, some 15,600 acres, is too large for economical exploitation. It is difficult to manage, especially when its manager is harassed by the party bureaucracy to meet the latest quotas. In addition, managers must deal with a labor force that would prefer to farm their own plots which are more productive than the collective farms.[18]

In March 1965, after the ouster of Khrushchev, the Russians adopted a five-year agricultural plan increasing investment and incentives. Beginning in 1966, investment in machinery and fertilizers was doubled compared to the prior five-year period. Prices were raised for grain and animal products, and compulsory deliveries of grain to the state were stabilized. A 50 percent premium was established for deliveries in excess of the plan, and farm officials were given more autonomy. To reduce labor migration from the rural areas, pensions and guaranteed monthly wages were introduced for workers on collective farms. Previously, collective farmers had to rely on the profits, if any, that remained after recovery of costs. Lastly, the ideologically motivated restrictions on private plots were removed.

In 1967 reforms were extended to state farms. Pilot state farms were converted to a profit system. After a study of results, it was decided to place the country's 12,000 state farms under a profit plan. The profit system introduced in industry is thus eventually to cover the agricultural sector also.

In the industrial sector, the goal of surpassing the United States which has existed since the time of Lenin represents not simply an economic objective but also an instrument for demonstrating the superiority of the system. In their desire to prove an ideological point, the Russians are not reluctant to indulge in statistics juggling.

The problem of raising labor productivity is tied directly to the mode of existence of the Russian worker. The remarks of a Russian university professor are pertinent:

> The problem of providing services to the population is an acute one. No tradition of services exists in the Soviet Union. In 1913, they existed for the rich. The revolution destroyed and then neglected them as planning was concentrated on capital production. When a worker has to struggle all day to buy a suit, do his own laundering, line up for a haircut and food, live under conditions of stress in multiple-family dwellings, the result is a sapping of his energies. When this factor is combined with a lack of auxiliary services in production, the result is low labor productivity. The problem is not only one of increasing consumer services, but also of developing a habit of their use.

Other factors complicate the matter of raising productivity. In an environment where everyone including the plant director is a government employee, there may be a tendency to wink at inefficiency. Statistically, unemployment does not exist in the Soviet Union. Yet after going through its industrial plants and observing worker performance, one is persuaded that unemployment figures are not published in statistical charts. The

[18] Lazar Volin, "The Agricultural Picture In USSR and USA," *ASTE Bulletin* (Philadelphia: University of Pennsylvania), Vol. 3 (Fall 1963).

Soviets have also belatedly discovered that productivity depends to a considerable degree on the consent of the governed. Finally, it is an enormous undertaking to construct an efficient labor force with people removed from grinding poverty by hardly more than a generation.

The official ideology has an important bearing on worker attitudes toward productivity. When the state decrees that higher productivity is in the interest of the country, it follows that it is also in the interest of the individual worker. Any individual attitude to the contrary is intolerable, but the inference to be drawn is not a simple one. The position of the state is likely to create stresses on the mentality of the average Russian, who is likely to feel constrained to follow the wishes of the state despite his personal inclinations. Even Soviet refugees have accepted the premise that if a particular need exists, the Russian citizen should recognize that this is necessary for the country and do something about it.[19] It would therefore follow that the exhortations in the press on productivity, although appearing contrived to an American, carry weight among Russian readers.

The wording of the productivity slogans changes, but the drive to make Soviet man efficient persists through time. Its first manifestation was the *Subbotniki* in the 1920s.[20] Then followed Stakhanovism in the 1930s. Stakhanov, a coal miner, was the Russian Frederick Taylor of scientific management. By rationalizing work processes, he became a model of efficiency for other workers to imitate. And later came the communist emulation teams during the Khrushchev regime, in which groups tried to outperform each other.

The shift in Soviet psychological theory from environmental determinism to individual responsibility places the blame for low productivity on the individual person. The determinism inherent in traditional Marxism is better suited to a party challenging the status quo than one already in power. Once in power, leaders cannot tolerate a recalcitrant citizen of low productivity pleading that prevailing conditions make him so. Consequently, with the change in regimes has come a shift in the Soviet concept of man.

The attitudes of workers toward mechanization and the manner in which the labor displaced by it is handled remain hidden under layers of official pronouncements. The official line is that Soviet industrial workers know from experience that capital works in their interest, that they therefore give their wholehearted support to mechanization, and this unquestioning faith is manifested in their voluntary efforts to invent new techniques.

Press statements indicate that employers, in effect, store labor that

---

[19] Raymond A. Bauer, *The New Man in Soviet Psychology* (Cambridge, Mass: Harvard University Press, 1959).
[20] The *Subbotnik* movement was initiated in the early days of the revolution by a group of young Communist workers in a Moscow locomotive station who elected to perform voluntary work on Saturdays.

has been made surplus by technological change. There are reports of displaced workers in the metal, machine building, and consumer goods industries running into the hundreds of thousands. A machine shop superintendent complains, for example, that the plant engineer failed to remove surplus workers from his shop. As a result, he exceeded the target for automation of the shop, but labor productivity rose hardly at all, and production costs failed to drop. Problems occur because of a lack of planning on how to redistribute workers displaced by automation. Consequently, employees are kept on as "supernumeraries."

This reluctance to lay off workers permanently arises from the attitudes of the employer, employee, and union. Plant directors hedge against the possibility of a sudden rise in labor demand because of breakdowns in automated lines or unanticipated increases in orders. The government requires managers to find jobs for displaced workers, and the union may not agree to terminations unless this has been done. Moreover, the workers are reluctant to move to other areas of employment and risk uncertainties in wages and conditions of work. Strong personal incentives are therefore necessary to lure them such as a guarantee of former earnings or a new apartment. Whether the new profit-sharing plan will cut down the tendency to use labor inefficiently is a matter of speculation. One would suspect that the economic reform generally will push management toward more displacement. If so, the problem of what to do with the unemployed is likely to become more acute.

The criteria used for measuring performance and wage payments may also have the effect of lowering efficiency. To cite an example, two women unloading bricks from a truck were doing so with such abandon that some 30 percent of the load was being turned into rubble. The women were being paid by the hour, and the driver was compensated on the basis of the number of bricks hauled. They had been told to hurry and fulfill the plan. As a result of using a volume index of productivity, all three workers earned high scores.

Russian press reports of phenomenal increases in productivity by workers are difficult to interpret. Do these sudden bursts imply that the workers are normally holding back? Are they reflecting a form of insecurity, a way of placating authority for previous malingering? Is the worker who sets a new standard really a hero in the eyes of other workers? Are the authorities concerned about the physiological consequences of such spurts in production? The answers to these important questions are not clear.

The role of the party in productivity varies according to the level of the party structure. At the top, the party sets production goals and publishes the ideological slogans to further them. At the local level, it acts as a goad to stimulate production and reports the facts upward through the party organization. As often happens in organizations, these reports are wont to be censored as they move toward the top.

The public ownership of production may have the effect of blunting the drive to higher productivity. Strong pressures exist for wages to rise faster than productivity. These pressures stem mainly from the tendency of managers to ignore planned wage disbursements so as to ensure reaching output targets. As stated above, labor tends to be hoarded for the same reason. But the system also appears to show a high degree of security for the worker despite the relentless preaching of high productivity.[21]

Summation

This chapter concludes by highlighting salient features of the Soviet system, pointing out differences between the Soviet Union and the Eastern European countries, and suggesting future trends. These features underline the decline of traditional ideology and the rise of a philosophy of scientific optimism.

The contemporary Soviet system is characterized by a flexible but planned use of labor and material to obtain a widening variety of output at increasing efficiency. Its educational system is responsive to changing economic and manpower needs. A high level of activity in the natural sciences and technology exists in the universities, research institutes, and enterprises. The Soviets are building new academic cities in Siberia, and local enterprises are encouraged to bring their problems to these centers. At Novosibirsk, they have built an antimatter smasher capable of producing ten times more energy than the biggest atom smasher in the United States. The scientific and technical activity integrated with production planning produces rapid innovation in the economy, including changes in occupational skills in the labor force and a continuing necessity for training and retraining.

Soviet society appears to be more experimental than that of the United States. Its educational system is subject to frequent innovation. Despite the universal tendency of entrenched privilege to slow up change, the U.S.S.R. manages to make sharp shifts in institutions once inquiry indicates the necessity of change. Its contemporary experiment is a move from state capitalism and command of resources to a controlled market system in which product supply and demand are employed to affect prices, goods, and consumption.

Soviet industrial production is based heavily on large-scale enterprise. There are several reasons for this: the economies it permits, its proximity to adequate sources of labor; the relative ease with which production can be increased by expanding existing facilities; and finally, the nation's

---

[21] See Robert M. Fearn, "Controls over Wage Funds and Inflationary Pressures in the U.S.S.R.," *Industrial and Labor Relations Review*, Vol. 18 (January 1965).

mania for bigness. The production system stresses such traditional concepts of efficiency as systematic work methods, remuneration tied to individual productivity, incentives for labor-saving inventions, and improvement of management practices. Worker attitudes are purportedly not hostile, as they would be if the workers were producing for private interests but are instead cooperative in promoting the general welfare. Frictions are inherent in the management-employee relationship regardless of the nature of ownership, however.

Another feature of the system is the heavy involvement of the government, which directs the following: the educational system; manpower and capital planning in industry, agriculture, and social overhead; extensive welfare services, such as pensions and health programs; cultural activities; the setting of employment terms; and the assignment of the respective roles of the parties in industrial relations. Therefore, the area over which managers and employee representatives can bargain is smaller than in the United States. Although the area for bargaining on such basic policies as wages is more narrow, it is, however, rather broad in programs and procedures to implement such policies. In all, the greater involvement of the government issues from a long tradition of centralism and from the strictures of Soviet planning.

The fundamental purpose of the Soviet labor unions is to promote the efficient utilization of labor. Because of this role, Western critics conclude that these organizations are therefore not trade unions at all. The problem is partly a semantic one, for the Russian term *profsoyuzy* suggests something closer to "occupational association." The conviction persists, however, that trade-union functions British-American style are "good" and if not found in the Soviet organizations, the latter must be "bad." There is a presumption that trade unions should be independent and autonomous, that those of the West operate in that way and that those of the U.S.S.R. do not. However, trade unions no longer grow like Topsy. Governments of developing nations push them along and try to make them behave in a manner thought to be consistent with economic growth.

The trade-union officials of the Soviet Union have important roles within their society that reflect the problems inherent in the formation of an efficient labor force within a patriarchal society that is undergoing forced economic growth. Their responsibilities include raising labor productivity (including the development of industrial health and safety habits); planning, construction, and allocation of housing; organizing plant production conferences; encouraging workers to develop initiative and assertiveness in social and economic affairs; processing the grievances of the workers; overseeing the observance of labor law; setting output standards jointly with management; and writing collective agreements.

Two questions about Soviet trade unionism remain unanswered: What perception do Soviet workers have of their trade unions and to what degree do they feel that these organizations respond to their needs and interests? The International Labor Organization investigation in the U.S.S.R. fails to shed any light on this question. The opinion polls and attitude surveys the Russians have begun to conduct in the Soviet Union do, however, indicate that the government is developing a more sophisticated attitude toward the use of social science techniques.

The official depiction of Soviet attitudes is not entirely meaningless. The slogans, exhortations, and heroic descriptions of achievements are an indication that there are forces pulling in an opposite direction from the one the Soviet leadership deems desirable. By developing a skill in unscrambling and correlating such communications, Westerners can make a record of actual events with considerable accuracy. Soviet reportage, although suggestive of a homogeneous outlook among the people, contains meaningful latent content.

The experience in the U.S.S.R. strengthens the view that a method of studying industrial relations is needed that develops the relationship between national character and the processes in a society, but its analysis should not introduce the national bias of the investigator. National character produces diversity in economic and political arrangements. An assessment of an industrial relations system on the basis of technology and income distribution does not come to grips with this problem. The style of an industrial relations system has to be appraised in terms of men applying their values.

What are the differences between the Soviet Union and the socialist countries of Eastern Europe? [22] In the economic sphere, one difference is the degree of worker participation in management. In Yugoslavia, for example, the board of directors of major enterprises is chosen by the employees, subject to the approval of the local government. Within the confines of the law, workers in that country also have a voice in the distribution of enterprise profits. They differ also in the degree of strike activity. Generally, the Eastern European countries either have more work stoppages or give them greater publicity.

The Eastern European countries have outpaced the Soviet Union in moving away from centralist planning to a market system and, at times, appear to be in a race toward capitalism. Most of these nations never reached the degree of centralization that exists in the Soviet Union. As a typical example, 60 percent of the Yugoslav labor force works for private enterprise. Price and output decisions are being pushed downward toward the enterprise level. Although the individual countries differ in the degree to which their enterprises generate their own investment funds, they are moving in the same general direction. The Soviet Union appears to be trying to match the Eastern European nations on the amount of the industrial sector that is not subject to planning. For example, it has removed consumer goods plants from central planning and has made

[22] Bulgaria, Czechoslovakia, East Germany, Hungary, Poland, Rumania, and Yugoslavia.

them subject to the demand of the market place. Moreover, it is becoming a nation in which the worker as a producer chooses his occupation, his employer, and his termination date of employment; and as a consumer affects by his choices the type and quality of goods in the market place. Consequently, the economic systems of the Soviet Union and the Eastern European countries are becoming increasingly similar.

Is a similar trend evident in their political systems? The existence of a monopolistic political party in the Soviet bloc countries tends to hide similarities in pluralistic decision making. Within the framework of a monopolistic party different institutions emerge whose common function is achieving consensus. The Soviet Communist party yields to the pressure for diversity and participation by shifting decision making downward. The system under which industry and agriculture were treated as two divisions of the Communist party has been disbanded, and the Brezhnev-Kosygin regime reiterates its intent to keep party and government separate.

The Soviet intervention in Czechoslovakia in 1968 suggests that those who hold the balance of power in the Soviet Union find intolerable a free communications and multiparty system and are inclined to use force to prevent their emergence in the Soviet bloc countries. Nevertheless, by their intervention the Russians have accelerated the disintegration of communism as a monolith.

While the Russians try to cling to the past in the political sphere, they renounce traditional ideologies in the economic sphere. They now encourage enterprise management decisions on prices, output, and wages, and the sharing of profits with employees. Factory directors in agreement with the union have the right to decide whether to pay workers at hourly or piece rates so long as total wages do not exceed the amount assigned to the enterprise, and they also have the right to determine the occupational mix. With profits now a criterion of success, the profit-making incentive has even extended to state and collective farms. One would suppose the emergence of a new slogan: What is good for the capitalist countries is good for the satellite nations, and what is good for them is good for the Soviet Union. In the face of these drastic economic changes and the attendant cultural changes, the political posture of the Soviet leaders would seem to be a delaying action.

In this climate of change, a new industrial relations system has emerged in the Soviet Union, and party organization has declined. The plant manager who achieves prominence in his community and obtains his share of party awards is a figure to be reckoned with by the party bureaucrat. His factory is not simply a production unit, but the web of life of the local community. This decentralization of decision making does not, however, imply an abandonment of the collective ownership of the enterprise. Both are compatible.

The Soviet trade unions have also changed in character. The party seeks to persuade union officials to stand up to plant managers. In addition to encouraging higher productivity, they are expected to be a strong voice in labor-management relationships. Their historical timidity can be expected to wane as a new generation of officials takes over. For this reason, Soviet trade unionism provides clues to the social transformations that are taking place in the U.S.S.R.

Out of these policy shifts the Soviet worker emerges as a more secure individual. He has a considerable degree of job security. If he wants work, there is work available, and with ambition and ability, he has considerable opportunities for advancement.

Although the party seeks to make itself less obtrusive, it continues to be the voice of moral outrage. Its villains are the makers and drinkers of moonshine, falsifiers of production accounts, executives on liberal expense accounts, foreign currency manipulators, and employers who go to extremes in hoarding employees, including good soccer players.

The locus of Soviet leadership has thus changed with economic growth. Its first problem was to develop an industrial base with the utmost speed. This the Soviet Union did with highly centralized planning and authoritarian party direction. The problems now are finding the means to greater efficiency and catering to more sophisticated consumer tastes, which the new enterprise incentive system is supposed to achieve. This shift implies a move in the direction of greater consumer sovereignty and allocation of resources at the enterprise level. Nevertheless, the flow of economic resources is still centrally controlled to a large degree, especially the amount and direction of investment. With this change, influence moves from the party ideologists to the industrial managers, scientists, economists, and professors. The party has become a goal-making and evaluation body and less of a managing organization.

One might conclude, therefore, that by some sort of historical perversion communism has paved the way for capitalism in the Soviet Union. But this outcome should not beguile one into thinking that the United States rather than the U.S.S.R. should be the model for the rapid growth of modernizing nations. The attractiveness of the Soviet Union lies in its development in a mere fifty years from a feudalistic subsistence economy and mass illiteracy to industrialization and mass participation. This growth was achieved by concentrating first on heavy industry and then on the development of human resources. The country grapples presently with problems of streamlining an authoritarian political and economic system. Should it be successful in solving these problems, and as the excesses of Stalinism and Khrushchevism recede from the memory, Moscow may become the model for developing nations. The country is demonstrating that an authoritarian society can peacefully yield to democratization and a fast rise in living standards without creating a crisis. This attraction is not likely to be dimmed by Western anticommunist policy.

A distinguished British student of Soviet economic affairs, Peter Wiles, suggests that several trends in the U.S.S.R. indicate that its economy is becoming similar to that of the United States: the decline of ideology and the rise of social science as a tool of Soviet decision making; the abandonment of the Khrushchev program increasing party tutelage over the state and economy; and the abandonment of the idea of collective consumption of goods. These events, Wiles believes, indicate that the systems of the two countries are converging from a different route. One can also add the manner in which modern technology stimulates the growth of an international community of professional persons whose common viewpoints stimulate amicable relations between East and West.

Adding to this convergence is the evolution of the corporation in the American economy. Many American corporations are becoming quasi-public institutions that are increasingly divorced from the vagaries of private markets. For over two decades, corporations have been founded and nourished exclusively by government contracts, and it is difficult to determine where government ends and private enterprise begins in their operation. They do not yield to market forces so much as control them to reach preconceived objectives by planning costs, prices, output, and profits. As John Kenneth Galbraith states in his book *The New Industrial State,* the time is coming when men will regard as fiction the idea that corporations such as General Dynamics and American Telephone and Telegraph were private businesses.

What does the Soviet experience imply insofar as it concerns our thesis of human resources development? The Soviet Union has been stable and efficient compared to other nations at similar stages of economic growth. The underpinning of this growth has been a widely accepted social philosophy. In addition, investment in human resources has taken place to an extraordinary degree. It is apparent that the rise of professional and technical manpower brings about a decline of authoritarianism.

10

ASIA

Asians do not think of themselves as Asians. To them, the word "Asia" is meaningful only as a reference to a land mass. They identify only with a particular group in a particular part of that land mass and, in uncommon instances, with a national unity. In fact, many Asian countries are not nations as the term is understood by Westerners. If the people of one nation are aware of those of another in Asia, it is apt to be in terms of an acute awareness of differences and nationalistic pride. Americans tend to overlook these facts about that continent.

This chapter comprises a general overview of Asia and a discussion of three strategic South Asian countries: India, Pakistan, and Indonesia. Focusing on South Asia via these nations serves a practical purpose. The nations in the southern belt east of Afghanistan have in common the fact that they are former colonies in a tropical or subtropical climate. In addition, there is more information available on them than on other nations in this part of the world. Third, in the west of Asia are the nations of the Middle East whose economic development is *sui generis,* and the nations to the north have communist-type economies.

The problems of the South Asian countries have multiplied since World War II. They have shifted from net exporters of food to importers. Their population increases have reduced per capita income gains. Caught in the grip of social conflict, they show weaknesses in instituting structural changes and in democratizing their societies. Moreover, their policies are affected by the power play of big nations. Their manpower is fragile and inefficient. The majority of their children either receive no education or terminate their schooling at a level below functional literacy. In sum, it is questionable whether these nations of South Asia can institute a successful noncommunist style of economic development.

GENERAL OVERVIEW OF ASIA

The Western-oriented economist who visits Asia is overwhelmed by its complexity and wonders whether his analytical tools can cope with it. Its intricate web of institutions, which vary by nation and by region, is many thousands of years old. The age of these institutions and the rigid social caste systems produce strong resistance to change. Yet throughout much of Asia, insurrectionists are bringing pressures for change.

Living standards of Asians have improved little over the levels that existed before World War II. For the vast majority of them, investment in economic growth since the war has meant nothing. Its only effect to them has been inflation. The average Asian, if not starving outright, suffers from serious dietary deficiencies. Large numbers of Asians own merely the clothing on their backs and their kitchen utensils. Within close proximity on that continent are modern plants wherein bestial human labor is extracted from frail bodies. The Marxist thesis fits Asia well in that there is an exploited proletariat; moreover, an enormous and widening gap exists between a small fraction of rich individuals and a vast, impoverished population.

It would be erroneous to associate the degree of this poverty with the ascent of communism. The extent of communist influence in Asia is associated more with the intervention and conflict of interest of Western powers than it is with the degree of Asian poverty. Communism has been brought to Asia by Western nations seeking to prevent its emergence.

Many of these countries like to refer to themselves as socialist; for an Asian intellectual to be a socialist is to be *au courant*. These countries generally have planning of sorts that is focused on public investment. Some of these plans are directed toward educational, health, and community development goals. The plans of the noncommunist nations are not, however, examples of an integrated pursuit of preconceived goals.

The per capita gross national product of Japan, the most advanced nation in Asia, is about twelve times greater than that of Burma, the poorest (Table 12). The percentage of the population in agriculture varies from 39 percent in Japan to 85 percent in Thailand. The actual extent of economic progress in these nations is difficult to assess because GNP figures are affected by such factors as inflation, changing foreign exchange rates, and foreign subsidies, and the fact that much of their economies rests on an agriculture whose per capita output is difficult to assess. Gross domestic product per capita at constant market prices is a more meaningful measure, but it is not readily available. When the figures are available, they reveal little or no increase in real product per capita in any of these countries except for Japan.

TABLE 12 □ Per Capita Gross National Product of Asian and Middle Eastern Nations, Educational Level, Percentage of Population in Agriculture, and Average Annual Change in Gross National Product Per Capita, 1969 *

Country	GNP	Education†	Agriculture	Rise in GNP‡
Burma	71	2	—	.014
Laos	72	—	—	—
China	75	—	—	—
Afghanistan	85§	—	85	—
India	87	3	71	.028
Indonesia	97	2	75	—
Yemen	110§	—	—	—
Pakistan	124	2	65	.024
Thailand	164	3	85	.022
Cambodia	150§	—	—	—
Ceylon	156	—	—	.026
Korean Republic	212	3	75	.044
South Vietnam	175§	—	—	—
Egypt	183	3	65	—
Philippines	208	—	—	.016
Syria	248§	—	—	—
Iraq	278§	2	81	—
Taiwan	322	3	63	.046
Iran	314	2	80	.044
Jordan	286§	—	—	.023
Malaysia	344	2	56	.026
Turkey	360	2	77	.021
Saudi Arabia	478§	1	—	—
Lebanon	496§	2	—	—
Japan	1571	4	39	.072
Israel	1611	4	17	—
Kuwait	4111§	—	—	—

Source: Agency for International Development, *Gross National Product: Growth Rates and Trends Data, 1967;* GNP figure for China and data on educational level from Frederick H. Harbison and Charles A. Myers, *Education, Manpower, and Economic Growth* (New York: McGraw-Hill, 1964).

* In U.S. dollars at constant 1968 prices.

† Total enrollment in secondary and higher-level education as a percentage of potential enrollment, with third-level education given a weight of 5.

‡ Average percentage change for the years 1966–1968 at constant market prices.

§ In current 1968 market prices.

A Westerner visiting Asia for the first time is struck by the underutilization of its labor. Much of the population seems to be idle, and those who are working almost seem to be trying to keep their productivity close to zero. In agriculture, for example, a peasant may spend half a day transporting one bag of grain on a bullock cart at a speed of a mile and a half per hour.

In the industrial labor force, the preponderant number of workers are traditional craftsmen in family cottage industries. They work with crude tools and equipment at what seems to be a casual pace, and their earnings are not too far above those of unskilled workers in the relatively few modern plants. In addition, there are workers in small urban shops and in the services. A general characteristic of the wage-earning force as a whole is its loose organization and transitory nature.

The underutilization of labor does not respond readily to policies designed to raise aggregate demand. The low stamina of the workers, their poor housing and work environment, the enervating climate, and Asian social institutions combine to reduce work incentives and make the workers resistant to change.

The agricultural yields are among the lowest in the world, whether measured in terms of output per unit of agricultural land or output per inhabitant. The more important agriculture is for an Asian nation, the lower does the yield tend to be. The inefficiency of labor is a major factor. Generally, the plantation type of farming is the most productive; paddy farming and changing crops from year to year are the least productive.

Economists may well be ignoring the important role of climate in Asia's economic development. An investigator in one of its hot and humid countries may serve a more useful purpose for the developing country by shifting his research from model building to climate analysis.

The Asian working population consists of work castes of different racial, religious, and social groups with little of the cross-fertilization that exists in advanced economies. This type of separatism can be found even in large-scale industry. What exists in Asia, therefore, is not so much an economy as a loose alliance of occupational and industrial enclaves that were perpetuated by Western colonial policy.

The vision of an advanced economy exists predominantly in the minds of Asian elites, many of whom either belong to ruling military oligarchies or are subject to their influence. Seeking the material achievements of the West while rejecting its values, these elites are trying to inject modernization and rationality into societies that are resistant to change.

Moreover, the elites are captives of their culture, for they cannot change it radically without placing their own positions in jeopardy. Their efforts to bring about change is further hampered by the gulf that exists between them and the rest of the population. Their attitudes toward the people may be characterized as aristocratic and paternalistic. As a result of this detachment, they are unable to deal realistically with particular problems and particular people. For a Westerner, it is difficult to determine what is real and what is not in this relationship between the managers and the population.

The same quality of detachment of elites is present in Asian labor organizations. Their origins are not industrial but are inspired by the political ambition of officials with a Marxist outlook. The labor organizations are created in the parlor rooms of the intelligentsia rather than the shops; they become pawns for rival political aspirations. If the intelligentsia (meaning generally a person with a high school diploma or a college degree) look upon labor organizations as an abstraction of their utopian dream world, the politicians see them in more practical terms of how to use them so as to acquire and maintain power.

Peasants are the backbone of Asian society, yet many of them lead a life of semibondage under traditional forms of land tenure. In many countries, much of the land the peasant tills is owned by absentee landlords. In nations where no land reform has taken place, pressures arise for active communist insurgency. Yet if land reform is threatened, one finds equally strong conservative resistance. Therefore, whether one foments change or does nothing, the problems are of the same magnitude.

The high degree of segmentation in Asian society makes it difficult for any single social class to govern. If a particular class seeks to impose its own point of view to the exclusion of others, the reaction may range from passive resistance to violence. Accordingly, a military government, if it governs with a loose rein, can effectively exploit its lack of identification with any particular group, especially if the regime has the support of the peasantry. It is because of the high degree of segmentation that a political solution is an important requisite of economic growth in Asia, yet such a solution is difficult to obtain. Military governments cannot stand still. They must either engage in repression or grant participation to other social groups.

Generally, the Asian worker makes a partial commitment to industry. Like Africans, the peasant moves to a factory in the city in order to supplement his income during the off-season, when agricultural chores in his village diminish. Accordingly, he views his labor commitment and his labor organization with indifference, or he may not even be aware that a labor organization exists. The labor leader in turn looks upon the workers as an amorphous mass who must be emancipated whether the workers like it or not.

Under such conditions, a major problem of Asian development is to encourage Asians to see matters as they are. The leaders appear to be involved in abstractions, whereas the poor are preoccupied with a concept of a good life that is not industrial in character.

The situation in Asia highlights the two mutually reinforcing factors that shape the course of economic development: the attitudes of the managerial class and the surplus of labor. The Asian mainland appears to be comprised of an aloof managerial elite and teeming numbers of undercapitalized human beings who are competing for subsistence wages. Up until the end of World War II, the managers were foreigners who often viewed Asian workers as chattels available for exploitation. Although the national origins of the managers have changed, these attitudes persist. Moreover, the availability of considerable quantities of labor for a few pennies per hour continues to be a depressant on capital formation.

The management problem is a serious one when one considers that the government in these countries is akin to a holding company trying to manage the economy. The political leadership appears to concentrate more on international power plays than on strategies of raising living standards. Economic decisions of any consequence rise quickly to the level of the prime minister, and on the way up, they are progressively censored to minimize repercussions. The ranks of competent managers are thin; as in Latin America, many of them are the offspring of the military establishment. The difference is that in Latin America they are generally less beholden to foreign powers. In Asia the foreign powers appear to be concerned not so much with the actual economic development of these nations as with preventing an unfavorable international alignment among them.

Everyone seems to be a socialist in Asia, but the term may be misleading. Often more a reaction to colonialism than a full-blown philosophy of economic and social objectives and techniques, "socialism" includes everything from the mild forms in India to the orthodox Marxism of mainland China. For example, India, the largest laissez-faire country, contains a number of small authoritarian states of different socialist hues. Up until the time the blood bath drove it underground, Indonesia had the largest Communist party of the noncommunist countries. Although the political system of North Vietnam is called communism, a better description may be nationalistic socialism. Parts of the constitution of that country paraphrase the Declaration of Independence of the United States.

Of all the world's developing regions, the countries of Asia make the least attempt at economic cooperation. The tensions produced by East-West antagonism mitigate such a possibility. Moreover, although Japan, which is much more advanced than the other nations, could probably provide the necessary leadership, there are too many authoritarian rulers in the other Asian countries who are unwilling to live in the shadow of a stronger nation.

Some students of Asian development believe that the ancient religious tradition in Asia may be a deterrent to economic growth. Professor Manning Nash, for example, believes that Buddhism is passive as regards economic change. It does not promote "a restless activity" as does the Protestant ethic. Although he is not required to abjure the goods of this world, the Buddhist has to see clearly the rewards of a new activity more than other Asians. Moreover, because he generally lives on a scale above subsistence, he is not under a compulsion to meet any needs. If Professor Nash is correct, one is led to the conclusion that practicing Buddhists may indeed be a deterrent to a society's economic growth.[1]

INDIA

Policy makers in India describe their economic system as democratic socialism, or development under democratic but centralized control. In

[1] Manning Nash, "Social Prerequisites to Economic Growth in Latin America and Southeast Asia," *Economic Development and Cultural Change,* Vol. 12 (April 1964).

this framework, they state, the criterion for determining economic policy is what is good for the community as a whole. Although India calls herself a socialist nation, the United States is much more socialistic than India in terms of the percentage of product spent by the government and the government's overall direction of the economy.

The Indian policy makers express several basic objectives in Indian economic development. They hope to increase real income per capita; set in motion a self-sustaining expansion of output and input flows of capital, technology, and labor; and reach a point at which the economy will pay its own way in international markets.

The economic development of India is an experiment to raise a big country from a subsistence level without employing the stringent command economy techniques of the Soviet Union. The strategy is supposed to be similar, however: concentration on the build-up of heavy industry. A crucial difference exists in the population characteristics of the two countries. The Soviet Union inherited a higher level of human capital and developed during a period of labor shortages; moreover, it has had a scarcity of males. India, on the other hand, has teeming urban centers filled with an unskilled ragged army of unemployed that is increasing rapidly each year.

India has controlled its economic development by means of a series of five-year plans that began in 1951. The device was borrowed from the Soviet Union by the late Prime Minister Jawaharlal Nehru, who hoped to achieve for India an economic growth similar to that of the U.S.S.R. Each plan stipulates a series of investment and production targets. Industrial expansion is stressed, and agriculture and manpower development are given a low priority. This relative emphasis reflects an early view of economic growth that held that as a nation progressively raises its industrial investment, a point is reached where growth becomes pervasive and self-sustaining. The Indian planners concede that low productivity, the high proportion of the population in agriculture, and large-scale unemployment are deterrents to growth. They believe, however, that these factors will be responsive to a policy designed to raise investment to about 17 percent of the national income.

These plans have produced increasingly disappointing results. In the first five-year plan, the government's objective was to raise the living standards of the Indian people. The planning document states:

> The central objective of planning in India at the present stage is to initiate a process of development which will raise living standards and open out to the people new opportunities for a richer and more varied life.[2]

At the inception of the first plan, per capita annual income was about $60. On the assumption of population growth and anticipated additional

---

[2] Government of India Planning Commission, *The First Five Year Plan*, Vol. 1 (New Delhi, December 1952).

output created by the investment rise, the target was set to double this figure in one generation. The ensuing plans have been successful when limited goals were set for increases in output and employment and when the country was favored by generous foreign aid and abundant rainfall. When foreign donors and the monsoons are not generous, India experiences inflation, foreign exchange crises, and famine. In addition, investment has failed to produce the expected rise in output. It is unlikely, therefore, that India will achieve the goal of doubling per capita income in a generation.[3]

The fourth five-year plan beginning in 1966 had to be abandoned at the end of the first two years. In early 1969 the National Development Council, comprising the Prime Minister, the chief ministers of the provinces, and the planning commission members, formulated a new plan for the period 1969–1974. They set an annual growth rate target of 5.5 percent, or 1.5 percent more than the Indian economy's performance in prior years. Other targets included reduction of foreign aid, including the elimination of food assistance, within a period of two years.

Why do these plans falter? The answer may be that Indians are more effective as intellectualizers than as doers.[4] A particular failing is that the plans do not grapple with the serious problem of underemployment and unemployment. During the second plan, for example, unemployment rose from 5.3 million to 9 million, and underemployment rose to about 18 million in a labor force of 170 million. The plan did not produce the jobs to match the increase in the labor force. Although the national income rises at a rate of about 3 percent, the population explosion reduces the gain per capita to an imperceptible amount.

Indian planning does not appear to be an indicator of realistic goals or actual accomplishments to be achieved in production and consumption. If a person were to study the Indian economy on the basis of its five-year plans, he would not know whence the economy came, where it is presently, and where it is going. Indian planning is misleading by its suggestion of orderliness in an economy that actually operates in a chaotic manner. Should present economic trends continue, by the end of the century the majority of the Indian people will by present Western standards be living in poverty.

India is a nation of contrasts. It contains an old industrial and commercial community that was developed under British rule and that has produced considerable wealth for some Indian families. But it also has a

[3] For a discussion of Indian planning, see Wilfred Malenbaum, *Prospects for Indian Development* (New York: Free Press, 1962). See also Jagdish N. Bhagwati and Sukhamoy Chakravarty, "Contributions to Indian Economic Analysis: A Survey," *American Economic Review*, Vol. 59 Supplement (September 1969).

[4] In *Asian Drama: An Inquiry into the Poverty of Nations* (New York: Pantheon, 1968), Gunnar Myrdal states: "The dichotomy between ideals and reality, and even between enacted legislation and implementation, should be seen against the background that India, like the other South Asian countries, is a soft state. There is an unwillingness among the rulers to impose obligations on the governed and a corresponding unwillingness on their part to obey rules laid down by democratic procedures."

substantial population that lives close to starvation. Children with bloated stomachs, a symbol of undernourishment, are a common sight. Side by side with modern industrial plants are shops with primitive methods of production whose origins date back to the fifteenth century. Some 80 percent of the population lives in village clusters of less than 2,500 inhabitants. There are also large numbers of people concentrated in old urban centers. Professor John P. Lewis estimates that by 1973 five Indian cities may each have a population exceeding 60 million inhabitants.[5] Neither the small village clusters nor the huge urban densities make economic sense, for they deter an efficient use of resources. India has too many births and too many persons in the wrong places.

The path to modernization of the rural area lies in its industrialization, but the Indian village is too small at present to support efficient methods of consumption and production. It cannot pay for specialized skills in marketing arrangements. The public services and capital overhead required for modern living cannot be supplied at low cost. A regrouping of village clusters is therefore necessary.

Because economies can be achieved in production and marketing, planners prefer developing old industrial centers rather than these rural areas. Big cities incur social costs and rising inefficiency as they attract unskilled rural populations, however. Housing construction becomes more expensive; costs of crime control rise; so do expenses of feeding the population. In addition, the siphoning from rural areas of manpower with high potential increases the difficulty of rural development. Although attempts at rural development have been made, such as the institution of *panchayat raj* (people's rule), these experiments have suffered from a lack of authority, talent, money, and political boundaries that make economic sense.

The population of India is increasing at a rate in excess of 2.6 percent annually.[6] This means 13 million more nonproducing consumers each year, a rise that makes food shortages an ever-present menace. With an already high unemployment rate of 10 percent, the increase also means that an additional 2 million persons will be looking for employment each year. The birth rate of India is twice that of the United States. If its death rate were to fall to the American level, the consequences would be disastrous.

A shift in strategy is taking place to curb the runaway population increase. The Indian Ministry of Health is seeking alternatives to the use of intrauterine devices, such as male sterilization. The government takes the position that with the annual increase of 13 million and an overall

5 John P. Lewis, *Quiet Crisis in India, Economic Development and American Policy* (Garden City, N.Y.: Anchor Books, 1964).
6 The burgeoning population has rendered impossible the education target of compulsory education for everyone up to the age of 14. In 1960, 40 percent of the children aged 6 to 11 were out of school; 80 percent of those aged 12 to 14 were not attending school. The figures are those of Stanley Wolpert, *India* (Englewood Cliffs, New Jersey: Prentice-Hall, 1965).

population beyond the half-billion mark more effective solutions are necessary. The intrauterine technique, hailed at the time of its inception as the answer to the problem of overpopulation, requires medical staffs in rural areas that far exceed the capacities of a developing nation. Vasectomy operations are less expensive and require no follow-up.[7]

Some 20,000 Indian citizens with scientific and technical training are either studying or working in Western nations. About 1,200 of these are believed to be teaching in colleges and universities of the United States alone. Nearly 10 percent of its physicians are practicing medicine in the United States and Great Britain. One would think that India would be concerned about this export of talent. In fact, the government is alarmed by a Ford Foundation grant designed to bring this talent home, a reaction that reflects the fear of unemployment. To cite an example, India trains about 20,000 engineers annually but finds it difficult to place them in jobs. Therefore, there is a concern lest anyone persuade the 3,000 Indian engineers who are studying in the United States to return home. The problem in human resource development is not only to prepare a technical elite but also to provide job opportunities for advancement. India appears to export unneeded talent.[8]

Kerala State has the highest literacy rate in India, and West Bengal has the highest proportion of university students. As a portent of the political effect of high educational levels and low job opportunities, both states have the greatest concentrations of elected government officials who are left-wing.

As mentioned earlier, the population of India is, to a large extent, underemployed. A good deal of the nation seems to consist of squatters who do little but who manage by some miracle to stay alive. Is this low productivity a manifestation of a lack of interest in worldly gains, an indication of an asceticism that is free of the appetites of the modern world? One suspects that the philosophy of asceticism is fed by malnutrition. The animals of India seem to fare better than many of its humans. By subsidizing the development of a better human being, India could break the vicious circle of low psychological states and low productivity. The philosophy would probably change with healthier bodies. It is unlikely, however, that this human condition will change materially under conservative economic planning.

[7] A report by an advisory commission of the United Nations contains highly useful information on the status of population control in India. After seven years of substantial efforts in family planning, with current expenditures estimated at 370 million rupees annually, the birth rate has not declined. Meanwhile, the death rate continues to fall. In the four-year period prior to the report, over 7 million couples of the country's 100 million couples were encouraged to resort to sterilization and intrauterine insertions. In 1968–1969, some 50 million condoms were distributed, although, as the report implies, nobody seems to know what the Indian population does with them. A serious drawback is created by the fact that most intrauterine insertions have to be performed by women physicians. The commission makes recommendations on abortion and the introduction of family life education into the educational system of India. The government is counting on extension of the family planning program to lower the birth rate to 25 per 1,000. United Nations, *An Evaluation of the Family Planning Program of the Government of India* (New York: United Nations, November 24, 1969).
[8] *The New York Times*, April 25, 1967.

The vast majority of the Indian population is not committed to modern work. Of the 29 percent of the working population in nonagricultural employment, only about 7 percent can be considered as comprising a modern industrial labor force, a figure that has changed little since the inception of economic planning. This 7 percent is concentrated in manufacturing, mining and quarrying, construction, utilities, transportation, and communications. The remainder of the nonagricultural population is mostly in single-craftsman enterprises and in government.[9]

Periodically, the workers in the small industrial force shift between urban and village life. Although the worker has some measure of security in the village with his family, the rigid caste relationships in the community trigger migration to the urban center, but then the insecurities of the urban center push him back periodically to the village. The resulting high turnover in industrial employment is a measure of the reluctance of the rural person to become a permanent industrial urban worker. When he does return to the city, however, he makes a strong claim to his old job and seeks the support of a labor union to get it back.

The social fragmentation of Indian society is well known. Taboos prohibit intermarriage and physical proximity between members of different castes. The effects of the caste system range from simple lack of communication between the castes to conflict and violence. Some students of Indian development believe that the system slows up economic growth. They assert that it stifles the rise of a national consensus on economic and social policy because of the difficulty in transferring loyalties from the castes to a common national view. In fact, these groups appear to be shifting their animosities from each other to the government. One group within a community may express its animosity toward another group by staging an antigovernment demonstration. Professor Richard Lambert suggests, however, that the routine character of these demonstrations robs them of any disruptive effect. Moreover, the conflicts are no longer on national lines. Since the Hindu-Muslim battles at the end of World War II, communal strife has been confined to particular regions and urban centers.[10] In all probability, the caste system, although illegal, inhibits the national consolidation required for rapid economic development.

This fragmentation of Indian society makes social change difficult. For example, the innovation of one particular group may not be considered a model for others. Therefore, the demonstration effect is lost. This indifference to the accomplishments of other groups also affects the relationships between the government and the people. The governing elites who seek to promote the welfare of the population may not be accorded the admiration they think they deserve. For example, the

---

9 Figures in this paragraph obtained from press reports and personal interviews.
10 Richard D. Lambert, "Some Consequences of Segmentation in India," *Economic Development and Cultural Change*, Vol. 12 (July 1964).

minister who believes he is bringing a worthy message to the community may be driven out of town. The managerial elite is judged in terms of the group that it represents, and the people may raise barriers against its efforts that may range from indifference to obstructionism. The system has a high potential for violence, which, curiously, runs high in a society whose philosophers teach nonviolence to the West.

Generally, Indian industrialists have a short-term outlook. They are low-volume–high-profit operators typical of the type one sees in southern Italy and Latin American nations. They consider a high return today better than small profits over a long period.

As mentioned earlier, unlike other former colonies in South Asia, a considerable number of indigenous entrepreneurs arose in India while it was still under British rule, the most prominent of them being the Parsi and Gujerati family groups. These managers, who originated in the textile, jute, and steel industries, are not the heroes among the Indian people that their counterparts are in the United States. Nor do they have a collaborative relationship with the government similar to that of managers in Japan. Instead, government officials tend to look upon them with suspicion, and they tend to look upon government officials with hauteur.

Industrial managers operate under a unique Indian institution called the management agency. Under this system, the manager is an agent who controls a firm either because his family owns it or because voting and managerial rights have been assigned to him. The family enterprise is usually the ancestor of the management agency. In such instances, the property and income are held by the family while the management agency is controlled by the oldest active ancestor. Professor Charles Myers points out that the concept is similar to the central office of a multiplant corporation, with the difference that Indian managers exercise a much tighter control.[11] Now, however, the government is becoming the proprietor of an increasing proportion of industry, mostly in capital goods production, and the management agency may be expected to wane as the public sector becomes more significant.

Indian law requires the managers of every firm of 500 or more employees to appoint a personnel officer, known as a labor welfare officer. Because of the wide social gap between managers and workers, the labor welfare officer has a difficult role to exercise. He is expected to gain the confidence of workers and at the same time be the hatchet man for the boss in matters of discipline and discharge. Nevertheless, this legal requirement is causing structural changes that favor the process of economic development. The labor welfare officer is evolving into a staff personnel officer who advises management on employee relations and assists in the professionalizing of the management function. The role of the first-line supervisor, who had formerly been the recruiter of workers, is

[11] Charles A. Myers, *Labor Problems in the Industrialization of India* (Cambridge, Mass.: Harvard University Press, 1958).

also curtailed as the personnel function is broadened. Although this shift takes status away from the supervisor, it is probably in the long-run interest of human resources growth.

The stated objectives of the labor organizations in India are to change the distribution of income (a hackneyed socialist goal) and to protect the workers from the excesses of the industrial system. To pursue these goals, they try to control technological innovation and nationalize industry, after which the labor-management problem is expected to wither away. They try to control technology by placing obstacles in front of the introduction of machinery and preventing the installation of work methods that may displace labor. They also seek to impose controls generally over the private sector and to increase worker participation in the management of enterprises. These policies differ in emphasis, depending upon the particular labor organization that pursues them. They seem to have little faith in developing positive relations with particular employers. Some labor unions, through the skillful processing of worker grievances and through the development of a stable relationship with an employer, do, however, succeed in creating a viable organization. But these seem to be the exception rather than the rule.

India has experienced the same phenomenon as some other developing nations in the growth of politically powerful labor organizations before an economic takeoff. As in the case of Argentina and Indonesia, this evolution of institutions may raise complications in economic growth. The pressure of these labor organizations may restrict employment, particularly of low-skilled workers. The labor leaders' indifference to raising costs may make employers reluctant to incur long-term employment commitments. As these two factions clash, the government may respond by devising ornate labor standards that fit the needs of everybody and nobody among the workers and that raise costs further. These labor organizations may be a threat to the extent that they retard technological change and reduce the workers' commitment to modern employment. The early growth of labor political power may thus deter efficiency.

There are four major labor federations in India, each with a strong political orientation. The rivalry among them reduces their bargaining effectiveness with employers. The oldest one is the All India Trade Union Congress, organized by the Congress party, which founded the new nation. The federation is now dominated by Communists. It stresses class conflict in labor-management relations. The second is the Indian National Trade Union Congress, which was the brain child of the Indian government after national independence and is a moderate force in labor organization. The United Trades Union Congress, the third federation and the one with the greatest employer orientation, consists of dissident socialists who have broken with the socialists in the *Hind Mazdoor Sabha* (HMS), the fourth labor federation. Each federation reflects caste alignments in Indian society. Their claimed memberships are exaggerated, for as many as half of their affiliated unions do not submit returns on their membership. Although there are some instances of a single labor union dominating an entire industry, the existence of these federations means a potential of four rival unions in each industry.

The nature of the relationship between these organizations and management varies, depending at the plant level on managerial attitudes and the impact of union rivalry. The labor-management relationship evolves in the context of extremely complex rules set by the national and state governments. Collective bargaining without third party intervention is not common, but when it is practiced, it tends to be industry-wide in a particular labor market. The plants in which collective-bargaining agreements do exist are usually those under foreign management. Formal plant grievance machinery is rare, although a few firms have established three- and four-step grievance procedures with joint labor-management committees as the last step. The initial procedure is for an employee to petition the labor welfare officer for assistance in a particular problem, which commonly may be housing, medical care, leaves of absence, or layoffs. Although only 2 percent of the labor force is organized in India, the concentration of labor organizations in a few urban centers in the modern sector of industry makes them an influential force.

The trade-union leaders are generally outsiders who use their organizations for their own advancement. They have so many commitments that little time is available for improving their organizations. Professor Charles Myers reports that one leader of national stature is the president of some thirty unions. Although some labor officials in the large plants may have come out of the ranks, this is an exception rather than the rule, for officials are more likely to come from the supervisory levels. Little serious attempt is made to develop leadership among the workers themselves.

An arm's-length relationship exists between the labor official and worker that is typical of the aristocratic style of leadership generally. The usual posture is one of benevolent authoritarianism. Shifts in attitudes are apparent, however, in the new generation, which seems to be increasingly concerned with self-examination and with a desire to look at facts as they are. As in developing nations generally, the effect of this change will depend upon the extent to which knowledge of social science will permeate decision making. But the Indian educational system is not geared to the development and use of quality social science thought.

The government is very much involved in regulating labor-management relations and in setting minimum labor standards. Up to World War II, its major interest was protecting workers, particularly women and children, from the excesses of industrialization. Since the granting of national independence, however, it has been moving rapidly toward a comprehensive control of relations between labor and management. A major reason for this evolution is concern over economic development. A conviction prevails in government circles that frictions in labor-manage-ment relations create serious obstructions and that conflicts can be minimized when the government acts as arbiter of differences. In conse-quence, the government has empowered itself to refer any labor dispute to compulsory arbitration. Government officials defend this procedure by stating that an economy of planned production and distribution can work only in an atmosphere of industrial peace.

The government seeks consensus by placing employer and labor representatives on a labor advisory panel within the economic develop-ment machinery. The labor disputes procedure consists of three levels. At the base, labor courts hear disputes over interpretation of company regulations and disciplining of workers. On the second industry level, tribunals adjudicate disputes over compensation and work methods. Disputes of major importance are referred to national tribunals.

The results of such intervention are not easy to assess. Strike statis-tics, as they do generally, partially reflect the competence of government mediators. A real case can be made for the possibility of a long-run decline in strikes in the absence of government intervention, for they are now a means of forcing the government to intervene. Another factor that makes assessment difficult is that the government is deeply involved in wage determination, the criteria for which have to be worked out as guidelines for changes. Whether the wages that issue would have done so even in the absence of government intervention is also a debatable question.

Government involvement does not assure the development of coopera-tive labor-management relationships. Such an outcome is often produced by management's desire, for one reason or another, to develop a coopera-tive relationship and by the union's desire to avoid being embroiled with rival unions by gaining the support of management.

To summarize, by concentrating on tangible capital growth and foreign trade, India does not appear to have come to grips with her human resources problem, which is enormous. The development of the rural population is crucial to the country's economic future. Their numbers have to be reduced and they have to be involved in a modernization process.

To conclude, two contrasting observations on Indian economic de-velopment are quoted. The first is by an economist:

India, for all of its sophistication, remains one of the world's most deeply impoverished countries. In many ways it is a prime case of a dual society in which an industrializing urban minority is drawing away from a stagnating traditionalist rural community. Labor reforms have been carried only part way to their intended target in most Indian states and may now have lost their momentum. Much of the social structure, organization, and traditional leader-ship in the countryside is still highly resistant to rapid economic change. Even in the cities, the appetite of policy makers, both public and private, for greater productive efficiency are being dangerously jaded by the omnipresence of un-employment. Moreover, the vaunted experience of the Indian business and financial communities is not an unmixed blessing. Some of their members still hold to the conservative, low-volume, high margin, Scotch banker traditions of the limited, stagnant market in which most of their experience accrues.[12]

These are the words of sociologists:

India's progress in this task since 1947 stands as one of the historic examples of human advancement. Proceeding through a program of planned social and economic development, India has increased her food and agri-cultural production by some 42 percent, has raised her low industrial output by an average of 93 percent, and has moved ahead with formation of the numerous policies and institutions, including education and community serv-ices, that are needed for realizing her goals of future growth. These achieve-ments are monumental and deserve recognition. It is probably safe to say that no other great nation has ever before made so many and so great gains in the short period of time that has passed since India began her first planned decade of development.[13]

Which assessment is closer to reality? On the basis of human re-sources criteria, it would appear that economic development in India is failing.

PAKISTAN

Pakistan was created as a solution to the religious intolerance between Muslims and Hindus and not for any reason of economic logic. Formed at the end of World War II after an unprecedented exchange of 14 million people in the short period of a few months, it is a nation divided into two parts with some 1,000 miles of India intervening. The languages spoken in West Pakistan are not intelligible to the Bengali-speaking people of East Pakistan. Since 1947 the country has had to use its energies, without much success, to develop political and economic cohesion between its parts. With the seizure of power by General Ayub Khan in 1958, the rule of Muslim landlords was augmented by high-ranking military officials and their families. In 1969 under mounting opposition of members of the oligarchy and amid violent disorders, Ayub resigned from the presidency.

The question of whether democracy is working in Pakistan is not at issue because it has not been given a try. Political control has been in the hands of a group of well-to-do politicians who are out of touch with the people and who engage in a periodic scrambling for government posts. There has not been a national election since the nation was founded. Former President Ayub Khan had been voted into power by 120,000 electors equally divided between East and West Pakistan, who were also empowered to elect the central legislature and the two provin-cial legislatures. These so-called "basic democrats" were a principal target in the violence of 1969.

---

[12] John P. Lewis, op. cit., pp. 4–5.
[13] Carl C. Taylor et al., India's Roots of Democracy (New York: Praeger, 1965), Preface.

For many years, Pakistan has been a showpiece for American advisors in economic development. Their strategy focused on increasing tangible capital, with little concern for social progress and the development of human resources. The 1969 rebellion suggests that economic policies that are oblivious to the cultural aspects of economic development rest on a shaky foundation.

Over half of the nation's population of about 110 million people live in East Pakistan, which makes that region one of the most densely populated areas in the world. Most of the economic investment, however, has gone into West Pakistan. Although this allocation has been defended on the basis that investment in West Pakistan has greater economic feasibility, it is causing a rise in political tensions in the eastern portion of the country.

The people of West Pakistan are of nomadic origin, but their movement has declined as irrigated lands have been developed in that part of the country. The principal products of East Pakistan are rice and jute, the latter of which is the nation's principal earner of foreign exchange. The economy as a whole has a net agricultural deficit, however, with food production lower than consumption, and the deficit channels scarce foreign exchange away from industrial products. According to the Pakistani government, the country has been moving in the direction of becoming a net exporter of food. As a result of the political crisis of 1969, the government may be impelled to raise the rate of social and economic progress of the population and to increase investment in East Pakistan, actions that would be likely to slow down the rise in indexes that have been used to conclude that economic development in Pakistan has been successful.

Sixty-five percent of the population is in agriculture, but only a small fraction of this number owns land. Some 50 percent rent the land that they cultivate, mostly in a sharecropping arrangement with the landlord. About 14 percent are day laborers. These day laborers are a prime source of new entrants to the industrial labor force. With an annual rise in population of about 2 percent, this rural proletariat is growing and industry is unable to absorb the excess.

The 32 percent of the population in the Pakistani labor force compares with 40 percent in India and 48 percent in Indonesia. The low participation rate for Pakistan reflects a higher death rate and opposition to female employment. The estimated number of women in the labor force, 4 percent, contrasts with Indonesia where the number amounts to 44 percent, a high figure for developing nations. Seven percent of the labor force is in mining and manufacturing. In absolute figures, this amounts to some 10 million workers in modern industry out of a total labor force of 32 million.[14]

Sixty percent of the Pakistani population is less than twenty-one years

---

[14] The data are from Willis D. Weatherford, Jr., in Walter Galenson (ed.), *Labor in Developing Economies* (Berkeley: University of California Press, 1962).

of age, an age distribution that results in a preponderantly young and unskilled labor force. Many of its members are recent migrants from rural areas, and many of them return to their villages for a good portion of the year. The universal rural custom of pooling family income acts as a deterrent to the ability of the most talented young to amass capital. The workers have little sense of loyalty to a particular employer, and the absence of a sense of permanent affiliation to the labor force creates industrial morale problems and low efficiency. Work planning in industrial plants becomes a matter of day-by-day improvisation. A fatalistic outlook is also common in the Pakistani labor force: In Latin America it is *Dios* who wills it; in Pakistan it is Allah.

After a shaky start, Pakistan brought forth its first five-year plan, which covered the period April 1, 1955, to April 1, 1960.[15] The plan envisaged a 20 percent increase in GNP and a per capita income rise of 12.5 percent during the period. Industrial production was to rise about 75 percent. To attain these goals, the plan proposed a total investment in public projects amounting to 9.3 billion rupees. The plan, a document of over 500,000 words, was not authenticated for publication by the government until three years after the beginning of the planning period. A majority of its projects had already been in execution prior to the beginning of the planning period. At the end of the period, the per capita rise in income was negligible, unemployment had risen significantly, and the balance of payments had reached a crisis stage.

The second five-year plan estimated a 60 percent rise in industrial production, a per capita income rise of 2 percent annually with a gross investment of 19 billion rupees, and a rise in food grain production of 21 percent, with self-sufficiency to be attained by 1965. East Pakistan's share of public expenditures was doubled. According to data issued by the Pakistani government, after two years of the second plan, per capita income had risen by 7 percent and industrial production by about 23 percent.

As in India, rural life in Pakistan raises obstacles to economic development. Most Pakistanis live in small backward villages as do the people in India. The fragmentation of the land around them is increased by a population growth that produces further subdivisions. The fixed amount of available land is divided among an ever-increasing number of people. Although caste consciousness is not as prevalent as in Indian villages, it does exist to some degree. The industry that does exist is based on production for the local market and is performed with primitive tools. A

[15] Albert Waterston, *Planning in Pakistan* (Baltimore: Johns Hopkins University Press, 1963). See also Gustav F. Papanek, *Pakistan's Development: Social Goals and Private Incentives* (Cambridge: Harvard University Press, 1967), and Clair Wilcox, "Development Planning and Programming in Pakistan" in Everett E. Hagen (ed.), *Planning Economic Development* (Homewood, Ill.: Irwin, 1963).

It is difficult to find in the literature a critique of Pakistani planning policy by individuals not involved directly or indirectly in the development of such policy. Mr. Waterston wrote his treatise as an employee of the International Bank. Mr. Papanek is director of Harvard's advisory service to developing countries, including Pakistan.

migrant trying to escape village life comes face to face with the uncertainties of the urban center: estrangement, subsistence wages, arbitrary treatment, uncertain job tenure, substandard housing, and loss of the freedom to pace himself at work. A major need in Pakistani economic development is the involvement of the rural community in a modernization process that develops industrial skills and raises real wages. The large-scale enterprises of the city, organized by paternalistic managers, do not satisfy this need.

Closed family groups tend to control top managerial posts in industry as they do in India. Nepotism is widespread. The typical manager is an authoritarian type whose attitude often produces submerged hostility in supervisors, trade-union officials, and employees. In an industrial plant three closed and unrelated groups exist: managers, supervisors, and workers. They seem to belong to different races and often do not speak the same language.

The weakest link in management is that between the executive and the supervisor. The latter is distrusted by the worker and kept at arm's length by the manager. Managers commonly obtain their labor by contracting a specific number of workers at a particular price, and the supervisor is given wide discretion in the choice of workers and in their terms of employment. As a result of this practice, many supervisors are open to bribes; consequently, the problems of even an enlightened management are compounded, because the unfavorable image the worker has of the supervisor is transferred to management generally.

The Indian institution of the management agency exists also in Pakistan, and it appears to encourage the financial manipulation of enterprises and the allocation of economic spheres of influence to the detriment of production expansion and plant efficiency. Although Pakistan pays only 50 cents a day for workers, it has high labor costs.

It is the government rather than labor officials that produces returns for the workers. Inspired partly by the pressure of world opinion, the government did ratify conventions of the International Labor Organization on minimum labor standards and on the right of association, but it has not gone out of its way to give labor officials any status. This attitude has not helped their position vis-à-vis management.

As in India, a suspicion exists that modern labor organization impedes economic development. This attitude has resulted in extensive labor legislation. Unions must register, and the law regulates the conditions under which they are to be recognized by employers. The law also specifies unfair labor practices of employers and unions as it does in the United States. Labor standards are set for hours of work, minimum age for work in industry, minimum wages by industry and by occupation in each industry, and vacations and overtime. Special standards are fixed for strategic industries. The law prohibits an individual from leaving his job or the location where he works in the event the government deems his work to be an essential service.

The law also provides that where either party to an industrial dispute is contemplating a strike or lockout, advance notice must be given the provincial conciliation officer, who then must attempt to reconcile the differences. Failing that, he must authorize the parties to take their dispute to an industrial court. No work stoppage and no change in employment terms are permissible while the case is in the hands of the court. In addition to producing long delays in resolving labor disputes, the law is, to all intents and purposes, a prohibition against strikes, and it shifts the determination of employment terms from collective bargaining to the government. Accordingly, it puts the unions out of any meaningful business.

There has been considerable discussion in Pakistan as to whether the government should give greater support to collective bargaining. American advisors suggest that the grievance machinery be streamlined so as to allow collective bargaining a dominant position in Pakistan industrial relations. A basic obstacle, however, is the need for a support- ing base of literate and enterprising workers, without which collective bargaining cannot flourish.

Although one-fourth of the industrial labor force is organized, the unions cannot produce substantial results for the workers. The provision of the law that allows any seven employees to organize a union creates difficulty by spawning labor leaders who compete with each other over trifles. The major labor federation, the All-Pakistan Confederation of Free Trade Unions, is under the dominance of the government and is not highly regarded by the International Confederation of Free Trade Unions. Arrayed on either side from the far right to the far left are six other federations, each of which may seek to enroll members in the same plant. The major sources of their strength are the railroad industry, the port of Karachi, and tenant farmers. The federations are symbols of ideological divisions inherited from India that have become aggravated since the secession.

The further to the left a federation is, the greater is its political orientation and the more likely it is to advocate nationalization of industry and worker control of plant management as cure-alls. Together, the federations are probably among the weakest in Asia, exerting little influ- ence on employers, public opinion, and economic development. Under the quasi-military rule of the government and the authoritarian attitudes of management, the unions tend to become minions of the government and the employer. The key to the democratization of Pakistani industrial relations lies in a change in this subordinate role.

The local organizations are ineffectual. They obtain little income either from the rank-and-file members or from the federations to which they are affiliated. Facing employers who have strong antiunion attitudes, their energies are consumed mostly in trying to become recognized. The union leaders, most of whom are outsiders, principally from the legal profession, are weak in talent, money, and employer acceptability. The rank-and-file employee hesitates to assume an overt position in the union because of fear of discharge and does not appear to show much confidence in the unions. The low level of literacy of the membership and the leaders' incentive to use the union as an avenue for political aspirations contribute to the alienation between leaders and rank-and-file members.

Professor Charles Myers finds three forms of labor-management relationships in India that to a considerable degree are applicable also to Pakistan.[16] First is occasional collective bargaining, which in some instances terminates in agreements, most of which are obtained through the intervention of the government in a kind of tripartite bargaining. Second are the relations developed through the works committees established by law at the plant level. Third are those that arise from the settlement of individual grievances. In collective bargaining, the scope of the agreements varies with the degree to which they are preempted by the unilaterally determined employment terms of the company and the government prescription of labor standards. A union negotiates matters not determined unilaterally by the firm nor prescribed by the government. Always in the background of such bargaining is the power of the government to compel a labor dispute to go to compulsory arbitration. Although required by law to bargain with a union, management appears free to decide whether to take the institution seriously or not and what its scope and depth should be.

The law on works committees specifies that their purpose is to promote amicable relations between employers and employees by joint solutions of production problems. The committees appear to be a failure. Generally, employers do not like them because committee members want to bargain and employers do not want to do so. Unions are suspicious of them because of a fear of losing their prerogatives. With regard to the settlement of individual grievances, such machinery is rare at the plant level, as it is in India.

To conclude, what stands out in Pakistan is the heavy involvement of the government in economic development. The largest employer in the nation is the railroad industry, which is owned by the government. One-third of the factory workers are employed in government-owned and operated plants. The unions live at the sufferance of the government, which pursues a policy of enrolling labor organizations into the federation it dominates. The country's economy can be likened to an authoritarian holding company whose majority stock is owned by the government. The government has not encouraged the growth of institutions that would raise

16 Charles A. Myers, op. cit.

the degree of political and economic representation of the population.

The political consequences of this type of development have come to the surface. The country is faced with a split between the Punjabis in the west and the Bengalis in the east and quarrels among the Punjabis themselves. Some lessons derive from this political situation: (1) a program of economic investment may be endangered by a population that is hostile to those managing it; (2) the population cannot be expected to accept a decline in their real wages as the rich become richer under the development program; (3) although Western political forms of democracy may not be requisites of development, some form of participation of the population is; (4) what is sometimes described as political stability by American policy makers is actually temporary political quiescence before the lid blows off; (5) although the United States government has frequently expressed the worthiness of social goals in economic development, it has no strategy to implement these goals.

Can Pakistan be rated as an example of successful economic development? Since 1959, the per capita product of the country has been rising about 1.5 percent annually. Using this figure alone, one might conclude that economic development has been successful. On the basis of criteria indicating the political, social, and economic progress of the population, however, one would have to conclude that it has not been successful.

INDONESIA

In economic resources, Indonesia is one of the richest countries in the world. It has good agricultural soil, petroleum, iron, tin, bauxite, teak, and rubber. Yet it contains the most impoverished and unstable masses to be found anywhere. The nation's per capita income has actually declined since World War II, and its food production has not kept pace with the rise in population. The pertinent question is why the country has failed to develop despite its abundant resources. To ascribe Indonesian poverty to the four centuries of foreign domination is too simple an answer. That a country becomes and remains a colony for a long period is suggestive, however, of characteristics of its people as well as those of the occupying power.

Indonesia poses the classical question as to whether developing nations have benefited from foreign investment. At the beginning of World War II, some 500 Western enterprisers had invested some $2.2 billion in the country, mostly in mines, oil fields, and plantations. Yet the living standards of the Indonesian people did not rise. A major reason for this is that Indonesia has two rather unrelated economies: a modern sector in the outer islands where most of this investment was made and a peasant–small-crafts economy in Java. Little trade takes place between these two economies, their relationships with the world economy being more important than those between themselves.

The foreign domination of Indonesia began with the Portuguese at the end of the fifteenth century. The Dutch colonial period up to World War II and the Japanese military occupation during the war left Indonesia with few trained native managers. At the inception of independence in 1949, the Sukarno government tried to remedy this situation by expanding the educational system at a rapid rate, especially higher education. In 1939, for example, the state universities had some 1,700 students, 800 of whom were Indonesian. By 1961, the figure had jumped to 45,800, up 27 percent from 1959 alone. Within a few years thereafter, the estimated number of students graduating annually rose to 10,000.[17] Yet few found jobs.

This rapid expansion appeared to be achieved at a sacrifice of political stability and quality of education. The turmoil that occurred in Indonesia in 1966 would seem to indicate that the headlong expansion of university education as a tool for acquiring the manpower necessary for economic growth may produce more problems for developing countries than remedies.

Three major power centers existed under the Sukarno regime. One centered around Sukarno himself. The second comprised the Communist party leadership and that of the trade union federation, SOBSI,[18] both of which were outlawed by the military government that succeeded Sukarno. The third comprised the army senior officers, who were the biggest stumbling block to a Communist takeover. For seven years beginning in 1959, Sukarno, the supreme spellbinder, ruled the country with dictatorial power through what he called a system of guided democracy in which he sought to balance these blocs. He failed. The abortive Communist coup and the blood bath that followed eclipsed the Communist party as an open organization, killed off most of its cadres, and placed the armed forces in command of the nation.

As a leader, Sukarno was a militant anticolonial who tended to play upon international tensions. He sought to unite antagonistic Indonesian groups against a foreign threat. The foreign posture of the nation controlled emerging domestic institutions. The imperatives of economic development seemed to escape Sukarno completely, and he sought to control events in terms of what was good or bad for his power. For example, he discouraged the rise of a new managerial class, which might have posed such a threat.[19] His two decades of power did not create a mechanism for economic growth. He died in obscurity.

With a population of approximately 120 million, Indonesia is the world's fifth most populous nation.[20] The island of Java, 7 percent of the

[17] From Bruce Glassburner, "High Level Manpower for Economic Development," in Frederick Harbison, and Charles A. Myers, *Education, Manpower, and Economic Growth* (New York: McGraw-Hill, 1964).
[18] SOBSI is the Indonesian abbreviation of All-Indonesian Central Labor Organization.
[19] For the origins of Indonesian entrepreneurship, see Clifford Geertz, "Social Change and Economic Modernization In Two Indonesian Towns: A Case in Point," Chap. 16 of Everett E. Hagen (ed.), *On the Theory of Social Change* (Homewood, Ill.: Dorsey Press, 1962).
[20] After China, India, the Soviet Union, and the United States. The figure is a 1969 estimate. The population is rising at an annual rate of 2.8 percent. Figures are from the United Nations Statistical Office.

nation's territory, contains 75 million people, or two-thirds of the total population. A major factor in the island's poverty is the huge concentration of people in its central and eastern portions who compete for the scarce agricultural land. The 75 percent of the population in agriculture produces two-thirds of the country's exports. A preponderant amount of these products comes from large estates that were created by the Dutch and are now run by the government; the remainder derives from small landholders. Indonesia's agricultural wage system is based on the practices of these large estates rather than on those of the small properties, where workers are usually paid in crops. The estate workers also dominate the Indonesian labor movement. The heavy concentration of laborers in Java and Bali tends to depress wages. Internal migration has little influence in reducing this population pressure or raising the food supply. Like Pakistan, Indonesia is a net importer of food. Rice, the principal staple in the diet, is a major import.

The same dualism of production scale exists in industry, where a small group of huge firms coexists with a considerable number of small handicraft industries. The big enterprises had been in the hands of foreigners including Dutch, Americans, British, Chinese, Arabs, and Indians. By 1956 the takeover of these firms was completed, but because Indonesian managers were mainly in the handicraft industries, the country had no established native managerial class.

Indonesian economic planning is not as sophisticated as that of India. Under the Sukarno regime, planning consisted of fixing and administering a series of investment targets by the National Planning Council, which had been appointed by the President. Its members had a high political coloration and represented different geographical areas, political groups, and associations. A major portion of the investment required foreign exchange, which was derived principally from oil, rubber, copra, and tin. The announced labor goals of economic planning were higher living standards, greater education, and more participation of the laboring classes in the operation of industry and trade.

The successor Suharto regime de-emphasized the political and participation aspects of economic planning. Its first plan, called REPELITA, an Indonesian acronym for five-year development plan, calls for a total investment of $2.6 billion. Its primary target is to make the country self-sufficient in food. Its other goals include road construction, housing, transportation, and communications. A heavy reliance is placed on foreign funds for this development. At the beginning of the five-year plan, Indonesia had accumulated a foreign debt amounting to $3 billion. Accordingly, like many other developing nations, the country moves in a direction in which funds acquired from abroad will approximately equal the interest charges of funds previously borrowed.

The cultural factors that affect Indonesian economic development resemble those found in South Asia generally. Ethnic segmentation is high, and national identity is low. The majority religion is Muslim, but it reflects Southeast Asian influences rather than those of the orthodox type found in Pakistan. Accordingly, the Indonesian Muslim is influenced more by Hindu-Buddhist values than those of the traditional societies in the Middle East. Organized religious groups exert a strong influence in political and labor affairs. In education, sharp differences exist that range from the European-oriented training of the Javanese elite to the illiteracy of the primitive people of Borneo. Among the non-Indonesian population, the Chinese are the largest force, amounting to some 2 million people. Caste divisions are not as important as they are in India and Pakistan. The schisms in Indonesian society are more along religious, racial, and educational lines.

A significant part of the male population would prefer to have women do the work, for they regard work as servitude that provides no vision of redemption. With the threat of jail sentences, however, the Dutch made compulsory labor a profitable institution for their colonizers, particularly on the sugar, rubber, and coffee plantations. The forced labor system did not disappear until the 1930s, under pressure from the International Labor Organization.

As noted above, some 48 percent of the population participates in the labor force, a quarter of which is comprised of wage earners. The rest are independent farmers, sharecroppers, and individuals in trade and commerce. The women are concentrated in agriculture and trade. Male industrial wage earners are mostly in handicraft rather than factory production. Based on government estimates, some 65 percent of these industrial workers perform unskilled labor. Precise figures on unemployment are not available. Urban unemployment is estimated at about 7 percent and the amount of underemployment at about 10 percent.

To reduce the absenteeism resulting from the aversion toward work, employers pay a bonus when workers show up and stay on the job all day. Those who come to work for six consecutive days are paid a seventh day's wages. The preference for leisure is no bar to rapid urbanization. From 1930 to 1956 the population rose 40 percent, six urban centers doubled their populations, and in six others the population more than tripled. This rapid urbanization contributes to the political turmoil that asserts itself in the political gyrations of Indonesia abroad.[21]

The trade-union leaders of Indonesia administer their organizations in a benevolently autocratic style that is compatible with Indonesian culture. Traditionally, the unions have provided the members with food, clothing, and health facilities. The rank-and-file member has a low degree of education and not too much zest for productive activity. Seventy-six percent of the adult population over twenty-one years of age does not have an elementary school education.[22] The union officials, who are

[21] Everett D. Hawkins, "Indonesia" in Galenson, op. cit.
[22] United Nations Educational, Scientific, and Cultural Organization, Statistical Yearbook (New York: UNESCO Publications Center, 1965).

politically ambitious, do not rise out of the ranks of the membership, unlike some of the officials in the outlawed SOBSI. Because of interunion rivalry the unions tend to be mettlesome and to make excessive demands.

Indonesian labor organizations date back to 1908. Rising originally in the railroad industry and government, they thereupon expanded into agriculture, trade, and services. A split between socialists and communists in the 1920s was followed by new organizations of social democratic and Christian trade unions modeled after the European trade-union movement. The unions played a major role in the drive for independence. For a short period of time following the Japanese occupation, labor was organized into a single federation, the SOBSI, but it became highly fragmented thereafter, with each political party organizing a subordinate trade-union division. One of them, a Muslim organization, was disbanded by the Sukarno government in 1960. Up to the time of the military takeover, some one dozen labor federations that were divided along political, religious, and ideological lines were active in Indonesia.

The labor movement has two lines of organization. One goes from the local level to the particular national union in an industry organizing the rank-and-file workers and the other organizes all unions in a particular geographical area associated with a federation and terminating at the headquarters of the particular federation. The national unions have more autonomy than is generally characteristic of those in other developing countries. They bargain collectively in varying degree, process grievances with the government central disputes committee, and operate regional and local offices. The federation has a greater political function, which manifests itself in bringing together the trade unionists of different national unions in a particular geographical area. By banding together in this fashion individuals with the same political and religious affiliation, the federation becomes a significant political entity in the country.

The number of affiliated trade unions varies from forty for the outlawed SOBSI to as little as one in other federations. In some plants, there may be unaffiliated local unions. Dual union membership among rank-and-file members is common. The unions estimate their affiliated membership to be 4 million, but 2 million, or about 25 percent of the wage ai.d salary earners, is probably closer to the truth. A particular labor demonstration may exaggerate these numbers because of the tendency to pick up sympathizers who are not affiliated with a labor organization but who join the crowd out of fear of ostracism. The unions estimate that only about 10 percent of the membership pay their dues. Possibilities for the growth of these unions lie mainly in the development of more large-scale enterprises. The opportunities offered by small shops are limited because they cannot afford the wage concessions that are needed to attract new members.

As for the actual influence of these labor organizations, they are supported by the sympathy toward labor and hostility toward employers that resulted from the period of colonial domination of Indonesia, and they are recognized by politicians as having political importance. On the other hand, the labor leader does not mix in Indonesian high society; the professional with a college degree is considered his superior. Moreover, although the labor official has some influence in fomenting crises that may produce structural changes, he has less weight in the management of the economy.

Multiple unionism raises a question of its effect on bargaining power. It generates extravagant demands, and the schisms give management and government officials an opportunity to play one organization against the other. To a considerable extent, the limits of concessions are set more by economic forces than they are by these organizational characteristics. The ability of these trade unions to raise the real income of their members reflects the product markets of employers, the surplus of unskilled labor, the ruinous government economic policy, and weaknesses caused by multiple unions.

The wages of most unskilled trade unionists are at a subsistence level. In a 1954 report, the International Labor Organization estimated that the wages of Indonesian skilled workers were on the average three times as great as those of unskilled laborers. The difference to some extent is offset by family allowances that tend to be greater among the unskilled, in some cases exceeding wages. Overall, the economy has failed to increase the real income of the working class since the end of World War II.

The quick shift away from management by foreigners caused a lowering of production efficiency and uncertainty in labor-management relations. Indonesian workers view efficiency as a capitalistic weapon, and the shift to government ownership does not appear to have changed this attitude. They view political freedom as freedom from work. A wage increase to induce more work may be less attractive than more time for dancing. Because the labor organizations defer to the culture of the people, the new management must thus deal with the possible political repercussions of labor-management decisions. With less of a technical orientation than their predecessors, the new managers waver between a continuance of paternalistic attachments and the development of genuine collective bargaining relationships. In short, Indonesia is paying a price for its political volatileness and its cultural attitudes.

An unstable government is the major employer, setting labor standards for some 2 million employees under the jurisdiction of national, provincial, and local governments. It decrees the number of hours of work per week and the number of paid holidays. Generally, it sets a tone of low efficiency. The scarcity of private foreign capital, together with the low rate of savings, requires the government to concentrate its energies on obtaining capital from abroad.

The post-Sukarno government has produced stability, albeit by repression. It is prolabor but also concerned lest wage and job security demands stifle economic expansion. The nationwide system of labor-disputes settlement manifests this conviction and has the effect of preempting collective bargaining and pushing disputes toward compulsory arbitration. Once governments have statutory power to settle labor disputes, such power tends to be used to the fullest. Indonesia is no exception.

This section on Indonesia concludes with an examination of the reasons for the mass killing and a suggestion of what it portends. First, the Communists were pushing cultural change too fast in the face of powerful conservative groups centered in the army. Second, the expensive saber-rattling ventures of Sukarno and his ornate capital displays in the midst of poverty and galloping inflation made a precarious situation worse. The mass killing was precipitated by a military coup in 1965 that was launched by a junior army officer. The role of the Communist party in that coup is not clear. Nor is the actual number of those who were later killed, but a large segment of the Communist-dominated teaching profession was wiped out. The Communist party, which had up to 3 million members, had to submerge, and a good deal of its leadership is presumably dead. The catalyst for structural reform was thereby removed from the society. The slaughter was reported in the Western press as a welcome setback for world communism, but some observers predict that a day of retribution will occur in Indonesia. These forces suggest that any effective grappling with Indonesian problems necessitates a dictatorship.

Summation

The shift from colonial to national governments provided Asian countries with an opportunity to break away from the past and create the institutions necessary for economic growth, but this has not happened. The traditions remain steadfast despite changes in the leadership, and the leaders themselves tend to be aristocratic and paternalistic. What structural changes do occur run into strong resistance, including armed intervention.

The governments commonly believe that labor organizations hinder economic growth, so they attempt to subordinate them to what is believed to be the national interest. As planners and principal employers, the governments set the pattern of labor relations and labor standards to a greater degree than occurred in the West in its early period of growth. Under such conditions, an economic takeoff must emerge under a considerably different set of institutions. In addition, the policies of these governments do not manifest optimism, but rather a psychology of limited opportunity ascribable to a considerable degree to a surplus of labor living at a level of subsistence. For Asian countries, the science of economics starts with the premise that there are too many human beings.

No broad consensus exists in these nations as to economic development policies or methods of achieving objectives. There is little ferment for improving the capabilities of the population and providing work opportunities for them. In many countries, the development managers are the military or their civilian representatives. The people feel that these individuals represent special interests. Social change is necessary from which may come institutions more propitious to economic growth, but such change is unlikely without foreign assistance. The advanced nations use Asia in a game of balance of power, rather than providing such aid as subsidizing the import of Asian manufactured goods and providing technical assistance.

The paternalism and detachment with which Asian elites—employers, politicians, and even labor officials—view their people mitigates against a broad commitment to economic development. The labor official who talks about worker councils often is not thinking of worker involvement but is performing his own pirouette. So long as this arm's-length relationship prevails, a rapid rate of development is unlikely. The elites are detached because the capabilities of the people are low, and the capabilities are low to some degree because the elites are detached. Such is the vicious Asian cultural circle.

A fundamental lesson to be learned from Asia is the enormous barrier that a labor surplus raises against creating a spiral of human and economic development. The methods of the West are not likely to penetrate that continent as they may in other developing regions. Asia is too old, and the people too many.

To conclude, the principal obstacles to Asian economic development are the high segmentation of society; the low psychological and physiological states of the population; an enervating climate; the power bloc rivalries; inefficient agriculture, which precludes the possibility of creating an agricultural surplus as a basis for industrial expansion; and a surplus of labor, compounded by the rise in population, that makes rapid industrialization an impelling necessity. The inefficient agriculture and the necessity for rapid industrialization require advanced nations to assist in raising agricultural productivity and to subsidize Asian industrial imports.[23]

[23] See Shigeru Ishikawa, *Economic Development in Asian Perspective* (Tokyo: Kinokuniya Bookstore Company, 1967).

11

LATIN AMERICA

Latin America stands at the threshold of convulsive change. Its growth rate is the smallest in the world, and its population increase is the greatest. Two out of three Latin Americans are undernourished. Three out of five cannot read or write. Because political forces are polarized in most of Latin America, at any particular moment in time, at least one country is a potential battleground for armed violence. Since World War II, armed conflict has taken place in Brazil, Argentina, Bolivia, Peru, Santo Domingo, Cuba, Colombia, Panama, and Guatemala. In many of the other nations that have not experienced violence, the authoritarian regimes have managed to avoid it only by suppression. A pattern of haves against have-nots is common, with the United States on the side of the haves, thereby contributing to the polarization of political forces and making needed reform impossible.

In discussing Latin American economic development, one must group together countries with such differences in human and economic resources as to make overall generalizations difficult. Nevertheless, similarities do exist, and the differences provide clues as to the general lag in economic growth. Our discussion focuses on Latin America in general and on Argentina and Mexico in particular, for these two nations provide examples of the weaknesses and strengths in the growth of Latin America. With the exception of these nations, the income of the people and the amount of foreign exchange available derive principally from agriculture. Consequently, a crop failure can be a disaster. The theme of our discussion is that the precarious position of these economies derives from characteristics of human resources that are not effectively altered by free market policies.

FACTORS AFFECTING ECONOMIC WEAKNESSES

In the middle of the nineteenth century, Latin America was approximately on a par with Japan in its level of industrialism.[1] Both had social protest movements that urged the emulation of the more industrialized nations in the West. Only Japan, however, succeeded in undergoing a transformation that pushed her people's standard of living up to that of the industrialized nations.

Why did Japan succeed and Latin America fail? The human costs exacted by Japan from foreigners and her own people in the period of aggressive expansion, although relevant to the answer, are only a partial explanation. So are arguments that stress the geographical disadvantages of Latin American nations and the dominating shield placed around them by the United States as compared with the economic challenges posed by Japan's insular geography.

To a substantial degree, Japanese economic development is explainable by two factors. At her period of takeoff, Japan had a greater cultural cohesion, which was manifested by a strong sense of national identity in confrontation with the foreigner. The Japanese people were thus able to accept innovation at a considerable pace without allowing the foreigner to dominate them and destroy their culture. The second major factor was the people's interest in learning. One of the first acts of reform at the beginning of industrialization was compulsory education.

Therefore, these advantages of a greater social cohesion between its elite and the population and the passion for education provided Japan with a powerful base for accelerated growth. Innovation did not create cultural chaos as it seems to have done in Latin America. In contrast with Latin American nations, the rising middle class in Japan became innovators who were acceptable to the population. Only Mexico among the Latin American nations has managed this combination of importation of technology, political stability, and a sense of national identity. To indicate factors that account for this disparity among Latin American nations is a primary task of this chapter.

The Latin American countries show considerable diversity. The geographical size ranges from that of Brazil, which is larger than the continental United States, to that of Panama, which is approximately the size of Rhode Island. There is considerable spread between the per capita income of Venezuela, the highest of Latin American nations, and Bolivia, the poorest country. Literacy rates range from 90 percent for Argentina to 30 percent for Guatemala. With the exception of Mexico, the greater the extent of dual cultures of whites and nonwhites, the lower is the per capita

[1] Ronald Dore in *items,* Social Science Research Council, Vol. 17, No. 2 (June 1963).

income. Lastly, these nations have appreciable differences in rates of population growth and pressure on the available agricultural land.

They have a common problem of financing economic development that reaches crisis proportions in some countries. The governments are inclined to pay their bills by printing money and causing inflation. Capital from the United States is offset by capital leaving Latin America. Terms of foreign trade often ride on the fortunes of a single crop or commodity in each country. They seek protective tariffs for their imports and free-trade policy for their exports. In two critical areas of development financing—

TABLE 13 □ **Per Capita Gross National Product of Latin American Countries, Educational Level, Percentage of Population in Agriculture, and Percentage Change in Gross National Product Per Capita, 1969***

Country	GNP	Education†	Agriculture	Change in GNP ‡
Haiti	65	1	83	
Brazil	354	2	58	.019
Colombia	301	2	54	.008
Bolivia	182	2	72	.016
Ecuador	258	2	53	.012
Paraguay	229	2	54	.009
Honduras	246	—	—	.007
El Salvador	283	—	—	.006
Nicaragua	387	—	—	.008
Guatemala	314	2	71	.007
Dominican Republic	305	2	56	.001
Peru	371	2	62	.002
Costa Rica	466	3	85	.019
Mexico	572	3	58	.021
Cuba	560	3	42	—
Panama	624	—	—	.016
Chile	619	3	30	.000
Argentina	763	4	25	.011
Uruguay	593	3	37	−.025
Venezuela	949	3	41	.012

Source: GNP data for all countries except Cuba are from Agency for international Development, *Gross National Product: Growth Rates and Trends Data,* 1970. GNP data for Cuba is from United Nations *Monthly Bulletin of Statistics.* Educational and agricultural data from Frederick H. Harbison and Charles A. Myers, *Education, Manpower, and Economic Growth* (New York: McGraw-Hill, 1964).

* In U.S. dollars at constant 1968 prices.

† Total enrollment in secondary and higher-level education as a percentage of potential enrollment, with third-level education given a weight of 5.

‡ Percentage change for the years 1966–1968 at constant market prices.

creating savings for capital formation and paying for imports—they have considerable difficulties.

Table 13 indicates the relative differences in growth levels. The national product figures of small nations, especially those with accelerating inflation, should be viewed with skepticism. A heavy capital project has the effect of pushing up the figure appreciably. So does inflation if the rise in prices is not counterbalanced by a decline in the value of the local currency vis-à-vis the American dollar. A more reliable figure during an inflationary period is a measure of product at constant prices. Some countries, as can be seen from the table, do not publish such figures, however.[2]

Greater meaningfulness would obtain if income in Latin America were broken down by social groups. For example, the per capita income of such countries as Peru, Bolivia, Paraguay, and Guatemala is small, but a substantial portion of the income is received by a group of wealthy families. Argentina has a high per capita income by Latin American standards, and its income is more diffused. As a general rule (with the exception of Venezuela), the higher the income the greater is its diffusion, and conversely, the lower the income, the greater is its concentration.

Generally, the minimum annual goal of the Alliance for Progress of a 2.5 percent per capita income increase is being achieved only in Mexico. Begun in 1961, the Alliance for Progress committed the United States to a contribution of $1 billion annually, but the plan has not produced any significant improvement in the income of the population.

In 1969 the United States Senate Foreign Relations Committee published a case history of American foreign assistance to Colombia under the Alliance for Progress program. Colombia had been chosen as being in the vanguard of the program. The survey indicated that since the end of World War II, loans and grants to Colombia have totaled approximately $1.1 billion. During the study period, which began in 1962, economic assistance amounted to $732 million.

The committee found that the assistance achieved a basic United States objective—political stability—but fell short of the economic and social goals of the Alliance for Progress program. Between 1961 and 1967, per capita gross national product rose from $276 to $295 at an average annual rate of 1.2 percent. During the same period, the peso depreciated to half its value. The average annual rate of inflation during the first five years of the alliance was 15.1 percent, greater than prior to the beginning of the program. In agrarian reform, land titles were provided to 54,000 out of approximately 400,000 to 500,000 landless families. The educational policies of the Colombian government vacillated from emphasis on primary education to emphasis on university education with the result, in the judgment of the committee, that little progress was made in either. Although the literacy rate remained constant, the absolute number of functional illiterates rose from 5 million to over 6 million. The nation of Colombia, the report states, barely tackled the problem of more equitable income distribution, and the country's social structure remains

2 One is reminded by these income figures of a story about economic development in southern Italy. In a small village lived the family of the local baron and two peasant families. The delicacy of the village was poultry, and the baron's family was consuming all of it. With the coming of development, the baron doubled his poultry consumption, and consumption among the population rose by a third.

essentially unchanged, with about two-thirds of the population not participating in its economic and political decision-making processes.
Furthermore, the limited successes of the program have had the effect of
postponing basic reforms in public administration, taxation, local government, and agriculture.

The weaknesses of bilateral aid are pointed out in the report as
follows:

> The administration of an economic assistance program to any less de-
> veloped country carries with it inherent obstacles, limitations, and contradic-
> tions, which often frustrate both donor and recipient in efforts to implement
> reforms. On the recipient side, the problems arise from the very characteris-
> tics of underdevelopment: (1) institutional vacuums; (2) lack of technical skills
> and statistical data; (3) political and economic instability; (4) political domi-
> nance by a social and economic elite; (5) strong nationalism and sensitivity
> to outside interference in domestic policies. The United States, on the other
> hand, has a tendency to project its own political, economic, and technical
> biases, to say nothing of its balance of payments difficulties, into its aid
> program.[3]

The report goes on to state how United States exports of capital goods
to Colombia intensify a dilemma that is common to all of Latin America.
On the one hand, increased imports of capital goods enhance Colombia's
industrial capacity and expand its long-term potential for earning more
foreign exchange. On the other hand, capital-intensive industry limits job
opportunities to an elite of highly skilled workers.

Countries with high literacy rates in Latin America also have the
highest per capita income. (Venezuela is an exception. Its income is
affected by oil operations based on foreign capital.) Is Latin American
income high because literacy is high, or is the association the other way
around? With greater income, more resources are available for education. On the other hand, the higher education and training of some Latin
American nations produces higher income. Another factor is at play.
Countries with the greatest diffusion of European culture are generally
those that have the highest living standards. This fact draws attention to
the effect of European motivations on income compared to those found in
indigenous cultures. Put another way, the greater the cultural dualism of
a Latin American nation, the lower is the income.

Where substantial growth takes place, it is generally found in a particular sector and involves only a small fraction of the population. The lag
in rural development offsets growth in urban centers. The rural exodus of
Latin Americans to national capitals is a growth deterrent for two principal
reasons: The migration creates a mass of unskilled underemployed in
urban centers who are sustained by resources drained away from capital
investment, and it depopulates the countryside of the talent needed for

---

[3] *Survey of the Alliance for Progress: Colombia—A Case History of U. S. Aid,* U. S. Senate,
Committee on Foreign Relations (Washington, D.C.: Government Printing Office, 1969).

rural development. Rural programs of self-help in Latin America produce meager results because of the lack of talent and the scarcity of resources.

POPULATION AND LABOR FORCE CHARACTERISTICS

Latin America is having the greatest population explosion in the world. At the current rate of growth, the present population of about 250 million will rise to 600 million by the end of the century. Efforts to raise per capita income are dissipated by this population surge. Although the average yearly rise in GNP for all Latin America is approximately 4 percent, the population is rising at a rate of 3 percent annually.[4] Educational resources are spread over a greater number of children whose proportion is rising in the population. Thirty-five percent of the children of primary school age do not attend classes. Three-quarters of the labor force does not have a primary school diploma. A significant rise in Latin American living standards is unlikely unless this population surge is curtailed.

The people of Latin America are sealed off from one another by natural barriers. Within each country, the population in the hinterland feels little association with the middle class in the cities, who are oriented more toward Europe and to a lesser degree toward the United States. For this reason, the countries look outward for their commerce. The isolation of the interiors encourages the preservation of feudal relationships and animosities toward the urban population. The middle class in the cities has little interest in investment to provide power, transportation, education, and other public services to the hinterland. This attitude is reflected in political decision making.

With the exception of Mexico, the greater the Indian population within a country, the greater is the schism in the population. The whites do not succeed in persuading the Indians to set aside their tenacious resistance to change and to integration with the white society. The attitude of the Indian toward whites ranges from aloofness to animosity. The whites are city dwellers. Some 45 percent of the overall population lives in a relatively small number of congested cities. In some countries, the agglomeration is one urban center, the country's capital. The trek continues unabated. In the city, the rural poor perform menial tasks, peddle goods in the streets, or work as unskilled laborers in the construction industry.

As small landholders, sharecroppers, tenants, or laborers, these former tillers of the soil have been among the most wretched in the population. Until the beginning of land reform in Latin America, much of the arable land was held in large haciendas that left a good deal of the land idle or inefficiently used. These areas were inaccessible to markets and

[4] United Nations Educational, Scientific, and Cultural Organization, *Statistical Yearbook* 1965 (New York: UNESCO Publications Center, 1966).

to have opened them up would have required considerable overhead expenditures and an efficient organization of the hacienda. Before the Castro revolution in Cuba, no substantial land reform had taken place in Latin America (except for Mexico). Beginning in 1960, legislatures begrudgingly commenced to pass laws on land redistribution. The conversion of rural areas into modern communities was slow and laborious, however. Decisions had to be made as to which land should be expropriated, and the form and amount of compensation to former owners had to be determined. A wily game commenced between landowners and government in which the one sought to frustrate the purposes of land reform while the other looked at the unfolding drama with an eye to its political consequences. In some countries, although the legislators were sympathetic to the tillers of the soil, the administrators of the law were more concerned with preserving the interests of the landlords.

Once the land is redistributed, the problems of the new owner have only begun. When governments do not follow through with investments in social overhead and technical and capital assistance to the farmer, the land reform produces a new variety of desperation and productivity may actually decline. In Venezuela, where capital, land accessibility, and administrative competence are greater than in other Latin American nations, this outcome has been minimized. In such nations as the Andean republics, where resources are scarce, the problem is more acute.

Differences between bordering nations with regard to land reform policy stimulate rural migration toward the country with the more liberal policy. Thus Honduras has experienced considerable migration pressure from El Salvador, where the land is owned by a small number of wealthy families. The migration has caused armed conflict.

In industry, the wide variation in skills among Latin American workers requires wide tolerances in output standards and industrial discipline. High turnover and absenteeism are common. Firms pay bonuses to workers for good attendance records, for getting to work on time, and for remaining with the company. The acute shortage of primary schools is reflected by the inability of workers to upgrade themselves in industry because of their lack of basic reading and writing tools. The government is deeply involved in prescribing terms of employment and in settling labor disputes. The extensive fringe benefits required by law raise labor costs, which have already been made high by the low labor productivity. Huge government bureaucracies administer social insurance programs on an industry-by-industry basis. A relatively high number of employees working for the government is common in Latin America. In Argentina, for example, 1.3 million, or 16 percent of the labor force, work for the government. The low wages encourage moonlighting, the effect of which is an overall decline in productivity and a stifling of the spirit of innovation.

Generally, the labor force as a proportion of the total population is declining. In Argentina the economically active population fell from 41 percent to 38 percent in two decades. In Chile, the decline during an interim eight-year period was from 36 percent to 32 percent. In Honduras, the fall has been precipitous—from 47 percent to 30 percent within an eleven-year period.[5] There are several explanations for this phenomenon. School attendance among the young is rising, particularly in secondary schools. The average age of the population is declining as the number of people rises. The U.S. Bureau of Labor Statistics ascribes the decline in part to a change in census methodology.

The relative proportion of wage and salary earners is rising as more persons enter the money economy. The increase is greater for developing nations at low levels of economic growth. By industry, a proportion-

TABLE 14 □ Population and Labor Force Characteristics of Argentina, Brazil, and Chile

Characteristics	Argentina	Brazil	Chile
Population (millions)	23.4	88.2	9.2
Population increase rate	1.4	3.1	3.3
Ethnic orientation	Spanish-Italian	White-Indian-Negro	Mestizo
Literacy rate	90	50	81
Labor force participation	35	33	33
Percentage of income from agriculture	17	28	20
Percentage of labor force organized	45	13	25

Source: *Labor Digest*, Nos. 38, 40, 42, U.S. Department of Labor, 1964. Population figures are 1969 estimates from projections of data in the United Nations, *Monthly Bulletin of Statistics* (December 1967). Population increase rates are from the UNESCO, *Statistical Yearbook*, 1965 (New York: UNESCO Publications Center, 1966).

ate increase is occurring in construction, transportation, communications, and services. For nations at low levels of industrialization—six out of a total of fifteen countries for which data are available—the proportion in manufacturing is falling despite the absolute rise. The phenomenon is explained by the fact that as the population expands in Latin America and manufactured imports rise, the relative number of jobs in manufacturing decreases.[6]

Table 14 compares the labor characteristics of three principal South American nations. Argentina has the highest literacy rate and the highest level of labor organization, and Brazil is lowest in each of these categories. Argentina has the largest industrialized labor force. The three nations have dissimilar racial stocks. Most of the population in Argentina is of Spanish or Italian origin. The population of Chile is largely mestizo, of Indian and white origin. The Brazilian population is a complex mixture

5 *Labor Developments Abroad*, U. S. Bureau of Labor Statistics (March 1965).
6 *Ibid.*

of white, Indian, and Negro strains. In Brazilian *haute société,* social distinctions are based on the lightness of skin color.

Latin American nations generally have disenfranchised populations. Rather than being participants in establishing consensus, they are used as props to support particular elites. Where the people are quiescent, there is stability, but where they are protesting or being manipulated by contending power leader elites, there is turmoil. The rapid urbanization of this disenfranchised base causes concern among conservative forces and produces polarization rather than integration in the body politic. Rapid migration to urban centers, which in theory is a prelude to economic growth, becomes instead a principal deterrent.

A structure is lacking that would integrate values and encourage a rise of leadership with a capacity to control events. The social structure of these nations impedes the evolution of commonly shared concepts of what constitutes progress. In brief, they are often archipelago societies with weak communication lines between the islands. Social sensitivity is low, and intergroup responsibility is not highly valued. To compete is a mark of inferiority, a sign of not knowing the right people. Under such conditions, the government becomes an instrument not of forging consensus but of quietly operating pockets of privilege.

Two major deterrents to economic growth issue from this condition. There is a lack of continuity in policy, as evidenced by former administrators being labeled traitors. Second, direct appeals to group efficiency are difficult in a society of individualists. If such a value is to be encouraged, it has to be done by appealing to the ego of the parties involved without fully revealing one's cards.

One of the biggest demoralizing forces in these countries is inflation. Economists who analyze inflation as an abstraction may underestimate the psychological barriers it raises to the growth of a sense of commonweal. It seriously damages the social trust in the governments and political parties that is necessary for economic growth.

Where Latin American countries operate on a market system of economic development, they flounder. In lieu of balanced economic growth, they obtain distorted economic structures, galloping inflation, and gross income inequality. Because of their social structures, these countries face a choice not between comprehensive planning and a free market system but between a variety of planned economy and the communist model.

INSTITUTIONAL RELATIONSHIPS

Extreme ideological fragmentation is a common characteristic of Latin American nations. When not suppressed by authoritarian regimes, the various ideologies find their outlet in numerous political and labor organizations. The schisms frustrate the emergence of institutions that are conducive to economic growth.

Labor Organizations

With the exception of Argentina, Latin American labor officials are ineffective in establishing themselves as an influential group in their societies. The governments generally tend either to suppress their organizations or to subsidize them to the point of converting them into willing servants. Rarely are they encouraged to become an independent force in the economy. In addition, the slow rate of Latin American industrialization has served to perpetuate the ideologies upon which the labor organizations were originally founded, and this inhibits the coalescing of power. A third factor is the demagogic approach of the labor officials, who, in pursuing their ambitions, are not averse to manipulating the rank-and-file members. The demagoguery is encouraged by a working class that is emotionally volatile, anarchistic in inclinations, and vulnerable to the pushes and pulls of ideological contention. Fortifying this ideological combat are hostile attitudes generated by the autocratic posture of Latin American employers. Lastly, the poverty of Latin American workers precludes the possibility of their accumulating funds with which to develop effective organizations.

Labor organizations are confined mainly to nonmanufacturing sectors of the economy—extractive industries, transportation, communications, and power. By occupation, their largest organization is among white-collar employees in government and banking. Total membership figures from labor sources are not reliable. Informed students of Latin America estimate that some 25 percent of organizable employees in industry and agriculture belong to labor organizations. As a general rule, these organizations are a product of both Spanish and United States culture. Their orientation to the more industrialized countries is greater than those of Asia and Africa. Like organizations on those continents, however, they are a reaction to low industrialization and colonialism, the latter being not one of physical possession but of foreign domination of economic structures.

The course of political history in each country is a principal cause of the differences in Latin American labor movements. As a result, government attitudes toward labor organizations may be hostile, indifferent, or favorable (with the latter attitude at times fatal). For example, some unions are bestowed with government favors and do not exert an independent influence (Mexico). Some are looked upon with hostility but exert a powerful influence in the economy (Argentina). The manner in which these government attitudes change has been demonstrated in Brazil, where the organizations manifest the strong domination that had been imposed by the Vargas dictatorship from 1937 to 1945. Prior to the dictatorship, the unions had emerged out of anarchist and syndicalist ideology. Later, with the advent of communism in the Soviet Union, the movement split into two factions, one with a communist orientation and the other anticommunist. The growing hostility of the government crystallized into a purge after the abortive communist revolt in 1935.

Using Italian fascism as a model, dictator Getulio Vargas of Brazil converted the labor organizations into a part of the corporate state structure. His intent was to destroy the unions as an expression of worker protest and to educate the worker into using the government as the agent for redressing his grievances. The unions were converted into social welfare organizations that provided workers with such facilities as clinics, schools, and libraries. The Vargas intervention served to establish a pattern for subsequent heads of state. João Goulart, who had been Minister of Labor under Vargas, turned to courting the friendship of labor officials after he became President. In 1964, however, the successor government reshuffled the leadership and made the trade unions a servant of the state once more. The government forbade the formation of a federation that would have included all of organized labor and removed all elected officers deemed to be communists or communist sympathizers.

The basic unit of Brazilian labor organization is the *sindicato,* each unit of which brings together workers in a trade or industry within a local area. Its essential function is welfare services, although the more militant unions do some collective bargaining with employers. Each of these local organizations is affiliated with a national federation, which in turn is associated with a confederation of industrial workers, white-collar workers, or transportation employees.

Chile has the longest history of political stability in Latin America, despite its numerous political parties and labor organizations. Unlike Brazil, it demonstrates a capacity to move toward the left without causing a violent reaction. Chilean labor organizations reflect the same anarchist-syndicalist origins with latter-day socialist-communist trimmings as other labor organizations in Latin America. Similarly, the intervention of the state gave unions, at an early stage in their growth, legal recognition and also specified their jurisdictional areas. The law places considerable controls on what labor leaders can and cannot do, regulates their finances including provisions for compulsory check-off of dues for those unions recognized by the government, and prohibits industry-wide collective bargaining with employers. Two types of organizations are recognized: the *sindicato industrial* and the *sindicato profesional.* Although the distinction between the two is complex, the one essentially organizes manual workers in a particular plant whereas the other has jurisdiction over craftsmen and white-collar employees. The law makes no provision for the recognition of national unions.

After the first federation in Chile, the *Gran Federación Obrera Chilena* (Grand Federation of Chilean Workers), was organized in 1909, political struggles ensued that led to a series of divisions in the labor movement.

Out of these schisms came the dominant federation, the *Central Única de Trabajadores de Chile* (United Central of Workers of Chile), comprising communists, socialists, and anarchists, but dominated by communists who managed to make effective use of the cliché of working-class solidarity. The other organization is the *Confederación Nacional del Trabajo* (National Confederation of Labor), which was organized in 1958 by elements that split from the communist-led federation.

As is common throughout Latin America, these divisions forestall the rise of a stable industrial relations system. To the consternation of the employer, strikes take on a political orientation, and a system of industrial relations does not issue that reconciles the values of employers with those of the working classes. A major problem in economic development is the evolution of institutions that create cooperative economic relationships that are based on the acceptance of efficiency as a value.

Some Chilean unions manage to organize nationally. The outstanding one is the Confederation of Copper Workers of Chile, the bargaining agent for the copper miners. The federations formed by the railroad workers and by the maritime workers are other examples of successful organization on the national level.

These Latin American labor organizations are often accused of playing a substantial role in producing inflationary pressures. By virtue of being in a strategic industry or government service, some of them acquire substantial bargaining power. The individuals with whom they negotiate are inclined to yield to union demands to the extent that they are capable of transferring their costs elsewhere: industry by raising prices and government by printing more money. Workers in these strategic industries may receive wages six times as great as the industrial average. A rise in their wages sets off a series of invidious comparisons that ripples through the entire economy.

Elite Groups

The traditional employer elite in Latin America derives from the landowner class and the traders, and neither group is a substantial source of new industrial entrepreneurship. In the traditional culture, work in industry is a manifestation of low social caste. Therefore, the innovators are not likely to come from old Spanish families, but from such recent European migrants as the Italians and Germans. These innovators often start in the retail trades and then enter into the production of goods they sell, a type of vertical expansion that has brought about the amassing of new fortunes. Although there are exceptions to this source of entrepreneurship, this seems to be the rule in Latin America.[7]

Industrial investment derives from two other major sources. The

[7] See William F. Whyte, "Culture, Industrial Relations, and Economic Development: The Case of Peru," *Industrial and Labor Relations Review*, Vol. 16 (July 1963).

cronies of top government officials may use their connections to obtain public funds, which are then invested in favorite enterprises. Another source is private foreign capital, principally from Western countries, which has gone mainly into railroads, mining, and manufacturing. Investment tends to be concentrated in one geographical sector of each country, generally in the principal urban center. The sources of this capital adversely affect the image the Latin American people have of the employer.

A slow evolution is taking place in the creation of professional managers. Management organizations in Latin American capitals clamor for increased efficiency. They run impressive conferences, sometimes with the support of the United States government. These groups seem to do little, however, in the way of seeking a consensus with the working class. Productivity to the Latin American worker means taking his job away from him. The managers these organizations train are predominantly engineers and lawyers who are inclined to use their respective professional formulas in problem solving and have a distaste or incapacity to seek solutions based on consensus. In the name of rising productivity, they tend to perpetuate a principal obstacle to economic development in Latin America: the alienation of the working classes from the economic elites.

With the exception of a few nations, such as Chile, Mexico, and Uruguay, the final arbiter in Latin America is the top military caste. Senior officers of the military have the support of the upper middle class and do not tolerate an innovation that they consider a threat to their prestige and income. The effect of United States military assistance is to strengthen the power of this military caste and to encourage the thesis among the population that the promotion of the interests of this clique in Latin America is not compatible with the economic development of these countries. To the extent development requires it, the military elite seems to tolerate the evolution of a broad consensus and participation but only so long as a clear threat to their position is not implied. The politician with the ultimate balance of power is the one who has the greatest number of guns supporting his position.

Political Systems

On the surface, Latin American political systems appear little different from those of the West. There are competing political parties, elections to bicameral legislatures, presidential officers, and a free press. The similarity is deceptive however. Forces of conservatism and change do not fall along the lines of the rich and the not rich in the manner of Western history. Young revolutionaries may be sons of the bourgeoisie, talented sons of the poor, or even sons of the military caste. The new elites emerging from the universities are a stronger radical force than those of the United States. Those at the top of the political power structure are often authoritarians or minions of conservative cliques who may look upon economic development with dismay. Latin American democracy is *pro forma,* and as such it is tolerated by the ruling oligarchy and the United States government so long as acceptable solutions issue therefrom. There are outstanding exceptions, such as Chile and Mexico.

The ideological cleavages are more similar to those of the Latin Europe of the nineteenth century than they are to those of the United States before its takeoff. Land, religion, and social caste act as forces for division and lack of consensus. The parties of the communists, socialists, and more recently the Christian democrats tend to be parties of reform. The conservative parties tend to be regarded by the people as parties of capitalistic reaction. These parties have not managed to establish the cross-relationships among organizations from which consensus can issue. Latin American policy-making style does not produce a comprehensive involvement of different groups in the population. It is more an unobtrusive pursuit of private interests.[8]

The decision-making process in Latin America should thus be viewed in terms of *clientelistic* politics rather than in terms of countervailing power among blocs as has been the experience of the United States. The only countervailing regulator of this *clientelismo* is the possible adverse opinion of the elite: the top politicians, military officers, newspaper publishers, bankers, industrialists, and landowners. If consensus exists in these nations, it is more likely to be found among these elites who share a common ideology than among the population generally.[9]

ARGENTINA

Argentina, both the most advanced nation in Latin America and the most stagnant, is one the student of economic development should study in depth. It appears to negate the thesis of this work: the association between high levels of human capital investment and rates of economic growth. The country's performance suggests a series of tableaux that other Latin American nations may go through when they reach higher levels of economic growth.

Economic Overview

Data on Argentine population characteristics are not extensive. As will be seen later, Mexico, with a per capita income about half that of Argentina, has a much more developed statistical system. The population

8 Morgan, Betz, and Choudhry (eds.), *Readings in Economic Development* (Belmont, Calif.: Wadsworth, 1963). For a discussion of style in Latin American policy making, see Albert O. Hirschman, *Journeys Toward Progress: Studies of Economic Policy Making in Latin America* (New York: Twentieth Century Fund, 1963).
9 For the picture in Brazil, see Nathaniel H. Leff, *Economic Policy Making and Development in Brazil, 1947–1964* (New York: Wiley, 1968).

density of Argentina is eight per square kilometer, compared to twenty for Mexico.

The economic structure of Argentina rests on a narrow base.[10] Its living standard, the highest in Latin America, has been supported historically by high prices and high volume sales of agricultural goods, principally grains and animal products, marketed abroad. These goods have been produced by the relatively small number of persons who own the bulk of the land in use. The landowners and those who derive income from their economic activity are prime sources of demand for producer and consumer goods, a considerable amount of which is imported from abroad. Such manufacturing as there is tends to be concentrated on end products and relies heavily on imports for its producer goods. The precarious income flow to the wealthy serves to exert pressure on the wages of industrial workers represented by the most powerful labor movement in Latin America. The narrow economic base causes economic instability, which, in turn, produces political instability. In short, Argentina is an example of the precarious colonial-type economy.

Beginning at the turn of the century, spurred by rising world demand for grains and animal products, the nation moved rapidly toward autonomous economic growth. The bubble burst in 1930 as world demand for Argentine agricultural products began to fall. The resulting decline in agricultural jobs, combined with the limited access to usable land, accelerated the rate of urbanization. The ruling agricultural class either failed to see the enormity of the new trend in the economy or did not manage to pursue policies that would stem the tide. During the fifteen-year period from 1949 to 1963, per capita production rose only 8 percent. Industrial employment remained at a standstill, although part of the slack was taken up by the public sector (for example, the number of railroad employees doubled to over 300,000). Inflation increased to an annual rate of approximately 30 percent, and the export market collapsed. The political manifestation of this crisis was the military dictatorship of Perón, which began in 1946 and lasted until 1955, when he was forced to flee the country. The political turmoil has continued since his downfall.

Since 1955 both real wages and wages as a relative share of the national income have declined. Government indexes indicate that wage increases are followed by price increases; in fact, in some instances, employers push up prices in anticipation of wage concessions. The effect of the price-wage spiral has been a relative decline in wage income since 1953, from 50 percent of the national income to 43 percent, after a rise of 2 percent during the Perón regime.[11]

The government's major effort to stop this backsliding was the tradi-

---

[10] There is little in English literature on the economic growth of Argentina. A basic comprehensive work in Spanish is Aldo Ferrer, *La Economía Argentina: las etapas de su desarrollo y problemas actuales* (Bueno Aires: Fondo de Cultura Económica, 1963).
[11] Arthur Smithies, "Argentina and Australia," *Papers and Proceedings, 77th Annual Meeting*, American Economic Association, December 28–30, 1964.

tional economic baggage of compensatory deficit spending and employer tax incentives to expand existing plants. A consequence of such policy is more inflation and more aggravated tensions among the urban proletariat. The old elite, the patricians in land and cattle, failed to provide the necessary leadership in building a new economic structure broader than the formerly successful agricultural base. The middle class that emerged from the short-lived economic expansion, more preoccupied with conspicuous consumption than innovation, also failed to fill the leadership void.

One-third of the entire population of Argentina is clustered in the most developed area—the province of Buenos Aires. The remainder of the nation, running some 2,300 miles from the semitropical north to the tundra of the south, contains only a small fraction of the country's human and capital resources, and that fraction is concentrated mainly in the region of the Pampa, the plain that runs northward from the capital.

The Argentine labor force amounts to approximately 8 million persons, or approximately 35 percent of the population. Some 29 percent of this number is engaged in manufacturing or mining, 25 percent in agriculture, and the remainder in commerce, banking, and government. Argentina has considerably more persons in these latter sectors than the advanced nations had at a similar stage of economic growth. Reliable unemployment figures are available only for Buenos Aires, but intelligent guesses for the nation as a whole place the figure at some 10 percent of the labor force.

The landholding pattern, which consists of enormous expanses of land controlled by a few and small, fragmented plots owned or rented by many, has a deterrent effect on growth. Little incentive exists in either case to modernize. The large landholders are primarily interested in land speculation and hedging operations against inflation. Small landholders have little incentive to modernize because of the availability of cheap labor and because they prefer consumption to investment. Both factors combine to push up the price of agricultural land. Hence, the anomaly of agricultural land costing the equivalent of some seven months' industrial wages per acre in a country with a very low population-to-land ratio.

The pattern of landholding pushes people into the urban centers. The heavy waves of immigration from Europe, relatively greater than those absorbed by the United States, have also tended to move into the cities. In so doing, an urban proletariat has arisen that is characterized by low productivity. Living in urban centers with deteriorating transportation, housing, education, and other public services, this proletariat is the prop for political demagoguery.

An expanding economy provides people with a sense of progress; a declining or static one evokes frustration. In Argentina, the social disorganization attending the economic decline is manifested in the defense mechanisms of organized labor and the use of violence for its own sake.

The working classes are almost obsessed with nostalgia for their former leader, Perón, and the good times that allegedly used to be. As their wages shrink in purchasing power, their disenchantment with the social system rises.

Ideological cleavages manifest themselves in the numerous political parties and in the labor organization. At the time of the Onganía coup d'état in early 1966, eight political parties had enough adherents for representation in the National Congress, which consists of a Senate and Chamber of Deputies. These eight parties, however, represented only part of the political spectrum, which could be classified into four major groups. At the extreme left were the Communists, Trotskyites, the *Movimiento Liberación Nacional* (MLN), and the left-wing Socialist party, the *Partido Socialista Argentino de Avanguardia* (Progressive Argentine Socialist Party). The center left comprised the Argentine Socialist Party and a series of Perónist organizations that centered around the *Partido Laborista* (Labor Party), the first Perónist party. The center right had five parties: Democratic Socialists, Christian Democrats, Progressive Democrats, the People's Radical Civic Union (the party of the deposed President Illía), and the Intransigent Radical Civic Union, the party of the deposed President Frondizi. The right consisted of the *Confederación de Partidos de Centro* (Confederation of Center Parties), which went under many names in the provinces. The far right was represented by the *Tacuara* (a right-wing organization), whose political name is *Unión Cívica Nacionalista* (Nationalist Civic Union). President Juan Carlos Onganía subordinated the legislature to the executive. In 1970, he was ousted by the military junta and replaced by Army General Roberto Marcelo Levingston.

The various political elements of organized labor are housed precariously in one confederation, the *Confederación General del Trabajo* (General Confederation of Labor, or CGT). This is more a matter of legal necessity than an indication of labor unity. Of an estimated 5.5 million wage and salary earners, some 45 percent belong to trade unions, most of which are affiliated with the CGT. Within the confederation are three major political blocs, with each individual union belonging to one of them. The blocs consist of Perónist unions, the so-called democratic independents, and the communist-oriented bloc, the *Movimiento de Unidad y Coordinación Sindical* (Movement of Union and Trade Union Coordination). The unions shift from time to time between blocs.

In early 1968 the CGT held a congress at Buenos Aires at which a rebel faction managed to pack an organization meeting and get itself elected to key posts. The regular leaders refused to accept the results of the election, and the rebels voted to impeach them. Although both factions call themselves the CGT, the rebel group (left-wing Perónists) is known unofficially as the rebel CGT and the original leaders as the collaborationist CGT.   The split may become permanent, much to the comfort of the government.[12]

The Perón dictatorship in Argentina left a legacy of a powerful labor organization with considerable political consciousness.   Whereas the Vargas dictatorship in Brazil had created a labor organization capable of being molded to the will of political authority, Perón left a labor movement with a truculent voice and notable bargaining skills.   Prior to Perón, the unions, which had been of anarchist origin, had refused to have any bargaining relationships with employers.   Subsequently, they split among anarchists, syndicalists, and communists and proceeded to institute bargaining relationships.   Perón, selling himself as the benefactor of the workers, did not disturb their collective bargaining relations but succeeded slowly in bringing negotiations into the government.   The labor leaders went along with his progressive accumulation of power, either because of sympathy for him or because of rank-and-file pressure to do so.

From 1946 until 1955, when Perón was overthrown, the history of Argentine trade unionism was one of increasing dominance by Perón and his wife, Eva.   By making the dispensing of social services her private preserve, she gave the working class a sense of status in the society.   At the same time, the locus of power moved upward to the headquarters of the CGT, which became an integral part of the Perón political machine.   Since Perón was deposed, its top-heavy union structure has remained intact.   The three succeeding military intercessions have created a hostile impasse between the government and organized labor.   Because embarrassing the government is trade-union policy, the military has been wary of a showdown struggle.

The two most important employer organizations in the country are the Argentine Industrial Union and the General Economic Confederation.   The former, founded in 1887, represents a majority of large manufacturers.   The confederation, which represents employers in commerce, industry, and agriculture, was formed in 1951 and made an official organization by Perón in 1953.   Employers generally identify themselves with the Conservative party.   The economic deterioration that began in 1962 aggravated an already combative relationship with organized labor.   When labor interpreted an employer attempt to increase productivity to mean arbitrary dismissal of workers, it reacted by seeking to force on employers a fixed guarantee of employment.   In addition, in seeking to redress their political grievances with the government, organized labor seized plants and created an atmosphere of insurrection.

The relationship between employers and organized labor is poisoned by factors introduced by either party.   The Argentine employer tends to be secretive and sees his enterprise as his private preserve instead of

---

[12] From a letter to the author written by Malcolm W. Browne of *The New York Times*.

part of an economy complex; he keeps his cards close to his chest. This attitude worsens a relationship aggravated by economic downturns. Nor does the political orientation of organized labor and its indifference to the needs of operating a plant efficiently serve to improve the relationship.

Employer-worker relationships in Latin America often assume a Marxist coloration, and Argentina is no exception to the rule. The issues are a contest between the interests of the ruling oligarchy, of which big employers are an important part, and those of the working class. From time to time, incidents arising from this conflict involve members of the Roman Catholic clergy championing interests of working-class groups. When such clashes take place, the hierarchy often appears to resolve the crisis by removing the priest from his post. Such an incident, of dramatic proportions, took place in Argentina in 1967. The bishop of an industrial suburb of Buenos Aires attracted attention by his criticism of the Onganía regime and attempted to promote worker interests through his preaching on a papal encyclical, "On the Development of Peoples." The bishop was asked to resign by the Vatican representative in Argentina on the grounds of ill health, and he was transferred to Morocco.[13]

Economic development in Argentina is planned by the *Consejo Nacional de Desarrollo* (National Development Council), an organization of some 250 civil service employees whose director is the minister of finance. With the stated objective of increasing per capita income, the strategy of planning rests on economic policies that seek to induce private industry through tax and loan concessions to make investments that would result in a more soundly structured economy. Out of this more balanced economy, an increase in exports relative to imports and greater industrial efficiency are expected to ensue. Social aspects of economic development are confined to programs of housing, public health, and education.

The planning is hampered by shortages of specialists and statistical information. The training of specialists has a classical orientation. For example, the training of an economist leans heavily on traditional value and distribution analysis, an approach that is remote from the necessities of economic development analysis. An absence of psychological and sociological insights is also a factor.

There is a lack of agreement on the fundamental concepts of economic development, and this produces delay. For example, low-cost housing, a goal of primary importance in the Alliance for Progress program, was postponed indefinitely because of a deadlock as to just what constitutes low-cost housing. More coordinated effort is also required among government agencies in order to develop an efficient system of priority allocation of available resources.

The CGT pays only lip service to economic development planning.

---

[13] From *The New York Times,* December 5, 1967.

More productivity, say its official spokesmen, is commendable, but the way to acquire it is to increase wages first so that workers can purchase the greater production forthcoming. In this way, each of the three parties in industrial relations (the government, the CGT, and the employer) places the responsibility on the others. It is as though they were seated at the bargaining table, each pointing his thumb at the other to make the first move.

How does the Argentine experience compare to other Latin American nations? For one thing, Argentina has no problem of integrating European and Indian cultures because Indians are a curiosity there. The integration problem raised by the successive waves of immigration is also unique to that country. The immigrant is too preoccupied with establishing himself socially to be sensitive to community needs and tends to associate in closed groups with little contact with others. A further point of contrast is Argentina's high literacy rate as compared to that of most of Latin America. Because of the quality of the education, however, its payoff in economic growth is less than one would expect. (On this question, more will be said below.) It should also be pointed out that, in contrast with Mexico, the rise of a middle class has not brought to Argentina a substantial group of innovators in production.

Unlike the less-advanced countries of Latin America, it is difficult for a nation such as Argentina to generate a new social thrust behind economic development once it begins to lag. New social schisms of economic crises are difficult to deal with after powerful contending institutions have been structured. A traditional society without entrenched industrial groups has more elbow room in developing a cohesive social system. Restraint is greater if only because individuals do not as yet have instruments of power.

With the exception of the northern frontier, the Argentine climate is more conducive to economic growth than that of most countries to the north. The fact that most Latin American countries lie on or near the Equator may be an important deterrent to their growth.

Education

According to available statistical information, Argentina has a high rating in education. In the composite educational index of Harbison and Myers, it rates even higher than Denmark and Sweden.[14] Its literacy rate is more comparable to that of advanced nations than to that of other Latin American countries. Its primary school pupil-teacher ratio is better than that of the United States. In numbers of college graduates, Argentina rates higher than Sweden relative to population.

Argentine children are subject to compulsory education between the

---

[14] The composite educational index is in Harbison and Myers, *op. cit.* Other data are In UNESCO *Statistical Yearbook,* 1965.

ages of six and fourteen. Primary school education lasts for seven years. Secondary education, which begins at age thirteen for a duration of five years, comprises *colegios,* which grant a bachelor's degree qualifying a student to enter the university; normal schools, which prepare teachers for primary and intermediate schools; and a variety of commercial and technical schools. Students graduating from normal and vocational schools can enter some university faculties directly without examination or completion of any required courses.

If education increases output, why the low payoff in Argentina? Why hasn't the system produced a trained group of pragmatic leaders? A clue to this puzzle is to be found in the ingredients of Argentine college education: faculty, courses, students, materials, and administration.

There are ten state universities in Argentina, the largest of which is the National University in Buenos Aires with a registration of some 63,000 students. In addition, there are five recognized private universities, four of which are Catholic universities and one is a private technological institute subsidized by the Argentine navy. The faculties in these universities include agronomy, architecture, economic and social sciences, natural sciences, humanities, law, engineering, medicine, pharmacy, and dentistry. Approximately 60 percent of the students are enrolled in medicine, law, and the humanities. The academic year runs from the fall term beginning in April to the end of the spring term in November. There are five grades: *sobresaliente* (outstanding), *distinguido* (distinguished), *bueno* (good), *aprobado* (passing), and *insuficiente* (insufficient). One gains the impression that in these universities there is a high ratio of students to facilities compared with the United States.

Students in the public institutions are exposed to more political diversions than their counterparts in the United States, for the political contentions of their society are played out in the university. Strike demonstrations of students, instructors, and administrative personnel are common. A work stoppage of university administrators in 1964 lasted sixty days. In a one-semester course in economics, a fourth of the lectures were cancelled because of one strike or another. At the time when workers of the CGT were participating in plant seizures, students barricaded themselves inside the university buildings out of sympathy for the workers. In such demonstrations, it is not wise for a *Norteamericano* to go through a picket line.

The extent of student political activity varies with the social origin of the student and with the employment opportunities of his specialization. The practicing Catholic is less involved than the nominal Catholic, who is often from a lower social class. Students in medicine are less active than those in economics and law, but this again is a mark of differences in social groups.

Generally, the universities are not residential institutions. Most are located in buildings at the core of the city. A few, such as the one at

Cordoba, have campuses outside of the urban concentration. The advantage of an urban location for students is that their demonstrations become visible.

The colleges are quite independent of the university administration with which they are affiliated. Up to the time of the savage attack on the universities by the Onganía regime in 1966 and 1967, the universities had been rather free of government controls. In effect, they were a loose confederation of colleges in the different disciplines. Although the central government provided them with funds, a minimal control was exercised over them.

The institutions are governed by a tripartite council (*Consejo*) of professors, students, and alumni. Each college (*facultad*) is similarly governed. Each group is elected by its respective constituents for membership in the college councils, which in turn select the deans and university presidents. The relative strength of each group varies with the institution, with student representation in a few instances running up to half the membership of the council. In the event of a deadlock, the deciding vote is cast by the appropriate administrator.[15]

Generally, the effect of these councils is to make the administration a cautious servant of faculty and students. Students, mostly upper classmen, have to qualify academically before they can run for membership on the councils. In some universities, student pressure may not go beyond complaints on housekeeping. In others, they may concern themselves with changes in educational programs and selection of professors. A vociferous minority of students can exert a considerable influence on the decisions of the councils, a situation that places the dean or president in the position of having to seek a consensus rather than institute changes at his own discretion.

The tripartite administration makes a significant departure in educational policy difficult where students and professors have to be persuaded of its merits. Any given proposal is likely to produce the opposition of at least one of the three groups on the council. Members can stymie business by frequent absences, and an issue such as support from American foundations can be escalated by students up to riot levels.

The educational content of the universities comes from traditional European models, chiefly Spanish and Italian. The first colleges were thus in the humanities, law, and medicine and were intended to create an intellectual aristocracy. (The Spanish term *educación* has a connotation of superior manners.) One gains the conviction that the courses in the universities lag in modern content to a considerable degree, with the

[15] Under the organic Law of the National Universities passed by the Onganía government in 1967, students are no longer permitted a vote in the councils. They are also prohibited from engaging in political activity. The act also does away with the use of the university as a sanctuary from government authority. At the same time, the government passed a sweeping anticommunist law. The legislation defines a communist as one who carries out activities that are motivated by communist ideology. It is retroactive and is administered by the state intelligence organization. Whether a law can in fact stifle student participation indefinitely remains to be seen.

vocational orientation of courses more superficial than real. With the exception of medicine, they are slow in catching up to the existing level of knowledge because of general inertia and inadequacies in library facilities and research.

The semiautonomous research institutes attached to the universities appear to have an inferior status. The people who do the research do not teach, and the research findings do not seem to filter through so as to improve the quality of instruction.[16] Lack of initiative in university research is common. Administrative complexities and low salaries tend to stifle the initiative of these institutes. They often run on the zeal of one person. When he is pirated by industry, the effort collapses. The pace of accomplishment is painfully slow. In one instance, the publication of a manuscript of major importance took four years.

Although students are supposed to undergo technical training in pursuing their undergraduate degree, their courses have a traditional orientation. Perhaps as a consequence, they do not find a ready market for the alleged skills they acquire, although some, such as those who attend colleges with practical subjects like accounting, fare better than others. Those who find jobs after graduation often manage to do so in the already crowded public organizations. No apparent effort is made to attract the most qualified of the graduates into public administration. The poor student with no influential connections often ends up in the pool of unemployed malcontents after his supposed professional training, or he may convert his undergraduate study into a lifetime profession. Though called a student, he is actually an unemployed person lingering in the university with a course in law or social science.

Few professors are available to guide the student.[17] Professors teach a course or two and spend most of their working time pursuing their outside professional careers. Their instruction tends to be divorced from the realities outside the university. For example, the professor who teaches trade unionism may not be concerned about current trade-union affairs. The professional careers they pursue are rarely as consultants to business. They react incredulously to accounts of the degree to which professors in the United States influence business.

The student who takes a particular course with ten subjects can pick one for his examination by selecting a numbered ball in a rotating cage. If luck is on his side, he picks a ball representing a topic he has crammed for, and he takes the examination and passes the course. If fortune should fail him in answering the questions he has to be given another

---

[16] To cite a typical example, because a serious gap exists in the statistics on the actual number of unemployed in the country, the government awarded contracts to an economics Institute to measure its extent in areas outside of the province of Buenos Aires. In the second largest city of Argentina, the institute did not take any Initiative to obtain funds for such an investigation. Asking the director why produced a puzzled look.

[17] As an example, repeated efforts to reach the chairman of a department were not successful. His distraught wife advised that the only way to talk to him was to catch him while leaving class or to call him on the telephone either before seven in the morning or after eleven at night.

choice of subject. Examinations are offered monthly, so if he should fail again, he will have another opportunity. He thus does not take examinations in one fell swoop as students do in the United States but can spread them out over a long period of time.[18] Examinations can be taken repeatedly. In such an event, the professor seems to weaken first.

Several factors may contribute to a certain superficiality in analysis on the part of some of the students. A student may be the victim of a lack of guidance on the secondary school level advising him on the situation at the university. Most students work during the day and come to the university to take courses that are given during the late afternoon or evening. They may not attend lectures because of lack of time. In such cases, the one who acquires by himself an integrated body of knowledge is outstanding. Still another factor is the tendency of the volatile and fast-reacting Latin American not to concentrate on courses requiring qualitative judgment and high levels of abstraction. He is inclined to do his pirouette before his assignment.

Another contributing cause is the right of any person with a secondary school diploma to enroll in the university. As a consequence of this open-door policy, the number of dropouts at the end of the first year is enormous, causing a waste of resources and a lowering of educational standards, but students resist strongly any attempts to institute a policy of admission requirements.[19] Their hostility has its basis in the manner universities used to discriminate against the poor. There is some movement in the direction of more technical and scientific training in both secondary and higher institutions of learning. Deans appear to be more aware of the need for experimentation, but they also seem to be impotent to make any significant changes. The educational problem is not only the need for more rigid entrance requirements and updating of courses but also the need for developing a sense of tolerance toward points of view that are not one's own.

The characteristics of Argentine universities described here apply less to the small but increasing number of Catholic universities. The Catholic institutions are more centralized and show a greater flexibility in educational policy. They appear to be less accessible to the children of the working class, however. A Catholic university at the site of a state institution is likely to reduce complacency in both institutions.

To conclude, college education in Argentina is a portent of what the trends in the United States toward decentralization of power may bring. There is a price to pay for universal college education and student involvement in policy making. The experience of Argentina also shows that countries vary as to the extent of the wealth they produce from a

18 The Education Law of 1967 requires students to complete successfully at least one examination each semester or be liable to dismissal. Examination fees were also increased.
19 As of this writing, some university faculties were moving cautiously in the direction of entrance requirements and entrance examinations.

given amount of college instruction. These differences occur for a variety of reasons. The investment payoffs reflect student selection and activity while in school, quality of instruction, course content, tangible capital, and administration. There are notable differences in student allocation of time for courses and extracurricular activity. Upon graduation, students may move toward jobs that are traditionally low in productivity such as government and services. Education may be used more as a manifestation of social status than as a means of solving pressing social problems. Finally, as is the case in Argentina, the best educated may leave the country and put their training to use elsewhere. The two most important factors accounting for the low payoff in Argentina are probably the quality of the instruction and student allocation of time.

Little can be done with hardened social attitudes once they gain entrance into the university. The Argentine university in some way has to develop a habit of inquiry removed from the intense spirit of partisanship. It can encourage emulation of respected professors and foster student exchanges with foreign countries so as to provide reference groups. Such techniques, however, require speculation as to what kind of total planning is needed for growth, and such speculation is unlikely under an authoritarian regime.

MEXICO

Since the end of World War II, Mexico has maintained a high real increase in per capita product and a rise in agricultural produce in excess of the rise in population. No other developing nation at a similar stage of growth has such a record. In Latin America, Mexico stands out in a general situation of instability and lagging economic development. The nation is moving steadily toward third place, after the Soviet Union and Japan, in the list of countries that have succeeded in building an autonomous mechanism of growth in the contemporary world. Therefore, a case history of Mexican economic development is indispensable.

Cultural Overview

As economic development progresses, a cultural explosion is taking place in Mexico that is destroying traditional values and creating a burgeoning new middle class. The *nouveaux riches* pursue the symbols of modern success, a major one being the automobile. They value education because of its income-producing ability. To those who aspire to higher living standards, the new middle class is enviable. To the older upper class and intellectuals, they represent a new breed of ill-mannered Mexicans.

Mexican social scientists assert that the traditional Mexican has a strong conviction of what is good and what is bad in society. With education, he believes one can get almost anywhere; therefore, education is good. Furthermore, he is sensitive to how justice is administered. He does not want to be trampled upon and is touchy about any suggestion that he might be. Moreover, he has a strong sense of national identity and common purpose. To some extent, his attitudes have grown out of the historical threat of the colossus of the North. His reaction is: Let's show the *Norteamericano* what we can do.

These social scientists state that Mexican conduct is subtle and therefore subject to misunderstanding by foreigners. An incident at the University of Guadalajara illustrates this subtlety of Mexican character. Some "juniors," the Mexican equivalent of American motorcycle gangs, were congregating at the entrance, waiting to swoop down on American girls enrolled at the school. Police action would have caused repercussions that would be difficult to handle. Members of the student organization, who were armed with guns and had the acquiescence of the authorities, cordoned off the street and gave the juniors a mass haircut. The tactic brought about their disappearance. To cite another example, a politician aspiring for high office must zealously avoid revealing his ambitions. He has to proceed in a manner consistent with the traditional ritual and text. In the meantime, his followers proceed to embarrass his rivals. Generally, such action means that the choice of the incumbent wins the nomination.

Samuel Ramos asserts that an important aspect of Mexican character is a lack of self-confidence because of repeated failures in life. A Mexican finds it difficult to resign himself to the idea that he is worth less than he would like to think. The extreme manifestation of this sense of inferiority is a high homicide and suicide rate. Its less extreme evidence is a posture of superiority and a touchiness as to any suggestion of inferiority.[20]

Although the Mexican revolution stripped the Catholic church of its political and economic power, Catholicism is a strong cultural influence among the people. Its influence differs by geography—it is strong in Guadalajara and weak in the capital city—and by social group. The laboring classes tend to indulge in relic worship and such rituals as walking on their knees to the church altar. With the upper classes, religion is more an instrument of social communication.

The established upper class of inherited wealth has made a relatively small contribution to economic development. In a typical upper-class view, economic affairs as the art of the practical is inferior. On the whole, however, no serious cultural schism exists to block economic growth. Unlike the situation in Spain, Mexican intellectuals in the 1930s and 1940s were directly involved in the nation's economic takeoff. For example, such intellectuals as Alfonso Reyes, José Gorostiza, Martín Luis Guzmán,

20 Samuel Ramos, *El Perfil del Hombre y La Cultura en México* (Mexico City: Espasa-Calpe Mexicana, 1968).

Octavio Paz, and Agustin Yáñez served as ambassadors and top government officials.

The Mexican masses have a rich cultural endowment. The *campesino* enters the urbanization process with a culture that is not considered inferior by the general society. In the words of his champion, Emiliano Zapata, the *campesino* feels important and wants to be listened to. This position contrasts with that of other countries where low-income groups are considered to be cultural freaks. This inferior position creates pressures on them to escape their culture and subjects them accordingly to the cultural tastes suggested by the mass communications media.

Much of the culture of the Mexican people can be found in their songs, which are called *corridas,* or current events. Frequently, the corrida is an account of a male who, in spite of his weaknesses, is *muy hombre*—very much a man. Self-pride is his forte. Industrialization tends to destroy this folk culture, but it lingers and has an impact on growth.

Mexico is the one Latin American country with a large Indian population that has had success in integrating the races socially and economically. Although there are still subtle distinctions—the person who shines shoes is apt to be Indian, and the plant manager is likely to be Caucasian —Mexico does not have the separatism that exists in countries to the south. The fact that there is a statue of the Spanish conquistador Pizarro in the central square of the capital of Peru but no statue of Cortés in Mexico is symbolic of the cultural differences with respect to race.

Sociologists divide Mexico into three cultural worlds: Indian; transitional, where the preponderant number of the so-called mestizos are found; and modern, where the whites are concentrated. The Indians speak a dialect of the Indian language, and some 2 million of them do not speak any Spanish at all. The government used to make this racial distinction in its census but for political reasons no longer does so. Sociologists continue to discern the difference, however, through census questions on language.

In a sense, the actual number of Indians in the population depends on whether one is making a *cultural* or a *racial* count. The Indian who gives up his customs and language is, from a cultural point of view, no longer an Indian. Accordingly, the question of how many individuals there are in the Indian population depends on one's definition of the term "Indian."

The preponderant number of Indians live at a subsistence level, but many supposedly aspire toward modern patterns of consumption. The transitional group represents the bulk of the population. Many of its members have come out of the peasant class to form the new proletariat in the cities. Representing the underdogs redeemed by the revolution, they are supporters of the ruling party. Mexican sociologists say just as a man running for office in the United States must have an Anglo-Saxon face, his counterpart in Mexico must have a face suggestive of Indian origin. The members of the transitional group tend to be small farmers, ward heelers, merchants, and industrial workers. Their number is estimated at about 20 million, and their language is Mexicanized Spanish. The modern group wields the most influence in the economy. The upper middle class comes from this group and comprises the managers, teachers, lawyers, doctors, and skilled workers of the society. They are Spanish speaking and look upon the transitional world of *tortillas* and *frijoles* with disdain.

The Political System

Under the Constitution of 1917, Mexico is a federal republic with twenty-nine states. The national government is led by a president who is elected by direct popular vote for a term of six years and is limited to one term of office. The presidential powers are sweeping: for example, he can expropriate land by decree. The legislative branch consists of the Chamber of Deputies, which is elected for three years and the Senate, whose members serve a term of office of six years. The states have their separate constitutions, governments, and bicameral legislatures. Under the law, every eligible citizen must register, vote, and serve as an election official if so appointed. He can avoid this civic responsibility only for justifiable cause.

The only effective political party is the *Partido Revolucionario Institucional* (Institutional Revolutionary Party, or PRI).[21] The other parties have little appeal. The influence of the Communist party, for instance, is confined mostly to the state universities. A principal factor in Mexican political stability is the manner in which the PRI succeeds in reaching an accommodation with big business and organized labor. The conflict of opinion that takes place within the party is not commonly disseminated in the press. Some Mexican political scientists believe that the number of individuals voting for the PRI and the relative percentages are rigged so as to demonstrate a high national consensus. Insofar as private pressure groups are concerned, they do not exist in the way they do in the United States. The voice of public opinion is expressed within the party. It is that of business, professional organizations, organized labor, and politicians reflecting popular sentiment. Out of this expression emerges a national consensus that is probably among the highest in Latin America.

The Mexican style of governing tends to make the national legislature a rubber stamp. Accommodation of different points of view takes place not so much in the legislature as among the different power centers. The outcome manifests their relative strength in the PRI. Because many

[21] The party has been in power since 1929. In the national elections in 1964, its candidates took over every seat in the Federal Senate. In the 1967 elections for the Chamber of Deputies, it won every seat but one. The reason for the single failure was that the party withdrew its support from its candidate for that seat because of a scandal. To minimize the lopsided victories, minority parties are allocated some seats based on the votes they receive.

of these power centers are creatures of the government, their performance is expected to be consistent with the necessities of national development as interpreted by the chief of state. Based on their relative strength, the power clusters are allotted legislative posts. The particular senators and congressmen who will win an election are predetermined. The rapidly rising population restricts the number of legislative posts that can be used to attract young people to the party.

In the pursuit of economic interests, it is more important to know the person who can make the desired decision than to rely on delegated authority. Some matters have to be taken up directly with the President or with a cabinet minister. All that is necessary afterward is a telephone call to a particular subordinate. To zoom up to top levels, the astute employer develops a relationship with a well-placed *padriño* (godfather) in the government who can open up the right door.

There is considerable talk in Mexico about the alleged corruption in that country, allegedly pervading all ranks of political life up to the presidency. Some social scientists estimate that about 20 percent of the money in government contracts is used in influence peddling. The gifts take a variety of forms. A high-ranking official may find, for example, that an industry suddenly wants to buy his land at almost any price. Another company may give him securities of the firm or some attractive real estate. These tokens of gratitude may be offered for such reasons as speeding up a government decision, ignoring a high import duty, reducing a tax liability, or avoiding indictment, and they are generally considered to be part of the cost of operating a business. Mexicans who describe these practices do not appear to view them with calamity. In Mexico, one might say that corruption is a form of fringe benefit for workers.

The extent and effects of this corruption are difficult to assess. One of the foremost Mexican economists has made an evaluation and says that there are three different types of corruption. First, there is a good deal of such petty corruption as tipping a civil service employee at the border for getting things through customs with dispatch.[22] Donors accept the practice as a fact of life. Second, there is the corruption of businessmen, who consider giving bribes to labor leaders, government officials, and other businessmen a means of expediting decisions. They also use them to obtain import licenses and to avoid payment of duties. Third, there is the corruption that exists at high government levels, although in the economist's judgment, this type of corruption is on the decline. He further states that the Mexican is not as sensitive to the question of conflict of interest as Americans are. To reward a friend with a government contract is a friendly gesture. One who uses one's influence as a service expects to be paid for it. A bribe is thus simply a payment for services rendered.

---

[22] The border corruption is not petty in terms of volume. The Mexico City Chamber of Commerce reports that smuggling along the border is a $240 million a year business and that the government loses about $80 million annually in taxes on clandestine imports.

Indeed, it is a major instrument for the creation of wealth and a stimulant to economic growth. The businessman who through friends in government succeeds in obtaining needed goods more quickly and cheaply outside of quota restrictions may be behaving in a manner consistent with growth.

Mexicans do not appear to feel the sense of crisis that American specialists on their country do and seem amused by prognostications of doom. Corruption? No problem. The population explosion poses no problem for most Mexicans. The population rise is caused by more food and better health standards and will level off as Mexicans become middle class. Mexican democracy? There is democracy within the monopolistic political party, and the party reacts to the needs of the population.

The Mexicans attribute this American pessimism in the face of Mexican optimism to the differences in cultural characteristics and to the bias with which a person from an affluent society looks at a country at a lower stage of economic growth. According to the Mexicans, the American takes a cursory look through an American-oriented calculus, sees things that are different from the United States, then escalates from perplexity, to rejection, to forecast of doom. They also state that they are acquiring their own bias vis-à-vis other Latin American nations and are amazed by the arrogance of the military in these countries, whom they believe to be subsidized by the United States.

As for opinion making, the state controls the press indirectly by selling all the newsprint available, and it also controls TV and radio, the programs of which are devoid of politics. The Mexican newspaper with the biggest circulation is a sports daily. *La Prensa,* the second largest newspaper, concentrates on crime and sports. Because of a lack of correspondents, newspapers rely heavily on press services that do not reflect the opinion of particular Mexican publics.

Who, then, belongs to the Mexican opinion-making elite? The President, certainly, is the foremost member. So is the Minister of the *Gubernación,* the overall administrative body of the executive department. Others would include big industrialists, bankers, especially those of the Banco de México and Nacional Financiera, and the general secretary of the labor confederation. Their power is more diffused than that of the typical Latin American nation and is subject to the general upward movement of a dynamic society. Moreover, although Mexican elites employ government as a tool to promote their economic interests, their actions serve to raise the living standards of the people.

On a major new policy formulation, the interest groups are not initiators as much as reactors to the new line proposed by the government. A major innovation usually comes from the President and may be motivated by a desire to make his mark during six years of office or by a need to perpetuate the myth of the continuing revolution. Once the executive makes a decision deemed workable, acquisition of support for the new line unfolds in a well-planned and fully orchestrated manner. To avoid the appearance of arbitrariness, the government consults the interest groups and seeks their acquiescence. This consensus seeking is remarkable when one considers the absence of structures in Mexico that can impose restraints on the unilateral use of government power. A challenge to this cooperative organized power is coming from students, however.

Is there democracy in Mexico? If one looks for British-American political forms, democracy would be difficult to find. Fraudulent elections are common at the local level. The monopolistic political party at times even decides who its opponents will be in elections. This is not to say that the government is not responsive to the views of the Mexican people. Although the people may show some indifference and cynicism toward elections, they are aware that these elections are not part of the consensus process so much as its end result after the give-and-take that takes place within the party organization.

Economic growth may broaden party representation. According to Professor José Luis Reyna of the Colegio de México, the greater the economic well-being of Mexicans and the higher their level of education, the greater is their opposition to the PRI. He suggests that as living standards and education rise more Mexicans will shift their votes to a minority party.

The national government is making a substantial effort to raise living standards. It is heavily involved in economic development and does not appear to shy away from difficult decisions designed to generate growth. It controls prices, output, and specifies components of products that have to be manufactured in Mexico, and it owns a substantial part of industry. One senses that the people are aware of this involvement. They draw a distinction between the President, a symbol of the nation, and subordinate government officials, whom they look upon with cynicism. The government has made mistakes, such as trying to grow olives in Mexico, but it recoups with new successes. In contrast to most Latin American nations, Mexico is inclined to take the political risks of economic development.

Economic Overview

For over a decade, the Mexican gross national product has risen at an annual average rate of 6 percent, or 3 percent per capita. Prior to 1940, the product was rising about 2 percent yearly, hardly more than the population increase.[23] At the end of 1966, the GNP stood at 2.72 billion pesos, after rising by 7.5 percent from 1965. The population during the same year increased 3.6 percent, for a real increase of GNP per capita of 3.9 percent. By sector, the product went up 11 percent in manufacturing, 15 percent in construction, and 1.6 percent in agriculture. The index of

---

23 E. Pérez-López, *México: 50 Años de Revolución* (Mexico City: Fondo de Cultura, 1960).

industrial production in that year was 309.9 on a base of 100 for 1950.[24] The *Banco de México,* the national bank, and *Nacional Financiera,* a lending agency and supplier of industrial managers, are competent institutions that make a major contribution to economic growth.   One indicator of economic growth is the time gap between an idea and its execution. Values and pessimistic attitudes can affect this indicator, and deficiencies in training are also a factor.   These lending organizations contribute to making the Mexican gap not typical of Latin America.

Noise is also an index of economic growth.   In the traditional Mexican area as the dawn breaks, there is the noise of animals exclusively: hens, roosters, braying donkeys, and barking dogs.   As the sun rises, one hears the birds take over and the soft voices of Mexicans walking to their fields. With economic growth comes the siren of the new factory, the noise of motorcycles, the roar of Diesel trucks with open exhausts.

The Mexican economy before the revolution was dominated by large landholdings of private individuals and the church and by foreign interests who controlled extractive and basic industries.   The image of the affluent person was not a Mexican but a foreigner.   The revolution, however, shifted power to politicians who identified with the population, a change that is reflected in Mexican art.   The *ejido* land system was instituted, based on the mystique that every Mexican had the right to work his own piece of land.   Under the system an individual is assigned a particular parcel, but he cannot pass it down as an inheritance.   The revolution also created a base for an innovative political party that claimed to be the champion of the people's aspirations.   Although the revolution initially increased tensions with the United States, the subsequent rapprochement opened the northern border to people, technology, and capital.   In short, the revolution provided a cooperative political base for an economic takeoff, a base that furnished successful economic policies in export-import trade, infrastructure, and land reform.   The demand surge caused by World War II furnished the final booster.

As in Latin America generally, the focal points of economic development are the principal cities.   The foremost is the capital, Mexico City.   It is in these cities that the visible evidences of growth are found.   The dilapidated condition of the rural towns, on the other hand, and their level of sanitation and personal hygiene are worse than that of the interior rural villages of Sicily.   The different examples of successful regional economic development reflect dissimilarities in leadership, location, and history.   The three principal cities—Guadalajara, Monterrey, and Mexico City—demonstrate these differences.   Guadalajara represents the most traditional type of growth.   Its economy has an agricultural base that produces above subsistence levels and stimulates small shop manufacturing and retail trade.   Its principal industries, food, shoes, textiles, and

---

24 Bank of Mexico, *Informe Anual* (Mexico City: Bank of Mexico, 1966).

construction materials, reflect this type of growth. Its leadership comes from the public sector and from top political leaders of its state, Jalisco. Monterrey, with its long ties to the United States and the Mexican capital, was propelled into a type of industrial growth without an agricultural base by a small group of families who were highly intelligent and highly aware of their personal interests. The development of Mexico City reflects the leadership of the nation's top political leaders and intellectuals. It has no agricultural base. The visible results of these styles differ also. Guadalajara reflects the nature and tastes of its Catholic people. Monterrey is a drab industrial town. Mexico City is a showpiece of intellect.

The common characteristic of these cities is an exploding population. The population of Guadalajara almost doubled during the decade 1957–1967. Hunger pushes the sons of marginal rural workers toward the city, where they congregate at the public markets and at the entrance of the city, seeking employment in loading and unloading trucks. They are a primary source of rising crime rates.

Thirty percent of the Mexican labor force is located in the Federal District, where the Mexican capital is located. Its population, which was approximately 2 million in 1940, climbed to over 7 million by 1967. With some 250,000 motor vehicles being driven in a city surrounded by mountains and the rapidly rising number of factories, the city promises to become the most polluted one in the world. It contains 30 percent of the total secondary school enrollment and more than half of the secondary school graduates. About a third of the professional and technical employees of Mexico live there.

Like other Latin American capitals, Mexico City attracts rural migrants, most of whom end up in peripheral districts of the city. One such place is Ciudad Netzahucayotl just outside the city limits, where an estimated 500,000 persons live. There is no water, sewerage, transportation, or police. Migrants buy a lot on the dry salt bed of a former lake, put up a shack out of scrap material, and live a life of daily improvisation.

In a real way, the ability of a nation to grow is reflected in what is happening outside the hothouse atmosphere of the capital city. To assess this capacity, it is useful to choose in each country some area at a low stage of economic growth that is not dominated by the capital city but whose economic and human resources have a growth potential. Morelia in the state of Michoacán is such a place. It does not attract tourists to the degree the capital city does. There are relatively more poor persons in Morelia, but far fewer than on the Yucatán peninsula. Lastly, Morelia has an agricultural base as a springboard for growth.

Since 1940 the core of its growth has been in agricultural industry, including vegetable oils, canning, wood products, rice, and wheat mills. This rising economic activity has triggered construction activity and the production of construction material. Of the sixty major employers in

Morelia, five manufacture construction material. From 1940 until 1967, the population of the city more than trebled, going from 44,000 to 140,000. During the same period, agricultural industry doubled in employment, and the social overhead industries, such as construction, electricity and gas production, went up 175 percent. In addition, typical of contemporary economic development, services trebled in the same period. As the level of economic activity increased, the portion of the population in the labor force rose from 28 to 35 percent.

For the nation as a whole, the major problem for economic growth is the population explosion, the biggest in the world.[25] It poses a threat to the increase in per capita income and the rise in tangible capital per head. The population goes up fastest in rural areas, where resources to cope with it are more scarce. Mexican economists estimate that some 2 million persons can leave the countryside without any appreciable effect on agricultural production. By fragmentizing the land and by stifling incentives to increase productivity, the *ejido* system of land tenure introduced by the Mexican revolution may contribute to the problem of modernizing the rural area. The burgeoning rural population reduces the size of farm units, and these smaller parcels of land mean more inefficient methods of production. Some enterprising farmers, however, put together economical land units by the use of subterfuge and are thus able to produce efficiently. Some Mexican economists—often orthodox Catholics or Marxists—scoff at the concern for the population pressure on the land.

A general feature of life in the rural area is that its active population works only during the growing season. In some instances, as in the case of the Toluca knitting mills, rural Mexicans do find off-season employment. When such work is not available, it is possible for the government to take advantage of this seasonal idleness by putting the people to work on capital projects that will help to increase capital formation and raise human capacities. Mexico has tried this approach to rural development through the combined efforts of government agencies and private foundations. By involving the people in the planning, an effort was made to motivate them to participate in the projects. The people of a village in the state of Guerrero were given extra food rations to plan and construct a bridge, school, or road. Or they might have been encouraged to build a latrine in return for a discount on commercial fertilizer. Done on a voluntary basis and without substantial funds, these were token efforts, however. Follow-through is necessary in resources, talent, and education.

The low level of rural development is a reflection of regional dualism.[26]

---

[25] The estimate for 1970 is 50 million. I suspect that the population increase is affected partly by the rate with which the Mexican census taker discovers remote rural areas.
[26] Some rural villages are so removed from lines of transportation and communication that to all intents and purposes the federal government does not rule over them. Rather, they are governed by local leaders who are challenged occasionally by federal troops.

The per capita income of the Federal District is over ten times that of such states as Guerrero and Oaxaca. The disparity is not between north and south so much as between highlands and lowlands, and it is heightened by Mexico City's proximity and transportation links to the United States border. There is evidence, however, that these regional differences are narrowing.

In an effort to step up rural development, the Mexican government raised public investment in agriculture by 40 percent in 1968 over the prior period. The overall $2 billion investment program represents an overall increase of some 11 percent, which was intended to obtain the capital formation necessary for a growth rate in excess of 6 percent. The increased agricultural investment was apportioned to such projects as irrigation, farm extension services, transportation facilities, health and welfare services, and industrial promotion. Mexican policy makers anticipate a decline in the rural population at a rate of about 1 percent annually. Their aspiration is a drop to about 25 percent of the total population of the nation. They anticipate an increase in the rural exodus as agriculture shifts from subsistence farming to crop diversification.

Mexico has an economic planning office, but its members are not inclined to label what they do as planning. They collect a variety of statistics and prepare economic projections that cover the public sector only. They hope to include private sector analysis some day, but their big problem is to ascertain what in Mexico is public and what is private. The casualness of Mexican planners contrasts with the high-level cerebrations of a country such as India. The nationalized industries in Mexico such as oil refining are under the administration of an organization called the *Patrimonio Nacional* whose chief executive officer is a member of the cabinet. The planners are primarily concerned with what role government-owned firms should play in the future, how to improve their efficiency, and what standards to use in measuring their performance.

As in Latin America generally, foreign capital enters the Mexican economy from three sources: private investors, lending institutions abroad, and the United States government. Mexican planners do not have the problem of shopping for funds from the last two sources as do most other Latin American nations. Mexico is more wary of American government aid, however, than are other Latin American nations. This wariness is reflected in her attitude toward the Alliance for Progress, and the CIA revelations increased it. The purpose of American government financing in Mexico is a puzzle. For example, financial assistance is given to an American educational institution in Mexico City, the majority of whose students are American citizens. This support is said to be given to offset Marxism at the college level.

Mexican policy makers were asked for their views on a variety of economic questions. On the subject of a Latin American common market, they were skeptical as to whether it would work, saying that Mexico is too diversified and growing too rapidly compared to other Latin American countries. Because of the high disparity in economic development, they felt that for such an idea to succeed, other countries would first have to develop basic economic structures. What can one get out of a banana economy in exchange? "Bananas," stated an economist. He denigrated the idea of integration as the metaphysical economics of American politicians.

These same individuals were also asked to account for Mexico's rapid economic growth compared to the rest of Latin America. All of them cited the revolution as providing the necessary economic and political base. The breakdown of the Spanish hacienda and its replacement by the *ejido* were mentioned as the critical factors in this overall reform.[27] In order of frequency, other reasons mentioned were the long political stability of Mexico in comparison with other Latin American nations, the relatively more efficient public administration, and the common border with the United States. The judgment on this common border was that its advantages have outweighed its disadvantages, the latter of which have been effectively held in check by the Mexican government.

Some of these specialists were skeptical about the ability of the Mexican economy to maintain its high rate of economic growth. The loose tax system, it was said, does not impose sufficient taxes to support the rising population. Moreover, public and private savings are declining relative to the national income. It was also pointed out that as firms become increasingly controlled by Mexicans, there is a rise in their tendency to distribute earnings. As indicated earlier, the issue over which Mexican specialists disagree the most is that of the impact of the population rise on future growth.

Professor Edmundo Flores is a prominent Mexican economist whose views command respect. Flores belittles the pessimism of American specialists who believe the Mexican economy is headed for trouble. He thinks that their view that Mexico has to choose between public and private enterprise is like asking a man to choose between his wife and mistress. When asked to account for Mexican economic growth, he says the foremost reason was the confiscatory nature of the land reform. An enormous number of persons were suddenly given land without a tax burden being imposed on the economy. Before, a handful of individuals had been obtaining 90 percent of the income. The distribution created a surge in demand because of new incentives to improve the land and political pressure to increase rural overhead through such projects as roads and irrigation. The policy was effective because it was quick and massive.

The former profits of the landlord began to flow to the government.

---

[27] Mexicans are becoming disenchanted about an ideological favorite in their country: the co-operatives. The criticism is that they are operated by cliques pursuing private interests. Co-operatives by law must belong to one of thirty-two federations. The federations in turn have to associate with a confederation under the control of the secretary of commerce. Most are of the producer variety. A common characteristic is a reluctance to pay dues.

Formerly a hostile force in society, the poor began to support the government. With such a wedding, the revolutionary party obtained backing in return for its social and economic programs for the advancement of the people. In the Flores view, the ensuing flight of foreign capital was a blessing in disguise because it forced the creation of an indigenous capitalist class. A chain reaction followed. The surge in demand boosted the demand for construction, which in turn increased the demand for complementary goods and services. The rise in consumption produced political stability, which encouraged talented individuals to migrate from Europe to Mexico. The political deification of the Indian led to the development of a $9 billion tourist business. Americans in the hundreds of thousands, with no knowledge of the American Indian, thus come to Mexico annually to learn about the Mexican Indian.

Flores seemed to be saying that what Americans see as a weakness in the Mexican system of political patronage is actually a strength in economic growth. He implied that the catalyst needed for Latin American growth is a sudden and massive land reform of a confiscatory nature or one subsidized by a foreign power. Flores also indicated that the Alliance for Progress serves to prevent an evolution similar to that of Mexico and that it promotes the interests of the United States government and the power structure of Latin American societies. He appeared to be optimistic about future Mexican growth. In his view, it will be sustained by the development of rural areas and by the emergence of a welfare state.

Professor Flores believes that American pessimists do not fully understand Mexican values. To try to predict the future outcome of Mexican economic growth, one has to become involved with the complex of values behind decisions. This is not easy because of the character of the Mexican. He is not straightforward. He feels that it is a sign of strength not to allow the world to penetrate his being; to reveal oneself fully is a manifestation of weakness. To predict his future behavior in the context of such thinking is difficult unless one is Mexican too.[28]

The impact of a government responsive to the needs of its people that Flores refers to can be better grasped by placing Mexican change in a historical context. During the Indian civilization, and more so after the Spanish Conquest, the government was a privileged caste supported by levies on the people. Taxes progressively mounted, committing the Indian to slow starvation. On an average, twelve Indians contributed to the support of one member of the privileged caste. The producer was thus a subject person, and the nonproducer was his superior. The Spaniards inherited this institution and assimilated the nonproducers into their public administration. This oppression was the basis for the revolutionary upheavals, which produced the change in the image of government.[29]

[28] For a view of Mexican economic growth by Mexican economists, see Enrique Pérez-López et al., *Mexico's Recent Economic Growth: The Mexican View* (Austin: University of Texas Press, 1968).

[29] For an analysis of the original text of early Mexican tax law, see Birgitta Leander, *Códice de Otlazpán* (Mexico City: Instituto Nacional de Antropología e Historia, 1967).

Mexican Enterprises

The typical big firm of Mexico has certain characteristics. It is likely to have a close association with a company in the United States, even in instances where the plant is operated and owned by Mexican citizens. A strong impetus behind the association with American firms is that the innovator in Mexico runs into technical and financial difficulties and decides to look for assistance from others in his industry. Many of these firms have direct retail associations because of weak wholesale links in Mexico or because the entrepreneur who founded them may have had his start as a trader. The expansion rate of the firm is likely to be considerable. In fact, Mexican firms are not expanding, but exploding; the restraint on their production volume is not markets but supplies and equipment.[30] In addition, the labor organization in the firm is likely to be employer-dominated. He may dominate simply because of his greater power or because of the susceptibility of the labor leader to bribes. Further, because the government has considerable latitude under the law in making administrative decisions, the firm makes a special effort to curry its favor in order to insure against arbitrary acts. As for its labor force, the firm prefers to train young persons of above-average intelligence with no more than a primary education. Lastly, the stock of many of these firms is subscribed to heavily by the government. Accordingly, it is difficult to draw a neat distinction between the private and public sectors of the economy and between who is a government worker and who is not.

These enterprises are crucial to the economic development of Mexico. They have considerable know-how and labor forces of sufficient size to develop diverse human capacities. Because the law requires that 60 percent of a firm's supplies must come from Mexican producers, these firms train and develop other manufacturers to supply such parts. By so doing, they achieve the two development goals of raising human capacities and broadening economic structures.

The Ford Motor Car Company in Mexico is typical of this kind of firm. The company develops its suppliers to meet the 60 percent standard. In the conviction that the payoff from occupational training is more immediate, the firm prefers hiring workers with no industrial experience. Its labor force therefore consists of a young, carefully selected elite with rarely more than a primary school education. The minimum starting age is eighteen, and the average age of the blue-collar work force is twenty-three. Wages vary from 40 to 100 pesos a day (one peso = 12.5 cents). The company resists efforts of the union in the plant to have a voice in the selection of employees.[31] The function of the labor organization is con-

---

[30] It was not uncommon for the plant managers to whom the author spoke in Mexico to state that their annual expansion rate was over 15 percent.

[31] As an indication of the relative power of the union, a company official stated in a discussion that if the union did not consent to a discharge, the company would go ahead and fire the employee anyway, with or without severance pay. Some firms in Mexico concede to the union the right of recommending candidates, with ultimate choice resting with the company.

fined mostly to handling worker grievances. Personnel in the top and middle management positions are about 80 percent Mexican. The engine and foundry plant started with a cadre of fifty American managers and technicians in 1961, a number that was reduced to four within three years. As in the case of blue-collar workers, young faces are very much in evidence.

The company has no problem recruiting employees. In fact, it has difficulty in resisting pressures from individuals seeking employment. Prospective workers are given a battery of tests to measure aptitudes, including comprehension, manual dexterity, and logical thinking. Interviews follow with the hiring supervisor. The firm estimates that one person is hired out of every forty interviewed.

Plant executives concede that the plant operates at a level of average costs higher than would be the case if the operations were located in the United States. The higher costs are not ascribed to labor charges, however, but to nonlabor costs deriving from government regulations prescribing local purchases; higher costs of machinery and equipment, which are common in developing nations; and the higher cost per unit of low-scale production. Accordingly, an engine costs about $500 to make in Mexico compared to $300 if the same engine were made in the United States. The relatively low degree of technological sophistication serves, however, as a means of reconciling technology with the existing level of skills.

A Mexican employer is required by law to belong to an appropriate industrial or commercial association. The industrial employer affiliates on a local basis with the *Confederación de Cámaras de Industria* (Confederation of Industrial Chambers of Commerce, or CONCAMIN). If in commerce, an employer affiliates with the *Confederación Nacional de Cámaras de Comercio* (National Confederation of Chambers of Commerce). If the number of enterprises in an industry does not warrant a local association, the employer belongs to a catch-all organization called the *Cámara Nacional de la Industria de Transformación* (National Chamber of Manufacturing Industry), which is an ardent supporter of the government. It is reluctant to see employers leave and affiliate with the regular associations.

A voluntary organization of bankers and industrialists is called the *Confederación Patronal de la República Mexicana* (Employer Confederation of the Mexican Republic, or COPARMEX). Having grown out of the intense labor unrest of the 1930s, COPARMEX is now an enormous organization that specializes in the international problems of firms, wage studies, management processes, and labor problems and political lobbying. Its estimated membership is about 13,000 employers, who pay a membership fee ranging from $250 to $7,000 a year.

These organizations are highly influential in the Mexican economy. If the government fixes prices in some industries, they are first consulted.

In industries where there is no price control, the employers get together and do their own price fixing. They have caused a shift in the government's attitude toward employers from one of suspicion to assistance, in which the employer is considered a client. What the employer does not have in votes at the polling booth he has in money and effective diplomacy. What is the effect of such a wedding of employer and government? For one, it tends to discourage structural reforms in the economy. The tax loopholes, for example, are likely to remain. Second, the collaboration tends to restrict the introduction of new products and new entrepreneurship. Third, economic planning moves in the direction of indicative planning of France, suggesting the amount of public investment necessary to achieve a predetermined level of economic growth. In sum, the association produces stability and little likelihood of drastic change. The conservatism is likely to continue indefinitely, barring new pressures that may arise from the rural population. The employer is cozy with organized labor also. As an example, COPARMEX took the leaders of organized labor on a trip to Europe.

Population and Labor Force Characteristics

Since its days of Indian civilization, Mexico has experienced periods of dramatic economic growth and equally spectacular collapse. These precipitous rises and falls in the economy have been attended by sharp changes in the size of the population. Historically, the Mexicans have taken the rise in productivity in more children and not in more income per person. This choice has been followed by downturns that were signalled by agricultural crises and the weakening of health and sanitation standards.

At the zenith of Indian culture, there were approximately the same number of people in Mexico as there are today. The decimation began with the Spanish Conquest, the population declining 2.2 million in less than 300 years. At the turn of the nineteenth century, it started to rise rapidly and then leveled off at the beginning of the revolution. During the revolutionary period from 1910 to 1921, the population declined by 1 million. In 1940 another accelerated rise began. By 1964 the population had doubled, and by 1985 it is expected to double once again. The death rate has declined since 1950 from 43.8 to 23.6 per thousand. Whether Mexico can avoid its historical fate remains to be seen. There are individuals in responsible positions who count on a rising middle class to stem the population explosion.

The gyrations in population and growth have left pockets of chronically depressed areas. There are clusters of Indians living at the same level of consumption that prevailed during the time of the Aztecs. Education is more a phenomenon of cities than of these areas. A third of the labor force in the countryside is unemployed and presents a source of future tensions. The population rise has caused a sharp decline in the percentage of the people participating in the labor force. In 1930 the figure was 72 percent and by 1960 it had declined to 52 percent. At present, it stands at 33 percent. The population rise means that about 1.3 million more Mexicans will require public services each year and that 450,000 new jobs will have to be created annually so as not to aggravate unemployment. The burden is reflected also in the decline of savings and family income per child.

Mexico presently is a net exporter of manpower, principally to the United States. Approximately 43,000 immigrants cross the border annually, most of them blue-collar workers. In addition, some 60,000 daily cross the frontier for employment in border towns. Considerable illegal immigration into the United States takes place. The record for the period 1950–1955 shows that 3.8 million Mexicans returned to their own country.[32]

The government has no official policy on birth control. Mr. Luis Echeverria Alvarez, the President inaugurated in 1970, took a position as secretary of the government against government sponsored birth-control programs. He is quoted as saying: "We have to populate our country and we have to have faith in our youth and our children." [33] The official reluctance toward population planning is not concerned so much with social attitudes as with difficulties of follow-through if such a policy were instituted. A private effort in birth control is an organization called the Planned Parenthood Association, founded by an American woman. Staffed by Mexican physicians, the organization developed a list of 13,000 patients within 8 years after its founding. Ninety-five percent of its donors are non-Mexican. The women who come to the clinics hear about them by word of mouth.

Economic growth is associated with shifts in the occupational distribution of the labor force. Compare the figures in Table 15 with those of the United States to see in what direction the Mexican data are likely to continue to move. The relative percentage of a particular occupational group in the labor force can decline, whereas its absolute number may rise. For example, the relative number of indirect production workers declined during the decade 1950–1960 while their absolute numbers were rising.

Another way to observe changing labor force patterns is through trends in employment status. For example, in 1940, some 42 percent were categorized as employers or self-employed. By 1960 the figure dropped to approximately 34 percent. At the same time, the number of clerical workers rose from 9 to 14 percent. These figures are for the nation as a whole. In the Federal District in 1960, 32 percent of the work force was classified as clerical workers.

Approximately one-third of the Mexican labor force is unionized. The

---

[32] Most of the figures in this section have been obtained through personal interviews.
[33] *The New York Times*, November 9, 1969, p. 26.

trade-union members are concentrated in mining, petroleum, transportation, manufacturing, and the government bureaucracy in such big cities as Mexico City, Monterrey, and Guadalajara. The most powerful labor organization is the Confederation of Mexican Workers (*Confederación Trabajadores Mejicanos,* or CTM). The organization claims about 1.5 million members, or about half of the country's organized workers. Founded in 1934, it has as affiliates 26 national unions, 29 state federations, and about 100 regional and municipal federations. The CTM is the labor voice of the PRI. For two decades, beginning in the early 1930s, the confederation was affiliated with the communist World Federation of Trade Unions.

TABLE 15 □ Percentage Distribution and Percentage Rise in Absolute Numbers of the Mexican Labor Force, 1950–1960

	Relative Distribution of Labor Force		*Percentage Increase in Absolute Numbers*
Occupation	*1950*	*1960*	
Professional, technical, kindred	2.50	3.64	4.39
Managers, except farming	.79	.85	.16
Clerical and kindred	4.66	6.16	7.60
Sales and kindred	7.83	8.88	13.88
Agricultural workers	58.16	54.05	.75
Mine, petroleum, gas workers	.98	.94	.58
Direct production workers	14.09	15.63	1.56
Indirect production workers	3.83	2.96	2.28
Service and kindred occupations	7.18	6.89	.92

Source: Colegio de México, Department of Economic and Demographic Studies, 1967.

Since the passing of its founder, the extraordinary figure Vicente Lombardo Toledano, the confederation has left the WFTU and affiliated with the Western-oriented International Confederation of Free Trade Unions and its regional arm in Mexico, *Organización Regional,* or ORIT. The CTM is now a respectable organization, and its top ranking officers are important personages in the party.

In common with other Latin American countries, Mexico has many other confederations. Second to the CTM is the Regional Federation of Workers and Farmers (*Confederación Revolucionaria de Obreros y Campesinos,* or CROC). With about 300,000 members, its strength is concentrated in the states of Baja California, Sonora, Veracruz, and the Federal District. It is a strong force among textile and transportation workers. Next in importance is the Mexican Regional Federation of Workers (*Confederación Regional Obrera Mejicana,* or CROM), which has some 200,000 members. The other confederations are of lesser importance.

There are important independent national unions in addition to the three major federations. The Federation of Unions of State Workers, of which the Teachers' Union is a part, ranks among the most important. Others of similar influence are the Railway Workers, the Mining and

Metallurgical Workers, and unions in the telephone, electrical, and entertainment industries.

There is no labor movement in Mexico in the sense of a unified group of workers conscious of their power and pursuing common political and economic objectives. In 1966 an organization was created to bring together the different confederations. Called the Congress of Labor, it is supposed to be an experiment in political influence.

At the company level are three general types of unions. There is the company-dominated union found in big firms. At the other extreme are the leftist red unions, more militant and more ideological. This type represents only a small minority of the workers, but it has a higher degree of rank-and-file participation. Red unionism promotes intransigence. Thus, in Monterrey in 1967, a large plant was shut down for forty-two days before a new contract was negotiated. When the union threatened to strike again fifty days later, the firm offered to deliver the factory to the workers. There were no takers. Between these two extremes are the so-called white unions, which are not controlled by employers and which try to do a businesslike job of representing rank-and-file interests.

In explaining Mexican trade unionism, a distinction must be drawn between the behavior of top-level officials and those representing the rank and file. The high-level organizations are administered by men with political aspirations who are inclined to use their organizations to serve these aspirations. As an example of such domination, the secretary general of a national union expelled a subordinate for having run on the ticket of a rival party. From time to time, the rank-and-file members rebel against such heavy-handedness. In the instance cited, the expelled official was reinstated by a membership vote.

Mexican labor officials are not immune from the values of the society in which they operate. It is alleged that they indulge in corrupt practices, such as selling jobs in the Mexican oil monopoly, PEMEX. Doubtlessly, some are opportunists. To assess their style, one has to take into account the weakness of their position with employers. It is difficult to develop a direct bargaining relationship with astute managers of huge corporations who offer highly desired jobs to workers who are living close to subsistence levels. Accordingly, the labor officials improvise their successes outside of the context of a bargaining relationship and become the children of government and the instruments of politicians. They become so heavily subsidized by government officials, employers, and party leaders that they have no independent voice.

Mexican labor law rests on highly detailed constitutional guarantees of worker rights that were set forth in the Constitution of 1917. These guarantees cover such matters as work shifts, overtime pay, minimum wages, welfare payments, profit sharing, and the right to strike. Eight hours is prescribed as the maximum workday. Overtime thereafter has to be paid on the basis of triple time. Heavy controls are also placed on the work of women and minors. For example, women are forbidden to work in commercial establishments after ten o'clock at night. The constitution also provides for compulsory rest on the seventh day and payment of wages in legal tender as often as once a week, with such payment prohibited in places of recreation. The specific amount of the minimum wage is determined by national wage commissions of the government. The constitution states that a worker can be dismissed only for just cause. If just cause is not found to exist, the employer has to reinstate him or pay three months' wages. The worker can also demand 3 months' wages if he leaves because of ill treatment or if his employer mistreats his wife, parents, children, or brothers.

From these constitutional guarantees a comprehensive labor code was passed in 1931. The labor code contains at this time some 700 provisions that deal with such matters as labor contracts, minimum wages, hours of work, holidays, strikes, labor courts, occupational risks, apprenticeship regulations, rules for the hiring of agricultural laborers, domestics, seamen, flight crews, and workers in the artisan industries. Typical of Latin cultures, this web of regulations is so intricate that one questions to what extent they are taken seriously.

Profit sharing is compulsory in Mexico, but new firms are exempt for a period ranging from two to four years. Although the formula is complex, the plan generally provides for the employee's shares to be based on the profits remaining after the deduction of taxes plus an allowance of 30 percent of profits for ploughing back into the enterprise. Shares are based on the number of days worked during the year and on the salary of the employee. The market for the employer's products causes the profit share to fluctuate, but the plan is often sold to workers on the basis of their productivity. They generally expect to get an annual share that approximates a month's wage.[34] The plan provides some employers with the incentive to come up with profits as close to zero as possible, thus providing employment for imaginative accountants.

In addition to these labor laws, there are similarly complex statutes on social insurance. Benefits include payments for occupational disability; pensions for total and permanent disability; maternity care; old-age pensions with provisions for early retirement on up to 67 percent of average wages; a marriage dowry based on the bridegroom's wages; and death benefits, which include a burial payment of one month's salary and pensions for widows and orphans. Big companies supplement these benefits with those of their own—death benefit plans, for example, because Mexican blue-collar workers rarely carry life insurance. A pension plan may also be offered, which employers use as an inducement to persuade a worker of low productivity to retire. There are also medical plans, mostly for white-collar employees who generally prefer not to use government social insurance for fear of losing status.

[34] According to a management consultant firm in Mexico, the profit share amounts to 8 percent of annual wages on the average.

These labor standards are administered by the traditional type of government agency, including the Departments of Labor, Health, and Industry and Commerce, and by quasi-independent organizations. The latter include the Social Security Institute for workers in the private sector, and the enormous ISSSTE for employees in the public sector of the economy.

The extent to which the Mexican laboring classes have benefited from economic growth is a matter of deep controversy. The average monthly earnings of workers are rising at a rate of 5 percent annually, a figure the PRI cites as proof of the success of the revolution. There is, however, a considerable disparity in the wage scales. Although precise data are not available, it is estimated that a worker in a big firm may earn three times as much as a worker in a small shop. The labor office of the United States Embassy in Mexico estimates that the monthly wages of unskilled workers in industry vary from $20 to $100. The higher paid worker also works shorter hours. The legal workweek is 48 hours, but the large firms are on a 40-hour week.

As for the actual living standards, at least a semiskilled worker in a large firm eats well. As mentioned above, a variety of social insurance benefits are available to him, and he is paid a month's bonus at the end of the year. Housing is another matter, however. The government states that 63 percent of the housing in Mexico City is below minimum standards, which in effect means that almost the entire working class lives in inadequate housing.

The rural population—half of the Mexican people—lags behind the urban population in living standards. Only a beginning has been made in improving remote areas, such as building feeder roads and making investments to attract industry. Social insurance benefits are slowly being extended to farmers.

The principal expenditures of the Mexican population as a whole can be broken down as follows: food, 42 percent; housing, 15 percent; clothing, 8 percent; household goods, 9 percent; amusement, 3 percent; other, 23 percent. This distribution is based on an allocation of an average monthly family income of $135. In less developed areas, the food component increases sharply. For example, in the city of Morelia, where the average monthly family income is $85, approximately 55 percent of it is spent on food. In remote areas, the proportion becomes even greater. In fact, if Mexican families were divided into three groups, the amount of income being spent on food by the bottom third would be about 80 percent.[35]

A controversy exists as to whether the number of poor is rising. No

[35] The figures on Mexico are from a sample study made by the Departamento de Muestreo, Secretaría de Industria y Comercio. The population of each city covered was divided into three sections: poor, middle class, and rich. The percentage of the sample from each component varies. The percentage of income spent by the poor on food ranges from 17 percent in the Federal District to 66 percent in Veracruz. For the city of Morelia, the distribution was 44, 35, and 21, respectively.

continuing studies exist on income changes at the base of the population. What has to be done is to define poverty and to estimate the number of persons falling below the poverty line. A fair judgment is that although the relative number of the poor is declining, the absolute number is rising. The crux of the controversy centers on the impact of the population explosion, which can be revealed in hypothetical figures. Let us assume that the population in 1940 amounted to 100 and that 50 lived in poverty. Twenty years later the population numbered 200. The number of poor rose to 75, but their relative number declined from 50 percent to 37 percent. Critics of Mexican economic growth concentrate on the 75 and sympathizers on the 37 percent. Another factor is also at play. The rural migrant to the city who previously received little or no wages, shows up in the statistics as receiving a minimum wage. Because the minimum wage has risen in step with the rise in prices and the industrialization process has created an increasing number of persons earning the minimum, the misleading conclusion is drawn that the poor of Mexico are falling behind.

Another approach to the controversy is to look at the gross national product (GNP) in the agricultural sector. At constant prices, the increase in the agricultural GNP was approximately half that of the entire product during the period 1940 to 1960. During the same time, the number of persons actively engaged in agriculture increased 60 percent even though their relative numbers declined. At the same time, the percentage of the total population consuming bread went up from 45 to 66.[36] The low-income groups of Mexico comprise small farmers, rural laborers, and unskilled industrial workers. The preponderant number of the latter category are recent rural migrants to the city. Keeping in mind that the minimum wage during the same period rose about the same amount as consumer prices, what do these facts imply? Again, some poor or the children of some of the poor have gone over the poverty line. They have shifted from tortillas to bread, from huaraches to shoes, from pulque to beer, and from burros to buses. They have not done as well in housing because of the burgeoning population and the movement of rural individuals into the slums of the cities. At the same time, however, principally in the rural areas, the absolute number of poor has risen mainly because they have elected to consume their increased product in terms of more babies.

In an attempt to control the rising costs of low-income groups, Mexican law establishes maximum prices on such basic commodities as cereals, cooking oil, coffee, meat, cigarettes, soap, bread, and milk.

[36] The GNP figures are from *Projections of Supply of and Demand for Agricultural Products in Mexico*, Bank of Mexico, August 1966. The population rise in the rural area is from *Nacional Financiera*, 1965. The actual rise in the agricultural product in millions is from 2,670 pesos to 4,260 pesos. Agricultural productivity per land area has gone up in Mexico, but is still far below American standards. The main crop, corn, has an average yield of 9 bushels per acre compared to yields 8 times as much in the United States. Interestingly enough, the increase in yield matches the population rise. Again, the rural Mexican tends to use his increased productivity not in rising out of poverty but in more children.

Prices are based on production costs and a "fair rate of profit." The law establishes criteria for determining costs and a price control commission composed of bank, industrial, agricultural, government, and labor representatives establishes prices. Sanctions include fines, jail sentences, and the closing of establishments.

Another factor that beclouds the issue of poverty is the paradox of the increased visibility of the poor. In the traditional stage of economic takeoff, the poor are hidden in isolated villages, which may take several hours to reach by foot or by mule, a fact that may discourage even rural sociologists. At the start of economic growth, however, the poor oblige social scientists by camping at the periphery of cities. They can then be seen from a comfortable auto.

In summary, how far down the economic pyramid is Mexican economic growth paying off? The payoff decreases the further down one goes on the economic scale and stops at the level of the semiskilled worker in large enterprises. For the small landholder in the rural area and the unskilled migrant to the urban center, the gains, if any, are modest. For unless the migrant is young, tests high in intelligence, has a primary school education, and is lucky enough to land a job in a big firm, he does not participate in the benefits of economic growth. If fortunate enough, he may end up making cement blocks at a dollar a day. Lastly, the relative number of Mexicans in poverty is declining, but the absolute number is rising.

Education

If present trends continue, about half of Mexico's citizens will in the near future be of primary and secondary school age. The population explosion is thus placing a burden on the country's education resources and on those who work and provide such resources. To cope with this problem, the nation has been expanding its educational system to train an increasing number of students.

The Human Resources Office of the Bank of Mexico estimates that in 1960, 2 percent of the gross national product was going into private and public education. By 1965 the figure had risen to 2.9 percent. The federal government is devoting about 18 percent of the national budget to education. Of this amount, 47 percent goes to primary instruction, 11 percent to secondary schools, and 11 percent to college preparatory, normal schools, and universities. The remainder is allotted to school construction and other educational services.

Mexican primary education begins at age six and continues for eight years. The nation places a high priority on getting all children of primary school age in school. In 1965, 6.6 million children were enrolled, or 68 percent of the primary school population, a percentage that is rising, despite the population boom. The figure for 1960 had been 64 percent.

Only 40 percent of the rural children were in school in 1965, however; most of them terminate primary education at the end of three years, and the number of terminations is rising.[37]

A manual issued to primary school teachers states a philosophy of education in terms of six fundamental objectives: protection of health and improvement of physical vigor; inquiry into the environment and into the exploitation of natural resources; understanding and betterment of social life; creative activity; practical activities; and acquisition of the elements of culture. Within each of these areas, the manual states that the following must be developed: knowledge, skill, capacity, experience, and attitude. From this structure, the teacher is expected to develop a lesson plan on a particular topic. The theory behind the six objectives is that the child learns through such goals. The child's advancement to the next grade is based on a final examination.[38]

Mexican secondary education is divided into two stages: a lower one of three years followed by a college preparatory course of two years. In 1960 there were 355,000 enrolled in the secondary schools. By 1965 the figure had risen to 399,000, or 6.5 percent more than the rise in population. The absolute number represents 19 percent of the total in the eligible age group. In 1960, 68 percent of the primary school graduates were enrolled in the secondary schools, including technical institutions. Five years later, the figure had gone up to 75 percent.

In 1965 there were eighty-two institutions of higher learning in Mexico. Enrollment in these institutions increased from 25,000 in 1940 to 131,000 in 1965. In 1960 only about 1 percent of the twenty-three-year-olds in the population had a college degree, but this figure is expected to reach 7 percent by 1975.[39] The number of persons with professional and technical qualifications is increasing at an annual rate of 7 percent, the preponderant number of them (74 percent) going into occupations in commerce and services, including the government. A high proportion of those in industry and construction are employed in the Federal District.

Mexican universities offer the following specializations: natural science, applied science, agriculture, economic and administrative science, medicine, social science (including law), and the humanities (including education). Engineering is also offered, as in European universities. The average course of study runs for five years. Course enrollments, in de-

[37] The 1965 figures are from the Centro de Estudios Educativos, AC, Mexico City. All other figures are from Victor L. Urquidi and Adrián Lajous Vargas, *La Educación Superior, La Ciencia y la Tecnología en el Desarrollo Económico de México* (Mexico City: El Colegio de México, 1967), unless otherwise indicated. I was not able to obtain a figure on the percentage of children entering primary education who complete the course. My estimate for Mexico is 43 percent. This compares with 35 percent for Argentina, a figure of Morris A. Horowitz in Frederick Harbison and Charles A. Myers, *Manpower and Education: Country Studies in Economic Development* (New York: McGraw-Hill, 1965).
[38] Programas de Educación Primaria Aprobados por el Consejo Nacional Técnico de La Educación, Segretaría de Educación Pública, México, D.F., 1961.
[39] By way of comparison, the figure is 7 percent for Sweden, 4 percent for Great Britain, and 37 percent for the United States. The figures should be interpreted cautiously. European instruction, and to a somewhat lesser extent Mexican instruction, is professional preparation compared to the United States where increasingly it is becoming a form of consumption.

creasing order of size, are: science, engineering, economics, medicine, and the humanities.[40] The enrollments are rising approximately 12 percent annually, considerably less than the increase in the number of secondary school graduates. The disparity is explainable to some degree by the introduction of admission standards in some universities. About 60 percent of enrollment in higher education is in the Federal District, but the figure is declining. Expenditures follow a similar pattern, with the Federal District making some 60 percent of all outlays on higher learning institutions.

What assessment can be made of Mexican education? For one thing, it is unlikely that university enrollments will keep pace with the growth in the eligible age group, principally because facilities are not keeping pace. The preparation of university-trained elites is being supplemented, however, by private schools and by education abroad.[41] In addition, because of the burgeoning number of individuals with college degrees, the net payoff of a college education is not commensurate with that of a technical secondary education. Although the quality of secondary instruction leaves something to be desired, it is nevertheless rising sharply. Moreover, the system would be more responsive to economic growth if more emphasis were placed on research. Studies have begun on the utilization of labor, the characteristics of college graduate manpower, and the impact of technological change on occupational patterns, and the findings should be useful.

Mexico faces difficult challenges in education. First, the problem is not only to keep pace with the population rise but to increase the amount of education per person. Second, the quality of instruction has to be raised, particularly in rural areas and in the national universities. Third, in secondary education, more emphasis should be placed on developing a habit of technological inquiry among the new generation. Mexico is still highly dependent on borrowed technology, often from Americans who would not command top posts in the United States. A nation is not really advanced until its citizens independently develop a technology suitable to that nation. Hand-me-down technology may guarantee a nation's inability to catch up.

The public education system of Mexico plays only a minor role in developing elites in two critical areas of the labor force, which are the warp and the woof of industrialization: skilled workers and elite managers. A substantial amount of this need in the Mexican economy is filled by employers and private educational institutions. This provides a lesson for developing nations in that alternative sources have to be developed if public instruction fails to meet this need. The Mexican experience seems

[40] Compared with Argentina, where the order is medicine, social science, law, humanities, and engineering.

[41] In the period 1960–1962, 1,271 Mexicans were studying in foreign universities, principally in the United States and Western Europe.

to suggest the wisdom of a quality universal primary school instruction and the need for the development of occupational elites by user organizations and private schools.

A preponderant number of students coming out of the social sciences in the national universities of Mexico are not prepared to perform graduate work in outstanding American universities. The economics student, for example, is not especially equipped with modern analytical methods and is more versed in social theory than in how to look at an economy. Nevertheless, one gains the impression that the government is more responsive to the need for quality education than most other Latin American nations. The Colegio de México is a case in point that fills this gap with high-quality curricula and staff. It has high entrance requirements and pays students allowances on the commitment that they take no outside jobs. Financial assistance comes from American foundations, Mexican banks, and the government. Professors work on a full-time basis, in contrast with those in state institutions who may be on campus for four or five hours a week.

The goals of Mexican education are stated by the government as follows: a universal primary education, an occupation-oriented secondary education, and a rise in the quality of state higher education. The poor education in the rural areas, the highly classical orientation of secondary education, and the political orientation of the national universities suggest the need for working toward such goals.

To cope with the problem of allocating scarce resources, Mexico has organized the National Council of Human Resources. The council, which furnishes technical assistance to the government, is comprised of members of the Education and Labor Ministries and representatives of organized labor and employers, with the Bank of Mexico providing the technical experts. Council studies focus on the best way to train and use human resources. Through analyses of labor force characteristics and manpower needs based on growth projections, the council presents a total education plan to the Education Ministry. It is handicapped, however, by the lack of comprehensive planning in Mexico and by the difficulty in measuring the private education expenditures of the economy, such as those of employers.

In concluding the discussion on Mexico, we can list some of the factors that account for Mexico's record of economic development. First, the revolution provided a base for growth by dispossessing the idle rich from economic resources and by providing a more competent public administration that was sensitive to the needs of the population. Second, the economy demonstrated a capacity to develop human resources in two critical areas: skilled workers and managers for the public and private sectors. Third, the proximity of the United States and its acquiescence to the revolution brought in modern technology and employers who were seeking markets and production facilities. Fourth, the Mexican government limited American activities to policies that were designed to broaden the country's economic structure. (Mexico is the most stringent of all Latin American countries in not permitting American interests to determine the course of its economic growth.) American technology thus comes into the country predominantly through joint company ventures, and to a lesser degree through engineering and management consultants, in a manner designed to serve the interest of a diversified economic structure. Fifth, the government has succeeded in avoiding inflation and was assisted in this by the capacity of the economy to increase production steadily. Sixth, Mexico's diversified agriculture and extractive industries provided a broad base for growth. Seventh, its climate in the highlands is less oppressive than that of much of Latin America and provides an agricultural and industrial environment that is conducive to work. Eighth, the Mexicans have so far succeeded in containing the population explosion by increasing effective demand and employment. Lastly, and probably most important, the economic development of Mexico profits from the sense of cultural identity among its people that has no precedents in Latin America.

The economic development of Mexico can be likened to a spider. Growth takes place along the north central highland, where the agricultural base of the nation rests. The legs reach out in all directions to sparsely populated areas with cultures not too different from those of aboriginal civilizations. The principal development weakness in Mexico is the rural area, and no nation has reached an advanced stage of growth with a depressed agricultural sector. Yet despite marked differences between the modern and traditional sectors, Mexico has considerable agricultural potential. Moreover, the Mexicans are tackling the rural problem by developing specific geographical areas with an endogenous economic base where imports can be progressively and economically reduced. The Mexicans thus not only can think in sophisticated economic terms but have the competence to convert ideas into practice.

The Mexican experience demonstrates the key indicators of successful economic growth. It has had a trade pattern of rising diversification in exports and a corresponding decline in the import of foodstuffs and consumer goods. Between 1954 and 1964, for example, major export commodities increased from 18 percent to 40 percent. The percentage of manufactured and semimanufactured goods exported during the same period rose from 5 percent to 30 percent. Mexico also kept consumer prices under control by confining increases to an average of 2 percent annually. Moreover, the degree of public investment contained in total gross investment has risen over a quarter century to about 40 percent. Another important factor is the change in the relative importance of agriculture and manufacturing as components of the gross national product. By 1965 agriculture had declined to 11.6 percent and manufacturing had risen to 25.3 percent.[42]

Mexico has also shown how it is possible to have a good measure of democracy within the framework of a single dominating political party. The PRI wins the important elections and determines to what extent the other party wins the less important ones. The President is never criticized but is reached indirectly through criticism of his ministers. The press is wary of doing either. Mexican Presidents since the second world war have been practical men who were sensitive to the aspirations of the population and without illusions of grandeur, a posture that contrasts with that of generals of other Latin American countries who often view themselves as God-appointed saviors and who are held in contempt by the people they rule.

Nevertheless, Mexico's substantial record leaves no room for complacency. The return on economic development is unevenly distributed. Only approximately 4 percent of the population has an annual income in excess of $1,000. In terms of relative income distribution, about 2.5 percent of the population receives 22 percent of the income whereas 55 percent receives 18 percent. The expansion of the population makes the correction of this imbalance difficult. (Anyone going through Mexican cities is impressed by the extraordinary number of babies and the relentless pressure of crowds.) Moreover, Mexico has no comprehensive policy for developing the rural area. It has no program, as Spain does, for developing an industrial skill in rural youths before they migrate to urban centers.

Two questions remain unanswered: Will the Mexican people support policies needed for further economic growth, and can such policies succeed in improving the status of the population base at a faster rate? The economic growth target is an annual gross increase in excess of 6 percent. This goal means a growth in agriculture of about 4 percent. If these goals are to be attained, the government has to undertake a serious research and policy-making effort in demography, technology, and rural development.

Some specialists looking at the student disturbances of 1968 may raise a critical question about Mexican democracy. University professors and students say that in that disturbance they were expressing a grievance against police brutality and that they were seeking to extend the democratic process beyond the confines of the ruling oligarchy. In their view, the government demonstrated a proclivity for arbitrary authoritarian rule. Government officials interpret the incident as a manifestation of emerging problems that have been produced by rapid urbanization and as a desire by student leaders to influence the coming presidential elections.

Since the fall of the dictator Porfirio Díaz, Mexico has experienced a

---

[42] The GNP figures are from *El Mercado de Valores*, Special Supplement, December 5, 1966; the remaining data are from *Nacional Financiera*, January 1965. (Both are Mexican publications.)

series of internal shocks, but it has always been successful in readapting its structure in response to them. In other words, the country has managed to convert cataclysmic events into continuing progress. On the other hand, the broad-based oligarchy that governs Mexico appears at times to suffer from hardening of the arteries and from an indisposition to meet institutional challenges by a rule of reason.

Summation

When asked what could be done to accelerate Latin America's economic development Latin American graduate students in economics gave the following answers:

1. Break up the colonial economies of selling land-based products abroad and relying on imports for finished goods and processed foods; use export earnings to develop diversification; compete in the finished goods markets of American employers in Latin America.

2. Discourage the flight of Latin American capital abroad; discourage economic development from becoming an instrument of political ambitions; avoid wasting resources by the spoils system in public administration; develop a new entrepreneurial class.

3. Develop the idea that economic growth is for man and by man rather than a tool for enriching those with political influence; involve the population in the development effort.

4. Develop attitudes favorable to economic development at preschool levels.

Pointing out that other nations with equally formidable problems of geography and economic resources have made more progress, the students cited some basic noneconomic factors that may be deterrents to economic growth in Latin America—values, political relations, and social structures. To ascribe difficulties to such factors as savings and capital formation is erroneous, they said, because economic indicators are symptoms of underlying human characteristics.

Traditionally, Latin Americans have valued leisure as a symbol of status, a more important one than the acquisition of money. In fact, economic dependency is not considered a sign of inadequacy. Property holding is also regarded as a status symbol rather than a means of economic exploitation. Particularly important to the Latin Americans are their ideological beliefs and their freedom to assert them with impunity. Moreover, the individual acting as an individual is more worthy of praise than a person who surrenders his individuality to the needs of the group. In sum, the individual proves his self-worth by noneconomic means; once asserted, noneconomic values produce their own income. The differences in Latin American economic development manifest the dissimilarities in the extent to which these traditional values are rejected.

Because there has been little change in the social structure in Latin American nations, except for Cuba and Mexico, these attitudes have influenced high-level investment and foreign trade policies. There appears to be no attempt to relate consumption to productivity. Responsibility to the community does not emerge, and without it growth is difficult. Moreover, there is a general lack of confidence in the leaders, who are viewed as squanderers of public funds. In one country, the view of such leaders as purveyors of organized gambling and prostitution led to revolution.

It is possible that the feeling of national honor in Latin American countries could be used as a building block for cohesion. In probing into this sentiment, however, one often finds national honor to be merely a sensitivity to suggestions of inferiority rather than a feeling of common identity and purpose among the people. In fact, it is often a means whereby a particular group promotes its own interests. Even if national honor could be harnessed to economic development, there is the problem of finding the kind of leadership that will use it to achieve practical results. The single, powerful authoritarian leader has been a failure in Latin America and has used his power to prevent the social and economic upward movement of the people. Whether contemporary examples may be exceptions to the rule remains to be seen. In any case, this kind of leadership works against time as the level of cynicism rises among the new generation. The alternative of cooperative multiple leadership, however, is a rare phenomenon in Latin America.

Latin America could make a unique contribution to economic development by extending the sentimental and generous attachments within its family groups to the community. But even if such a shift could be made through the education of the young, a generation would be necessary for a payoff.

Each of these countries has its own particular problems and opportunities. In Argentina, organized labor must be made a positive factor in growth so the country can move toward democracy; Venezuela has a bounty of resources that could be used for the general development of its people; Brazil has to find a way to involve the population without risking rightist reaction; Bolivia, Ecuador, and Peru could learn from the Mexican experience in the integration of Indians.

If one could measure the gap between the expectations and fulfillment of a people, one would find an association between the extent of the difference and the degree of political turmoil. Latin American political systems fail to produce consensus and decisions of quality. Yet one should not exaggerate what to Americans may appear as a climate heavy with crisis. Conflict may connote progress. The Latin American variety appears more convulsive to the Anglo-Saxon than to the people involved in it.

The Punta del Este Conference of Latin American nations and the

United States in 1967 confirmed indirectly that the Alliance for Progress, which had begun as a revolutionary enterprise, had become an agency of international finance. At the conference, eighteen nations signed a declaration in favor of putting a Latin American common market into operation by 1985. According to the blueprint, the Latin American Free Trade Association and the Central American Common Market would be merged, and those countries not belonging to either organization would be brought in. Some concern was expressed, however, that such a market would be dominated by the economies of Mexico and Argentina.

The Latin American university could be a focal point for a critical exploration of economic development, but such an effort would have to be shielded from the political cauldron generally found there. The university is not tainted in the minds of the people as are the government, the political parties, employers, and organized labor. The quality of instruction and research would have to be raised and courses developed that look outward to the community. Social processes would have to be explored with the help of experts in industrial relations so that human resources could be used more efficiently.

The evangelical spirit kindled during the administration of President Kennedy has been lost. The American labor movement arm in Latin America—the American Institute for Free Labor Development—might conceivably have been a strategic source of change, but it does not have a sufficiently broad base to influence the Latin American power structure. Moreover, the CIA revelations cast a pall on its efforts. Its policy of channeling money, training, and Cook's tours into Latin American unions that are considered anticommunist is essentially negative in character.

Juan Bosch, the former President of the Dominican Republic, has some observations on where the revolutionary thrust for changing the Latin American power structure may come from. He rejects the Communist parties as being too bureaucratic and respectable. It will come from Latin American youth, he asserts. Rejecting the reformist parties within their own countries, they are likely, in his view, to be at the vanguard of insurrectionist movements under the inspiration of Castro. Mr. Bosch does not indicate the effective conservative power that can be coalesced against such insurgency.[43]

To conclude, the principal politicoeconomic features of Latin American growth include: (1) a high tolerance for inflation; (2) a failure to develop economic structures that favor balanced growth; (3) a failure to obtain a consensus among the people and to secure their trust in the government; and (4) a tendency of United States policies to frustrate the rise of a new class and to promote the interests of American employers rather than to advance balanced economic growth.

[43] *New York Review of Books,* October 26, 1967.

12

AFRICA

Of all the developing continents, Africa is the most diversified. From north to south, the continent contains three different civilizations that live precariously at their contiguous points: Arabic, Black African, and Western. The Arabic nations on the northern tier, Egypt, Libya, Tunisia, Algiers, and Morocco, have a gross national product of approximately $200 per capita. In the heartland, the GNP runs below $100 and in South Africa it is about $600.

This chapter focuses on the economic development of the new black nations south of the Sahara. By eliminating the Arab states north of the Sahara, the old nations of Ethiopia and Liberia, and South Africa, one is left with a fairly homogeneous group with which to make meaningful comparisons of rates of progress. All these nations of Black Africa acquired their independence in the 1960s, and all of them, with the exception of Ghana, are underdeveloped and have low levels of educational attainment.

This big land mass contains a population of 165 million that is expanding at a rate of 2 percent annually. One million are European, and .5 million are Asian. The dispersion of the population is uneven, ranging from 63 per square mile in Nigeria to less than one in Botswana. Only 10 percent of the population lives in towns larger than 5,000. The population is very young—perhaps half of the people are younger than 15 years of age. Observe what this implies for the political style of these new countries.

Some differences do exist among these countries. For example, most of them on the western side of the continent are French-speaking, whereas those in the east are predominantly British-oriented (see Table 16). According to economic growth potential, the most important of the former are Senegal, Guinea, and the Ivory Coast; the most important English-speaking countries are Ghana, Nigeria, and Kenya. The countries on the western side tend to have higher incomes, but some of the poorest countries, such as Upper Volta, can be found there too. Gross domestic product (GDP) per capita figures at constant market prices are available for five countries: Ghana, Nigeria, Tanzania, Sierra Leone, and Uganda. The last two nations show some progress, but the others none at all. As for political style, they range from Senegal and the Ivory Coast, which lean toward the right, to Guinea and Tanzania which have a leftist orientation; the remaining countries fall somewhere in-between.

As stated, with the exception of Ghana, the new Black African countries are at a very low level of development. The relatively higher per capita product figures of some nations reflect differences in the number of Europeans relative to the total population. In a sense, there is no such thing as an African economy. With the exception of some movement of migratory labor between countries, each one looks to the world beyond Africa for imports, exports, capital, and technical assistance. However, the economy of the Ivory Coast, which is steering a middle course that combines state capitalism with a moderate Africanization policy, does show some signs of dynamism. Uganda and Tanzania are also relatively dynamic, but both nations have some special problems. Uganda is landlocked, and its potential is therefore limited. Tanzania started her growth from a low base because of neglect during the colonial era. At this low level of development, the short history of these new countries suggests that a stable government with a reasonably efficient public administration and a strong but technically minded ruler is a critical requisite for growth.

These countries are probably the most difficult to study with regard to regional economic development. For one thing, the historical record is meager. Perhaps more important is the fact that Westerners do not know how Black Africans really think, and one must have this understanding to determine what their development problems are. After much study of its ritual and artifacts, the African mentality remains essentially an enigma to the West. When people do not understand how other people think, there is a tendency to conclude that they do so in an inferior manner; but after some serious probing, we often find that the reasoning may be different but that it works in the context of its environment.

The Black African countries, more than any other large land mass in the world, have experienced the greatest foreign exploitation. Their borders follow not ethnic lines but the empires the former colonial powers cut out for themselves beginning in the nineteenth century. The colonists also imposed a Western political structure. Out of the enormous re-

TABLE 16 □ Cultural Orientation, Per Capita Gross National Product, and Increase in Gross National Product Per Capita of New Black African Nations by Region, 1968*

Western

	GNP	Rise†
French Orientation		
Cameroon	143	—
Congo (Brazzaville)	200	—
Dahomey	75	—
Gabon	417	—
Gambia	95	—
Guinea	174	—
Ivory Coast	312	—
Mali	55	—
Mauritania	155	—
Niger	90	—
Senegal	220	—
Togo	120	—
Upper Volta	50	—
British Orientation		
Ghana	244‡	.003
Nigeria	120	—
Sierra Leone	137	

Central

	GNP	Rise
French Orientation		
Burundi	53	—
Central Republic	136	—
Chad	78	—
British Orientation		
Rwanda	45	—
Zambia	348‡	.014
Belgian Orientation		
Congo (Kinshasa)	78	—

Eastern

	GNP	Rise
British Orientation		
Kenya	129‡	.011
Malagasy	111	—
Malawi	46	—
Mauritius	225	—
Tanzania	76‡	.009
Uganda	100‡	.004
British-Italian Orientation		
Somalia	62	—

Southern

	GNP	Rise
British Orientation		
Botswana§	95	—
Lesotho	90	—
Swaziland	175	—

Source: Agency for International Development, *Gross National Product: Growth Rates and Trends Data*, 1969.

* In U.S. dollars at current market prices.

† Percentage change for the years 1966–1968 at constant market prices.

‡ In constant 1968 prices.

§ Formerly Becuanaland.

Note: Per capita GNP for other African nations includes Algeria ($270), Libya ($1,644), Morocco ($204), Tunisia ($224), Ethiopia ($63), Rhodesia ($240), and Liberia ($225).

sources drawn from Black Africa by the empire builders, only a handful of Africans profited. The industrialization left at the time of national independence was primarily at the mines and plantations, and those managing them were predominantly Europeans.[1] Therefore, these nations are sensitive to being managed by members of a different race. Their lack of toleration of white managers differs only in degree.

The environment of Black Africa presents formidable barriers to economic development. Up to a hundred years ago, the Sahara to the north and the lack of natural harbors on the eastern and western coasts isolated Black Africa from the world mainstream. If the coasts were penetrated, ensuing land barriers and unnavigable rivers prevented further penetration. If the white man succeeded in surmounting the coastal swamp lands, he was confronted inland with a tough climate and enervating tropical diseases that destroyed both men and beasts over wide areas. The absence of communication lines between the Africans themselves added to the problem of penetration. These barriers, even today, make transportation a major factor in production costs. In addition, the human element—the attitude toward work created by the slave trade and forced labor, the tribal wars, the debilitating effects of the environment—add to the deterrents to production.

These factors shape the economic structures of these countries. Their base lies in products of the land: bananas, coffee, cocoa, peanuts, rubber, tobacco, cotton, iron ore, bauxite, and a variety of animal products. Imports, more than half in consumer goods, are traded against these exports. Large-scale activity tends to be concentrated along the coasts. Acute shortages of social overhead capital exist. External economic assistance comes into these countries at a rate of some $1.5 billion annually. The capital projects into which much of this assistance flows have little effect in involving the population in employment, education, and consumption. Moreover, the projects, which are confined to developing power sources and exploiting natural resources more efficiently, provide little income for the government.

Developing Africa for the Africans emerged as an idea during World War II. With the influx of capital and Europeans produced by the conflict, the idea gained currency that governments should assume responsibility for accelerating growth and that advanced nations should have a responsibility in developing Africa for the Africans. As the demand for African goods rose in world markets, so did per capita income. Up to 1960 the growth performance was good, with the exception of countries in equatorial Africa where population growth tended to cancel out gains. The

---

[1] Generally, the intrusion of colonialism in the form of a small commercial enclave controlled by foreign entrepreneurs with export interests in an environment of general stagnation serves to hinder the rise of social overhead and thus general economic growth. For an expression of this view, see John C. H. Fei and Gustav Ranis, "Economic Development in Historical Perspective," *American Economic Association, Papers and Proceedings,* 81st Annual Meeting, Chicago, December 28–30, 1968.

second phase of growth began in 1960 with the drive for independence. Unfortunately for the new nations, the timing also coincided with a leveling off of demand for African primary products, a concomitant decline in prices, and emerging political instability. With this slackening of demand, the flow of private capital ceased, and production and administration were disrupted by the precipitous transition in the management of the economy as the Africans took over under a system of state monopolies. National independence thus had the effect of retarding economic growth.

A general characteristic of developing nations is that they do not grow sufficient food to feed themselves at minimum standards of nutrition. Raising food production and releasing some rural labor to industrialization are requisites of growth. The Black African nations are no exception to this rule. They have to strike a balance among rising agricultural output, modernization of the rural community, and industrial expansion, and like other developing nations, they have to allocate scarce resources economically in achieving these goals. Yet the Black African nations do not have comprehensive economic and manpower plans with which to pursue these objectives. Perhaps the weakest link in their economic development is the absence of a highly trained public administration.

Several institutions in Black Africa have a bearing on its growth. They are the land tenure system, tribalism, and labor migration. (The last two are discussed in the section following.) In contrast to the institution of private property rights in Western civilization, a substantial portion of Black Africa looks upon the land as being at the disposal of the whole community. The principle of the community controlling land use varies among the different regions. Generally, land is parceled out by the tribe to a family and reverts back to the group when it is no longer used. In most areas, farmers owe tribute to the chief, which may take the form of payments in kind or a work obligation of a stipulated number of days on the chief's land.

This characteristic of land tenure is breaking down, however, because of the urbanization of the population, the commercialization of agriculture, and the introduction of a money economy. In countries of British influence, such as Kenya and Malawi, individual farmers have full title to their land. The rising practice of leasing land and tilling land by hiring contract laborers is also making inroads in the traditional system. Pledging land—the practice of surrendering the use of a portion of land in return for a liquid asset such as cash, livestock, or food—is also contributing to the change. Pledging is encouraged by the surge in demand for liquidity on the part of the African population. The shift in the land tenure system represents a continuing evolution from the traditional African economy. The first stage was a subsistence economy based on nomadic pastoralism. In the next, cash crop agriculture and land tilling by persons with no ownership rights emerged. Concomitant with the present evolution is a shift of the rural population to wage employment outside the agricultural sector.

POPULATION AND LABOR FORCE CHARACTERISTICS

The borders of the new African countries divide the same ethnic group and force different ones to live together. This heritage of colonialism is a source of friction within the nations and an obstacle to the structuring of an integrated labor force. The population of the British sphere is more homogeneous than that of the nations with a French orientation. A major exception is Nigeria, where the precarious relationship between the Muslims in the north and the Christians in the eastern region has exploded into violent secessionist movements. The indigenous population in the French sphere ranges from nomadic Moors of mixed white origin in the north to Black Africans in the south. The nonindigenous people are for the most part Europeans, predominantly of French origin. The foreign population in the former British territory includes Indians, Pakistani, and Arabs in addition to Europeans. In east Africa, the population is concentrated around the Lake Victoria region and the high plateau areas of Kenya in contrast to the relatively greater dispersion on the western side.

The Black African nations differ as to the degree that they have moved against the privileged occupational and salary positions of the nonblack population. To a considerable extent, the differences in restraint manifest differences in the policies of human resources development of the former colonial powers.

A precise estimate of the percentage of the population in the labor force and its distribution by occupation is unavailable. The ILO estimates that 13 percent of the population in these countries are wage earners, with the percentage varying from country to country.[2] Half this number is in agriculture; a preponderant number of those not in agriculture work for the government. The participation rate of the population in the labor force is somewhat greater in the British-oriented countries, where mining is the principal means of entering the labor force. On the western side, workers are more likely to start out in agriculture than in mining.

Professor Elliot Berg estimates that the wage-earning labor force of French Africa comprises about 4 percent of the population, with a third of them in agriculture. A great majority of the rest are unskilled workers who earn wages that are barely enough for them to subsist in the towns and who consequently shift periodically from work place to village. Labor turnover is high. Berg reports that a new textile mill in Dakar had to hire 908 men in a seven-month period in order to maintain a work force of 170 employees.[3] The remainder of the wage-earning force is divided between

2 *African Labour Survey* (Geneva: International Labor Organization, 1958).
3 Elliot Berg, "The Development of a Labor Force in Sub-Saharan Africa," *Economic Development and Cultural Change*, Vol. 13 (July 1965).

skilled blue-collar workers and white-collar employees. The higher up the occupational scale, the greater is the number of workers committed permanently to a wage-earning class established in the towns. A considerable portion of this urbanized group works for the government, as do most European wage earners in French Africa.

White-collar employees have a strong preference for office work and law and care less for the technical positions required for economic development. This preference may change, however, as the Africans' need to prove their worth vis-à-vis the white man declines and as a factory system rises in Black Africa. Table 17 indicates the occupational distri-

TABLE 17 □ Absolute and Relative Distribution of the Ivory Coast Labor Force, 1962

Occupation	Number	Percentage
Managers	1,560	1.5
Professional and technical	2,700	2.6
Supervisory	2,750	2.7
Clerical	16,240	16.0
Skilled	9,200	9.9
Semiskilled	15,400	15.3
Unskilled	53,300	52.0

Source: Elliot Berg in Frederick Harbison and Charles A. Myers, *Manpower and Education: Country Studies in Economic Development* (New York: McGraw-Hill, 1965).

bution of the labor force for the Ivory Coast alone. Although the occupational groups are not strictly comparable, the student should compare these figures with those of a more developed country like Mexico.

A major problem of structuring a labor force centers on the low incentive to work outside of meeting minimal village needs. As a result of British and French measures forcing males to work, the men were pulled away from their villages and developed a habit of working intermittently for money. The introduction of money into the villages, together with the new consumer tastes brought back by the workers, caused a rise in consumer demand. The wage earners acquired more status than those who had remained behind. By producing expectations for goods that cost more than current income, these factors disrupted traditional society.

A wide disparity exists between the population estimates made by the new nations and those of the former colonial powers. Under the colonial regimes, because head counting was associated with tax paying, many heads tended to disappear. A contributing factor was the degree of laxity with which the colonial powers approached the population survey. As a general rule, the French and Belgians made more thorough studies than the English. Because of the barriers to precise counting, the census taker tended to be careless. He was confronted—and still is—with suspicion, ignorance, and such complexities as which children belong to whom in polygamous households. When Nigeria announced the results of its first national census in 1963, the figure was 70 percent greater than that of the 1952 census. These overestimates are common in Black Africa, including Liberia, which has been consistently overestimating its population so as to attract more economic aid and investment. The greater exactness of present methods of counting, together with political pressures to overstate, may be producing an overestimate of the actual population rise.

The work of T. E. Smith contains a wealth of insights on African population characteristics. Only 9 percent of the people live in towns, according to his estimates, and a trend toward urbanization is not apparent. The fertility of Asians in Africa is higher than that of the black population. Although most of the black girls marry within several years of the beginning of puberty, abortion, male migration to urban centers, and disease keep the number of their offspring down. Smith cites as a typical case a Gambian village where almost half of the children die before reaching the age of seven.[4] One should add that in some regions of Black Africa half the children die the first year.

Africa has the highest illiteracy rate in the world: 85 percent of the population. The extent of educational improvement varies. (See Table 18.) Considerable variation exists in the percentage of children of primary school age enrolled in school. Enrollments are generally lower in the French-speaking nations. For example, the total in Gambia is 14 percent; in Guinea, 23 percent; and in Senegal, 27 percent. These figures may be compared with those for Kenya (53 percent) and Ghana (54 percent). Some 5 percent of the primary school graduates enter secondary schools. The overwhelming majority of teachers in secondary schools are not Black Africans. A doubling of enrollments at both levels would require some 450,000 teachers compared to the present 344,000.[5] These countries have set for themselves the goal of universal primary education by 1980. Achieving such an objective may mean that the growth in education will outpace the growth in job opportunities.

An association exists in these countries between gross national product and educational level. That is to say, the country with the highest product is generally one with higher levels of enrollment beyond primary school. An inverse relationship obtains between gross national product and education, on the one hand, and the percentage of the population in agriculture, and the other. For example, in Tanzania and Uganda, which have low GNPs and educational levels, 90 percent of the population is in agriculture, compared to Ghana with 70 percent.

[4] T. E. Smith, *Population Characteristics of the Commonwealth Countries of Tropical Africa* (New York: Oxford University Press, 1963).
[5] The percentage figures are for 1963. The number of teachers was obtained by adding the number of primary and secondary school teachers of thirty-one Sub-Saharan countries for the latest available year 1963–1964. The figure comes to 344,062. Data are from UNESCO, *Statistical Yearbook*, 1965 (New York: UNESCO Publications Center, 1966).

Up to the time of independence, Africans were only minimally involved in education. When an African was educated, he was generally trained as a subordinate to a European. Since independence, the surge of interest in education has brought several weaknesses to the surface. First, the system is not particularly adapted to the needs of development in an African environment, reflecting instead the European influence inherited from the colonial period. Second, the schools are inefficient as producing units; they are in the wrong places and of the wrong sizes. Third, such practices as importing instructors, principally from Europe, add to the already high costs of education. Fourth, the high dropout rates at lower levels also adds to the costs. Elliot Berg estimates that in the Ivory Coast it requires twenty-six pupil years of instruction to produce one primary school graduate.[6]

TABLE 18 ☐ Increases in Enrollment in Primary and Secondary Schools, 1954–1960, for Selected Black African Nations
(In Thousands)

Country	Primary		Secondary General		Secondary Technical	
	1954	1960	1954	1960	1954	1960
Senegal	56	129	4.4	9.5	1.8	2.9
Guinea	28	97	1.0	5.0	7.0	1.8
Ivory Coast	57	239	2.4	11.4	.8	1.7
Ghana	396	477	97.0	147.0	6.9	15.1

Source: Elliot Berg in Harbison and Myers, op. cit.

The Black African countries have not placed equal emphasis on education. Table 18 indicates the dissimilarities among four nations. Accurate figures do not exist on the number of Black African students in institutions of higher learning in Africa and abroad, but the African-American Institute has made some rough estimates. According to these estimates, there are some 57,000 students receiving higher education. The number of students abroad is calculated at 8,000 in the United States, 9,000 in Soviet orbit nations, and 30,000 in other countries, principally Great Britain, France, and West Germany. Some 10,000 are estimated to be enrolled in the forty-odd universities in Africa. The fact that a high proportion of such students are enrolled outside the African continent can be considered an economical use of scarce African resources.[7]

[6] Elliot Berg, "Education and Manpower in Senegal, Guinea, and the Ivory Coast," in Frederick Harbison and Charles A. Myers, Manpower and Education: Country Studies in Economic Development (New York: McGraw-Hill, 1965). Strictly speaking, a dropout rate is not a real measure of inefficiency. Dropouts receive some education. The real question is the amount of resources used relative to the education they acquire.
[7] The author made an estimate of Black African college students by using the 1965 UNESCO Statistical Yearbook. Data are given for 17 African countries listing total enrollments within each of them and for fifteen non-African countries showing the total number of African students enrolled. These include Western European countries, Czechoslovakia, Australia, Syria, United Arab Republic, and the United States. The figure comes to 29,380.

A fundamental problem in African education is how to raise the speed of learning in modern subjects. Investigators in education research have found that the culture of the teacher and the book writer enters into a subject that is being taught, even mathematics. The disparity between this culture and that of the learner has a bearing on the speed with which the learner absorbs the subject. The implication is that the cultural content within the subject and within the student has to be reoriented in a manner that increases the rate of learning. Experiments with children of the Kpelle tribe along the west coast of Africa sustain this observation. Once these cultural hurdles are overcome, Kpelle children perform as well as white children.[8]

As in the case of education, the controversial question of low African labor productivity is beclouded by a lack of study as to the relative importance of contributing factors. For many years, Black Africans had been forced, directly and indirectly, to labor by a white boss, but by the time of national independence, forced labor had been generally abolished. The French began to prepare a labor code at the end of World War II and introduced it in 1952. The code represented the most liberal legislation in Black Africa. The labor standards that were developed during the colonial administrations were in most instances carried over into the period of independence. The French extended family allowances to African workers. Wage differentials among whites, Asians, and Black Africans were abolished officially during the colonial period and actually began to decline, a process that still continues. Nevertheless, the legacy of forced labor persists. Moreover, the rewards for any increase in a worker's productivity tend to be wiped out by inflation.

There is little question that the output of the African worker is low. It is substantially lower than that of European workers, whose productivity is lower than workers in the United States. It is not clear, however, to what extent such factors as climate, poor health, training, and communication problems between employers and employed contribute to the low productivity. Many studies that suggest that the Black African is inherently a man of low productivity seem to rely more on bias than fact and reasoned thinking. The African often works in a condition of physical impairment that would place a Westerner in a comfortable bed. There are apparently also cultural factors at play. Little in tribal mores conditions the African worker to accept the virtue of high productivity, a preachment that historically came from the white man. The work system outside the tribe may conjure up servitude in his mind. Work, to him, is not a virtue but a task that should be done in collective doses (preferably by women) with the rest of the year spent in leisure. The real man may be the one who succeeds in avoiding work.

Migratory patterns of African workers show a sensitivity to differences

[8] Michael Cole, "The Puzzle of Primitive Culture," *Psychology Today,* Vol. 1 (March 1968).

in employment terms. Workers are aware of which employers are paying the higher wages and offering the better conditions of work. This labor mobility means that the higher wages go to the workers of higher productivity.

To raise labor productivity, incentives are needed to raise African skills and motivation. Some evidence exists that male Africans respond to competent training, supervision, adequate medical care, and incentive systems of wage payment. They are responsive also to rhythmic mass production techniques and to group activity because of their gregariousness. The British tried joint consultation as a means of raising productivity. This East African experience was unsuccessful, however, because of employer impatience and a lack of worker responsibility. It was premature to discuss with workers how to raise output before determining under what conditions they would do so.

Professor Berg sums up the causes of low productivity as inadequate diet, crippling disease, lack of training, climate, and managerial incompetence. He reports that studies indicate that the African either does not care for or does not have the ability to perform precision work. The real questions remain unanswered, however. Under favorable working conditions and with a desire to raise his living standards, would the African worker respond to investments designed to raise his productivity? At present, he may have little incentive for steady employment. If he does take a job, he may be motivated not by a wish to raise his standard of living but rather by a desire to meet a particular exigency, such as the cost of a bride or bicycle. Once having met such a need, his interest in work declines.[9]

What is the evidence as to work dexterity? There is no scientific basis for the presumption that his low capacity for skilled labor rests on hereditary differences from other races. In the capacity to absorb information, he shows the same aptitude possessed by illiterates in general. His ability to apply a body of technical knowledge to an involved and novel situation is, however, another matter. The reason for this difference is not clear. The fact that this problem also exists in Asia suggests that the reason may be differences in values and motivation.

In machine-paced output, the Black African is inferior to Europeans both as to quantity and quality, given the same combination of equipment. But again, the underlying reasons for this difference are not clear. Turnover figures for Africans are much higher than those for Europeans. The reasons here are rather apparent. As stated previously, once he has achieved his limited material ends, the African worker quits. Moreover, unskilled jobs are considered unattractive universally, regardless of race. Income sharing by a family also probably curtails the incentive to make a permanent wage commitment and to accumulate savings. Sooner or later

9 For an analysis of this question, see Elliot Berg, "Backward Sloping Labor Supply Functions in Dual Economies: The African Case," *Quarterly Journal of Economics*, Vol. 75 (August 1961).

the family of the wage earner may descend on him and wipe out his gains.

A discussion of population characteristics would be incomplete without touching, at least briefly, upon the institution of tribalism. This institution can be defined as an extended family concept that embraces the entirety of life's activities and stresses tradition as a criterion of behavior. It bears a striking similarity to the extended family tradition of Sicily, where the *cumpari,* or close family friends, assume a status equal to, if not stronger than, blood relationships. The question at issue here is whether the some 800 African tribes will be a force for divisiveness or cohesion in economic development. The bloody three-year Nigerian civil war, which terminated in 1970, exemplifies the horror to which tribalism can escalate.

Arguments that tribalism inhibits development can be summarized as follows: It perpetuates the attitude that work outside the tribe is a temporary expedient, and such a view toward labor is intolerable in a modernizing economy. It overshadows loyalty to a labor organization, government, or industry and works to the disadvantage of these institutions. Because of pressures to organize political parties on a tribal basis rather than on national lines, tribalism reduces the possibility of developing a national consciousness. Furthermore, political patronage tends to be dispensed on the basis of tribal influence rather than competency. The argument is also put forward that tradition tends to place a religious sanction on customary practices, such as in production, and to impose the odium of sacrilege on innovation. Finally, the belief that tribalism can lead to bloody conflict is borne out by the experience of such countries as the former Belgian Congo and Nigeria.

Certain characteristics of tribalism are alleged to have beneficial effects on economic development. Under the institution, the family is the source of moral principles governing man's relationship to other men and to nature. Tribal members believe that a supernatural power controls the world, that life continues after death, and that the dead control the destinies of the living. Furthermore, each member of the tribe, by tracing back his ancestry, develops a linkage with every other member. Out of these beliefs and relationships comes an involved system of mutual obligations that circumscribe individualistic tendencies and provide a cohesive force for economic development. This sense of cohesion could be a potential means of energizing the people of the new nations. The supporters of this view consider tribalism's potential for conflict as exaggerated. Just as there are examples of tribal conflicts, there are also relationships on a live-and-let-live basis. The necessary strategy, it is therefore alleged, is to extend the forces within the tribe outwardly to the nation.

Some countries, such as Ghana and Guinea, have sought to curtail tribal power by insisting that the exercise of power in Ghana enter the national political process or become illegitimate. It is believed there that any human relationship is likely to be a political relationship and should therefore be subject to national review. A person who uses the tribe as an instrument of pressure on the government may be accused of treason. This view, encouraged by Kwame Nkrumah during his period of power in Ghana, tends to persist. Inevitably countries have to face the institution of tribalism as it affects economic development. Production has to be taken out of the confines of the tribe. In any case, it is not clear what form tribalism will take after the onslaughts of modern technology.[10]

Labor migration is another characteristic of Black Africa. Young males customarily leave the tribal community to seek employment for wages, either within their own country or across the border in another. Unlike the migrants of Latin America who settle permanently in the urban center, the Africans work for only a temporary period and then return to the tribal community, although permanent migration in Black Africa is growing. The extent of the labor migration is not precisely known, but it has been estimated that up to half of the able-bodied male adults are away from the community at a given time.

The motives behind the migration vary from region to region. Poverty may force the males into the money economy on an intermittent basis. They may be simply bored with community life. Other reasons may be that migration is a ritual of initiation into manhood, an escape from personal difficulties in the tribal home, or a simple habit transferred from one generation to the next. The indispensable condition, however, seems to be an economic need that, combined with some other factor, triggers off the movement. It would seem, then, that a wage-earning activity in the community might tend to keep the migrant at home.[11]

A majority of the migrants seek employment in agriculture and mining; others look for industrial employment. Some move between countries in search of seasonal employment during the dry season and afterward return to their homes. Some migration is regulated by government and some is not. A few governments take the position that the phenomenon is not consistent with economic growth and seek to reduce the movement by providing local work opportunities. Employment terms may be set out in a contract between the employer and individual worker and supplemented by agreements between countries. A considerable degree of the movement is neither controlled nor organized but flows informally between countries. There is some evidence to suggest that those who move over country borders tend to be marginal workers.

The critics of such uncontrolled migratory labor allege that it has deleterious social effects. The floating manpower, it is claimed, causes vagrancy, disruption of family life, spread of disease, and sexual license in both the tribal village and migratory camps. They propose to control

[10] For an optimistic view, see Colin M. Turnbull, "Tribalism and Social Evolution in Africa," *The Annals* (July 1964).
[11] J. Clyde Mitchell, "The Causes of Labour Migration," *Migrant Labour in Africa* (Brazzaville, Republic of the Congo: Inter-African Labour Institute, 1961).

the movement through such means as community development, better housing in the industrial center, and planned resettlement.

Generally, the workers migrate from a less developed country to one that is more developed. For example, migrants may go from Nyasaland to Rhodesia and from Zambia and Tanzania to the Union of South Africa, although a reverse movement may also take place, such as a migration to the Zambian copper mines.[12] Migrants may also move back and forth among Ghana, the Ivory Coast, Nigeria, Upper Volta, Guinea, Mali, and Senegal. These movements make a planned structuring of an efficient labor force difficult and make less likely strong loyalties to labor organizations and employers or an interest in productivity. Migration also raises problems as to the relationships between governments. What returns, for example, should the migrants' home countries expect, and should they come from the governments of the countries to which they have migrated or from employers? Who should bear the cost of services for migrant labor? How should wages be controlled, and what special fringe benefits should be given to migrant workers? Some migrant contracts go into specific detail such as "a pliable mat of good quality replaceable every six months," and "the right to gather firewood for cooking."

Migration to towns is increasing at a rate of 10 percent annually. An urban population of unskilled workers is accumulating and threatens the ability of these countries to produce the agricultural products vital for their foreign exchange. The rise in education creates an aversion for work on farms and plantations and encourages further migration to urban centers. The urbanization may result in a decline in the influence of tribalism and two-way migration.

MANAGERIAL ELITES

The emerging managerial elite in Black Africa is in such a state of flux as to make generalizations difficult. In the 1966 overthrow of Nkrumah in Ghana, 1,100 political prisoners were freed, and 500 new ones incarcerated. A total of eight successful and eight abortive coups took place in the new nations between 1960 and 1966.[13] The change in fortunes of government officials is not always achieved without violence. To cite an example, in the former Belgian Congo, an ex-premier and three of his cabinet ministers were arrested on a Monday in 1966, condemned the next day in a ninety-minute trial by a military court, and hanged on Thursday before a holiday crowd of 100,000 men, women, and children.[14] At the

---

[12] Liberia is an example of migration between black nations at similar levels of economic growth. Semiskilled workers from Ghana and Nigeria migrate to that country seeking skilled employment opportunities. The matter is one of supply and demand.
[13] The New York Times, February 27, 1966. For an analysis of these coups related to human resource questions, see Dorothy Nelkin's article in the September 1967 issue of the Journal of Asian and African Studies.
[14] The New York Times, June 3, 1966.

time the Congo became independent, there was a semblance of an integrated leadership; but the honeymoon was short lived. The emerging pattern seems to be the replacement of the old revolutionaries with the military.

Attempts to develop African elites by countries with scarce managerial talents can cause declines in efficiency. Part of the problem arises from the fact that the people have little sense of national identity and therefore do not view their managers as national symbols. A tribe may look upon a political leader belonging to another tribe as an outsider. In filling administrative posts in government and industry, there has not been sufficient time to develop African models of efficient performers. Nations with a very low tolerance for white managers may allow emotions to prevail over reason. Those colonial powers that encouraged the development of African human capacities laid the groundwork, however, for an orderly transition to black management. The consequences of those that did not are evident in the subsequent political deterioration after independence.

The elites who came to power with independence did so in a political climate that seemed favorable to economic development. Some came to the top with a substantial mass following. Initially, no conflict existed between the political leader and the labor official. With the major exception of the former Belgian Congo, they did not assume the reins of government amid the factionalism that is typical of Asia and Latin America. Instead, they represented the successful conquest of foreign domination. It is difficult to imagine more favorable psychological circumstances in which an elite could energize a population in behalf of a development effort. Yet these favorable circumstances waned quickly.

The alienation was due partly to differences in education between the elite and the rest of the population. During the colonial period, the impulse behind the education of the African by the white man was to remove him from "savagery" and make him European as much as possible. Some of these Europeanized Africans came into power with independence without substantial support from Africans who had remained African. Their support came from the colonialists they replaced and from Africans of similar educational experience.

Statements of some leaders that ascribe their difficulties to the colonial domination are apparently something they feel they have to say for the record. They inherited a cultural climate that discourages the rise of the industrial antagonisms between labor and management that are typical of Western economic history. The absence of such conflict provides opportunities. On the other hand, the absence of genuine mass political parties means that there is no mechanism for upward communication and accommodation. The foremost preoccupation of the political leaders is the consolidation of their power. Some imitate the arbitrariness and coercive tactics of former colonial rulers. Their experience highlights the fact that democracy lies in its substance rather than in its form. African political leaders have to develop a political process out of conditions quite different from those from which Western democracy emerged. Those leaders who practice democracy with some degree of success do so either because they voluntarily exercise restraint on their power or because events have imposed restraint on them.

The shortage of competent managers has led some countries, such as Senegal and the Ivory Coast, to rely heavily on the use of the nationals of their former colonial administrators. About half of the top positions in government, industry, trade, and education in these countries are filled by persons who are not Black Africans. In agriculture and mining, the proportion is greater. In order to attract and keep these managers, the government and other employers pay salaries that are greater than those paid for similar positions in Europe. When one considers that these posts are also supplied with Black African trainees, one can appreciate the enormous cost of managers in Black Africa.[15]

For the most part, labor officials in these countries are civil servants, former civil servants, or white-collar workers in industry. They are in effect the better-trained and the highest-paid persons in the labor force. The posts these individuals man in the labor organization structure are rarely full-time jobs. With the exception of confederation and territorial officials, trade-union responsibilities are discharged on a shared-time basis with government duties. The labor-union official is a close associate of the politician. His post is a stepping stone to political office and a transmission belt to the people of the monopoly political organization in the country. In a sense, it is difficult to make a neat distinction between political and labor leadership. The first President of Guinea came out of the General Confederation of Labor. The late Tom Mboya, who had been a competent leader in Kenya, rose out of the ranks of the labor movement. The marriage of political and labor leaders weakens, however, as the political imperatives of economic development emerge.

Many African labor officials had been educated in France, where they were influenced by Marxist ideology. Their clichés on capitalism and imperialism are similar to those uttered in metropolitan France. Communism has had little influence on the population, however. The anticapitalist expressions are really an expression of anticolonialism. Moreover, the labor officials who use them have a European orientation that may serve to alienate them from their own people. Their organization is the child of the government and of trade-union officials of France and Great Britain. The British, unlike the French, did not try to build outposts of the Trades Union Congress in London. Yet, in their own way they also left their imprint on the Black African labor official.

---

[15] A manager who earns $15,000 in the United States would earn $25,000 in salary and allowances in Liberia.

INSTITUTIONAL RELATIONSHIPS

Institutional relationships in Black Africa are a blend of the style of the former colonial powers and the traditional cultural patterns they found there. The difference in colonial style was manifested in the way the colonial officials viewed indigenous human resources and in the institutional relationships that they created. The combination of colonial imprint and African culture created institutions at an early stage of economic development that were different from the legacy of the Western nations. The political and economic institutions of the West evolved from internal class conflicts, whereas those in Africa emanated from differences in the confrontation against an alien master. The West controlled Black Africa for over a hundred years but did not transplant its own institutions. Even if these new leaders are now disposed to import Western institutions, they have to reckon with the tenacity of African culture.

A majority of these countries have a dominant political organization that originated in the anticolonial protest movement. This monopoly control of political communication lines is in some countries administered at the top by a person whose image is being deified. This organization is the fount of all legitimate change, and any new structures arise within its mantle. This monistic view of society allows little toleration for organized opposition. Those who promulgate the rules of the game at different functional levels are expected to express a single purpose that is symbolized in the person of the ruler.

Trade-union organizations are expected to conform to this monistic view of society. Generally, the French left competing trade-union federations in their territories and the British single federations. There are some sixty such organizations, and their membership is concentrated in government agencies, extractive industries, and large plantations. The largest single employer is often the public works department of the government, where union organization is concentrated. Accordingly, the government is a principal employer and plays the principal role in setting employment terms. Because only a small number of Africans are stable workers, only a small segment of the labor force can actually be organized. Of those organized, about half are white-collar employees.

On the international level, the majority of federations are affiliated with the International Confederation of Free Trade Unions. The others belong to either the International Federation of Christian Trade Unions or the World Federation of Trade Unions. In addition, the move toward Pan-Africanism has brought about the formation of the following two organizations: the All-African Trade Union Federation and the African Trade Union Confederation.

African trade unionism began to have some influence as colonial regimes liberalized their policies during World War II. Trade unions had existed previously, but they had operated under strict regulations. In the former French colonies, the structure of the unions was made similar to the unions in France to which they were tied. The three-way split of unionism in France served to create a split in the union organization in the colonies. In the British zone, no attempt was made to create close ties with the organization of the mother country.

The basic trade-union unit in the French colonies was the *Syndicat Professional* comprising all workers in an area in a particular trade or industry. In turn, all trade unionists in the area belonging to the same confederation were brought together into a city central. At the next level, the structure in theory rose vertically in the form of an industrial union and spread horizontally in relationships with labor organizations in different geographical areas. In practice, however, the industrial type of union was not common. Mass organization on a local basis was more practical in the function these unions actually performed.

In general, it is the city organizations and the national headquarters of the unions that are the dominant bodies of African labor organization. The individual local unions are often ineffective. They have little staying power in a dispute, and their strikes are more in the nature of political demonstrations against the government than contests of economic strength. Therefore, as a consequence of a strike, the government could break the union. The seasonal nature of some trade unionists' employment, such as in agriculture where workers disperse after the growing season, lessens the possibilities of creating an effective organization. The bargaining power of such workers reaches a peak during the harvest season, but because a work stoppage would cause a decline in the size of the year-end bonus, the workers are not inclined to use such power. Paradoxically, the small number of trade unionists in Africa gives them a prominence that places them under close government scrutiny.

The break with the trade unionism of the mother country accompanied the drive for independence and was more pronounced in the French territories. Ties with European labor organizations meant a relationship with the International Confederation of Free Trade Unions, an organization looked upon, in the French colonies especially, as one that had promoted the foreign policy of the colonial nations. The drive for Pan-African trade unionism that began with independence was impelled by a desire to gain freedom from the dominance of European unions and by the myth of a united Africa. The movement in the former British possessions was blunted by the greater mutual respect that existed between officials of the British Trade Union Congress and those of the new African states. Two factions prevail in Pan-African trade unionism. One centers around a bloc of unions with a religious base. The other is more influential, more left wing, more dominated by the Arab nations of Africa, and by the philosophy of neutralism.

African governments are becoming increasingly suspicious of trade unionism. Guinea is a pivotal country that furnishes some clues as to the

general trends of trade-union organization. In 1961 the executive committee of the Guinean teachers' trade union distributed a pamphlet critical of
the conditions of employment of teachers, asserting that they were worse
off than before independence. The members of the committee were
denounced by Sékou Touré, the President of Guinea, charged with treason, and given heavy prison sentences. The teachers' union was then
instructed to select a new committee. A twenty-four-hour sitdown strike
that followed was suppressed brutally by the police and the army and led
to further arrests and a denunciation of the affair as a plot managed by
Moscow, the Vatican, the French Foreign Ministry, East Germany, and the
editor of the *Financial Times* of London.[16]

In Tanzania, when a government was formed in 1960 dominated by
members of the trade-union federation, the ensuing honeymoon between
the government and the unions was short-lived. The ministers concluded
that strikes and pressures for wage increases jeopardized economic
progress and should therefore not be tolerated. From 1962 onward, the
government began to take a series of steps to control the trade-union
movement. These acts culminated in the establishment of a single trade-
union organization with different industrial sections, the general secretary
and deputy of which became appointments of the President of the Republic. The government decreed that trade unionism was to become an
instrument of economic development and that wages could be increased
only as productivity rose.[17]

The relationship of African trade unionists to government has shifted
over time. Before independence, their role consisted of harassing colonial governments and employers. In the transitional period after independence, the same persons held positions in both the government and
the trade unions. In the third phase of institutional growth, the labor
leaders were no longer government officials, and the government began to
assert its dominance over them. In a country with a single party and
military rule, it is prudent to leave to Caesar what he thinks is his.

As these single-party and military-rule governments emerge, labor
leaders tend to shy away from big political issues. This tendency is
probably in the interest of the survival of the labor organization because
political questions in the African countries often become ethnic questions,
with workers preferring to pursue their interests in a tribal union rather
than in a labor union. In addition, this attitude keeps them out of trouble
with the national government. As in the case of Tanzania above, African
governments also look warily at the economic role of the trade unions,
arguing that the unions may frustrate national economic goals.
Accordingly, some countries have made the strike illegal. They either are

16 In *Africa Report*, June 1964.
17 W. Tordoff, "Trade Unionism in Tanzania," *Journal of Development Studies*, University of
Manchester, Vol. 2 (July 1966).

convinced of the validity of the argument or employ it as a means of containing the rise of a competing power center. Consequently, the political and economic constrictions tend to focus union activity on the needs of workers in particular places of employment. By so doing, a genuine African trade unionism may evolve. For local collective bargaining to evolve effectively, what is needed is a permanent commitment by workers to the labor force and sufficient education to enable them to pursue effective courses of action. These factors are lacking at the present time.

The confining political and economic climate of African trade unions should not suggest they have no influence in their countries. The unions are among the more important organized forces in the Black African states. Much of our judgment of these unions derives from listening to the rhetoric of African government officials and labor leaders. Experience in the United States suggests what a misleading activity such listening can be.

Summation

Black Africa is in a period of transition. Although it may take decades for a sustained economic development to become apparent, political and economic structures are evolving rapidly in spite of an acute shortage of highly trained indigenous managers. Because these countries are at relatively similar stages of economic growth, it is difficult to discern which one is more "successful" than another. There is no pacemaker country like Argentina in this group of countries to suggest the stages through which each is likely to pass. The older nation of Liberia cannot serve as a portent of the development style that is likely to issue in Black Africa because the circumstances and timing of its independence were quite different.[18]

The need to adapt Black Africans to an efficient system of work is one of the most difficult problems anywhere in the developing world. Western experience provides only limited lessons. There is need for a study of the problems and possibilities of economic growth in a tropical environment. The goal of an effective utilization of labor is universal, but the strategies for achieving it must be adapted to the environment. There are aspects of African character that are unique and that should be studied in terms of their possible use in economic development. The tendency to ascribe growth difficulties to the colonial era and to racial sensitivities makes such a quest difficult, however.

[18] Liberia has developed a reputation for authoritarian rule by an aristocratic clique. Stories about this tendency are numerous. One is an account of a pilot being arrested by the Vice President for taxiing his plane in such a way as to obstruct the Vice President's view from the airport building.

Some of the more immediate prospects for labor in Africa are clear. The seasonal labor migration is likely to diminish. The countries will probably raise their demands for the use of their labor surpluses and impose increasingly severe restrictions on such movement if only because of national pride. Growing antagonisms will also serve to curtail the migration. In addition, as the wants of African workers rise, they will be more interested in becoming a permanently urbanized work force. The type of urbanization that will emerge may, however, be different from the urbanization that has taken place in Latin America. The contrasts between rural area and urban center are not as sharp in Africa. The Africans also appear more disposed to the modernization of rural life.

Some trends in the evolution of the ruling elite are also apparent. The first round of rulers is being toppled by army officers who are not disposed to allow the emergence of rival power centers. This replacement of leftist revolutionaries with the military tends to move the nations toward more conservative economic policies. The change may bring more trade with the West, more private investment (if it can be made attractive), and a greater staffing of administrative posts with technicians. If the military fails to fulfill the aspirations they generate by their conquests, however, the outcome is likely to be suppression or replacement by another group of generals. Political stability can be achieved only if the generals in power can prevent other generals from arousing the population to support another coup.

A principal difficulty for African governments is drawing a distinction between domestic challenges to their existence and legitimate opposition. Opposition to government policy may be interpreted as a challenge to the existence of the state, and the leader of the opposition may end up on the scaffold. There is substance to this fear because opposition takes the form of separatism based on ethnic and economic differences and differences in living standards and values between regions of the same country. The richer groups do not like the idea of carrying the poorer groups, and the poor do not like the superior attitudes of the rich. The new countries of Africa are thus faced with anarchy because of an inability to reach an accommodation between these different groups within their boundaries. As in the case of Biafra and the split of the French West African countries, the opposition groups attempt to solve the problem by seceding. So long as this conflict remains unresolved, it is difficult for the new nations to make significant gains in economic development.

Of all the world's developing countries, those of Black Africa have the greatest potential for change. As the government takes power away from the communities and as most of the educated elite work, either directly or indirectly, for the government, these countries are an experiment in the process by which primitive societies can become more complex under the centralized control of government.

In achieving balanced growth, African women can play a strategic role. In such countries as Ghana, they are an unobtrusive but important driving force behind the accomplishments of men. If they are discriminated against in education, if their greater energies are not channeled into growth, African development will evolve below its potential.

13

THE MEDITERRANEAN BASIN: SICILY

A considerable disproportion exists between the rates of economic development in northern and southern Italy. In traveling southward from Rome, one seems to slip back a century for every hundred miles traversed. The disproportion is evident in land use, education, industrialization, social overhead, and living standards. Culturally, northern Italy is oriented toward Western Europe, whereas southern Italy is Mediterranean in climate, soil, and outlook. In seeking to industrialize the south, the government counted on public works and incentives for private investment to produce an economic takeoff. Two decades of such policy has not narrowed the per capita income differences between the two parts of Italy.[1]

Sicily is at the end of this southern Italian region. Because historically the island has been a more or less closed economic system, it is useful as a case history of economic development in a traditional Mediterranean society. Sicily fell into decay as its role as the center of a flourishing Mediterranean economy declined. A historian described her people at the time of the Renaissance as living in caves and working on church lands like beasts of burden.

Today, Sicily, with a population of 5 million, is at the center of the lines of transportation and communication of a potential market of some 160 million people in North Africa, southern Europe, and the Middle East.

[1] For a review of southern Italian economic development, see Gustav Schacter, *The Italian South: Economic Development in Mediterranean Europe* (New York: Random House, 1965). See also Allan Rodgers, "Regional Industrial Development with Reference to Southern Italy," In Norton Ginsburg (ed.), *Essays on Geography and Economic Development* (Chicago: University of Chicago Press, 1960). Also Hollis B. Chenery, "Policies for Southern Italy," *Quarterly Journal of Economics,* Vol. 76 (November 1962).

The nations of this Mediterranean group are committed to accelerated economic growth. Sicily's semitropical climate, soil, and topography are typically Mediterranean in character as are the individualism and volatility of her people. Typical also is her population problem in the sense that the wrong people are in the wrong places. A community in Sicily may be perched on a mountain top for protection against twelfth century barbarians and not for reasons of modern economy. Those who do move are often the more talented, making the problem of modernization more difficult. A development policy that does not consider the need to regroup the population would probably be an exercise in futility.

Although Sicily's physical and human resource problems are enormous, its representativeness and its location make it an appropriate site for a center of Mediterranean economic development. What is applicable for Sicily has implications elsewhere in the Mediterranean.

CULTURAL OVERVIEW

After centuries of dormancy, the interior villages of Sicily are feeling the shock of change. Traditional societies are being changed by an economic development that assumes grotesque forms. The peasant who travels two hours by mule in order to reach the plot of ground on which he works is overtaken by a Fiat automobile with its radio antenna at full mast oscillating in the wind. Juke boxes and pinball machines are delivered in picture-postcard donkey carts. A young girl in high heels and elaborate coiffure steps out gingerly to avoid the manure piled up on the stone street. Not too far from the Bar Moderno, a peasant woman scrubs the stone threshold of her home in a futile gesture to keep the rubble at a respectful distance. Next door, the animal a peasant uses to take him to the fields lives in the same room as a television set, the peasant's reason being that the animal might soil the street.

What is there about the island that makes economic development such an enormous task? A variety of historical factors have combined to make inertia difficult to overcome. Illiteracy is widespread, corruption in high places a commonplace, murder the exercise of moral justice, religion an instrument of resignation. The abyss between the individual with a formal education and the illiterate breeds suspicion and divisiveness. Hypocrisy is a characteristic of social relationships. Objective inquiry is difficult because no one gives the real facts. Reality is what is convenient at the moment to have reality be. The toughness of this social milieu is more than matched by a brutalizing physical environment. The burning heat of summer and the harshness of winter make life a malediction.

There is little economic activity that can be used as a means for developing human capacities and institutional changes. Those who do labor expend a great deal of energy merely to make a pittance and spend a considerable part of the year idle.

One Sicilian institution, the Mafia, is subject to many misconceptions. The membership of the Mafia is as exaggerated as the generic manner in which the term is used. The bandit who holds up automobile drivers on the road and the Sicilian with a chip on his shoulder are both considered *mafiosi.* Similarly, the cattle rustling that takes place in rural communities and the contraband activity on the sea between the coasts of Sicily and Africa are considered the work of the Mafia. In the United States, the Mafia is viewed as an international cabal. In Sicily, the members of Danilo Dolci's social reform movement are perplexed by the fact that the Mafia does not lay siege to their headquarters, yet it is impossible to get any of them to point out a bona fide *mafioso.*

The Mafia originally grew out of certain institutional arrangements in Sicily and certain character traits of the Sicilian people. The *mafioso* was the administrator of the landlord, hired as the *campiere,* or he was a *gabellotto* who rented the land to the peasants. In either case, he rose from the ranks of the peasants as a leader and became a symbol of authority, a mediator in situations of conflict who acted outside of the legal institutions of the government, which appeared to the people to represent interests that were foreign to them. In this respect, the interests of the landlord and the peasant converged. Both felt a common interest in subverting demands of the state.

Therefore, there arose a belief in justice by individual initiative because organized society could not be counted upon. Accordingly, a person against whom a wrong had been committed was under pressure to avenge himself or else seek the intervention of a *mafioso* to correct the moral imbalance; otherwise, he would suffer unbearable criticism from the community. Homicide is an act of morality. Sicily continues to have the highest homicide rate in Italy.

As the feudal estates were broken up, the power of the *mafiosi* gradually began to decline. In a struggle over the declining opportunities they began to exterminate one another. Of those who survived, some became racketeers in Palermo on the western side of Sicily; others in the rural towns became wholesalers or politicians or hired themselves out to do dirty work for others. The *mafioso* learned to gain a livelihood in the countryside by stealing cattle and controlling the marketing of produce. Behind him could be found a respectable businessman or a politician. The assertion that the *mafiosi* are part of a conspiratorial organization is only a partial truth. It would be better to say that they develop authoritative spheres of influence and do not like competition. If crossed, they restrict their numbers by killing one another off.

Linked to this lingering attachment of the Mafia is a web of traditional rural values. Sicilians are quick to rub against each other's sense of pride. They give innocently developed situations an exaggerated importance and seem incapable of social intercourse without moments of turbulence and rage. (The one who shouts the loudest is always right—

cu grida chiu assai havi ragiuni.) To accede to another's point of view is
to lose dignity. They are preoccupied with a concern as to whether or not
they have been offended. The people themselves describe this characteristic as *la falsa dignità spagnolesca* (false Spanish-type dignity).

The Sicilian peasant has little confidence in those in positions of
authority and trusts no one outside of his family and friends.[2] He has a
low estimate of involvement in an organized society. He keeps his cards
close to his chest, and what he sees "remains in his stomach" (*cu sulu
joca cu nuddu si sciarria*). He who plays it alone, says the Sicilian
proverb, will never quarrel with anybody. He works alone in the isolated
countryside for long hours, an isolation that over the years makes him
closed within himself.

Because he is illiterate, the peasant relies on the volatile accounts of
those who can read for his sources of information. The newspaper is
important only to the degree that there is someone in the community who
can read it to him. His other sources are radio, television, and news from
the organization to which he belongs. His cynicism derives partly from
the fact that his perception of reality is not firsthand but is distilled
through the intellects of others in the community. This is a real problem
for the illiterate: reconciling a mass of contradictory points of view tainted
by the embellishments of different individuals and organizations.
Therefore, his difficulty in determining what is real strengthens his suspicion of society. Because he has not experienced the joy of creating with
his own faculties an abstraction of the real world, his ties with his family,
with his closest associates, and with his work are the only authentic life.
Industrial society appears fraudulent to him. The assumption of a modern
society that a voice on the telephone can be trusted is difficult for the
Sicilian to accept.

He approaches religion as a supplicant, for it promises a respectable
existence after the bestial one on earth. Catholicism for him is also fear
of power. Christ or God—no distinction is made—is a force to be
reckoned with. He is exacting at times, and little can be done about it.
In contrast, the Virgin Mary and the saints are not symbols of awe but
intermediaries who can be appealed to for supernatural intercession.
There are thus masculine and feminine aspects of the peasant's faith. His
outlook in religious matters is rather pessimistic, however, and that of the
women is even more so. He expects adversity rather than success to be
the normal course of events. Religion is part of the defense against
forces outside the family, but it is a relatively weak defense that becomes
easily broken with literacy and rising living standards.

If he has any associations outside the family, they are with organiza-

[2] The extended Sicilian family has a similarity with that found in Asia, Africa, and Latin America.
It is restricted not to an association of blood relations but to intimate associates who call each
other *cumpare* and *cummare* (for women). Although the term refers to godparents, it has gained
a wider connotation. Associates expect financial assistance of each other in time of need with
no questions asked on when repayment will be made.

tions that may include his political party, trade union, veterans' group, cooperative, or social club. Each elicits an acceptable type of behavior. He is never alone in this sense because he cannot escape the morality of his own group.

The unquestioned authority in the peasant family is the father. The dictum, *il padre comanda* (the father commands) has brutal aspects in a tyrannical will that stifles the development of those it subjugates. The father's outbursts of rage thunder down on the children and women in the family. The older children retaliate by becoming *prepotenti* (tyrants) themselves over their juniors. They play games in which the loser's toys are destroyed by the winner.

The women are claimed by proprietary attachment by the males as wives, mothers, sisters, daughters, and fiancées. In any such capacity, it is prudent for a man to assume that for every Sicilian female there exists a sensitive male claimant. As a good wife, the Sicilian woman is submissive, passive, and cloistered. Her vision of life does not extend beyond the street on which she lives. Although such a woman satisfies acceptable standards of virtue, her qualities of restraint create an unsatisfactory relationship with her husband. The warnings of her priest during childhood and her forced isolation at the first signs of puberty contribute to her passivity in adulthood. Accordingly, the need she does not fulfill is discharged by village prostitution and by a masculinity that reaches bestial proportions.

The most precarious existence is led in Sicily, as in depressed areas anywhere, by the person who has no industrial skill and no land. Such a person has to rely on the uncertainty of part-time employment in agriculture and possibly on building construction and public works. In areas where the agricultural season is short, such as where cereals are grown in contrast to fruit and vegetables, his employment is confined to a few days during sowing and harvest. The adverse psychological impact of this intermittent employment is not due to low wages as such—these people adjust remarkably well to low income—but to its uncertainty and the lack of social institutions that might support the worker when his income is curtailed during the rest of the year. The impact of such involuntary, intermittent unemployment is more severe in an underdeveloped area than it is in an advanced economy, where the length of industrial employment during the year may be more easily anticipated and where unemployment is cushioned by a social insurance system that maintains customary consumption levels.

What are the consequences of a long history of unpredictable, involuntary unemployment? It produces a person with a low level of future expectations whose imagination cannot be excited. He is wary of innovation in production because of disastrous past experiences. It also has an effect on fertility rates by encouraging the creation of more male children who can be put to work. What appears in the abstract as folly to economists and sociologists is the only available solution to poverty for the impoverished.

There is a significant implication for development policy here. The longer the history of unpredictable subsistence employment, the less does the community respond in a desired manner to traditional development policies. There is a progressive decline in both initiative and interest in education and training. A correspondingly longer time will be necessary for a program of human resources development to produce changes in the social structure. Consequently, the longer a society tolerates precarious subsistence poverty, the more expenditures in human capital will be needed to reduce it.

The emotional ingredients of Sicilian poverty can be summed up as a sense of ceaseless improvisation and conniving in order to make ends meet, a feeling of isolation from the mainstream of life, and a lack of empathy for other human beings to the point where a man becomes converted into an object that neither laughs nor grieves.

The general climate of the community in Sicily thus suppresses the rise of an engine of growth. The increase in income occasioned by more government expenditures and migrant remittances has not been associated with an increase in the productive effort of the community. The fellow down the stone street who is consuming more is astute or lucky. Life is a daily improvisation on how to survive rather than a sustained pursuit of a series of higher level goals in a lifetime. It is difficult to find anywhere in the world a better example of how poverty bestializes people.

THE INVESTMENT POLICY

At the beginning of 1950, when the Italian government started its development program, Sicily presented the classic picture of underdevelopment. The island was essentially agricultural with the exception of several urban centers on the coast. The agricultural land, largely in inaccessible areas, was owned by absentee landlords and was highly fragmented. The government administration was inefficient. The people were underemployed, and savings and money exchange were low. The people felt that the society was divided into exploiters and exploited and that poverty could be solved only by latter-day Robin Hoods. To these characteristics, which are common in underdeveloped areas, Sicily added a special flair for rural violence. Its effect was to make the police force the most developed human resource.

The stated objective of the Italian government's development program was to reduce the difference in income between the south and the rest of Italy. To achieve this goal, the government was to provide a new economic base by investing in social overhead and by inducing employers to invest and to continue the process of capital formation initially launched by the government. The initial thrust was to be accomplished by a heavy investment in public works, by land reform essentially involving the parceling out of the large estates, and by special tax and loan incentives to employers to create and expand plants. In brief, the strategy was to construct through public expenditures an economic environment that once formed would produce the conditions necessary for a takeoff.[3]

Up to the time of the land reform, side by side with the cultivators of the large estates were peasants on highly fragmented and dispersed plots of land. The uncertainty of tenant rights on the large holding discouraged the cultivator from capitalizing it and made it uneconomical. If savings could be eked out, he would place them in another piece of land, under the mattress, or if he were venturesome, in a bank. In the fragmented and dispersed plots, the possibility of capitalization was even smaller because savings were less. Therefore, the land reform program should have considered combining some of the fragmented plots so that they could be economically viable and developing a strategy for human capitalization. Instead, the policy of the land reform organization, Ente Riforma Agraria Sicilia (ERAS), became a political phenomenon of parceling out land to a land-hungry people. The reallocation to individuals of low productivity provided a strategic opportunity for kindling the attitudes and motivations necessary to increase the effective utilization of labor. The redistribution also provided opportunities for planning for the expansion of industry allied to agriculture. But ERAS bungled because of managerial incompetence.

An initial step in this initial goal was the formulation of an investment plan. Two classes of investment were conceived: those involving social overhead capital and those stimulating the growth of industrial plants. The first meant roads, dams, transportation facilities, water control, and irrigation. The second was intended to promote the building of industrial plants through loans and tax policies. The first plants to be built were to be those nearest the sources of raw materials and power. Basic social reform was to follow through the operation of the market place. No study was planned of population characteristics and strategies of human development.

The prime source of investment in Sicily was the Fund for the Development of the South (*Cassa per il Mezzogiorno*) of the central government. After twelve years of operation, the fund had committed some $3 billion to operations in southern Italy.[4] Other sources of investment besides the *Cassa* included special credit agencies of both the Italian and Sicilian

---

[3] See SVIMEZ, *Summary of Measures to Promote Industralization in Southern Italy* (Rome, 1961), In which Rosenstein Rodan describes the strategy as the development of agrarian and social overhead capital and the attraction of private capital, with planning being limited to scheduling projects in agriculture, utilities, public works, and housing. See also Schacter, *op. cit.*; B. Singh, "Italian Experience in Regional Economic Development and Lessons for Other Countries," *Economic Development and Cultural Change,* Vol. 15 (April 1967).

[4] In terms of approved projects, the sum is apportioned in percentages as follows: land reclamation, 27; water control, 17; roads, 10; tourist facilities, 8; railways and ports, 6; and industrial enterprises, mostly in loans to small and medium business, 32. In addition, the fund reports in the planning or construction stage educational facilities for some 13,000 agricultural students, 34 vocational schools, and 697 nursery schools.

governments. The Regional Institute For Industrial Financing in Sicily (*Istituto Regionale per il Finanziamento alle Industrie in Sicilia*—IRFIS) offered loans to small and medium-sized industries for new or modernized plants. The Sicilan Society for Investment in Securities of the regional government of Sicily (*Società Finanziaria Siciliana per Azioni*—SOFIS) helped to finance enterprises by purchasing up to 25 percent of their stock. Its major area of operation became the construction and modernizing of industrial plants and the extraction of oil and gas deposits. In addition, private banks such as the *Banco di Sicilia* contributed loans to industry. A precise estimate of investment from these private and public sources is not available. Existing figures suggest that such funds may have amounted to some $300 million.

The general pattern of investment was to begin with the search for a local economic resource that could be exploited, such as natural gas. Second, the center of development of such a resource was to be located near an already fairly industrialized urban center, such as Catania or Syracuse. Third, outside investment funds were to be used—either from northern employers or from a state organization such as the Fuel Trust of the *Cassa,* or a combination of the two—to construct and operate light industrial plants, such as textile fibers and plastics. Fourth, this economic base would, it was hoped, encourage northern employers to build additional plants for the production of producer and consumer goods in order to meet the rising local demand for such items as cement, plastic containers, and plumbing fixtures for the new housing that would be stimulated by the development.

The interior of Sicily does not have the first two of these requisites for starting the spiral processes of growth. Government efforts to counteract this lack are stymied by the enormous problem created by the character of the people themselves. To ascribe failures to the policies of the government is an oversimplification.

RESULTS OF THE INVESTMENT POLICY

That was the way economic development in Sicily was conceived. It was hoped that a point would be reached where self-operating growth would issue from the government assistance. Thereupon, such assistance would be reduced, but new plants would continue to rise. In addition, there would be a rise in the skill levels of the people and in agricultural productivity.

A decade later, the government had second thoughts. The hoped-for response had not been forthcoming. Consequently, the policy shifted in the direction of human resources investment to develop human capacities. As a result, Sicily is now a laboratory that through trial-and-error experiences tests the responsiveness of difficult human problems to a range of development policies. The lesson to be drawn, however, is that although traditional economic policies may be ineffective, a mere increase in educational and training expenditures may also produce small payoffs.

Government data on the impact of this traditional approach to economic development are limited. According to one government publication, employment went up 15 percent and per capita income 73 percent in the ten-year period that began in 1951.[5] To what extent the higher employment figure reflects changes in the meaning of employment and the migration of workers to jobs on the European mainland is not known. Nor is it known to what extent the rise in income is due to remittances sent home by those migrant workers. Agricultural money wages increased by 100 percent during the same ten-year period,[6] an increase that can be accounted for by the low subsistence base from which the wages rose, inflation, and the reduction of the agricultural labor supply by migration. In any case, the income gap between north and south has not been narrowed. Moreover, despite the considerable migration, which has drained the island of its best young manpower, the population rose about 5 percent in the first ten years of the investment program.[7]

The program has produced an increase in consumption. For example, the same government source, in citing the blessings of Sicilian development, states that tobacco consumption rose 60 percent and expenditures on entertainment 50 percent during the ten-year period that began in 1951.[8] Part of the increase in consumption can be attributed to the remittances sent home by the migrants. The people tend to believe that it is due, not to an increase in productivity, but to the fact that some individuals are more astute than others.[9]

There has been little change in the outlook of the peasant who has little or no land. Although he aspires to own land or acquire more, the price of agricultural land is prohibitive. This reflects not so much its income potential as the craving for land as a way of life.[10] The peasant views the community in terms of the good and bad behavior of specific individuals in the range of his personal experience. He remains a chronic pessimist. Of all the groups in his society, he is the most asocial and isolated, with little trust in government, political parties, trade unions, and clergy. If pushed too hard with changes that are intended to better his situation, he turns against his self-appointed benefactors. To him, the new consumer goods are evidence of soft living rather than products of industrial complexity and human skills. A television set is desirable, but the best way to acquire it is by some improvised maneuver rather than through work. He looks upon his environment not as something to dominate but as something to submit to or shy away from; his land is not a

5 *Italian Report* (New York: Italian Information Center, August–September 1962).
6 *Ibid.*
7 *Ibid.*
8 *Ibid.*
9 The assertion derives from in-depth interviews undertaken by the author in Sicily.
10 Good agricultural land sells for $3,500 per acre, a small fortune by Sicilian standards.

means of exploiting market possibilities but an instrument for supporting his family and mollifying his spirit. It can thus be seen how accelerated economic growth can be deterred when the consumption patterns of rural individuals are raised but there is no personal effort to raise their own skills.[11]

The trade unions perform a minor role. Originally, they had participated in protest actions prior to the beginning of the development program. The issues that would have sustained a protest movement have waned, however, and the unions do not have the funds and competence to assert a new role in the development process. Their offices, whose major function seems to be to provide a place for socializing, are manned by individuals working part time. The principal economic role of the labor organization consists of pushing for wage gains and more social insurance for their members in agriculture. Added to the emigration of agricultural workers, the effect of such pressure is to embitter landowners who require the services of the workers and to add to the divisiveness in the community.

A similarity exists with regard to the labor organizations and labor-management relations of Italy and India. In both countries, interunion rivalry provides an opportunity for management to play one union against another and increases the importance of worker representation at the plant level not accountable to any particular trade union. There is a similar wariness in granting any one union the right of exclusive representation. Similarities also exist in the forms of compensation; for example, annual bonuses are a significant part of employees' compensation in each of these countries. Why such similarities exist between two countries that are so diverse in geography, history, and culture would make for a useful inquiry.

The change in consumption patterns that comes with economic development is initially reflected in the dietary habits of the people. With more income, they shift from such basic food staples as spaghetti and beans to meats and pastry, which are considered luxuries. Next comes more housing, clothing, a radio, movies, and more leisure at the cafe and club. The so-called *casa terrana,* consisting of one room on the ground floor shared by men and animals, is raised to include a second floor. The new consumption patterns may extend to publications of the lurid press for those who can read and the greater use of such services as barbers and retail shops, principally those selling food. The new demand creates a plethora of retailers in the stores and in the streets, which is caused not only by the rise in consumer demand but also by the relative ease with which a landless agricultural worker can escape into retailing. With still more income comes more tobacco, a piece of land, and industrial goods.

---

[11] For a similar finding, see Martin Brofenbrenner, "Second Thoughts on Confiscation," *Economic Development and Cultural Change,* Vol. 11 (July 1963).

For many, a television set is the ultimate luxury. Because of differences in consumer preferences, however, the individuals who purchase them may be looked upon as the irrational elements of the community.

For those who leave for the north—generally the young—the chief advantage of the new environment is the opportunity to save money. As mentioned earlier, emigration speeds up a change in the consumption patterns of both the migrant and his relatives at home due to the sharp rise in the migrant's income, his sudden exposure to the variety of goods in a highly industrialized center, the money he sends back to Sicily, and his influence on tastes when he goes back home.

A universal response these migrants make to the question of why they leave Sicily is the lack of work in their community. Every male states that he would return if he could find a job there that would net the same savings. (This is extraordinary when one considers the difference in physical amenities between Milan and a Sicilian village.) In time, the migrant becomes disenchanted with the new environment. The bad aspect of the northern urban center, he feels, is the social estrangement and the lack of authentic man-to-man relationships. He complains that the relationships are exclusively economic ones in which men are rivals.[12]

From the point of view of the social factors necessary for economic growth, the traditional Sicilian value system is obsolete. It was a means by which the Sicilian had historically adapted himself to an exploiting environment, but that environment has been changing rapidly since World War II. To the traditional Sicilian, the value system appears rational. To policy makers, it serves as a dam that obstructs the ground swell that would project Sicily into rapid economic growth.

On the other hand, some social factors may serve as catalysts to development. The Sicilian spirit of controversy, for example, could possibly be used as an instrument of critical inquiry into the requisites of growth. The logical mind of the peasant, his ability to spin a web of logic from given premises, could also be put to use. In addition, the protests against the old order voiced by the intelligent sons of the poor may serve to expedite development. Movies, television, and visits to urban areas may encourage them to challenge traditional relationships and habits of thinking and the fatalism and violence of Sicily. They may discern that there are socioeconomic techniques that can be used to reduce poverty and privilege.

A strategy of development may be found in this ferment. The essence of the strategy would be acceptance of the *esprit critique* of the young as a means for institution building, together with success images from the modern sector of the economy. Its vehicle would be modern industrial

12 Professor Bert F. Hoselitz describes the alienation the rural migrant of Asia and Africa feels in the city. He never feels part of the metropolis and his only association is with his own kinship group who speak the same dialect. They become demoralized and an easy prey to rioting. He observes that the traditional function of the cities of converting rural migrants into efficient factory workers is not fulfilled.

plants and its locus rural towns of economic size. As the traditional social structure is destroyed by the free market, a new class may emerge from the talented sons of the poor. Not all the sons of the poor are likely to join the protest, however. Some do not have the perception to give the matter much thought, or they may fear the retaliation of the community. Others are landowners or have otherwise acquired status and vested interests within the old social structure. Some leave the community with hatred in their spirit and do not return.

The Sicilian experience thus supports the thesis that without radical social change no appreciable economic growth is likely to occur. A rise in per capita income has occurred, attributable in no small measure to the rise in immigrant remittances. The change cannot be taken for granted. A situation may evolve in which the leaders of the poor and the managers of capital become separated by a wall of mistrust. The pressures may come from intelligent lower-class youth. But social change propitious to economic growth just does not happen automatically. To be sure, there is merit in abstract statements by such economists as W. W. Rostow on the stages of economic growth. Events do not occur in neat fashion, however, with one unfolding the necessary requisite for the next. They occur haphazardly, and the particular configuration of social circumstances necessary for development may not appear. Therefore, we turn next to a model for developing human capital suggested by the Sicilian experience.

A MODEL FOR DEVELOPING HUMAN CAPITAL

The primary goal for the economic development of a depressed area is to secure the greatest increase in output from the resources that are available in the area. Through this objective, the living standards of the people can be progressively raised without the need for a permanent subsidy. The area can raise output in two ways: The supply of the factors of production—labor and capital—can be increased, or the way in which these resources are used can be improved. Labor quality emerges when efficient and resourceful persons are able to produce cooperatively in a spirit of technical inquiry. As mentioned earlier, this is the single most important factor in a developing area. In its absence, capital goods can be squandered; in its presence, if capital goods are scarce, they can be created.[13]

By an investment in human capital is meant any activity whose primary effect is a sustained increase in the physical and mental capacities of an individual. Such activities can include general education; training; acquiring knowledge of politicosocial environments; training in health and

---

[13] For background material on human capital processes, see Gary S. Becker, *Human Capital* (New York: Columbia University Press, 1964), and T. W. Schultz, *The Economic Value of Education* (New York: Columbia University Press, 1963).

sanitation; democratic planning, including the preparation of goals and involvement in the subsequent processes; morale studies and follow-through. The basic strategy of such investment should be to structure a social system that encourages participation in these activities and rewards such participation.

The duration and extent of governmental intervention necessary to develop human capital is dependent to a considerable degree on the length of time subsistence poverty has existed in the depressed area. If the community has managed to afford individuals some measure of security, the cumulative process of the demoralization and bestialization of the poor is lessened. Without such collective security, a human investment program that pays off is apt to be more costly.

The investments have to be allocated between human and capital resources so as to maximize total returns. That is to say, they have to be apportioned to one class of input so long as the increased productivity obtained by so doing is greater than that obtaining by allocation to the other. In matters of practical policy making, however, this approach should be tempered by the realization that expenditures on human resources should be given priority soon after the initial capital outlays for social overhead.

Strategically placed model communities are useful in achieving maximum involvement in human capital growth. Although they should be located within the depressed area, they should grow as a distinct entity in which a representative population is controlling its destiny. The choice as to the number of communities is dependent on locational factors that reconcile costs of productive factors, employment opportunities, and social impact. To develop oases of efficiency in a sea of poverty is defensible on the grounds that the entire population of the area will eventually be involved. A basic objective of the model community is to change the economic and social structure of the depressed area within its range of influence and to shift power away from the traditional structure. The model community should be controlled by the democratic planning of its members.

These communities can arouse among the people an interest in growth that is not obtainable otherwise. Channeling production, distribution, planning, education, and training into cooperative activity breaks down the divisiveness that impedes growth. The communities have the advantages that accrue from starting at a zero point. Their managers have the task of converting traditional forms of agricultural cooperation into modern equivalents. The rural values of reciprocity and group responsibility can furnish an important thrust to these communities.

The optimum size of the model community can be sought in several ways. Keeping down the cost of social overhead capital per capita is one. Such overhead includes public buildings, housing, telephone services, water, roads, parks, power, sewerage, and drainage. An optimum point is established in which population size reduces overhead costs to a minimum. Another approach is to increase the size so long as the ability of the community to support itself rises through a widening tax base. A third is to reconcile the diminishing returns in maximum relationships among its people with the rising usefulness of diversity caused by increasing numbers. Other practical considerations also enter into the decision. The size depends on the necessary population shifts and the reallocation of political boundaries. It is influenced by the need to attract different income groups and by the capital projects needed for its development. Population size is affected by the attraction of the community as a place to live and work. Nevertheless, the size should be controlled, preferably by natural buffers. One standard would be to make the community small enough so that all its members could walk to the community center.

The desired outcome of the community is the shifting of decision making toward cooperative choices that accelerate development. Its element of human investment must change with the development of economic structures. A principal objective of this investment is to redistribute power and knowledge. To reach this objective, a public corporation should be employed as an organizational tool. The corporation should plan, finance, and control the development of the community, seeking the maximum involvement of the people in production, education, and social action. The corporation should acquire land in the developing area and plan its use for industry, housing, and the community center. At the beginning of growth, the corporation should plan for a production technique requiring labor skills that is commensurate with the need to involve as many of the people as possible. As capital is deepened, training should increase in complexity. The public corporation, in a conscious policy of enlightened paternalism for its shareholders—the community members—should thus initially subsidize the development of simple forms of production, a rise in manpower skills, and the practice of cooperative relations.

Out of the corporation's activity should issue a flow of output and of household, enterprise, and public capital stock. Its purpose should be to develop and implement new ideas. A tangible criterion for determining the degree of accomplishment is the extent to which the enterprises spawned by the corporation become self-sustaining. The organization of development based on a corporate structure meshing public and private resources provides for the participation of the people and integration of the various phases of the development process. Profits are a measure of the corporation's efficiency in achieving its objectives. If the government wisely restricts its authority over the corporation, the latter can shield itself from the climate of ineptness that may surround it in the early periods of growth and that may constantly exert pressure to cause its failure.

It is of the utmost importance that the corporation be staffed by the more talented and motivated individuals in the nation. The choice of persons solely on the basis of political influence may prove to be a decision of irrevocably serious consequences. If political appointees are inevitable, their influence can be neutralized by giving them innocuous positions in the government posts away from the developing area. Once broad policy goals are established, the public corporation should be given a high degree of autonomy. An initial failure to anticipate problems that will emerge and to fortify the organization against the ambitions of mediocre bureaucrats leads to an eventual loss in timely decision making.

Technically qualified leaders in the public corporation are crucial to the success of the program. The people must have confidence in the managers who lead the effort and who must break up the traditional power structure's monopoly in decision making. The need of societies that are undergoing change is to ferret out the real power wielders and to develop challenging clusters of power. The challenge has its own dangers. The new managers may be inclined to manipulate the population rather than to develop its potential. The new charismatic leaders may be authoritarian or merely poseurs. They may be neither innovators nor trustees of the poor and may raise obstacles or simply maintain neutrality as to goals so long as they remain in power.

The isolation of left-wing elements in the community may weaken the thrust of development if the left-wing ideology is not replaced by an alternative philosophy that is acceptable to the people and that can serve as a symbol of protest. The people are not inclined to the ideology of the traditional power structure, yet an ideology is necessary to overcome their lethargy and mistrust. The weakness of the West in providing such an ideology is in common evidence in the world of economic development.

As a matter of practical policy making, the creators of model communities should seek quick and highly visible results. Resources should be concentrated and quickly applied so as to make change dramatic in its impact. A well-conceived plan that demonstrates the results of capital and human investments can produce a high level of morale among the population. The benefits of democratic planning in making choices and controlling their evolution are also so demonstrated. There is a danger, of course, that such participation may degenerate into a debating society. Nevertheless, the risk must be taken. For most of the present population, the returns of development are substantially limited to *processes* and not to higher income.

Human investments in the model community at a particular point in time should be chosen from a series of alternatives, the priorities of which will shift from one period to another. Drainage programs, for example, reflect the peculiar needs of a particular area and short-term versus long-term goals. The investments are controlled in two ways: by taking an inventory of the human capital stock before the inception of the program and by evaluating the results at different stages of its evolution. The planner should check progress by plotting results against goals so as to control community activities.

Evaluating results poses problems of measurement. The particular effect of investment is dependent upon varying allocations between human and tangible capital investments and upon anticipating the effects of different combinations. The components of these combinations include *manpower, economy,* and *environment.* A particular investment in the social system affects the relationship of all its parts and thus the returns on all investments. Therefore, one has to switch from an analysis of individual investment components to a study of interrelationships, or the morphology and physiology of the entire development system. In addition, budget allocations are affected by the value judgments of managers as to the desirability of particular outcomes. Changes in relative influence between the population and the traditional power wielders may be considered desirable by one set of policy makers and undesirable by another.

The ultimate payoff of the investment will be in human behavior. Whether the human behavior will be production, investment, or consumption is difficult to determine. The activity of an individual shifts among these three categories. An act of consumption can include elements of production and investment. Moreover, investment returns are both monetary and nonmonetary. Returns accrue in earnings and in status. A rise in the income of the community is a practical demonstration of the effect of human investment. By estimating investment per person, rates of return can be computed. The real value of psychic returns should be considered, however, in evaluating human investment payoff by monetary means.

Choosing a particular input to obtain a desired result is also a problem. A human return at times can be gained more economically by a tangible rather than a human capital input. For example, if factories are introduced that attract women workers, the consequence may be postponement of marriage and a rise in population quality more so than through a direct educational effort. A reduction in family size has the effect of raising population quality. A more enterprising individual may result both from the opportunity to exercise influence in the community and a job. An overall measurement of the effect of development such as changes in income does not reveal the contribution of each type of investment to the end result. Information on the overall development process and an understanding of it are thus not synonymous. Information on the separate human and tangible capital inputs is not the same as a comprehension of the dynamics of the system. Once these dynamic interrelationships are grasped, cost-benefit technique is useful in making choices as to particular inputs.

Cost-benefit techniques should not ignore the subtleties of human costs and fulfillments. Human costs are an input in development. On the output side, how is one to measure a new sense of expectation or an increase in human creativeness? Is the newly acquired power of the people a benefit? If so, how should it be quantified? Implicit in the choice of input and output criteria is a judgment as to what is important in life and the relative values of what is important.

A danger exists in this approach to community development. Such an effort attracts social workers, and it may degenerate into a talking society obstructing and diluting efforts to achieve quality. The social worker who seeks to humanize the effects of development can serve a useful function. A development effort is not a relief project, however. Too frequently, technicians have to take over the complications created by the well-intentioned. The humanistic approach to community development has to be controlled by competent management.

Industrial plants are indispensable to the success of the model community. The argument that plants are costly in depressed areas overlooks the price that is paid for both the inundation of established urban centers by the unskilled and the stagnation in the rural area. That an accelerated rise in the productivity of the rural unskilled can be achieved in a decade has been demonstrated by the experience of the Olivetti Company in southern Italy. Olivetti started the plant with a nucleus of skilled cadres from northern Italy, and he kept the number of highly skilled operations to a minimum. Beginning an industrial operation at deliberately planned low levels of capital does not imply prohibitively high labor costs. From a social point of view, such a strategy raises skill levels more quickly and more cheaply. Government incentives are necessary to start such plants and to encourage them to adopt initially a technology that employs a high proportion of labor to capital. Plants of high capital intensity offer limited opportunities for a massive change in the cultural and occupational levels of the population in the depressed area. The Olivetti experience suggests the possibility of a gradual rise in skill levels and capital intensities. The experiment also indicates that the democratic, paternalist employer who develops industrial skills in the rural area makes a significant contribution to human capital growth.

The Olivetti phenomenon is unusual, however. The economic incentives of the more typical businessman assure neither industrial plants in the depressed area nor a general rise in skills. His actions can be expected to produce instead a little oasis of efficiency surrounded by walls to keep out the unemployed. If Adriano Olivetti had relied solely on the advice of cost economists, he probably would not have made the decision to build a plant in southern Italy. To a Western-oriented manager with an orthodox cost-benefit approach to decision making, Olivetti's choice may have been considered an act of irrationality.

IS COMMUNITY DEVELOPMENT WORTHWHILE?

Community development means the integration of development efforts at the community level—including industrialization, land reform, education, health, housing, social overhead, family planning, and democratic participation—by which a comprehensive population effort is tied to national planning. It is a rational approach to the *selective* development of particular communities through optimum investment allocations and the social control of an emerging market economy. In assessing the question of whether such development is worthwhile, one must compare the returns of marginal government expenditures in rural areas with returns from established urban centers. In broad terms, the more depressed the rural area, the less visible may be the return on a unit of investment compared to the same unit expended in an established urban center. Visibility is important not only for the political showmanship it offers but also for its usefulness in motivating low-income groups in both the developing and peripheral areas. Secondly, in assessing relative returns one has to estimate social charges accruing from a rural exodus to established urban centers.[14]

The development of depressed areas has to be highly selective. Economic resources and human talents have to be concentrated at points where a self-sustaining potential exists that will produce results quickly. The potential can be almost anything, even sulphur water if enough people can be persuaded of its value.

This selectivity implies concentrating resources on the development of model units of production and consumption. It also implies a mass exodus in some depressed areas, abandonment of entire towns, cessation of overhead expenditures, and conversion of areas into a preserve as the last of the elderly die. A buckshot approach to community development produces little in the way of visible results.

The young people in selected development communities should be committed to education and to remunerative employment that will progressively raise their productivity. (The dilemma this objective raises, however, is how to reconcile the surplus of unskilled and underemployed labor in the development community with the profitability of adopting highly capitalistic methods of production.) Furthermore, the young should have a political and social commitment as well. If a particular site is in the midst of insurrection, investment may have to be postponed. If no problem of rebellion exists, investment may be worthwhile to the extent

[14] For a discussion of selectivity in terms of a growth pole concept, see Albert O. Hirschman, *Journeys Toward Progress: Studies of Economic Policy Making in Latin America* (New York: Twentieth Century Fund, 1963).

that the community contains a large proportion of highly motivated young.

The core should be built on new land requisitioned by the government rather than be submerged within existing sites. In addition, political boundaries may have to be realigned so as to reflect the needs of efficient development.

Community development implies the participation and consent of the poor. Such involvement is difficult. Few institutions exist other than those in the Soviet type of economy that can be drawn on in an effort at change through mass participation. Therefore, there is a possibility of converting such an involvement into a welfare boondoggle of low productivity.

The central development authority will have to deal with local authorities who may not have the same point of view or the same sense of urgency and who are likely to be those who have made a significant contribution to stagnation. Problems may arise as to respective rights and responsibilities. Competent instructors and leaders may be lacking because of forces that operate to drive the talented out of the area. Moreover, in seeking to encourage the participation of the poor and to develop a sense of individual responsibility, the planners may instead bring to the surface long-standing resentments against the conservative elite controlling the development funds, who in turn may look askance at the genie of their creation and who may feel offended at the lack of gratitude. The participation of the poor may thus produce an atmosphere of mutual suspicion and mistrust.

Briefly, the arguments against community development are: (1) It may be simply a means of making living on the land more tolerable. Although this outcome is defensible on humanitarian grounds, it is self-deceiving to consider such gains as economic development. (2) The effort may actually accelerate the rise in population and lock people into the agricultural sector. On the other hand, community development may remove individuals from farm work to the industrial sector, raise productivity, and keep the talented in the rural area. Moreover, land reform in a community development program is defensible not just on the grounds of raising agricultural efficiency (it may not) but in the expectation of social and political changes that would accelerate economic development. These changes include the breakup of isolated baronial economies and the rise of a new entrepreneurial class.

To conclude, community development should be judged on a cost-benefit basis. *All* costs should be estimated and the benefits should be judged on the basis of whether the development is setting the scene for the rise of a semiautomatic mechanism of economic growth. In judging whether the project will be worthwhile, one must weigh the comparative advantages and disadvantages of a series of possible alternatives between rural sites and established urban sites. Furthermore, although we have been discussing only rural depressed areas, a depressed area can also exist in an urban center, where the same principles of community development would apply.[15]

Summation

Sicily is an example of how well-intentioned development policies can be frustrated by the enormity of the human resources problem. The history of many developing regions of the world is one in which the population is exploited by foreigners. Sicily has been the exploited land par excellence: Greeks, Phoenicians, Romans, Byzantines, Arabs, Normans, and Spaniards have all taken their turn.

The reformist attempts have dwindled down to exerting pressures for more public works expenditures. The Mafia, viewed as a set of traditional social attitudes, is exposed to the inroads of mass communications media, education, contact with foreigners, and modern industrial employment. Nevertheless, it is remarkable how these attitudes resist the inroads of change. Current government policy does not offer any measure of hope.

---

[15] For an economic behavioral model of the unemployment effect of rural migration to urban areas see Michael P. Todaro, "A Model of Labor Migration and Urban Unemployment In Less Developed Countries," *American Economic Review*, Vol. 59 (March 1969).

14

THE MEDITERRANEAN BASIN: SPAIN

Spain is our second example of Mediterranean economic development. It poses challenging questions as to the relationship between political systems and development.

CULTURAL OVERVIEW

Spain is in ferment. A national wager goes on there on the impact that the passing of Franco will have on the ground swell of change. It is difficult to obtain a precise picture of this change. Each time the prism through which one sees Spain is turned, a new aspect of Spanish reality appears. There is the contrived picture-postcard one fabricated by tourist agency advertising—that of traditional songs and dances, of monuments and churches, all of them relics of the traditional Spaniard rather than the one of today, relics of a civilization that is fast fading away with economic growth. The traditional culture is disappearing so rapidly that recording it in books and on phonograph records has become a new industry there. There is the life of Spanish *haute société* to which an American can be easily attracted, but which is removed from the climate of change. Then there is the life of the people. It is difficult to penetrate, not only because people do not say what they think, but because of the way reality changes with the Spaniard who describes it. Truth becomes a convenience of the moment that varies with the individual's needs.

This rapid change is taking place under the perturbed eyes of a conservative leadership, for renunciation of the past is not part of the formulas of the economic planners in Madrid. The change has resulted from two conditions whose impact is incalculable. One has been the investment and consumption effect of a torrent of tourists who amount annually to one foreigner for every two Spaniards. From France alone, 8 million people cross the Pyrenees every year in pursuit of a low-cost vacation. The other reason for the rapid change has been the opening of jobs to Spaniards in the common market nations of Western Europe. At any given moment, these workers can number about a million. They come and go across the frontier so frequently and in such numbers that a substantial portion of the Spanish labor force has already been exposed to advanced economies. Although other nations have had an influx of tourists and an emigration of workers, there has been no situation comparable in the degree to which a formerly closed society has been subjected to massive and sudden change.

The vast exposure to foreign ideas has created a consumption revolution. New consumer tastes have emerged. The sudden increase in money has pushed up precipitately the total demand for goods. Out of such demand have come jobs and symbols of modern living—the transistor radio, the automobile, the complex camera. The symbol of modernity for the not-too-bright nouveau riche is a transistor radio played at maximum volume and held high on the palm like a votive offering and for the Spanish *chicas* (girls) tight pants of a matching color.

Coupled with the movement across the border has been the internal migration from rural areas to urban centers. This urbanization has been manifested in the precipitate closing of rural schools. In the northern province of Castile alone, some eighty elementary schools closed in 1965 because of the lack of children. Part of this internal migration joins the trek abroad, principally to France, Germany, and Switzerland. Over 90 percent of these persons are less than forty years of age, and about 20 percent are women. Most of them leave Spain with no skill and come back with an occupational specialty.

With this migration a shift in power has been taking place. Agriculturists have been losing their influence to industrialists and bankers. The power of the church has been declining. Moreover, a new form of collaboration between employer and employee has been emerging. Despite Karl Marx, the workers of the world do not unite with one another but rather with their managers.

The labor migration has created an increase in the number of small villages. As the population has been rising in the urban centers, the number of villages with fewer than 500 persons has been increasing. The latter has come about from the sharp decline in the size of the labor force in the rural towns. Some have been abandoned altogether.

The various regions of Spain differ from one another. The major regions are Catalonia, Castile, and Andalusia. The regions themselves are not homogeneous. Andalusia, for example, is divided into the provinces of Córdoba, Granada, Almerida, Seville (as its fulcrum), Cádiz, Jaén, and Huelva to the west of Algeciras. The topography of Granada alone changes in the short distance of forty miles from a snow-covered mountain cap over 10,000 feet high to banana plantations at sea level at the Mediterranean coast.

With growth, a population acquires the characteristics of the individuals who are fomenting change. Regional differences disappear as transportation improves and as internal movement rises. If this is true for Spain, the Castilian represents the future Spanish man. What are his traits? For one thing, he has a highly developed *esprit critique.* He has a fondness for contrariness. The Spaniard's fear of his own penchant for violence imposes a check on this spirit, however. According to the rules of the game, one does not rub against the other fellow's sense of personal dignity.

The character of the traditional Spaniard is to be found in the literature on Castile rather than in scientific works. With the exception of Ortega y Gasset, Spanish books on the social sciences tend to be sterile; therefore, one has to resort to poetry, drama, and the novel to understand Spanish character: the poems of García Lorca, Cárlos Bousoño, Blas de Otero, Gerardo Diego and Antonio Machado; the undertone of a life of no expectancy in the novels of Camilo Cela, Sanchez Ferlosio, Miguel Delibes; the rebellion against do-nothingness in the plays of Sastre and Buero Vallejo; the anguish of the literary giant Miguel de Unamuno. These are the sources of the cultural base from which Spanish economic growth is emerging.

Their works reflect the male orientation of Spanish society. Unless they are young and pretty, women in Spanish literature are often nondescript. They are a backdrop, the ones who fill the churches and bear the children. The men insist the women are better off by staying home and not working while the men bear the arduousness of work places and cafés.

An important character trait of the Castilian is his *sentido de dignidad.* To translate this term is to destroy its meaning. It is not sense of dignity but perhaps nobility in action. It means controlling one's behavior in a way consistent with one's idea about oneself and resisting the hypocrisies of society. This *sentido de dignidad* does not necessarily rise with the level of social classes in Spain; indeed, the Spanish peasant appears to retain this trait most. It vanishes with modernity. To individuals who do not feel this *sentido de dignidad,* a person who lives consistently with this feeling may appear as a fool.

Spanish mass communications media do not reflect these character traits but rather the official posture of the power structure. Not surprisingly, there is an absence of lively dissension in the Spanish press. The news is bland, rarely coming to grips with the nuances of particular events in Spain. It concentrates on ceremonial acts and speeches of govern-

ment officials, their trips in Spain, and their extraordinary accomplishments in economic growth. The following are typical headlines: "Soraya
has cried in Spain over her lost love." "The Pope blesses the Caudillo."
A local newspaper, reporting the visit of two "august persons," Prince
Don Juan Carlos and Princess Sophia, said that the visit would serve the
purpose of providing them with the tribute they well deserve. One paper,
in its report of the official opening of four new industrial plants, expressed
gratitude for the wisdom of the Caudillo and the government. The new
firms—a metal fabrication plant, a mattress-making plant, a poultry-proc-
essing plant, and a machine tool shop—provided 461 new jobs. The
president of the machine tool plant, when asked by a reporter the principal problems he had encountered in starting the enterprise, said that he
had encountered none, thanks to the authorities.

Miracles are reported with regularity. For example, a person may
regain a physical power long lost, and after a famous scientist is quoted
as saying that the event cannot be explained on scientific grounds, the
suggestion is made that a miracle has occurred. Newspapers reach
ecstatic heights over Spanish economic growth. They also cite her low
mortality rate, which, with the exception of the Netherlands, is the lowest
in Europe. Soon, they say, there will not be one adult illiterate in
Spain, and only 20 percent of the labor force will be in agriculture. A
more healthy, more cultured, more skilled Spaniard will emerge, with the
help of God and Franco.

The poor in Spain are highly visible. There is no mistaking them for
their elegant brethren. Centuries of poor diets of dry vegetables and fats,
of poor hygiene, and of general neglect have created what appears to be
a different race at the bottom of the social structure. One sees many
deformed persons in Spain; perhaps the United States hides them better,
but that is doubtful. When one travels in a bus from one village to
another, one can even smell the poor.

Spanish poverty does not have the neuroticism popularized by American sociologists and anthropologists. Family life is expressive and rich in
affection. A poor district is noisy and untidy, but there is no violence, no
alcoholism, and no rape. The Spanish family is a solid institution, although it is becoming subject to the inroads of the free market and the
consequences of what is indiscriminately called progress. The poor
seem to be more effective at improvising solutions to their problems. The
nonpoor are not only better able to afford psychiatric treatment, but they
need it more. Being poor brings rewards and privileges as well as
deprivations.

On the other hand, some characteristics of poverty that are universal
elsewhere can also be found in Spain. The poor boy who leaves school
at an early age to become an apprentice is marked as a member of the
laboring class for the remainder of his life. The high debt levels of the
poor make improbable an ascent from poverty. There are also the similar

social attitudes—the scorn for constituted authority and for the affluent who indulge in patriotism, the high sense of gregariousness, and the comforting fatalism. Although it does not reach the same level of barbarism found in other nations, there is also the same cult of the male and the subordination of the female to the needs of men.

Spain has lived in mass poverty because of poor land, poor land use, and poor economic concepts. The successive land reforms that have gone on for 800 years have been ineffective. Her enormous international power was undermined by an obsession with gold as wealth. Instead of searching for ways to make agriculture more efficient and to increase industrialization, Spain engaged in international conquests in search of precious metals. It was believed that the key to affluence was in laying claim to the production of others. Her steadfastness to this mercantilist view led to a series of declines down to the humiliation of 1898 and to the civil war four decades later.

Historically, a handful of Spaniards and the bountiful religious and military establishments have lived on the inefficient labor of others. In the north, the peasant has tried to produce on highly fragmented land. In the south, he has worked at subsistence levels on estates belonging to others.

ECONOMIC OVERVIEW

The annual income of Spain is approximately $15 billion, or about $500 per person.[1] Twenty percent of this income is from the rural sector. According to the National Economic Council of Spain, real income is rising at an annual rate of 7 percent over and above price increases in the range of 5 percent. Typical of developing nations, wide regional differences exist in income distribution. For example, the richest province, Viscaya in the north, earns four times as much as the poorest, Granada in the south. The differences are smaller, however, than those of the other countries covered in this book.

Much of Spain is Mediterranean in culture, geography, climate, and soil, and its economy reflects this important fact. The principal products of Mediterranean Spain are olives, fruit, and vegetables, which are grown in Andalusia and Valencia. Its other main agricultural product—grains— is cultivated in Castile, León, Aragón, and Extremadura. Compared to Western Europe, the grains are grown at high cost. Farm size is small: 64 percent of the farms are less than 5 hectares. (One hectare equals 2.471 acres.) Two-thirds of the total arable land of 21 million hectares are tilled by owners, and the remainder is divided between rented land and sharecropping. The small number of large holdings are mostly in the south. No precise figures are available on the extent of farm capitaliza-

[1] My figures indicate that with 1963 as a base, real per capita income in 1966 was approximately $515, rising at a rate of 5 percent annually. The computation was made from data of the United Nations *Statistical Yearbook, 1967* (New York: United Nations) and data of the Bank of Bilbao.

tion. The government estimates the number of tractors at 1 per 2,200 persons.

Geography and history have determined the location of Spain's economic growth. At the center of the country is a vast high plateau encircled by formidable mountain barriers. The capital was established at the center of this plateau. The country's major developed areas are along the coast and along the French border, and its communication lines radiate outward from the capital city to these areas. The quickest investment returns lie in the expansion of these growth clusters and transportation routes.

The population of Spain is approximately 33 million and is increasing at a rate of 1 percent annually. Forty percent of the population is in the labor force, and 20 percent of these are women. Seventy percent of the labor force is in agriculture, and two-fifths of the agricultural workers earn an average of $1 per day. Both the overall size of the agricultural labor force and the proportion of agricultural workers in the total labor force are declining. As mentioned earlier, a considerable flight is taking place from the rural areas. In 1963 some 200,000 persons were estimated to have moved to the urban centers of Spain. In addition, approximately 96,000 Spaniards left for foreign countries during that year, and a similar number returned.

Total employment has been rising more slowly than industrial employment. For example, in 1964 total employment remained about the same, but industrial employment increased 5 percent. Increases were made in construction, metal manufacturing, food, and transportation equipment, but they were offset by declines in agriculture, coal mining, leather goods, minerals, textiles, and basic iron and steel. During the same year, total man-hours rose 4.8 percent as a result of a growing shortage of skilled workers. Unemployment that year was about 2 percent, reflecting job losses in mining, agriculture, and textiles. The figure would be higher except for the number of unemployed who go abroad for jobs. As stated, the gap between the number of workers going abroad and those returning is small. In 1964, for example, about 87,000 workers emigrated and some 75,000 returned. The overall movement is declining as is the net difference in movement. By exporting unskilled unemployed and importing skilled workers, Spain transfers its training burden to the common market countries.[2]

One of the most difficult facts to obtain in Spain is the exact wages that industrial workers earn. It is in the interest of both employers and workers to indulge in the game of hiding the actual amounts from the tax collector. The data available are official wages bargained by the labor organization, known as *Organización Sindical Española* (Spanish Syndicate Organization, or SSO). They consist of minimum rates of pay rather

[2] The data in the preceding section were obtained from interviews with the staff of the National Economic Development Council in Madrid.

than gross earnings, however, and their usefulness is limited in estimating yearly wage increases and comparing them with price rises.

For a worker to live modestly well in the north, he has to earn some 7,000 pesetas monthly (1 peseta equals $.017). By "living well" is what Spanish workers feel is a necessary minimum wage in order to eat *chuletas* (pork chops). To do so, a family of four persons needs to spend some 4,500 pesetas on food alone. If the worker lives in a new dwelling unit, he spends another 1,000 pesetas on rent. Although few make such money, a skilled worker in industry, receiving full seniority pay and working six days a week with overtime opportunities could reach that figure. If he spends wisely his two yearly salary bonuses (at Christmas and Liberation Day), he could be in the living-well category. Most workers, however, could live at such a standard only if there were two breadwinners in the family.[3]

In a sample of northern households taken by the present writer, a family of four with one semiskilled worker had a daily spending allowance of some 100 pesetas. This sum took care of food and other basic household necessities. (To place this figure in perspective, a middle-class Spaniard would spend the same amount for his lunch.) The diet centered heavily on bread, about a pound per person per day. This typical family spent about half its monthly income on the rental of an apartment that consisted of two bedrooms, a living room–dining room, and a closet kitchen. Consumption beyond the basic necessities would require either that the wage earner work more than the standard forty-eight hour week or that a second person in the family work.

According to official government figures, when wage increases of agricultural and unskilled industrial workers are deflated by the rise in the cost of living, the increase in real wages is negligible.[4] The government points out, however, that the appreciable rise in employee shares is evidence that it is achieving a basic objective of its economic plan. To a considerable degree, the rise in relative shares is due to the relative decline of unincorporated enterprises and the change in the industry mix of the economy.[5]

There are competing pressures in Spain to abandon the rural areas or to seek a new economic base for their survival. Abandonment of the area is the only course if the government provides agricultural workers with industrial skills but has no concomitant policy of rural industrialization. In the four years prior to 1967, some 700,000 persons took these training

[3] It should be pointed out that workers with less than an annual income of 60,000 pesetas are entitled to complete medical and pharmaceutical care.
[4] According to data of the Spanish Syndicate Organization, average industrial wages, excluding construction, rose 17.5 percent during the period 1963–1964. The same source estimates an average rise in wages of agricultural and service workers of 12.5 percent during the same period. The National Institute of Statistics cost of living index rose by 12.7 percent in 1964. From U. S. Bureau of Labor Statistics, *Labor Developments Abroad*, June 1965.
[5] For income shares behavior in the United States and other advanced countries, see *The Behavior of Income Shares—Selected Theoretical and Empirical Issues*, Bureau of Economic Research Studies of Income and Wealth, Vol. 27 (Princeton, N.J.: Princeton University Press, 1964).

courses. The government believes that the resulting outflow to urban centers in search of employment creates incentives to regroup land holdings, shifts people away from marginal land, and channels production into cooperatives. As the agricultural labor force declines and agricultural production becomes more concentrated, the expectation is that the number of rural towns will diminish also.

The region of Old Castile is a grain-producing area that typifies this change. The Castilian peasant is generally an underemployed small land-holder. He may own five hectares of land in as many as 30 scattered plots. Every day he must make a decision as to which ones to go to, and he may have to travel as much as two miles. Because the growing season for wheat is short, he must spend a good deal of the year in idleness. No labor surplus exists during the growing season, however. Then he sleeps no more than five hours a day, and no hands in the family can be spared. The rhythm of his work is seriously curtailed if his male children acquire an industrial skill and leave the village to seek employment in an industrial center.

Agricultural capital is expensive for him. A pair of oxen, for example, costs 50,000 pesetas. A horse that can be worked for twenty years is worth 15,000 pesetas. Therefore, harvesting is often done with a hand sickle. Threshing is performed with a horse-drawn *trillo* (thrasher) on which the children sit to apply pressure on the grain. A day's operation involving the entire family may produce about thirty-five pounds of threshed grain.

The bulk of the Spanish labor force works in small *talleres* (workshops) that use antiquated equipment. As is common with most developing countries, however, a small sector of the Spanish economy is modern and efficient, and the productivity gains in the economy derive from this sector, which is comprised mostly of large firms, often of foreign ownership. The big industrial employer in Spain faces highly favorable prospects. If he has domestic competitors, they are apt to operate at low efficiency. Moreover, he acquires a subsidy through government protectionist policies that excludes the competition of Western European firms. A third source of assistance comes from matching modern technology with low wages. The Spanish worker's wage is so low that a substantial wage increase does not raise the average costs of a modern plant significantly. These factors, together with the pent-up demand, place the big firm in a very favorable position.

ECONOMIC PLANNING

Economic planning in Spain is based on the economic development law of 1963, which stipulates as its fundamental objective a rise in living standards of all Spaniards that is consistent with the needs of social justice. It goes on to state that living standards in depressed areas are to be stimulated by the industrialization of these areas, by a rise in their agricultural productivity, and by modernization of public services. Furthermore, their development is to be encouraged by on-the-site educational and occupational programs to raise the capacities of the population.

Economic planning is indicative. That is to say, the economic plan is not an instrument whereby a goal is set for the total amount of goods to be produced and the economy is commanded to produce them. The government does not plan every aspect of economic life but rather proposes a rate of growth for the economy, works out the public investment implications of such a proposal, and thereupon states what it proposes to do so as to achieve the planned rate of growth. The plan stipulates the amount and type of government investment and indicates the amount and type of demand for goods that private enterprise can expect. The plan also delineates broad social objectives and subsequently assesses the degree to which these goals are met.

This economic planning arose out of the studies of the International Bank's mission in Spain in 1961 and 1962. The report of the mission is an important indicator of the focus of Spanish economic development. As agreed to by the mission and the government, the objective was to "assist the Spanish administration in the preparation of a long-term development program designed to expand and modernize the standard of living of the Spanish people while, at the same time, maintaining financial stability." [6]

The mission's approach to economic development is that of the conservative banker:

> The prospects for the growth of the Spanish economy are very favorable, and, with suitable policies and the requisite public and private investment effort, an annual growth rate of 5 percent per capita should be possible over an extended period. This would make it possible to raise the level of income in the industrial and service sectors twofold within a decade; income would also grow in the agricultural sector, but necessarily at a slower rate. Total employment could increase by about one million persons over the decade; at the same time, there should be a large shift of manpower out of agriculture into industry. . . . It should be possible for per capita incomes of those who remain in rural areas to rise at much the same rate as those in the rest of the economy and, subsequently, for the level of agricultural incomes to approach more closely those elsewhere in the economy.
>
> Cost consciousness in the market economy can be promoted through the discipline of the price mechanism. Distortions that prevent the price mechanism from functioning properly should be eliminated as far as possible, in particular through:
> a. removal of price controls either immediately, or, where absolutely necessary in stages;
> b. abolition of subsidies taking the form of special prices between state enterprises.[7]

[6] The International Bank for Reconstruction and Development, *The Economic Development of Spain* (Baltimore: Johns Hopkins University Press, 1963), p. viii.
[7] *Ibid.*, pp. 4–5.

Most of the mission's report is devoted to an analysis of monetary and fiscal policies and of the major industrial sectors. The summary thus concentrates on the following subjects: budgeting, fiscal management, monetary management, foreign economic policy, transportation, agriculture, industry, and power.

With regard to labor, the report states as follows:

> The Government has been attacking the problem of rural poverty directly through the programs of the Instituto Nacional de Colonización. These programs are commendable and have achieved important results. But since they reach a relatively small number of rural families and tend to fix agricultural resources in areas where, for natural reasons, their return is relatively low, alternative approaches should also be considered.
>
> One such approach would be to facilitate the movement, already taking place, of families either to other rural areas where returns are higher or to industry and services. Relocation should be supported by other programs such as education and vocational retraining and the concentration of grants and credits in areas of greatest need.
>
> The expansion and modernization of industry will involve not only an increase in total employment but also changes in employment among industries and in particular trades within industries.
>
> Dismissals for "economic" reasons can be made only through a procedure involving governmental approval. Wage rates and other conditions of employment are regulated in considerable detail. This system has tended to impede changes in the employment pattern; it has also tended to impede changes in productivity and reduced the incentive to introduce new machinery or to undertake new ventures.[8]

In their first report to the Cortes, the national legislative body, in 1968, the directors of the plan claimed notable successes. Real income, it was stated, had risen 6.9 percent, more than that of the majority of European nations. The relative labor share of the national income had risen also, and the major objective of the plan, an accelerated rise in living standards, had been substantially achieved. The report also noted a rise in tensions in the economy however. These included inflation, the rural exodus, and the shift in the nature of labor demand.[9]

The report estimated the number of workers leaving the rural area in 1964 at approximately 250,000. The outflow was partly counterbalanced by migrants returning from abroad. No offsetting rise in the capitalization of farms was noted. The exodus was having a self-feeding effect. That is to say, the emigration was causing a deterioration of both the services in the rural area and the ability to produce; this in turn was creating further emigration.

Regional economic development is a vital part of the plan. Relying on

---

[8] *Ibid.*, pp. 30, 34.

[9] The performance of the Spanish economy between 1965 and 1967 shows two unsatisfactory tendencies: inflation and its evolution as a service economy. Within the three-year period, the cost of living index rose from 154.9 to 175.1, with 1958 as a base. Income in agriculture fell from 18 percent to 17.1 percent, in industry from 36.2 percent to 34.5 percent; it rose in the services from 45.8 percent to 48.4 percent. Figures are those of the Bank of Bilbao.

such factors as availability of local resources and demonstrated capability of economic growth, the regional development planners specify particular areas of Spain as primary or secondary development targets. Local areas vie for the primary designation because it means that the government will provide more financial incentives for employers to invest in such areas. The incentives consist of tax reductions, loans, and expropriated land. For each developing zone, bids are solicited for the different types of industry that are assumed to be needed there. The winners are chosen by the number of jobs that would be created by the prospective employer and the amount he intends to invest. The minimum requirements under the plan are thirty jobs and 1 million pesetas in investment. For most industry, foreign investment is allowed up to 100 percent. Any employer can invest in a developing area regardless of whether he is awarded financial incentives or not. In obtaining qualified personnel, each employer can seek the assistance of the Labor Ministry. He thereupon makes a commitment on the types and numbers of skills he needs but has the right to set qualifications for the jobs and to test applicants. By 1964 an industrial commitment was obtained amounting to 530,000 jobs and 31 billion pesetas in investment. At the then rate of exchange, each employee thereby represented an investment of about $10,000. In other words, it takes $500 million to create 53,000 jobs in Spain.

In the industrial sector, the report noted that half the new jobs were either in construction or in the manufacture of materials for construction. Wages for semiskilled and unskilled workers did not rise higher than the increase in the cost of living. Industrial production was reported as rising 11.6 percent. Coal production declined, mainly because of labor disputes. Major expansion took place in electrical energy, transportation equipment, construction materials, chemicals, whereas a less than planned rise occurred in machinery, but this was offset by imports amounting to over $400 million. The housing boom continued with the construction of 257,000 units.

In the agricultural sector, the increase in wages together with the 10 percent decline in production combined to depress farm income. Because agricultural prices are geared to the small inefficient producer, the small farmer was hit hardest. Spanish agricultural policy was restated in the report to consist of reforestation, irrigation, credits for capitalization, and resettlement.[10]

The report reiterated the government declaration that the basic objective of Spanish economic development is social. This goal is defined as the *elevación de la cultura* of the population, a better distribution of property and income, and the establishment of a more open society. To

---

[10] The conversion of land into irrigation farming raises productivity in Spain by a factor of 4. The rise is due not only to more product but to products commanding higher prices in the market.

achieve these social objectives, the report reaffirmed government reliance on full employment, education, and health and welfare policies.

This first significant report of the Spanish planners is suggestive of several characteristics of contemporary economic development in a market economy. First, the rise in jobs in the nonagricultural sector can misleadingly overstate the extent to which a manufacturing infrastructure is being created in the economy. Unlike British-American growth, a rise in services is more important than the rise in industrial production and industrial jobs. The key to the industrial commitment of the labor force in the more advanced countries was the availability of a large number of factory jobs for semiskilled laborers. However, the factory in presently developing nations is a highly capitalized modern corporation with a small elite of industrial workers. Second, urban development runs far ahead of rural development. The big cities of Spain are a match for those of the advanced nations, despite minor irritations such as the excessive noise and inadequate public transportation. The rural areas, on the other hand, lag by three or four centuries. Finally, the burden of an economic takeoff is borne by the unskilled in the urban centers and by the laborers and small landholders in the rural areas. At the same time, the income of the middle and upper classes is rising at a faster rate than it did prior to the economic takeoff.

The long-term projected outputs in the Spanish economic plan are 1 million new industrial jobs, 340,000 of which would be filled by rural migrants; universal primary education up to fourteen years of age with a corresponding rise in secondary and higher education; an improvement in social insurance benefits; and 727,000 new dwelling units. These targets are expected to reduce inequities in income and broaden equality of opportunity.

At present, the biggest business in Spain is tourism, which is able to narrow appreciably the unfavorable balance of trade between imports and exports. (Some 500,000 tourists yearly visit the Alhambra alone. The sudden disappearance of that vestige of Arabic culture would be an economic catastrophe.) Tourism has created a boom in consumer goods, including housing, food, appliances, and motor vehicles. There is a possibility, however, that it could seriously distort the Spanish economic structure into a service economy and as the boom becomes spent, cause a letdown in expenditures and a rise in unemployment.

The Spanish educational system was in a serious state of obsolescence up until 1955. Since that time, serious efforts have been made to modernize and expand it. Primary education begins at the age of six and is supposed to continue up to the age of fourteen. A significant number of children, however, particularly in rural areas, terminate at the age of twelve. The building construction program initiated in 1957 added a total net additional capacity of 540,000 pupil places by the end of 1962. By the end of 1964, 95 percent of the children between the ages six and twelve were attending school and about 82 percent of those between six and fourteen.[11]

About 15 percent of the children of secondary school age are in school. The bulk of this enrollment is in the general high school for children between the ages of ten to sixteen. In addition, a variety of technical schools enroll students from the age of seventeen to nineteen. University education starts at the age of seventeen and generally is of five years' duration.

MAJOR DEVELOPMENT PROJECTS

The province of Badajoz near the Portuguese border is the site of Spain's first experiment in rural development. The essentials of the plan involved harnessing river waters, land redistribution, irrigation systems, and the creation of new villages. Whether the plan has been a success or not, indeed the manner in which it should be evaluated, is a matter of controversy among Spanish experts.

The land being farmed was once a prairie of some 400,000 acres that was used for cattle grazing because of the absence of rainfall. The first vision of the possibility of irrigation dates back to 1902, when speculation began on using the Río Guadiana for such a purpose. The current plan dates back to 1949. A quasi-independent corporation was set up under the law known as the *Instituto Nacional de Industria* that used the services of the Ministries of Agriculture, Public Works, and Industry. Its total budget by the end of 1970 was 15 billion pesetas. The plan includes: (1) control of the river; (2) channeling of water into canals and troughs totaling 5,500 kilometers in length; (3) construction of forty-eight villages, each with some 300 houses with three bedrooms; (4) reforestation, principally in the area of the dam; (5) new communication lines, including roads and improved rail service to the seaport of Huelva; and (6) industrialization on a level that would provide incentives to start factories processing agricultural products.

The land was assigned to former day laborers, a group that is difficult to reeducate and train. They came out of old towns in the Badajoz area, where each town was assigned a quota depending upon its degree of unemployment. For both humanitarian reasons and the need to have several farm hands on each parcel of land, those with large families were given preference in the filling of quotas. Critics of the plan assert that this flexibility led to discrimination in favor of individuals with connections.

Each new village has approximately 4,000 inhabitants and contains homes, shops, a church, a school, a drug store, a medical clinic with a physician, and central storage facilities. In some instances, the farmer's home is located on the land, as in the case of farm homesteads in the

[11] United States Bureau of Labor Statistics, *Labor Developments Abroad*, June 1965.

United States. This arrangement is not popular, however. The farmer, his wife, and their children prefer living in the close quarters of the village. The village staff includes an agronomist, who has overall supervisory responsibilities in crop raising, tree planting, control of diseases, irrigation techniques, and marketing, and a foreman, who provides formal agricultural training and goes from one farm to the next offering advice and assistance. A trained and permanent employee, he is a graduate of an agricultural institute and may come from anywhere in Spain. The farmer is also a vital link, for he teaches the former agricultural laborer a new way of life. His big problem is teaching the intricate details of irrigation farming.

There are some 12,000 farmers, or *colonos,* in the area. The farmer is charged a rental of 4,200 pesetas annually. If he succeeds in managing his farm profitably, he eventually becomes owner of both the farm and his home. Some 5 percent fail, either because of inefficiency or because of the attraction of industry. Their average landholding is five hectares, and the average family has four children, although there are larger families in the villages and they appear to prosper. The average distance of the farms from the village is a mile and a half. The farmer sells his wheat to the state, his cotton and milk to cooperatives, and his cattle at the periodic fairs. His annual earnings average 140,000 pesetas, with his net, not counting his labor, running at approximately 40,000 pesetas. His debt is payable in twenty-five years. The land cannot be divided but can be sold by the farmer in the same parcel he received from the state.

The economic and social progress of the families seems to be considerable. In one village, the school teacher is the alert daughter of a farmer who signs with his thumbprint. Her mother is an assertive woman who grows flowers in an attractive small courtyard. The economic planners in capital cities who criticize this type of land reform as being inefficient do not place these human intangibles into their economic calculus. The improved spirits one sees in the lives of these people are not possible to describe quantitatively. The school teacher described above is a symbol of the potential of rural development.

This discussion concludes with details on two other important development sites in Spain. Seville in the south is one of them. Its plan calls for the construction of 133 plants, representing a total investment of 7 billion pesetas; they will provide 5,400 jobs. It is estimated that these factory jobs will create four times as much employment in the services. The major plants in the plan will produce construction materials, metal fabrication, chemicals, food, textiles, and paper. The choice of Seville as a major development site was based on a combination of interrelated political and economic factors. Because the area has a strong economic base, it also possesses political influence. Economic justification for the selection stems from the strong demand for goods there, and the strong base for the production of goods. Plants are needed to process locally grown cotton and olives and also to manufacture materials required in the processing of agricultural products, such as containers. A housing scarcity exists, and hence the necessity for construction material. Electrical energy to meet anticipated demand can be developed relatively easily. Lastly, the canal in Seville gives the city an outlet to the sea.

As these complementary industries evolve, a change in employment patterns takes place. Many of the rural people move to the urban center. Assisted by mechanization and irrigation, the productivity of those who remain rises. Emigration out of the province slows down. As a shortage develops in skilled labor, the unskilled must be trained. The participation of women in the labor force rises as they are attracted to factory employment. A spiral of rising employment, rising productivity, and rising income thus begins.

Burgos to the north of Madrid is another major development site. This provincial city of some 100 square kilometers is spread out in the shape of a butterfly. At its center lies the cathedral and an army cavalry stable. At each extremity of its wings are new industrial parks, which are located there because of transportation facilities and unused land. Beyond, the town ends abruptly and the wheat fields begin. The five-year development plan contemplates the opening of new plants that would create 30,000 jobs. The new plants (which read like a guest list at a diplomatic reception) are French, German, English, American, Italian, Dutch, and Japanese. They are attracted by generous government concessions, cheap labor, and increasing transportation and other social-overhead facilities.

There is a big Jesuit occupational training school at Burgos that attracts fourteen-year-old boys who have terminated public school instruction; the students are housed on the school grounds and undergo five years of training as carpenters, electricians, and machinists, training that seems to be of a high level. In addition, the province of Burgos is dotted with occupational training sites of the government.[12] Each training course comprises a series of well-developed lesson plans that are geared to actual industrial methods and run from a simple whole operation to a complex one. A bricklaying course was given in the village of Cedano. The young men would rise about five in the morning and work in the fields until one. At three in the afternoon instruction would begin. The young men were building a community warehouse with material supplied by the community. The trainees were laying brick forty-four days after the beginning of the course.

Road and rail traffic coming from France and northern Spain passes through Burgos and flows toward the central and southern regions of the country. The new motels and restaurants are suggestive of this flow. Its

[12] The government estimated that by 1964 some 170,000 students were enrolled in all the vocational training schools. This represented an estimated one-fourth of the trained manpower needed each year. The government target was some form of occupational training for 1 million workers by the end of 1967.

climate is that of the high plateau: long winters and dry, cool summers. Its industry includes paper, food processing, sugar, small metal fabrication, and machinery plants. Petroleum has been discovered in the province.

What does the initial stage of accelerated economic growth mean to the Burgos laboring class? For those without industrial skills, it may mean a job in services, such as in the many new restaurants and hotels. Those with an industrial skill can obtain a coveted job in a modern factory. The boom may, however, make those who do not experience a rise in job opportunities worse off than they were before it began. The motivation for self-improvement is obvious. If the opportunity is available, workers often work double shifts. A thirteen-hour day in the services during the tourist season is not uncommon. A pervasive desire exists to raise skills and find better jobs. The only people who sleep the siesta seem to be the tourists.

THE POLITICAL SYSTEM

If calling Spain a totalitarian country conjures up a Hitler or Stalin, the term is misleading. Its political system was totalitarian in its origins but has not remained so. The government no longer seeks to impose a full-blown philosophy from the top down. The Falange as a way of life has given way to a light-handed despotism that governs with the participation of different elites, who are the instrument of consensus making.

Spain is not a democracy in the British-American tradition. But neither is it the totalitarian society envisaged by its critics. If abstract labels are needed, the system can be described as a kind of authoritarian paternalism that permits a degree of expression and consensus that often escapes the Westerner. Contrasting political forces exist and are tolerated so long as they do not indulge in overt activity. Spain is the only nation in Western Europe where both communists and anarchists came to power. They have continued as underground movements since the civil war. Spanish anarchism is not just a conversation piece. These forces exist in a country where the Catholic Church has considerable political and social power, where an archbishop can be the chairman of a legislative committee.

According to the official line, political parties are instruments for encouraging distasteful struggles between competing interests. As proof of this contention, the press cites the United States Congress where each member declares publicly which group interests he defends in the legislature. In the official Spanish mind, justice is not a process of mediating between contending powers, but an abstract idea that can be grasped by pure reason. A clash of interests precludes the possibility of justice, which is more likely in an organic whole in which no stratum of society is excluded. The representation of economic interests of the worker is thus a function of the labor syndicates, whereas the representation of political interests is that of the *Movimiento,* the new name of the Falange. In such a system in which all groups are brought into a single unity, a parliament of conflicting political parties is considered a liability.

The leftist bloc in Spain is unofficial but formidable. Although predominantly from the laboring classes, it is nurtured by middle-class intellectuals and the children of the wealthy who are rebelling against the traditional social order. In an open political system, they would become communists, socialists, and left-wing Christian democrats. They share a common interest in wanting fundamental changes in church-state relations, trade unions, and education. They have no legitimate channel of expressing themselves openly, however.

Political power shifts among four groups: the Falange elite, the church, the military, and the financial elite. The composition of the cabinet in the national government reflects the shifting flow of power in this inner circle. The major disenfranchised groups are the intellectuals and the working class, where a generation of political eunuchs has risen. If the peasant and the industrial worker eschew political discussion, it is more because of ignorance than of fear. They are not used to the democratic process.

The law in Spain permits the right of association only for expressed legitimate objectives. Banned are organizations that are expressly contrary to the law, those that conflict with morals and the public order, and those that are a danger to the political and social unity of Spain. The law excludes from its provisions organizations formed under the canon law of the church, the Catholic Action organization, and the military. New amendments to the law make its provisions subject to judicial review. A retired foreign diplomat (in Spain delicate political questions are not raised by a Spaniard but by an unknown retired foreign diplomat) is cited as saying that the new amendments cannot be interpreted as allowing the formation of political parties.

The Cortes is the legislative arm of the government. In a typical session, the Cortes passed a law to reorganize the universities after the demonstrations by students and professors in 1965. None of the Spanish newspapers in Madrid indicated the association between the demonstrations and the reorganization of the universities.

The Minister of Education described these demonstrations to the Cortes as resulting from the universal problem of large student enrollments and the increasing complexity of courses. Enrollment, he stated, had increased from 62,000 in 1960 to 77,000 in 1964, producing a depersonalization of the faculty-student relationship. The attending stresses provided an opportunity for subversive elements from abroad. He lamented the ideological confusion into which the students had fallen. He went on to say that it is the duty of parents, teachers, the "directors of conscience," and the more enlightened students to liberate them from this confusion.

Politics must be removed from the campus, he asserted. Such apoliticization, however, should in no way imply a lessening of loyalty to the fundamental principles of the Nationalist Falange movement just as no country can tolerate a violation of its constitution. Nor does this mean the denial of academic freedom. On the day of this presentation, the Cortes met at eleven in the morning. The President swore in the new *procuradores* (attorneys). He then presented a proposal on the control of installment buying, which was passed unanimously. Next came the presentation of the Minister of Education. His bill was passed with two dissenting votes. The session closed at 1:25 p.rn., just in time for lunch. The student demonstrations for freedom of organization have since continued.

LABOR ORGANIZATION

The SSO, the Spanish labor syndicate, stirs up deep controversy in Spanish intellectual circles. At the end of the Spanish civil war, the organization was modeled after the Italian fascist corporations on the theory that the class struggle could be abolished by placing employers and employees into one organization. Institutions have a way of changing, however, despite the intent of their founders. The employer has never felt at home in the SSO, preferring his own organization. Sensitive to the necessity of placating the working class, the government has used the syndicates over the years as a means of increasing the bargaining power of the workers. Accordingly, as the SSO evolves, it increasingly resembles the trade-union organizations of the West.

The syndicates are a mixture of authoritarianism and grass roots democracy. The secretary-general of the SSO is head of the *Movimiento*. He controls the leadership down to the middle of the organization structure by appointing the presidents and the provincial secretaries of each of the national syndicates. At the rank-and-file level, the workers select their representatives at the factory and the first level of representatives in the syndicates. Historically, the tendency has been moving in the direction of selecting officials by democratic vote. Each syndicate is a public corporation that gives representation to all employers and employees in a particular industry or service. There are twenty-five national syndicates, twelve in industry, six in agriculture, and seven in services. Each one has three basic functions: *ordenación económica* (economic), *ordenación social* (social), and *asistencia* (welfare). The economic function is to provide guidance for the economy, the social office is supposed to implement postulates of justice through such instruments as collective bargaining, and the office of assistance is designed to promote the cultural, rehabilitative, and leisure activities of the worker.

The law lists the more detailed functions of the syndicates. They are to study and propose minimum standards for labor; see that the minimum standards are enforced in plants; process individual grievances of workers; collaborate with the Social Security Ministry in the administration of the social security law, which covers family allowances, old-age pensions, disability pensions, sickness benefits, workmen's compensation, and protection against occupational disease; and study the economy and advise on its operation.

Each syndicate is organized on a local and provincial as well as national level. Each plant has syndicate representatives of the basic components of the labor force: administrativos (administrative), técnicos (technical), specializados (skilled blue collar workers), and peónes (common laborers). In theory, the plant, through such representation, is a community of labor. The government maintains this structure to the extent of an annual budget in excess of $7 million.

Collective bargaining in the labor syndicate takes place within an individual company, within an entire industry in a province, or within an entire industry nationally. The bargaining frequently ends up in the offices of the Labor Ministry. Theoretically, the strike is permitted so long as it is economically motivated, but in practice, it has been outlawed by decisions of the Spanish courts and suppressed by government force.

In the official view, the syndicates are the instrument of popular democracy in Spain. They are the means by which the people participate in the functions of government. Evidence of this participation is the representation of the syndicates in the Cortes and the right of heads of families to elect members to that legislative body. In the words of Franco, the syndicate provides an instrument for a dialogue between the people and the government and an opportunity for the people to express their aspirations and anxieties through their petitions.

Syndicate officials view the trade unions of the West as representing selfish class interests. In their view, the trade unions are associations designed to promote the private interests of the workers. As a result, they scorn solidarity and often indulge in a violent struggle against society. This type of organization evolves, they say, when the government ignores the safeguarding of justice and when the common interest is conceived as the expression of the majority without any recognition of lasting values. Lastly, the officials draw a distinction between the Spanish syndicates and the corporations of the Italian fascist state, which they refer to as mere organs of the state administration.[13]

Accordingly, the syndicate is conceived as an expression of social unity that integrates the worker with the state. They claim as their ancestry the guilds of the Middle Ages, the corporate organization of Spain under Primo de Rivera, and the unitary movement of the Falange.

13 From La organización sindical española (Madrid: Escuela Sindical, 1961). The material on the Spanish syndicates was also obtained from interviews.

In more practical terms, the officials refer to the syndicates as a reaction against the intense political and trade-union struggles that erupted into civil war. They say that these organizations have evolved as the needs of the people have changed.

The syndicate leadership is driven by two aspirations. In any major changes in Spain, the top leaders of the SSO expect a seat at the decision-making table along with the church, the military, and the financial interests. If they do not obtain one, they are likely to foment disturbances in order to acquire one. As to the other, they have the problem of selling themselves to workers who do not choose them. To gain their support, the SSO leaders encourage the development of democracy as a by-product.

Accordingly, the syndicates bear watching as the bellwether of things to come in Spain. Whether they actually represent the Spanish working class will be reflected by what might happen if genuine freedom of association were granted. Conceivably, the present Catholic worker organizations, the only legitimate groups other than the *Movimiento* by virtue of the concordat with the church, would group themselves into a Catholic trade-union federation. There would probably be two other major federations with a communist-socialist orientation. The rest of organized labor would be represented by the SSO.

The tabloid newspaper of the SSO, *Pueblo,* frankly caters to mass interests. In a typical issue, a headline announced that in a decade American and Russian satellites with nuclear bombs would be circling over the heads of Spaniards. The columns are filled with news of film stars, bullfighters, and athletes. No one can accuse *Pueblo* of practicing uplift trade unionism.

Collective bargaining sessions between employer and employee representatives provide clues as to the extent of industrial democracy in Spain. In one of them, the discussion involved the extent of a wage increase in the food industry. The chairman was an appointed officer of the SSO. The employer and employee representatives faced each other at a long table. The labor people talked about the rising cost of living, and the employers urged an appeal to reason. A complicating factor was the way in which the previous agreement had been settled in the form of a ruling by the Labor Ministry. Since that time, new job classifications had been created in the industry, and the labor representatives felt it would not be fair if the increase were applied only to the new classifications. A battle of statistics ensued, and the parties succeeded in confusing each other. The chairman then suggested that the negotiators look at the problem in terms of the workers rather than job classifications; he proposed that every worker should receive two increases, the one ordered by the Labor Ministry ruling and any new increase that would come out of the present negotiations. When the provincial general secretary of the SSO walked into the room, everyone rose to his feet.

To conclude, the reader should not gain the impression that Spanish trade unions and collective bargaining are of the Western variety. They are not, although there are pressures that are moving them in that direction. The manner in which Spanish workers form clandestine labor commissions to pursue their economic interests suggests that the syndicates do not provide all workers with authentic representation. Moreover, as stated, the government seeks to stop all strikes, regardless of their purpose, and to resolve disputes under government auspices. Refusal to terminate a strike can lead to the imprisonment of strikers.

FUTURE PROSPECTS

The patterns of economic growth, employment, and inflation in Spain indicate that the rewards of economic development in its initial stages are meager to those who are below the level of the skilled worker. For the semiskilled and the *peónes,* inflation wipes out the rise in money wages. The major opportunity that economic growth offers them is the chance for a second member of the family to become a wage earner. Housing also typifies this relative disadvantage. Because the government did not set aside land in anticipation of the expansion of urban centers, land values have skyrocketed, pushing up housing costs beyond the reach of the working classes. Those who do acquire new housing must pay high rents, and their apartments deteriorate rapidly, partly because the worker lacks the incentive and money to check the deterioration and partly because of a general dearth of public services.

Nevertheless, because of the very nature of the poor in Spain, the government has a considerable opportunity to gain high rates of return on its investment in human capital. They grasp and accept the association between education and income. In addition, their highly motivated family life provides an interest in learning. Both of these are vital factors in rapid human capitalization.

Numerous anthropological tracts have described poverty as a pathology of violence, sexuality, prostitution, and drunkenness, suggesting that the poor of the world have a system of values of their own that is different from those of the higher-income groups in their society. Viewed in this light, the poor would pose serious obstacles to rapid economic development. There is no way of telling, however, to what extent these case histories are representative of the population from which they are drawn. Therefore, there is no way of making deductions about them. Even if the deviations from middle-class rectitude they describe are typical of the poor in the societies they describe, such may not be the case in other societies. The Spanish poor do not indulge in such peccadilloes. They are not saints, but they are fortified by the mutual affection and respect in their close-knit family life. Nor are their values radically different from those of the middle class. To be sure, there is in their ranks more fatalism, more of an attitude of living from day to day, and more alienation from the society. They carry their poverty with dignity, however, and aspire to better housing, food, education, and more control over their lives.

The low degree of politicoeconomic representation of the poor has been a drawback in the Spanish ascent from poverty. Although this factor does not appear to have been a serious deterrent in setting off a rise in the rate of economic growth, there are few examples in history of a successful ascent from poverty without a diffusion of power. Another possible drawback is the lack of a sense of social solidarity among Spaniards. History has made the Spaniard mistrustful of his society, which, as Ortega y Gasset states, is as much *dis*society. Nevertheless, the government expects that the cooperative nature of modern production will break down this mistrust.

The poor in the rural areas face a troublesome future. Because of Spain's long isolation, there has been an increase in the use of marginal land for high-cost production. The problem is how to eliminate these marginal lands from production, make the remainder competitive with Europe, and shift displaced labor into industry.

Some industrial workers are critical of the Spanish labor syndicates,[14] whereas others believe that these organizations do promote their interests. This low degree of group consciousness is not unique to Spain; it is characteristic of individualistic Latin societies. Workers in a country like Sweden may have a greater faith in problem solving through group action, but the Swede is concerned about the group's attitude toward him. The Spaniard, on the other hand, feels less intimidated and less inclined to modify his vision of reality to group perceptions. As far as group consciousness is concerned, the Spaniard is more likely to identify with a social group of his immediate experience rather than to engage in a day-to-day pursuit of collective action.

What of the future? Ambivalent pressures in Spain make the outcome of Franco's passing uncertain. As the cold war in Europe recedes from the memory of Spaniards, so does the grip of Franco's followers on the people. Only with increasing difficulty can they use a fear of communism as a means of obtaining support. Franco has set the scenario to unfold after his departure. In 1967, he submitted to the Cortes a new constitution that incorporates his plan for the succession. It was approved by acclamation. Although the new constitution provides for a king as chief of state and a premier to head the government it is difficult to anticipate the political process that will unfold from this. Franco will not be able to control from the grave the actions and counteractions that his passing will cause.

With economic change, the Spaniard's traditional scorn for modern

[14] It is impossible to make a judgment as to the extent of the disaffection either from a handful of interviews or from press reports.

Europe has been breaking down. That process of change has brought into power men who readily accept the technology and culture of Western Europe and has weakened not only the scorn for modern society, but the anarchical spirit and the hold of the church. Time therefore has eroded the support of the political and economic monopoly that rested in the hands of the nationalist revolutionaries, their children, and their friends. Although they may try to control and perpetuate the system after Franco, they cannot prevent the secularization that economic growth brings. Forces have been unleashed in Spain that are increasingly beyond their control. The forces of greater democratization are in the ascendancy.

At the international level, Spain's entrance into the European community of nations means a further relinquishment of traditional points of view. Because the employer must know his new competitors and standardize parts, equipment, and materials, he may make pejorative comparisons between his own culture and what he considers to be modernity. The attitudes of youth are also affected by the exposure to the more advanced economies. They reject authoritarianism. The change is likely to accelerate as the national revolutionaries pass away and the generation born after the civil war takes over positions in the power structure.

The big issues are whether an obsolescent political and social system can change peaceably and to what extent modern industrialism will contribute to such change. There is strong evidence that the Spaniards will make the transformation without violence. The way in which the goddess of technology will make its imprint is not clear, however. In this transition, Spain's possibilities are considerable. When an underdeveloped country has a population base of people with a high motivation to learn and with a mass cult of intellectuality, that nation has considerable potential for rapid economic growth.

Lastly, as in the case of Mexico, Spain appears to demonstrate that a successful economic takeoff and an authoritarian style of governing are not compatible.[15] Although Spanish power is more centralized in the chief of state and the cabinet ministers, a process of diffusion is evident. The election of members of the Cortes has been liberalized. The Spanish system of governing is becoming more pluralistic. The pluralism may be small, deliberately confined, de facto, but it is there to see. In actual practice, the authoritarian law is losing its force as the groups originally controlled by the dictator begin to control him and new power clusters emerge. The authoritarian law on the basis of which the state is supposed to be administered may become a scrap of paper. Scholars who base their descriptions of the Spanish political system on the written record may be describing a system that no longer exists.

Our overall assessment of Spanish economic development is a guarded rating of successful.

---

[15] For a study on a parallel evolution of democracy in Spain and Mexico, see Juan J. Linz, "An Authoritarian Regime," in Erik Allardt and Yrjo Littunen (eds.), *Cleavages, Ideologies, and Party Systems* (Helsinki: Academic Book Store, 1964), Vol. X.

part four
THE UNITED STATES AND ECONOMIC DEVELOPMENT

15

ROLE OF THE UNITED STATES IN ECONOMIC DEVELOPMENT

The basic problem of contemporary economic development can be simply stated. It is how to create an infrastructure of educational, employment, and government institutions that will set off a spiral of rising tangible and human capital. In spite of the enormous outlays that have been made in words and funds, only Japan and the Soviet Union have succeeded in launching such a mechanism in the twentieth century. Both directly and indirectly, the development of these two nations resulted from European influence. Russian economic growth began before the communist revolution and represents a forced and at times brutal accentuation of Western European economic history. Despite its anti-Western propaganda, that country has been disposed to copy the capital investment techniques and technology of its ideological adversaries. As for Japan, we have observed how that nation learned to borrow selectively from the West, harness its social processes to economic growth, and thereby generate an internal revolution.

In the current race for forced development, no latter-day Japan or Soviet Union has emerged. Moreover, those countries that are presently modernizing face considerable problems. They are hostile to Western ideas or remote from them. Their physical environments are tough. Their situations are such that domestic turmoil and international mischief are likely.

By the sheer weight of its income alone, one-third of the world total, the United States has been under pressure to become concerned with these problems. Yet, there is no urgent economic or cultural reason why the American people should be deeply concerned about the developing nations. Were it not for its military preoccupations, the United States in its present atmosphere of middle-class affluence would likely exercise a policy of minimum foreign commitment. Because of the bigger markets, American employers find investment in advanced nations more attractive than in developing nations. Accordingly, any political support for the rationale of foreign aid is dominated by political questions of international power and subject to shifting sands of time. Development problems of particular nations are ignored or stressed depending on the feelings of American citizens for particular foreign countries. The varying interpretation of the communist conspiracy has become a principal catalytic force behind development policy. The slogan is meaningless, however, to those who see the problems of these nations in a development context and who observe the government assuming differences in the use of the concept to suit its political ends.

A donor country affects the economic development of a country in a variety of ways through private and public institutions. This chapter concentrates on the foreign aid of the United States government, the foreign investment of American business, and international labor activity. By government foreign aid is meant policies to provide the recipient nation with goods and services without lowering in the immediate term its foreign exchange position.

TYPES OF FOREIGN AID

It is useful to trace the sequence of United States foreign aid since World War II. From the end of that conflict until the beginning of the cold war and its spread to developing countries, the United States government concentrated on recovery in Western Europe. The effort was successful. The quick recovery of Europe did not, however, provide useful lessons for those who formulate developing policies for underdeveloped countries. Western Europe already had a structured labor force of high skills and motivation for work. Furthermore, the pent-up demand for hard consumer goods and the destruction of capital goods primed the channels of production. A soldier who left Germany in 1944, for example, and then returned only six years later would have found the recovery incredible.

In the second phase of foreign aid, assistance was given to developing nations in a setting of big power rivalry. By 1960 the major part of foreign aid was being given to Latin America, Asia, and Africa, half of it in the form of military assistance. The impact of this military aid is not easy to assess. For the United States, it provides opportunities to dispose of obsolete equipment and to restock American arsenals with new designs. It also produces a psychological effect of treating the development and nationalism of foreign countries as a military problem.

In the recipient nation, the military may use the equipment to suppress protest movements in their country. The foreigner who is given a gun by the United States may use it to promote the interests of a privileged class. By inhibiting popular support of the government, the political suppression by the military may curtail attitudes that are favorable to a rise in productivity. Conceivably, innovators may be attracted to military service who might otherwise be available for industrial entrepreneurship. In addition, the recipient may not act in the interests of the United States government and may generate conflicts that draw in the United States. On the other hand, military aid can generate investments in education, transportation, public health, water supply, and communication systems as a backwash of building a military machine.

Military aid can increase significantly the economic dependency of the recipient nation. Thus, subsidizing the pay of the soldiers of the recipient nation releases resources for use in economic growth. Eventually, the foreign nation may find it necessary to support United States military objectives in order to maintain its economic growth.

The economic phase of foreign aid includes long-term loans to the recipient nation that are repayable in dollars. The terms of these loans may range as much as fifty years with a nominal interest charge to cover servicing. These hard loans shift to outright grants if the recipient nations find it difficult to pay back their debts. In any case the use of these funds is controlled so as to minimize any adverse economic effects on the American economy. For example, restrictions are placed on purchases in order to encourage the buying of American goods in the expectation that the balance of payments position of the United States will be thereby improved. The argument against such a restriction is that the recipient is then unable to shop in other nations for equipment more suitable to economies of low labor skills.

A major problem of developing countries is how to increase their per capita food supply at stable prices and at the same time attract agricultural labor to industry. Few such nations succeed in solving this problem. In the course of development, many shift from net exporters of food to net importers. The agricultural shortages in these countries contrast with American surpluses that cannot be disposed of in domestic markets. The surplus commodities program authorized by the Agricultural Trade and Assistance Act of 1954 has attempted to resolve this paradox. Under agreement with such nations as India, surplus products are sold to the recipient country and paid for in local currencies that are placed in the account of the donor. These counterpart funds are usable only for expenditures in the recipient nation. The hoped-for effect of these transactions is to hold down the rise in agricultural prices in the recipient's economy by the dual effect of introducing more goods in its markets and by withdrawing money from public hands. In addition, under special conditions of famine relief, outright gifts of food are made.

The disposal of such surplus agricultural products has other ramifications. These products may have possible adverse effects because of altered diet balances of persons consuming such food. The surpluses may also enter the international markets of nations that have an interest in preventing the price declines produced by the increased world supply. Furthermore, the American government has to devise ways of using its accumulating accounts of local currencies. Liberal expense accounts for itinerant Congressmen help dissipate them.

A third approach to economic aid is to facilitate American exports through the Export-Import Bank of the United States. The major source of the bank's funds is the Treasury of the United States. Through the extension of credits to importers and guarantees to exporters, the bank seeks to promote increases in American exports. The guarantees include insurance against such contingencies as the inability of the exporters to convert foreign currencies, losses due to expropriation in the recipient country, import restrictions, civil disturbances, and war.[1]

Technical assistance, the exportation of human resource skills rather than goods, is another form of commitment. At a particular point in its development, a nation requires a particular order of skills to gain further momentum in growth. In the short run, these skills may be more economically imported than developed in the recipient nation. Accordingly, technical assistance can have a useful role as long as offsetting disadvantages do not accrue, such as hostility to foreign experts in the recipient country.

In the United States, technical assistance has declined in the foreign aid agency, and the Peace Corps has offered a variety of its own. The Peace Corps workers are not exact substitutes, however, and operate at different levels. The stated purpose of the Peace Corps is to channel idealistic American youth into service for developing nations and to create thereby an increased awareness and sympathy in the United States for the problems of these nations. A preponderant number of these volunteers are secondary school teachers of limited experience, principally teachers of English. The remainder include agricultural technicians, medical technicians, construction specialists, engineers, and college graduates with a liberal arts education. Some are in quest of a little adventure before settling down to the business of becoming established in their fields. For some, a paid tour abroad can be a palliative for difficulties at home. The Peace Corps can serve a useful purpose in the host nation, however, to the extent that its token programs stimulate an interest in human resources planning.

Congressional disenchantment with foreign aid has not affected its favorable consideration of Peace Corps appropriations. If this outcome reflects popular sentiment for the program, the Peace Corps has attained

---

[1] In 1967 press reports indicated that a substantial and increasing proportion of the Export-Import Bank's credits was going into the sale of arms to developing countries.

one of its expressed objectives. To weigh the cost-benefit of a vaguely defined educational and training effort is not easy. One would suspect that the resulting output in the recipient country in relation to the annual cost per volunteer is small. Perhaps the propaganda effects at home and abroad make such expenditures justifiable.

Two issues in the economic foreign aid program are worthy of mention. One is whether assistance should be shifted from repayable loans to outright grants.[2] The argument put forward in favor of loans is that they increase efficiency in the use of capital by the recipient. The counterargument is that the pressure to repay such a loan curtails the efficacy of the development effort because it forces investments into a use that readily produces a rate of return in the short run and compels the recipient to develop export industries in order to acquire foreign exchange for repayment. Moreover, outright grants, by not hamstringing the recipient, allegedly produce more ideological adherents for the United States. In reality, however, the loans tend to shift from credits payable in dollars to credits payable in local currency and then to outright grants.

The economical use of aid funds has more to do with the educational levels and morals in the recipient country than with whether the capital is in the form of a loan or grant. Equipment may lie in warehouses because of a lack of knowledge of how to use it. The corrupt may take their share regardless of whether the aid is a loan or a grant. Moreover, it is difficult to estimate the rates of return on the different uses of such capital funds. How should one compare returns on such uses as building a school, a steel mill, a communication line? Assuming such a feat of computation can be made, how should a time limit be set in which the entire amortization should accrue? Productivity is indivisible. If an individual raises his productivity, judgments have to be made as to allocation among intellect, motivation, equipment, buildings, administrative support, social overhead capital, and perhaps even his wife.

The other issue is how much of the capital should go to public versus private projects. The issue is beclouded by old-time religion on private enterprise. In the Clay Committee report to President Kennedy on the question of foreign aid,[3] there is the implication that an inadequate share of capital funds goes to private enterprise in the developing nations. If one lumps together the loans of the major development agencies that provide hard currency loans, one finds as much as one-fourth going to private borrowers. Moreover, on the basis of frequency of loans, private borrowers are in the majority.

A developing country is not apt to have a considerable number of good

---

[2] For some interesting thoughts on the subject of grants and loans, see Harry G. Johnson, *Economic Policies Toward Less Developed Countries* (Washington, D.C.: Brookings Institution, 1967).
[3] The Clay Committee Investigation of foreign aid in 1963 was conceived by the Kennedy administration as an instrument for gaining support in Congress for the program. The report had the opposite effect of mounting a Congressional attack on foreign aid.

risks among its private borrowers. This fact has a special bearing on loans of the United States foreign aid agency, which is more inclined to underwrite a safe venture than to support a risky one. It has the mentality of the conservative banker: You can have the money if you do not need it and you cannot have it if you do. With Congressmen keeping a watchful eye on its administrators, the agency is reluctant to extend loans to private enterprise. Moreover, such loans may encourage scandal in the recipient nation, for the potential borrowers are often not particularly shining examples of virtue. They may be get-rich-quick artists who could tarnish the image of the United States rather than entrepreneurial types. If the loans are to be effective, the private endeavors of the borrowers have to be consistent with the overall capital planning that is likely to build a modern and diversified economic structure.

Consequently, although Congress commits the government to the promotion of private enterprise, the realities abroad do not lend to its encouragement. Entrepreneurs are a scarce commodity in developing nations. The law of the Congress itself imposes restrictions on loans. Nor does the Congress seem disposed to underwrite a foreign firm whose goods could successfully compete with products made in the United States. Therefore, talk about using foreign aid to promote private enterprise has little basis in reality for most developing nations.

What are the criteria officially expressed by the United States government for granting foreign economic aid? The government states it takes into account the extent to which the recipient country exerts energies along the following lines: creating a favorable climate for private enterprise and for American investment; taking measures to improve food production; making economic, social, and political reforms; increasing efficiency in raising taxes; land reform; allocating government expenditures in a manner conducive to economic development; contributing to the projects for which assistance is requested; and increasing the role of the population in the development process.[4]

DISENCHANTMENT OVER FOREIGN AID

The support of the liberals in the Congress is vital to the continuance of the foreign aid program, yet they are becoming as disenchanted as the conservatives. If the goal of economic development is to raise the living standards of the poor, they ask, where is the evidence that this is occurring? In addition, they see no demonstration of the ability of

[4] An *economic* rationale of the importance of foreign aid at different stages of economic development has not been sufficiently developed. Professor Hollis B. Chenery and his associates have worked on a model associating external assistance in three stages of growth: skill-limited phase, a saving-limited phase, and a trade-limited phase. The model consists of eight variables: GNP, investment, consumption, saving, capital stock, imports, exports, and foreign aid. For a critique of the model and rejoinder, see J. C. H. Fei and Gustav Ranis, "Foreign Assistance and Economic Development" (comment), and H. B. Chenery and A. M. Strout (reply) in *The American Economic Review*, Vol. 58 (September 1968).

developing nations to accumulate their own capital. Moreover, liberals state that the use of foreign aid to support governments that do not have the confidence of their population serves to turn these people against the United States.

Congressional disenchantment also reflects the attitudes of an uninformed public, which has been nettled by depictions of foreign aid recipients as virtue receiving its due and American policy as full of misconceptions and selfish motives. In this stereotype, the modernizing nation is sensitive, abused, and misunderstood, whereas the donor country is wicked and stupid. This attitude is reinforced by politicians' claims that developing countries have not demonstrated sufficient gratitude for the assistance they have obtained from a generous United States, and by accounts of mistakes and corruption in the foreign aid program.

There are a number of reasons for these attitudes. A foreign aid program is likely to be complex. In its hiring of certain types of personnel, the foreign aid agency seems to be using a criterion of political influence rather than maximum competence and of caution rather than imagination. The agency does not lack competent economic technicians as much as it lacks a broad view of economic development and an overall ideology. Congress itself and the executive department contribute to the weakening of the agency by the manner in which it is used for political purposes. The periodic reorganizations they impose contribute to instability and lowered efficiency. The lack of experience of the United States as a colonial power and the gap between affluent Americans and the "natives" of developing nations are also contributing factors.

Public attitudes range from small pockets of hostility or support to general indifference. The support comes mainly from a small circle of specialists and power strategists in and out of government and from international-minded Easterners with favorite developing nations. Their support tends to move the program in the direction of a power game against international adversaries. The aspiration of the Kennedy administration to shift the program in the direction of a long-term effort to raise the living standards of the poor in the world was terminated abruptly by the shots of an assassin. Subsequent events indicate that international power needs dominate development efforts. The need to reduce poverty in the world is not presented forcefully to Americans who live in the heartland. Even if it were, there is a real question as to whether such an objective would stir a sense of mission in an environment of affluence. The suburban middle class holds the balance of political power, and its members appear to be too overworked matching rising costs with more income to have the time to understand the problem of world poverty.

Lack of timeliness has been an important element of development mistakes, particularly in Latin America. Improper timing eventually produces a situation whose only solution, as conceived by the United States, is military intervention. The Guatemalan revolution of 1954 was a portent of the future, but the United States government responded by taking a tough position against communism. As a result, a polarization ensued in that country that brought the gunning down of American officials, including an ambassador. In 1958 no quick response was forthcoming to the proposal of President Kubitschek of Brazil for a joint attack on Latin American economic development. The precipitous political events that followed thereafter led to the hasty organization of the Alliance for Progress but not with a full-blown strategy behind the effort. Inaction followed by precipitous action reflects the slowness of democratic procedures and the need for development problems to crystallize as a communist threat before they are taken seriously.

The offer of economic assistance by one government to another unavoidably is a political act. To say that politics should be eschewed in economic aid is to suppose that such assistance can be made in a vacuum. A foreign aid program, in the very gesture of offering assistance, cannot be undertaken without strings attached. More pertinent are the political events that would occur in the absence of the program and those that do occur in its presence. Recipient nations do not divorce foreign aid from their own politics. Often their gauge of political accomplishment is to obtain maximum assistance from rival powers without becoming involved in their ideological conflicts. Their success in this international power game must be weighed against the political consequences within their own nations for failing to build a mechanism of sustained economic growth with such foreign aid.

The persisting crisis in American foreign aid is reflected in the periodic changes in the name of the government agency directing it. In some two decades, the name has shifted from the Economic Cooperative Administration (ECA), to the Mutual Security Administration (MSA), the Foreign Operations Administration (FOA), the International Cooperation Administration (ICA), and now to the Agency for International Development (AID). The names change, the top managers come and go, but the nameplates and style of the bureaucracy remain substantially the same. As a new crossroad in the mission of the agency appears, a crisis in title emerges. In shifting from international brotherhood, to security, to economic development, the titles do not lack in imagination.

AID is not master of its own house, for its top policy makers are subject to the swing and sway of domestic American politics. A Congressional attempt to authorize the agency to dismiss top personnel for inefficiency met the opposition of the AFL-CIO as an attack on the integrity of the civil service system. Such an accusation is intended to elicit the same response as an attack on motherly love.

ROLE OF ORGANIZED LABOR

The American labor movement has a significant influence on the foreign aid program. It is represented in the organizational structure of such agencies as the State Department, the Agency for International Development, and the Peace Corps. It is affiliated with the International Confederation of Free Trade Unions,[5] the International Labor Organization, and an organization with considerable activities in Latin America, the American Institute for Free Labor Development (AIFLD). In the agencies of the United States government, organized labor has a role in making and implementing policy and in selecting personnel for employment at home and abroad.

These functions include training foreign labor specialists who come to the United States from developing nations; staffing labor posts in American embassies abroad; processing requests for technical and monetary assistance coming from foreign trade unions; providing tours for foreign labor dignitaries; and representing organized labor in various economic missions of the American government. This involvement implies taking a position in a foreign nation that is allied to the foreign policy interests of the United States government rather than those of the laboring classes in the particular country.

The discharging of these functions has produced mixed results. Its role in public administration involves organized labor in functions of long-term planning and control. Yet the techniques learned at the collective bargaining table may not be suitable to the administration of public policy. The manner in which they fill posts with individuals no longer suitably employed in the ranks of organized labor is also questionable. These jobs become sinecures for those sponsored by a labor leader while the more talented remain in organized labor positions. As overseers in personnel recruitment, the labor officials are excluding individuals with a university preparation who have aptitudes in foreign labor affairs but no friends in the American labor movement. Government officials play their part in such an outcome by accepting the veto power of organized labor.

Another effect on the labor effort abroad derives from organized labor's negative approach to ideology—that is, American organized labor appears to know what it is against, but it has no positive philosophy of economic development. The old anticommunists in the American labor movement whose monolithic vision of communism is colored by the experience of the Stalin era exert a considerable influence on the position of organized labor abroad. They tend to focus their efforts in developing countries on flushing out communists and rewarding anticommunists rather than on developing human resources.

What brings about such a state of affairs? In order to gain support for

[5] In 1969 the AFL-CIO, smarting from the manner in which the United Auto Workers was treated by the International organization, announced its intent to withdraw from the ICFTU.

its foreign aid efforts in the Congress, the government must solicit the assistance of organized labor. In addition, the reluctance of the more effective labor leaders to participate in these matters preempts the field to those in the secondary ranks. Another factor is the assumption that an official with modest responsibilities in a labor organization is by that fact a student of the labor problem in economic development.

The AIFLD states that its purpose is to build strong democratic unions in Latin America. By such an objective is meant unions that are controlled neither by the governments nor by communist leaders. This purpose is traced by the AIFLD to the principle expressed in the Preamble to the Alliance for Progress charter for the establishment of trade unions in Latin America in the interest of social and economic development. In the first full year of operation, the income of the AIFLD amounted to approximately $1 million, of which a third came from trade unions, a third from the American government, and a third from a source the organization lumps together as "foundations, corporations, and other private sources." Two American firms with economic interests in Latin America, Pan American Airways and Grace Lines, are heavy contributors.

The organization pursues its objective of building strong anticommunist labor organizations by training Latin American labor officials and by social projects. A substantial number of trade unionists go through its course in Washington every year. In addition, regional centers throughout Latin America attract hundreds of men and women. Course content comprises trade-union organization, American labor movement history, international labor organization, labor education techniques, role of unions in a democratic society, collective bargaining, economics, and anticommunism. In addition, specially selected groups take an advanced course that includes travel in such countries as Italy, Germany, and Israel. These participants also spend some time in Washington for indoctrination. The social projects department of AIFLD includes a program on housing, clinics, cooperatives, and credit unions. The American government also authorizes the organization to distribute government surplus food.

The impact of the AIFLD is not easy to assess. Communication lines to representatives of the Latin American working classes are officially granted as a monopoly to the organization. Its program is self-validating in the sense that foreign recipients of its benefits are inclined to evaluate their experience in a manner their mentors would like to hear. The organization advertises itself as free labor working with the Alliance for Progress for evolutionary change in Latin America. In its approach, it transplants American trade-union technology and the message of anticommunism to Latin Americans and rewards those who accept the message. The AIFLD uses its social projects to woo Latin American workers from communist-dominated organizations to trade unions that receive its blessing. The organization is influenced by the anticommunist spirit of the AFL-CIO Federation headquarters. Some individuals in the federation are former communists themselves who have since seen the light.

The labor leaders of developing nations are in a delicate position. They require a stable environment with which to develop a power relationship with the managers of the economy. At the same time, they have to respond to the shifting and charged points of view of their constituencies. Reconciling these needs is more difficult when the labor leaders are viewed by their own nationals as owing an allegiance to an organization supported by the United States government. The schism that arises among Latin Americans in consequence of this allegiance affects the development process. The United States citizen demanding an oath of fealty in return for rewards may blunt the spirit of protest and strengthen the position of privileged groups who wish to inhibit change. When Americans have actually intervened in local conflicts, such intervention has pitted groups of workers against one another under the initiative of members of a foreign power.

In addition, the training of the AIFLD does not appear to come to grips with the problem of developing a mechanism for the effective utilization of labor. Indeed, its intervention may have an opposite effect. Moreover, in countries that are ripe for revolutionary change, a question arises as to who these noncommunist leaders of labor are. Are they men of principle with the confidence of the people or are they anticommunists simply for convenience? These are difficult questions.

The facts do not indicate that the participation of American organized labor in foreign aid is entirely wise in principle. Implicit in economic development is the idea that people do not wish to live in poverty and that they need not do so. The United States often appears to behave as though it is against the poor of the world. The government may appear to support the effort of American organized labor as an instrument of its foreign policy. American organized labor, with its anticommunist slogans, does not put forward an ideology that is persuasive with developing populations.

ROLE OF AMERICAN BUSINESS

American business investment abroad takes different forms. It may be the creation of sales agencies in the host nation, the construction and operation of enterprises, joint sales operations with nationals of the host country, or the granting of patent rights. The changing political situation in the United States and the host nations has varying consequences depending on the nature of the investment and the terms thereof. The total investment of American business abroad amounts to approximately $57 billion. A third of this amount is invested in Canada, whereas somewhat less is invested in Europe. A considerable portion of the remainder is in Japan, Australia, and South Africa. Consequently, little of this investment—about 20 percent of the total—finds its way into the developing nations, and most of it is in advanced nations with consumption patterns similar to those of the United States. (Canadians, more than Paraguayans, are likely to buy American power back scratchers.) One-third of the investment in Latin America is in Venezuela, and more than three-quarters of that is in petroleum. The rest of the world total for developing countries amounts to $1.2 billion in the Middle East, about $1 billion in Africa (outside of South Africa), and a similar amount in Asia (outside of Japan).[6] The principal goods attracting American investment in developing nations are raw materials or products from the soil and to a lesser extent consumer goods, principally foods, household goods, and pharmaceuticals. The American employer plays a minor role in the two prime necessities of developing countries: producer goods and social overhead capital.

The typical American producer in modernizing nations tends to be an opponent of the ideology of their laboring classes. He needs stability for his operations. Of necessity, he has dealings with the conservative elements who hold power and who may not have the confidence of the population. In this way, he may become identified with entrenched privilege and become anathema to insurgent groups, even though he often provides employment terms better than those of local manufacturers. In Latin America, such a position creates a dichotomy in American foreign policy. On the one hand, the government aspires to structural changes in Latin American countries that would produce a rise in the status of their people. On the other, it is expected to protect the interests of American employers who identify with Latin Americans averse to such change.

The advantages that may accrue to the economic development of recipient countries are in the transfer and spread of technology and in the training of indigenous personnel. Unless a deliberate policy exists to pursue such outcomes, however, these advantages do not automatically follow. It would be significant to study in detail the effects on the development of preconditions for a takeoff in nations where American capital represents a substantial portion of industrial investment.

The divergence of interests between the American investor and the development interests of the foreign nation can be decreased by transferring ownership of the American business to nationals, for it is in the long-term interest of the developing nation that these operations become owned and operated by local personnel. In addition, the company's products and their local purchases have to be consistent with the overall need to establish a diversified economic structure. Moreover, from a political point of view, the conspicuous American employer who is welcomed at an early stage of development in the host country may be considered an imperialist at a later stage. A deliberate policy of transferring ownership in this fashion also eases pressure on foreign exchange.

6 The figures are those of the United States Department of Commerce.

The prospects of such changes are not too bright, however, because many American companies, supported by the banking profession, do not view such a change as being in their interest.

The policy of the General Electric Company in Brazil is a model that serves the interests of the host country. The firm builds plants that are staffed with Brazilian personnel, although initially started with an American cadre of skilled workers. Both subassemblies and end products are produced in Brazil. Wholesale and retail outlets are developed and staffed by Brazilians. In addition, Brazilian suppliers of the company are assisted in developing their own human and material capital. The policy suggests the road on which private and national interests can be reconciled. Its demonstration effect lies in showing how skill levels can be raised, job opportunities provided to put skills to use, and how indigenous capital can be diversified.

IDEOLOGICAL DILEMMA OF THE UNITED STATES

The Brazilian experience is a case history of the ideological dilemma confronting the United States. The biggest source of Brazilian foreign capital is the United States. Economic development in that country contends with a general demoralization of the working classes. The crushing inflation and the use of labor organizations as a political spoil of ambitious politicians contribute to the demoralization. Workers must spend the preponderant amount of their wages on food. Rural migrants moving to the periphery of the cities to obtain the housing they can afford must spend as much as 20 percent of their wages on transportation, and after paying for their food, rent, and transportation, there is hardly any money left. Workers believe that the inflation is caused by friends of government officials who obtain money in ways that border on corruption.

The military regime that installed itself in 1964 set a 25 percent limit to the annual rise in prices as a gauge of successful economic policy. Its original goal of a 10 percent limit had to be abandoned. The regime's price-wage policies resulted in a decline of real wages by 40 percent in the period 1964–1967. The extent of worker discontent is unknown because of the censorship. The historical fate of the Brazilian labor movement continues under the military regime. Major unions are under the control of what the government calls interveners. Another potential source of protest, students, was neutralized by the dissolution of the National Student Union. Brazil is typical of the Latin American country where a redistribution of power in favor of the population base produces a reaction by privileged groups with the help of the military.

Brazil is a nation of educational contrasts. The managers of its big enterprises are highly educated and trained. Fifty percent of the people, however, are illiterate, and the majority of the children do not go beyond the third grade. Not too far from the glittering beaches of Copacabana, the unskilled line up in almost a solid phalanx in the streets selling sugar-coated peanuts at three cents a bag.

What should American policy be in such a climate? The United States government propped up the regime with liberal dollar credits, but the population is indifferent to its rationale: anticommunism. It is difficult to institute a massive interest in development in an atmosphere in which the managers and the people view each other with indifference or open hostility.

In an oblique reference to the United States, the Roman Catholic Archbishop Dom Helder Camara of Brazil had the following to say about economic development in his country:

> Often, a great power is concerned only with the short-term approach; it is concerned with maintaining the status quo. It does not introduce any big change in underdeveloped countries on the grounds it is opposed to communism and it wants to safeguard the free world. This same great power imposes economic sanctions. Sometimes it even resorts to military occupation.
> It is illusory to speak about the free world when referring to underdeveloped countries. Poverty also is slavery from which the masses must be freed, these masses which are not yet able to be, in faith, people. If one prevents rapid changes in underdeveloped countries, then that is nothing but a contribution to the provocation of social upheavals, civil wars, and chaos.[7]

In this dilemma, the United States approach appears to be negative. When asserted, its philosophy tends to be expressed in vague generalities about freedom and democracy and protecting the free world. A policy of deemphasizing anticommunism risks the accusation that the United States is being soft on communism.[8] One effect of this anticommunist position is to submerge the spirit of protest and to appear to be supporting the enemies of the people. The United States is thus put in the role of being the principal opponent of revolutionary change in the world, an adversary of the world's masses.

Can the image of the United States be improved as a champion of the poor in the developing world? The task is difficult. Communism has a strong appeal. It rides the crest of nationalism and articulates a philosophy that advocates rejection of the existing order, and the poor are in a rejecting mood. The United States often comes into their country and supports enemies of the people. Americans seem to be sympathetic toward anticolonial revolutions in developing countries. The feelings of many become ambivalent, however, when the revolution is led by a communist, even one who is supported by nationalist sentiment.

No alternative, effective philosophy appears to exist. A possibility for

---

[7] Quoted in *Center Magazine,* Vol. 1 (October–November 1967).
[8] By a quirk of history, at a time when anticommunist policy appears to be obsolescing, a President of the United States comes into power whose political career was based on exploiting the anticommunist issue.

developing nations is a pragmatic nationalism, Tito-style or Mexican-style. The plea to foreign populations for economic liberalism falls on deaf ears. The American habit of viewing crises in international loyalties as a military problem does not capture the loyalties of the poor. At home, the urging of support for foreign aid on the basis that it acquires friends and desired political institutions is on shaky ground. Such exhortations lay the groundwork for attacks against aid programs when these results are not forthcoming. Forced economic development presupposes institutions un-like those of the United States at a similar stage of its growth. A rise in the human capacities in modernizing nations may have to be its own recompense.

If the good will of people in developing nations is a necessary con-comitant of effective foreign aid, how is it attained? Oddly enough, some of the most favorable attitudes are found in countries where little or no American presence exists. Eastern Europe is an example. The senti-ment there is explainable on the basis of what their people believe to be the experience of fellow nationals as immigrants in the United States. Where contacts in depth occur, any good will that does exist derives only in modest part from the American government official or from the arms given to the foreign government. Rather, as in Mexico, it appears to come from the relationship between American professional men and their coequals among the nationals. In the public sphere, the more persuasive representations seem to derive from those who assume a temporary role in discharging public functions. In a world of ferment, frank idealists with a professional bearing seem to be more effective representatives of the American image.

If these assertions are correct, policy implications follow. The less blatant the foreign aid as a unilateral instrument of power play, the more unobtrusive the official American presence, the more likely will the objec-tive of rapport be successfully attained. A policy of multilateral aid from a group of nations is indicated. In addition, some phases of foreign aid could be channeled into an economic development foundation staffed by professional individuals and assisted by public funds but administered by individuals with a flair for implementing ideals with practical policies. Such an administrator is rare, however. Expecting creative and workable ideas from administrators of large organizations may be asking too much. Assuming that the powers that be are willing to hire such a person, how can he be allowed to operate without the dead hand of group policy-mak-ing and accounting controls?

A quasi-independent development foundation need not be an impracti-cal effort. It could have the advantage of flexibility and divorcement from the immediate power interests of government. The organization could evolve as a kind of National Science Foundation in the area of develop-ment policy. The work of the Peace Corps, the Alliance for Progress, and the development of effective institutional structures to increase the effective utilization of labor could be assumed by such a foundation. Such an organization could easily become a supporter of the aspirations of the talented poor of developing countries, a role that American government officials cannot perform. Its merit would be greater flexibility, more professional attachment, and less timidity.

If such an organization were to draw its staff from government agencies, however, its efforts could well be rendered ineffective. The caliber of some American personnel employed in foreign aid programs suggests an inclination to put one's worst foot forward. The top bureaucrat on the American side may be chosen because of political connections, and he in turn selects subordinates with similar assets. When a dignitary is due to arrive in the United States for assistance, the top-dog politician in whose jurisdiction he falls communicates with a lower-level politician, who in turn ferrets out a crony with a vital attribute similar to that of the foreigner, such as a hobby or similar ethnic origin. With each step in the procedure, the caliber of the American representative falls precipitately.[9] The international long-run equilibrium suggested by this tendency is that foreign governments choose their representatives on a similar basis.

Ruling hierarchies in many parts of Latin America and Asia do not have the confidence of their people. They are not on talking terms. By its relations with such officials, the United States inherits the burden of this lack of rapport. It is exacerbated by the tendency of middle-class American officials to prefer counterparts who fail to live up to an ideology that rouses the interest of the poorer classes. The Peace Corps is an exception, but probably not a significant one. The problem of lack of rapport is aggravated when the foreign poor are regarded as a statistic, as inferiors. The collaboration between ruling hierarchies and middle-class American officials stifles the growth of the people's confidence in both.

Summation

The stated American policy of foreign economic aid is a democratic approach to economic growth. This policy implies involvement of the people of a developing nation in the processes of economic development. The United States has the job of persuading the poor people of the world that its foreign aid policy is for them and not for their affluent compatriots. From the American record, the persuasion is not easy. The United States has been a principal party to the frustration of revolutions that have occurred in developing nations of Latin America and Asia. In that role, it has also tended to frustrate their economic development.

---

9 In one such confrontation, an official spokesman complained to a university professor that he (the professor) was not explaining the United States Labor Management Relations Act properly to a group of officials from a developing country. As it turned out, the official guide, a former trade-union official, had never read the law.

Its policy has appeared at times to promote the economic interests of a conservative elite. Its fundamental thrust has been a belief in the existence of a centrally controlled communist conspiracy to dominate the world.

The absence of an ideological force behind American foreign aid reflects the inhibitions of a conservative government. The request for foreign aid funds is merchandised to Congressmen on the basis of combating communism abroad; they thereupon consider this a cue to begin offending the people of developing countries. Moreover, the tolerable range of competing ideas is so narrow as to appear indiscernible. The debate tends to place the initiative in the hands of those who consider the communist challenge in developing nations as one of military power rather than as a need for an alternative development philosophy that could compete effectively for mass allegiance. If the crucial question is raised as to why the poor should abandon the clarion call of Marxism, the answer seems to be unconvincing.

If the goal of Western-style economic development is to raise human capacities within a setting of democratic institutions, the United States appears to shy away from the implications of this goal. Freedom implies diffusion of power and challenging established seats of influence. To seek such an objective means supporting dissident individuals of revolutionary zeal who come into conflict with conservatives disposed to defend existing institutions and seats of power. In the absence of such individuals, a basic question of policy for the United States is what philosophy it can support to encourage their rise on a large scale.

There should be a willingness to experiment with new forms of social relationships in order to bring to the fore a new group of innovators. In this objective, the United States is at a disadvantage with the Soviet Union, which had to cope with the problem in recent years. By promoting a leadership of middle-class timidity and by not encouraging experimentation in social processes, the United States may be hindering the growth of the developing nations. They require not only capital but new institutions.

A curious paradox of economic development is the manner in which Marxist ideology exerts a haphazard influence on the extent of government involvement. Marxist slogans have an appeal to the people of Asia and Latin America. Their simplistic clichés are directed against Western economies, especially the United States, in spite of the fact that growth in the countries where the slogans were formulated was brought about by imitating the processes that led to Western growth. To the extent that these catchwords cause an indiscriminate rejection of the European legacy that brought about economic change these nations impose on themselves obstacles to their development.

The Marxist slogans together with those of the West present a choice to modernizing nations that is specious. The founts of economic growth —critical inquiry, optimism, equality of opportunity, initiative—are indispensable to East and West. The degree of government involvement in development will be determined by the pressing needs of the society rather than by slogans, and whether the government will play an effective role will depend to a considerable degree on the type of men that it attracts. The slogans are mischievous also to the extent that they become a basis for political intransigence and rightist military takeover of the governments. It is a game played frequently and a source of continuous embarrassment to the United States.

As noted earlier, the economic takeoff of the Soviet Union took place before its revolution. The ensuing events, despite the intermittent penchant for excesses, were based on pragmatic choices from Western methods of capital investment and technology after due hosannas were made to Marxism-Leninism. Successful economies seem to be a product of competent solutions to existing problems rather than the appurtenances of ideology, bombast, and blather. Those economies that flounder often are the victims of a self-inflicted ideology that has managed to escape the superficial chitchat of cafés and to ensconce itself in development planning. One doubts whether competent individuals in positions of power take ideology seriously.

The ideological conflict was created in Europe and is likely to be buried there as economic and cultural integration on that continent make it increasingly meaningless. In the meantime, it imposes more severe handicaps on nations that take the slogans seriously than on those who originated them. To a considerable degree, the United States and the Soviet Union are adversaries with common problems. Each employs foreign aid as a means of increasing its power vis-à-vis the other. Each makes mistakes in the process. The only difference is that the mistakes of the Soviet Union are less publicized. In this struggle, both the United States and the Soviet Union may find that their international power is disintegrating and that they may be damaged by the countries they allegedly assist, for small countries may refuse to dance to their tune. Each country may thus be incapable of controlling its respective constituency.[10]

To restate the arguments on foreign aid, the administrative machinery moves cautiously in its operations in a fermenting environment abroad. It does not appear to attract the best talent in the United States for work in the field, in the labor function especially. Occasionally, aid takes the form of armed military intervention in support of those receiving it, and when the intervention is over, the amount of aid usually rises. Where no intervention occurs, the operation probably gains more friends than enemies. Although foreign aid has not produced a rise in living standards or governments in the American image, its processes have contributed to

---

[10] In addition to the United States and the Soviet Union, the principal sources of foreign assistance are the Western countries, China, and the United Nations. The operations of the UN include the World Health Organization, the International Labor Organization, UNESCO, the Food and Agricultural Organization, the Atomic Energy Agency, UNICEF, and a variety of special funds for food distribution, technical assistance, and other matters.

some extent to the growth of pluralism in the recipient countries, even in those with a tendency toward authoritarianism. This influence makes them less autocratic, and this is perhaps the best that can be hoped for in the transfer of American ideology. When foreign aid is military aid, however, the arms are used in some instances to help a right-wing military clique to take over the country. These failures are quite visible.

Several factors affect the foreign aid agency's commitment to economic development. AID has been influenced for two decades by the economic principle that the most important cause of growth is a net rise in tangible capital formation. This emphasis on capital formation may, however, cause inflation in the recipient country, lower the real wages of its working class, and increase unemployment. The agency is hampered also by the use of development policy as a power play. It tends to be impatient to see the results of aid quickly and clearly, although results are difficult to assess in the short term and may initially in fact have a tendency contrary to that intended. This impatience for results contributes to the reorganization craze that periodically sweeps over the agency in the expectation that out of such administrative changes the organization will acquire a new boost. The labor factor in economic development is in the hands of organized labor, whose philosophy is anticommunism.

Our growing knowledge of the importance of human capital in economic development has important policy implications. The policies needed include massive programs to raise labor productivity, opportunities for the upward movement of the poor, increased expenditures on education and training, participation of the people in the planning, and general institutional changes that will use labor more extensively and more efficiently. These targets appear similar to those employed in the Soviet Union. Development planners are too preoccupied with capital formation to devise a more balanced approach to development.

A question also arises as to whether a rising middle class that is preoccupied with refined forms of consumption can effectively counter the sense of mission of its government's ideological adversaries. This concern occurs at a time of mounting policy difficulties and increasing attraction to authoritarian forms of growth.

The United States government has been ineffective in coping with the revolutionary surges in developing areas that have been inspired by nationalism and directed against entrenched privilege and tends to react to these surges by supporting privileged social castes with military aid. The threat of military force as a means of grappling with development reflects a failure in Western culture to provide a persuasive counterforce among the poor of the developing world. Although military force may succeed in stabilizing power relationships, its end result seems to be the frustration of a massive improvement in the condition of the poor. The military intervention in Southeast Asia also exacerbates the deep feelings on that continent toward white colonialism. The war appears to demonstrate that a revolutionary nationalistic thrust behind development by ideological adversaries is effectively checked only by a similar thrust acceptable to the population.

It may well be that for Asian and African countries at least the more prudent policy would be one of maximum aloofness. No matter how well prepared in language, culture, and economics, the American represents Western man in these areas and reminds the people of their century's loss of self-respect. Even in the matter of anticommunism, there is evidence that left-wing militancy is nationalistic in character and tends to ebb if not interfered with but becomes consolidated if strong American initiative is exercised. The case for detachment and restraint is a good one.

The United States experience in Latin America suggests the advisability of reducing military aid, converting bilateral aid into technical assistance, and channeling other assistance through multination organizations. As indicated in the confrontation with Peru in 1969, Latin American countries, rightist or leftist, are faced with nationalist pressures to break away from United States domination and to find an accommodation with the Soviet Union and, eventually, China. Existing United States foreign aid policies appear to assure this eventuality. The Rockefeller report in 1969 to President Nixon, from what is publicly known of it, suggests another slogan in United States relationships with Latin America: partnership. The term appears to be a euphemism for the decline of United States influence.

Some Latin American military leaders are asserting their independence. Military governments, such as Peru, and to a lesser extent Bolivia, are pursuing an economic philosophy between that of Soviet and United States economies. Its thrust is nationalism, planned public investment, and state enterprises to achieve a diversified and autonomous industrial sector. The philosophy looks askance at both private domestic and foreign investment. The clue to the change is in the opposition the new philosophy has created among landowners and conservative businessmen and in the search by the military for popular support. The impulse seems to be nationalistic independence, which requires state directed industrial development and rising mass consumption. The effect of this nationalist economic policy can be the decline of the traditional social structure, the rise of a new class of industrial managers, the emergence of an influential working class, and the decline of United States political and economic influence in Latin America.

In trying to place foreign aid on a firmer footing, the United States government has to encourage a debate on the issues. The government does not appear to take the public into its confidence, however, with a realistic appraisal of foreign aid. Although a few senators talk about these issues, there is no general involvement. The journey toward economic development is long and difficult. If we are impatient for its rewards, the world will be in constant ferment and developing countries will be led by authoritarians for many decades to come. Despite the enormous outlays that have been made, the gap between rich and poor widens because the population explosion wipes out the modest gains. So long as vast poverty areas exist in the world, the United States will be insecure. The poor will be exploited by politicians and institutions to promote interests that may have little to do with the dictates of economic growth. In these situations, a technically competent society may not issue. Rather, there may emerge instead economies subsidized by people beyond these nations' borders who woo them for their allegiance. The development of human capacities, the means and end of development, may become lost in the shuffle.

The need to control these forces may compel nations to relinquish more of their sovereignty. As more regions of the world enter into the stream of international economy, the conflict of interest between dissimilar nations at different stages of growth may create a need for international cooperation. More and more countries are finding that the control of their destiny is dependent on the behavior of other countries. The modernizing nations face the psychological danger that reliance on aid from advanced economies will deflect their energies from dealing with the needs of their people. Relying on a permanent subsidy to low human capital is self-defeating.

The United States has been hesitant in its role as benefactor. Its artless use of power and its moral conscience have been its weakness and strength. The covert commitment to the use of power often becomes exposed to a political accountability. There is no similar example in modern history in which a country has risen so swiftly to enormous power and has used it with such gaucheness and moral self-recrimination.

The United States use of military power and its promotion of political alignments have produced a record of mounting failure due, to a substantial degree, to the inherent conflict between the moral basis of assistance and the amorality of promoting foreign power interests. The containment of communism by the threat and use of arms appears obsolete. If the purpose of foreign aid policy is to serve national interests, it may be better to return much of the military and civilian personnel from abroad and to reduce official personnel in diplomatic missions. Such a general disengagement may not increase good will but is likely to achieve greater respect and economic solvency. It may also be more conducive to the economic development of nations.

In sum, the essence of foreign policy is the manipulation of power to promote a country's own interests. It is difficult to divorce foreign aid from such an objective. But the manipulation of power or its supporting premise does not have much to do with the rise in human capacities in developing nations. The rationale for bilateral foreign aid between the United States government and the government of a developing country rests on two premises: promotion of the interests of the United States and assistance in developing the capacity of the foreign nation for its economic growth. The record of two decades does not provide much encouragement.

part five
CONCLUSION

16

ECONOMIC DEVELOPMENT: PRESENT AND FUTURE

Our discussion in this concluding chapter includes a general interpretation of economic development, the future prospects, and some implications for a theory of contemporary economic development.

A GENERAL INTERPRETATION OF ECONOMIC DEVELOPMENT

The end purpose of economic development is to raise the income of the poor at a faster rate than that of other groups. A policy of improving tangible capital alone will not achieve such an outcome. A more comprehensive policy is needed that will alter the economic, human, and physical environment in such a manner as to improve the utilization and efficiency of labor in remunerative employment. Such a total plan shifts the orientation from macroeconomic policies formed in the capital of a country to the human condition at the lowest income level of its society. This is where the focus belongs if one is not to lose sight of the end purpose of economic development as stated above.

Types of Poverty

To learn the dimensions of the problem, a country must first of all determine just who are the poor. What is an acceptable minimum income in the society, and how many people receive less than that level of income? Once these facts have been established, then the policy makers must focus on the causes of poverty in a specific region and develop a strategy to reduce it.

The poor of the world can be put into three general categories. In the first are the large masses of people in the underdeveloped nations who live at a subsistence level. In the second category are those members of an industrialized society who become impoverished as a result of a major depression. The third category takes in those who live within persisting pockets of poverty in an otherwise affluent industrialized nation, such as Appalachia in the United States. The second category is not our concern; it yields to modern fiscal and monetary techniques. A human resources approach to economic development is concerned with the first and third categories.

At first glance, it may appear that the nature of poverty in underdeveloped countries and that in a generally advanced and prosperous economy are sufficiently different in degree as to constitute differences in kind. In some respects this assertion is valid. Most of the poor in the United States receive incomes that are in excess of the average income in less-developed countries. The absolute difference between the poverty level income in industrially developed countries and the average of such nations is in the magnitude of several thousands of dollars. In contrast, the difference between those receiving an average income and the worst off in underdeveloped nations is small. The per capita income of the latter group is typical of much of the population.

Despite these differences, a striking similarity exists with respect to the characteristics of the poor in both types of economies. They seek a livelihood on land of low productivity or lack the skills that would command earnings in industrial centers that would raise them above the poverty line. They commonly have had a long experience of unemployment and underemployment, debilitating sickness, and conflict with society. In both cases, no investment in human resources development has been made on behalf of the poor such as has been made on behalf of the wealthy in both types of economy and on behalf of those receiving average income in the United States. The longer the history of such hard-core poverty, the greater the resources that will be necessary to diminish it. It is difficult enough to eradicate the poverty that has lasted for generations, but the problem is formidable if the poverty has lasted for millenniums. In any case, the policy maker for Appalachia and the policy maker for a developing nation can each profit from the other's experience.

Strategy of Economic Development

The human productive capacity of a society is measured not in terms of the size of its population, but in terms of the level of its human capital; that is, by the quality of the people who do work or can work and their number in proportion to the total population. We can call the raising of this capacity human resource development. In its broadest sense, the term is synonymous with education. But formal education is only a part of the totality of the many-sided development process. Human resource development requires a change in the attitudes of the people; in their political, social, and economic skills; and in their health and physical environment.

To ensure that investments are wisely made, the characteristics of a particular population that are associated with rising incomes should be defined and measured in such a way that the deviations of the poverty stratum of the population from the norms can be established. The next step is to determine what strategies will narrow the difference between the poverty group and those above the party line in the society. The lower the average income and the larger the poverty group, the greater the amount of investment needed. The end purpose of such investment is to raise the human productive capacity of the society by increasing the quality and the relative number of its producers.

Economic development planning must, therefore, focus on this question: What combination of inputs in the society is producing a particular outcome and what new combination of inputs would achieve a better one? To put it another way, a development outcome is the consequence of the social system of a particular area. Secondly, this social system derives from the relationship of its parts. Therefore, the problem is to determine what new set of relationships would produce a more desirable result.

For planning purposes, the social system should be geographically defined and its natural resources, tangible capital stock, and human resources calculated. As economic development proceeds, institutions will evolve in the social system that will accelerate the rise in productivity, participation in decision making, rise in income and social movement. In such a social system, the potential for the use of modern technology should be explored, and a search should be made for indigenous resources that could be efficiently put to use. If no indigenous resources are found, a judgment must be made as to whether the area should be abandoned and human resources shifted elsewhere or whether aspirations should be revised downward.

The individuals in the social system comprise a linkage of beliefs, institutions, and roles. By beliefs is meant the cultural pattern of the system; by institutions, those habitual ways of doing things and the interrelated organizations in which action occurs; by roles, the behavior of individuals in the discharge of their official capacities in the system. These three complementary components have a mutual cause-and-effect relationship.

Every social system "works." Up to a certain point, differences are resolved in routine fashion. As goals are reconciled the system may change, but more often than not its stability is not impaired. The working out of accommodations need not produce growth, however.[1] Because of different goal orientations, different social systems have different input combinations, which may not be conducive to economic growth.

In sum, comprehensive development can be conceived as an evolving input-output social system in a specified geographical area. Although some resources may emanate from outside its boundaries, a basic objective of development is to make the site more autonomous through the export of its specialization. The pressure for development and the resources needed for it may originate elsewhere, but the area is delineated for practical necessity along the lines of political subdivisions, such as a country or province. Its inputs comprise the flow of outlays of human behavior and matériel, whose relations determine performance. Its outputs are end products in real income and improved human capacities, which in turn become further inputs in an on-going societal process that can be described as a means-ends-means cycle.

TABLE 19 □ Components of a Development System

Human	*Environmental*
Individual characteristics	Productive plant*
	Education plant
Values	Water
Education and training	Power
Nutrition	Natural resources other than water and
Perceptions	power
	Housing
Social behavior	Transportation
	Communication
Work place	Health and sanitation plant
Economic and political organization	Other service facilities†
Planning organization	
Geographical mobility	
Occupational mobility	

* In agriculture and industry.

† Recreation, tourism, other leisure activity.

Human inputs include values (particularly as related to production), education, and human relationships arising out of jobs, housing, economic and political organization, and leisure. Human inputs at the poverty base of the population are of particular importance because their characteristics fix the potential of growth to a considerable degree. The environmental inputs include productive plant, educational plant, natural resources, health and sanitation plant, transportation and communications, and other service facilities.

The components of a development system are summarized in Table 19.

The strategy of economic development consists of shifting the flow of inputs in a manner that raises the capacities of human resources in an environment of rising job opportunities. To achieve such a goal, one changes *men, institutions,* and *environment.*

[1] See Talcott Parsons, *The Social System* (New York: Free Press, 1951).

The development model can be simplified further into an input-output flow of human resources. The inputs are divided into subjective states and the external stimuli that exert an influence on them. In proper combination, they bring about an economic system that is conducive to growth. Outputs are both the consequences and causes of growth (see Table 20).

TABLE 20 □ Input-Output Flow of Human Resources

Inputs

Individual

    Entrepreneurial drive
    Social equality beliefs
    Self-improvement motivation
    Production-oriented occupational attitudes
    High value for efficient work
    Economizing spirit
    Managerial ability

External

    Housing
    Equal opportunity education
    Health and sanitation
    Job opportunities
    Income proportional to effort
    Economic and political organization
    Planning institutions

Outputs

    Rising earned per capita income
    Reconciled values
    Rational resource allocation
    Saving
    Technology
    Upward social movement
    Respected entrepreneurial roles

Note: Reconciled values produce other outputs, such as fiduciary relations beyond the family and competent leadership. Morale studies and evaluation detect what input shifts are necessary to maintain development momentum. Such inquiries, formal or informal, are in fact inputs. Quantitative relative importance scales can be devised as a percentage of 100.

Prior to the application of development policy, the situation is stable but is producing what is considered to be an undesirable outcome. In the first phase of change, a comprehensive inventory should be taken of men and material inputs, and their relative importance to the outcome should be ascertained. The next step is to fix a series of realizable goals, and the one thereafter is to make investments that will move the system toward these goals. These components are graphically presented in Figure 1.

The flow of cause and effect between individual and environmental

Figure 1
Input-Output Flow in an Economic System

Individual Inputs

Behavior in the
Economic System

Outputs

Environmental Inputs

inputs [2] is reciprocal. The effect of external inputs on economic performance and on attitudes is probably greater than the effect of attitudes on
the external variables. An effective strategy of rewards for acceptable
personal behavior brings about such a causality.

The inputs are not mutually exclusive. Investment in some has the
effect of raising the level of others. For example, housing, health, and
sanitation affect motivation toward self-improvement and economy. The
more economical way of raising some inputs at a particular moment in
time may be by investing in others. Moreover, investment allocations
must take into account the necessity for conspicuous payoffs for morale
reasons even at the expense of greater returns in the remote future.
Outputs are both manifestations and causes of growth. Variations between such outputs and predetermined goals indicate the changes in
inputs that are necessary to obtain desired results.

Education

Economic development is a total social process around which individuals
cluster in a frequency distribution. The physically and mentally handicapped—the lower part of the distribution—require special arrangements.
For others, the relative importance of inputs varies in each development
context. The strategy of development lies in affecting these inputs in a
way that increases labor productivity and jobs through the resources that
are available to the developing area in the long run.

Formal education plays a crucial role in the reconstruction of inputs.
It not only prepares people for jobs but affects their values, perceptions,
nutrition, and disposition to change institutions. It affects their behavior
at the work place and in economic and political organizations and their
geographical and occupational mobility. Therefore, education is important not only because it provides the base for an efficient labor force but
also because it encourages a quest for new values. This does not mean
that developing countries can afford to place an undue stress on values in
their classrooms. They have to employ their funds in a way that will help
to create a dynamic economy. To do so, they must devise a strategy that
issues from manpower needs.

[2] See Appendix for a more detailed description of inputs.

Manpower planning is an art more than a science, however, and is therefore subject to error. If serious mistakes are to be avoided, manpower planning must be subordinated to the demands of the economic expansion program. That is to say, if the economic planners do their job properly and estimate economic expansion over a future time period, manpower planners can make prudent estimates as to what types of skills will be in demand and in what amount. Manpower planning thereby is a cautious exercise in marginality, and any other approach is risky. For example, to ascertain what skills are required for a particular stage of growth and then nudge the educational system in that direction is to risk serious error. The more cautious approach is an economic expansion program that may generate manpower shortages, for the market can adjust more easily to a manpower shortage than to a surplus. Some developing countries ignore this deference to the needs of economic expansion and use educational funds to produce a bumper crop of secondary school and university graduates in the anticipation that an expanding economy will absorb them. The result is frustration and political instability.

The critical area in which trained personnel are needed for growth is in industry. If industry is able to develop its own skills, however, and if the new educational elite, once graduated, gravitates toward government employment, the educational investment will produce a low payoff. Consequently, the importance of higher education at a stage of low economic development may be exaggerated. If the United States had needed college graduates for its takeoff, it might still be an underdeveloped country.

Consequently, developing nations have a difficult decision to make as to what to expand at the greatest rate: primary, secondary, or higher education. Generally, with the single exception of Mexico, the tendency is to think that the higher the educational level, the greater the relative increase in qualified personnel. Often, the choice is influenced more by the social status implications of education than by the actual need for facilitating growth. Moreover, the countries that expand secondary and higher education too fast produce students of low quality. Although countries that err in the other direction may appear to create shortages, the quality personnel needed can emerge if employers upgrade talented young individuals and assume responsibility for their education above the primary level.

In short, the concentration of marginal increments of public funds on the development of college manpower can go too far. In the immediate term, the most pressing need for the developing economy is for a nucleus of high-quality secondary school graduates who are not all seeking government posts. The next most pressing need is for a quality primary school education with an occupational orientation that is attuned to the needs of production at a low stage of economic development. The primary education creates a base for an efficient labor force. Pegging educational requirements for jobs beyond an elementary education is often arbitrary. Some employers change their employment notices with changes in the labor supply. For example, when a scarcity exists, the sign reads: "Wanted: able-bodied men." When there is a surplus, the new sign reads: "Wanted: high school graduates."

Moreover, a primary education is less costly than secondary or higher education. The general consensus is that some ten primary school children can be kept in school for one year for the same money developing countries spend to maintain one secondary school student. Lastly, a high payoff in an educational investment is not just a matter of seeing that the right number of persons acquire the right amount of education. Salaries have to be pegged to needed skills in an amount that attracts the best talent. Consequently, salary differentials are an important factor in maximizing educational investment.

Is the concept of human capital formation useful in a scheme of economic development? The merit of this concept is that it focuses on the problem of raising human capacities in a context in which scarce resources must be allocated in such a way as to maximize benefits. Its drawback, however, may be that it appears to make monetary value the overriding value of education and education the only form of investment in human capital. Although education need not be defended at all stages of economic growth in terms of the production of goods, its primary aim in a developing nation should be to increase production because otherwise its people may never become free. For an advanced nation, an education calculus based on material value may produce apparent success in terms of a rising GNP in the midst of failure in social and spiritual goals. In addition, such other forms of investment as health services, birth control, and housing may be more economical than education at a particular point in time in raising the level of human capital.

Motivation

It is important in overall development strategy to motivate the poor to raise their capacities and to convince them that in doing so they will be rewarded. They require a sense of self-worth and must be persuaded that they will have influence in an environment that is providing opportunity for rising talents. As the growth process commences, their participation in the control of its evolution can produce effective results. Without such persuasions, only a fragile basis exists for the economical introduction of investments. The importance of such motivation is demonstrated by Mexico.

Lack of motivation may be due to the hostility of the poor toward the social system. The reasons for this hostility may vary from country to country. Therefore, the effort to motivate them must be adapted to the particular situations in each country.

In the effort to raise the productivity of the poor, government officials and social workers may at times produce unwanted effects. The government official may accede to pressures to use scarce resources in subsidized consumption in return for political loyalty. The social worker may inhibit the structural changes necessary for the growth of human capabilities. Their efforts may produce fewer productive individuals among the poor than would be the case in their absence.

Moreover, urban centers that utilize modern technology are not effective sites for a massive growth in human capacities. If maximum growth is to be achieved, industry must be set up in rural areas because the rural workers are not ready for the sophisticated technology in urban plants. Otherwise, when these workers migrate to the cities, they will not be able to find jobs and will have to be subsidized. The wealthy may feel indifferent to their plight and hostile to policies designed to ameliorate it. As a result, existing urban tensions may be exacerbated, causing a political instability that actually may be a deterrent to growth.

Institutional Changes

The relationship between evolving human capacities and institutional changes is not neat and orderly. An interaction takes place as a series of continuing disequilibriums occur between segments of the growth process. Beginning with the traditional economy, the different rates of change may be triggered over time in such a way as to produce the desired result of a more productive society. If successful, this evolution may occur in a manner similar to the differentiated genetic control in the development of human cells. If not, chaos may ensue.

If we know little about human capital growth, we know less about the emergence of institutions as a process. Man knew more about biological evolution a hundred years ago than he knows about social evolution today. He conceives of its hereditary component as tradition and its environment as the changing perceptions of new generations. His knowledge does not go much beyond that point, however.

Every society appears to have a social system that consists of strata ranged in order from lower class to upper class by the collective estimate of the society itself. Whether this scale of superiority is established by law and social custom as in traditional societies or only by the informal judgment of the people as in modern ones, each stratum has a different political and ideological orientation. These dissimilarities cause the stress under which the system operates. The extent of this value cleavage between groups varies as does the ability of the groups to create a mechanism for resolving conflicts that will reconcile these differences and produce satisfactory solutions. Moreover, the members of the various groups differ in their attitudes toward the critical question of rising productivity as a value. They differ also in the functional relationship between their economic and political spheres.

As a traditional society modernizes, the rate of upward movement of its people rises also. An innovating class moving upward in the social system draws political and economic power away from the old aristocracy. The pursuit of knowledge increases. Fatalistic values are challenged by optimistic outlooks. Mutual trust and reciprocity between groups rises. Differences in values and ideologies narrow. The criterion of superiority shifts from land and idleness to the political and economic power inherent in certain occupations. The landed aristocrat in the traditional society was a man of prestige whereas his counterpart in the modern one is an innocuous fellow mentioned in the society column of the newspaper. Out of this change comes an engine of human capital improvement and employment and a decline in poverty.

An effective integration of economic and political spheres is a vital aspect of this stage. Unresolved conflicts in the economic arena are diverted into the political sphere where they are reconciled. What is polity and what economy become blurred. Furthermore, as this countervailing system emerges, productivity issues as a value, as does an elite group of managers of high motivation and ability who obtain monetary and social rewards for their efforts. If there are considerable social antagonisms in these systems, as in Argentina, the returns from human resource investment are small. To minimize this effect, a common education is necessary for contending social groups. The channeling of children of warring social groups into separate educational flows serves to perpetuate these antagonisms.

Once a development program has been started, economic growth is not necessarily inevitable. Traditional elites may frustrate groups at the population base who want to acquire political and economic power. Once having gained influence, those in the ascendancy may not develop an efficient engine of growth. The people may not yield to the demands of technology. Economic development may comprise only a few symbols of modernity in a desert of indifference and traditionalism. Or the moral tone of the community may shift from its traditional values to new ones influenced by movies, television, popular newspapers, and magazines before a cooperative mechanism arises. If presently developing areas want a change in human resources that will be favorable to rapid growth, they have to plan for it.

Societies differ in the extent to which people of low productivity are willing to raise their potential. The obstacle may be social, as in the case of Argentina where preachment on higher productivity is made by a mistrusted class. Or it may be economic, as in the case of a nation with a highly modern sector and a land surplus. Under such conditions, labor moves either toward new land areas, where low productivity is relatively more tolerable, or to modern urban centers, where highly efficient enterprises prevent the less productive from becoming involved in the work opportunities that increase human capital. This tendency is strengthened by the fact that rural persons have fewer wants than those who have had a long period of acclimatization in the cities. After fundamental needs are met, the opportunity for increased earnings loses its attraction. This is especially true when such individuals live in areas not exposed to advertising pressures to consume more.

A social system may obstruct a human resources takeoff, or it may abort one in process. The crisis may reflect itself in any of several ways: a low level of political accommodation between groups, as in Brazil; an economy of deadlocked organizations with few cross-relationships, as in Indonesia; a cynicism toward community efforts, as in Sicily; an educational system that is unresponsive to changing exigencies, as in Argentina. There may not issue either rising levels of common aspirations or quality institutions. A power bloc system may emerge before an economic takeoff that causes its deterrence. Presently modernizing areas are faced, on the one hand, with unprecedented pressures to develop sophisticated producer technology and mass marketing and, on the other, with a politically conscious population of low productivity.

The Growth Spiral

How is the traditional social system initially fired? Economic development can begin by a surge in the aggregate demand for goods and services, which brings about new technology requiring higher human capacities. The surge in demand is more often fortuitous than planned. In Argentina the spurt was created by World War I, in Spain by a sudden massive burst of tourism and labor migration, and in Mexico by World War II. Countries differ in the manner in which they take advantage of these fortuitous turns of events, however.

The most potent weapon such a surge creates is a tight labor market with its concomitant necessity for training manpower for higher skills and adopting modern technology. This has a pump-priming effect on the level of technology. By forcing the upgrading of the labor force, the skill shortage pushes up wages of the unskilled as well and enables them to share in the initial rewards of growth. The increase in per capita income that this economic growth brings about also provides the wherewithal to tailor welfare concessions to the poor. Used adroitly, these benefits prime the labor force for a rise in productive quality.

Neither ample economic resources nor educational investments alone assure rapid growth. Critical inputs of sustained growth are dependent on institutions that will develop a system of education that is pervasive in effect and that stresses quality group performance and provide job opportunities that will create productive and cooperative individuals who forge an environment favorable to growth. In so doing, the timing of institutional development is crucial.

One of the most important of such institutions is an efficient industrial relations system that reconciles technology, the mosaic of contesting values in the society, and the array of political and economic power. These forces can be resolved with the guidance of managers who serve as mediators, who maintain fiduciary relationships with their respective constituents, and who establish processes that produce goods and distribute income with a minimum of conflict and at the same time encourage habits of efficiency. Ideally, these processes emanate from the maximum enfranchisement of all segments of the population. At its best, an industrial relations system generates a cooperative climate of rising capacities. At its worst, as in Argentina, it fosters hatred, inefficiency, and alienation.

The power allocation of these industrial relations systems changes in dynamic economies. It shifts among the managers and between the managers and their constituents. Today, the critics of the system may be ignored. Tomorrow, they may be fomenting change. These shifting patterns of influence vary from area to area. For example, in one nation, as in the Soviet Union, the power may be moving away from the government toward the base of the system. In another, as in the United States, political authority may be growing more centralized.

Is there a relationship between the evolving quality of human resources and this shifting power balance? Power appears to shift to the group that is better equipped to deal with pressing problems, and conflict is the means by which the power balance is readjusted. However, it also appears that as the level of human capacities rises, decision making concentrated at the top of political centers becomes difficult to exercise. Political and economic democratization does not appear to be of primary importance in the initial stages of growth. Nevertheless, if it is postponed indefinitely, an eventual crisis in growth is likely to occur.

With such a spiral of growth, the relative number of poor falls even though the income level or other standard by which they are defined begins to rise. The widening involvement of the poor in political, economic, and social processes develops institutions of semiautonomous growth. Such a rising involvement may not occur, however. Or once begun, as in Indonesia, it may falter. It can be seen thereby that a fundamental task of contemporary economic development is to foster institutions that commit the entire labor force to processes that progressively raise human capacities. Since the pioneering work of Arthur Lewis, it has been common knowledge that such a goal requires job opportunities that will raise labor productivity. A desire to adopt the highly capitalistic production methods of advanced economies may, however, conflict with this objective. Furthermore, if productivity is to be raised, the program must ensure not only jobs, but also the economic, political, and social involvement of the poor. The disappointments in contemporary economic development are attributable to a failure to provide both.

Role of Technology

As stated earlier, technology plays a crucial role in economic development in the sense of using men and matériel in production and distribution at maximum efficiency. Be it called automation, systems engineering, information systems, or operations research, the common thread that runs through modern management is the use of massive and systematic techniques to achieve a precisely defined end at maximum efficiency.

Generally, technology is a product of the knowledge, motivations, wealth, and structure and scale of the enterprises of an economy. It is evidenced in the way men think and behave when faced with a problem in the production and distribution of goods. Technology creates new types of men not only through its production processes but also through its consumer artifacts, such as mass communications media, motor vehicles, and television. Technology is a catalyst in human resources development.

The particular level of technology a developing economy achieves depends upon a combination of factors, including the extent of the surge in demand; the education and training level of its workers and managers; the existing level of technology; the degree to which managers prefer high current profits at the expense of plowed-back earnings; the scale of production at which enterprises are operating; the extent to which the government prescribes purchasing within the borders of the country so as to expand industry; the higher cost generally of machinery and equipment compared to that of advanced economies; the greater profitability in using cheap labor because of such costs; and the degree to which the developing nation establishes a technological transmission belt with an advanced nation. The relative importance of these factors varies from one country to the next.

That technology is indispensable in raising the wages of the poor is clear. It is a necessary means of committing workers to modern methods of production, which provide a basis for raising their wages. Technology also poses a threat however. By rapidly breaking down traditional values, it produces a change in interpersonal relationships. In the traditional society a man's relationship to other men is defined by a community system of mutual obligation between intimates, but economic development changes this into an exploitational relationship as the functions of production and distribution enter large markets and dominate the relationships among men.

Accelerated change also causes a breakdown of family values and substitutes those of the market place. In addition, it provides a chance to acquire political power before a mass rise in economic capacities has occurred. The poor may become a political force and threaten the stability of government. There is little that is new about these pressures. What is novel is that they are appearing more suddenly and more intensely than they appeared in the advanced nations without allowing for anything other than an abrupt transition from traditional man to modern producer. If independent and enterprising spirits are outmoded in old industrialized nations, they are a vital necessity in modernizing ones.[3]

Moreover, the modern plant in the developing area requires a relatively small group of workers. The stage of technology that produced a massive involvement of the unskilled in production in advanced economies appears to be skipped by presently developing ones. Consequently, the plants cannot be used as a tool of industrial discipline and human capitalization, and this contributes to the creation of a man different from his counterpart in the early stages of growth in the West.

In sum, modern technology has ambivalent effects. It requires the cooperative talents of highly trained individuals because advanced technological systems cannot work without the responsible efforts of many skilled individuals. Yet the rapid introduction of technology in a developing area may stifle the necessary massive growth of these responsible producers.

Community Planning

Total community planning based on strategically placed model communities provides opportunites for controlling technology. The number and locations of these communities should be based on a series of compromises that reconcile production requirements, efficiency, and social impact. The model community can change the economic and social structure of the rural area within its range of influence and thereby draw prestige away from the traditional seats of power. Furthermore, it can provide an enthusiasm for growth that is not otherwise obtainable. The interest generated by a new school in the community can fan out to other groups who educate, such as the labor organization, industry, the family, and the social center. An eagerness for self-improvement should be stimulated. The model community should be assisted in the performance of its function through comprehensive local planning and through the organization of a public corporation to finance and develop jobs, housing, and education. These inputs represent the core of community development. To have separate programs for them is a waste of resources.

The working classes within these communities should be involved in a

---

[3] A controlled religious society such as that existing in Spain may have a better opportunity of bringing about this transition than one that is not. I refer not to the authoritarian aspect of Spanish Catholicism but to its teaching of social obligation.

variety of projects, including discussions on such matters as the meaning of development. The projects should include producer and consumer cooperatives, housing, agronomy, credit alliances, the planning of adult education programs, personal and public health services, and home economics. The people should help to fix tangible and realizable short-term goals that are consistent with the overall plan. If they are allowed to participate in this way, human capitalizing may occur in a series of successful steps, and a widening gap between expectations and results may be avoided. Without such an involvement, the investment in hard goods may be wasted. The ability of illiterate or semiliterate peasants to participate in, and even contribute to, such projects can be easily underestimated. Although there is a danger that such participation may degenerate into an ineffectual debating society, assuming such a risk may produce higher returns. Moreover, for many of today's poor, returns from development are in the form of participation in its processes rather than increases in income.

FUTURE PROSPECTS

In the *Divine Comedy,* Dante has an appropriate punishment for soothsayers. Their hands are tied behind their backs and their heads can only look back to the past. Economists are risk takers, not in the employment of capital, but in soothsaying.

Despite the risks, prognostications should be made because some trends are apparent. Developing nations are resorting increasingly to one-party or one-clique rule for the guidance of their development. Political patchwork rather than long-range planning dominates decision making. The supreme authority is the military. The urbanization problems of these nations are acute because their rural area policies come too late. Added to the poverty of money, the subproletariat of the city slums acquires a poverty of spirit. Such is the reality of contemporary economic development.

Urbanization does not abolish the dilemma of contemporary society—the problem of human capital growth—so much as it converts it into a new form and makes it more difficult to solve. Rather than a single individual of human worth, man becomes a collective object whose value depends upon his usefulness to men of influence who are seeking their own economic and political ends. Growth has to take place in an atmosphere of alienation and hostility. This exploitation is not unique to any one country and it varies only as to who the exploiters are, the manner in which the new urbanites are treated, and the processes and purposes the exploiters have at their command.

Although one hesitates to use the term socialist in describing them because of the confusing variety of politicoeconomic forms the word suggests, modernizing nations can be called socialist as a distinction from the economic liberalism of the nineteenth century Western models. After it is found that the shedding of colonialism does not bring the millennium, the clamor for quick results in economic development pushes these nations in the direction of a locally adapted nationalist-socialist type of economy. In countries where an intransigent polarization of forces exists, crises and revolutions ensue, and the supreme authority is vested in the one who can claim the largest number of guns. Authoritarian forms of development in the initial stages of growth thus appear inevitable.

This evolution may be galling to students of economic development. Nevertheless, the surge of aspirations beyond a nation's capacity to fulfill them and its inability to involve the population in a responsible exercise of power may make such an outcome inevitable. To be sure, systems of pluralism and consensus may prove to be more compatible with the long-term growth of human resources. In fact, the emergence of a society of affluent technicians may well be the undoing of authoritarianism. The facts indicate, however, that authoritarianism will be unavoidable for many decades in the future.

Will all economic systems eventually tend to be similar? To find an answer to this question, we must first examine the three types of systems that exist now. One is government-dominated, the second is the countervailing pluralistic type, such as that of the United States, and the third is the arm's-length variety that is characteristic of many nations in Latin America. In the first, the only quality leadership is concentrated in government positions. To a substantial degree, the industrial relations rules are fixed by the government, and employers use them as a means of resisting the emergence of pluralism. In the countervailing type of economic system, no one group clearly dominates the others. There are highly involved lines of interrelationships between employers and working groups as well as between each of these groups and the government.

The arm's-length type of economic system is a phalanx economy in which each phalanx, or producer group, is solidly organized to control its prices, offer unilateral employment terms, and quietly pursue political interests. A group achieves accommodation not so much by cross-relationships as by its direct lines to the government, which it uses in an attempt to manipulate governmental processes and to promote its own particular pocket of interest. An effect of the arm's-length system is the difficulty of reaching a consensus on the purposes and means of economic development.

These three systems appear to be dissimilar. In the countervailing system, the role of the leadership elite is to mediate between groups and among their respective constituencies. This contrasts with government-dominated economic systems, in which managers are mere symbols of acquiescence, and with the arm's-length variety, where government acts as a conduit in the mediation of differences between groups.

There also appear to be significant differences in worker-employer relations. The least amount of worker servility appears in the countervailing system and the greatest in the government-dominated types. Similarly, many conflicts of interest are resolved on a day-to-day basis within the enterprises by employers and worker representatives dealing with each other as equals. This contrasts with the other types where the plant manager is in a clear position of authority.

In addition, the countervailing system appears to have the greatest degree of public orientation. In the United States, private consultants, arbitrators, mediators, and university professors trained in these skills have a direct or indirect influence on the system. This insertion of a sophisticated public point of view differs from the other two types where third-party positions are symbols of government.

To repeat the question, are these systems converging toward a point of similarity? The thesis of Clark Kerr and his colleagues on this point is fascinating. Briefly stated, they advance the idea that countries at the beginning of economic development have a variety of cultures, forms of economic organization, and managerial types. The latter may be dynastic, middle-class, revolutionary, intellectual, colonial, and nationalist administrators. The overriding demands of production techniques (and one might add the course of political history) tend to make these elites and the cultures in which they operate increasingly similar. The universal demands of technology force the rise of a managerial class whose style and outlook resemble those of American managers.

The thesis is captivatingly simple. For those who have grappled with the problem of international comparisons, its focus on managerial types is an effective way of capturing the forces inside an industrial relations system. The behavior of a manager is an expression of underlying forces. To say that all future managers will come from the rising middle class is to state the inevitable. The pressures for increasing similarity are enormous. As economic development advances, an educated mobile labor force is rising whose members in different parts of the world have similar occupational requirements that produce similar outlooks on life. Economic techniques are freely exchanged among governments. The technology of a particular industry tends to be universal, and the people who work in it tend to be attuned to that technology in much the same way—with due allowance made to modifications that arise from value differences between countries. Moreover, this technology forces into similar channels not only occupations and production techniques but also education and relative income disbursements.

Forces for differences, though, have a way of persisting. Religion, dissimilarities in child rearing, and the stubbornly persisting different antecedents of history serve to scatter pressures for similarity. Moreover, the forces for conformity that rapid industrialization produces in its early stages create reactions against them. Those who seek to submerge cultural characteristics may bring about their own undoing.

One way of examining this question of whether economic systems are becoming similar is to compare trends in countries that began their economic development in different situations. The United States and the Soviet Union come to mind. In these countries, the rising similarity in technology and the impact of technology on education are apparent. Occupational specialization in the Soviet Union produces individuals with outlooks similar to those of their counterparts in the United States. Equally significant is what is happening to the power distribution of these nations. In the United States, as technology has gained supremacy, the government has asserted its right to participate in, and control the determination of, employment terms; to fix the relationship between employers and unions; and to control the administration of labor organizations. In the Soviet Union, on the other hand, power has been pushed downward away from the top party structure. The union has been criticized for not countervailing sufficiently against the position of employers. Workers have been encouraged to take the initiative and to be critical of the leadership hierarchy. It is difficult to assess motives for this democratization. Suffice it to say that if such a policy is effective, it pushes the system in the direction of the pluralism existing in the United States.

Consequently, it would appear that long-term forces operate in the world that force economic systems into a common mold. The universal communication that burst forth at the end of World War II is causing countries to recognize common problems and to try similar solutions. Accordingly, much of the seeming differences in practices may be vestiges that obscure the convergence toward similarity.

If economic problems and practices become increasingly similar, do they eventually make for similarity in culture? If the United States is the principal exporter of such practices, will all the people of the world become like Americans by the twenty-first century? What comes to mind is the similarity in problems and practices of Scandinavian countries and their persisting differences in national character. The Swedish worker has more in common with other classes in his society than with Norwegian and Danish workers.

Does this mean a world of countries that are integrated within themselves and have dissimilar national characteristics but similar economic and political institutions? Does such a picture make sense? These outcomes give substance to the thesis of Kerr and his associates. To be sure, their point of view of rising similarity is modest in its claim. Their observations were made in the context of the enormous export of American ideas in the decades following World War II, ideas that are now undergoing a period of gestation. Still, the idea has substance.

Economic development has to address itself to the position of the laboring classes—that is, it must create human controls and processes for human ends. If development is regarded in this light, the indicators of economic output have a limited usefulness in measuring the extent of the success of the development policy. A nation can have the beginnings of a diversified industry, a sound trade balance, a modest international debt, efficient input-output combinations—and social injustice.

Such humanistic development requires a labor-oriented strategy and a social philosophy that attracts the loyalty and participation of the poor. Rural reform should become a principal vehicle of development, with industrialization of the rural area an integral part of the policy. Migration to existing urban centers should be discouraged by incentives to remain in developing rural areas. There, a productive job must exist for everybody who wants one, and efforts at self-improvement through education and training should be rewarded socially and economically. Organized labor should have a leadership acceptable to the people and should consider the raising of labor productivity a major responsibility. Lastly, this effort should be guided by national and regional planning with the participation of the poor.

If manpower development does not take place in an atmosphere that takes into account national cultural characteristics, economic growth is apt to run into difficulty. It may disrupt the collective sense necessary for growth. It may evolve into a struggle between interests in which contending groups seek to impose their will on one another rather than to reconcile their differences. Achieving rising productivity and living standards by a system that does not extinguish the individual creative spirit is unfinished business even in old industrial societies. In presently developing ones, by their sheer numbers, the future belongs to the young. Whether they are likely to make profound changes in the direction of the current stream of development remains to be seen.

In sum, economic development comprises a series of successful interactions among evolving economic, social, and political institutions, whose effect is a society of rising consensus, human capacities, and income. Therefore, it is not measurable by economic calculus alone, which does not indicate what countries are doing and what they should be doing. Economic development is not concerned primarily with raising output as much as the status and dignity of man. In short, growth is the development of human capital in a particular cultural context, and, as such, it has moral overtones.

The national case histories presented in this work suggest the factors that produce self-sustaining growth. The instrument of total development is a net rise in aggregate output per capita. The factors in a country that produce such a result include political stability and efficient government; an unwillingness to be dominated by the interests of a foreign power; land reform; a production-oriented population with a sense of national identity and a willingness to undergo sacrifices for education and training; mass support of development policy; an economic base that can sustain a diversified economic structure; innovational energy; a surge in demand, often induced by forces external to the nation; an attempt to meet that demand by industrializing; and a rise in internal sources for financing growth by raising per capita savings; and narrowing the gap between imports and exports. The fact that it is difficult to measure and assess the relative importance of some of these social, political, and economic factors does not detract from their importance.

Since the end of World War II, the evidence has been mounting against the assumption that a rise in net capital formation alone triggers an economic takeoff. The facts suggest that practically every advanced nation entered the phase of sustained growth at investment ratios much less than those of presently developing nations. It seems clear that the rise in net capital formation is more a consequence of growth than its cause. The key to starting the process appears to lie in raising labor efficiency. Until this is done, developing nations face the prospect of continued low productivity and income.

What are the policy implications of their experience? Greater emphasis has to be placed on the education and training of the labor force. The emphasis on capital should shift to more rational choices and more efficient use. Second, the evidence suggests that whether tariff restrictions help or hinder the growth process is dependent on the type of entrepreneurs the economy has. Tariff protection for industry does not per se produce a psychology of restrictionism. It does in some countries and does not in others. Third, the kind of role that the government should play in economic development depends on the men it attracts rather than upon an ideology that rationalizes the government's role. If the government attracts incompetent, politically minded individuals, as in the case of some developing nations, they are likely to be a serious deterrent to growth. Similar government roles in different countries produce dissimilar results. In brief, the single most important factor in the growth of developing countries in all probability is the quality of its men as producers.

The physical setting of some developing nations is not favorable to the construction of an economic base for such human growth. Their land is poor as a source of food, raw materials, and power, and their climate is enervating much of the year. Little can be done economically about the climate in the foreseeable future. Atomic power may provide a source of power, however, and water from desalination plants, fertilizer, and chemicals can be used to make the land productive. Without such a breakthrough that would furnish an economic base for agriculture and industry, there is little prospect for self-sustaining growth in many areas of the world.

What a developing nation has to do actually in economic development is analogous to the blueprint of life in the nucleus of a human egg cell.

The nucleus represents a programmed computer. It contains the information and commands necessary to initiate and phase out processes at the right time, to integrate evolving processes, and to maintain a synchronous organism as these functions increase in complexity.

A majority of nations have made some progress in developing such an organism. They have new plants, schools, houses, equipment, and power stations. Some countries, such as Mexico, have made substantial progress. Nevertheless, the typical condition of the vast majority of people in the world is not well-being but abject poverty and conflict. The population rise together with the exclusion effect of modern technology means that the primary goal of economic development, an increase in the utilization of labor, must take place in agriculture and related industries. Will the developing countries assume accountability for their situation and undergo sacrifices for future rewards? Can the affluent of the world collaborate with the have-nots? Can starvation be eradicated from the earth? The challenge is enormous.

In what kind of world environment do emerging nations pursue this challenge? The principal motivating force in these countries is nationalism; their principal political instrument is an authoritarian elite; their principal threat from abroad is the power interests of the two latter-day imperialist powers: the United States and the Soviet Union.

IMPLICATIONS FOR A THEORY OF ECONOMIC DEVELOPMENT

The following postulates are suggested by this work as appropriate for a theory of economic development. Economic development is a social process involving an interaction between rising human capacities and their employment, on the one hand, and an environment and institutions that are favorable to them, on the other. The thrust behind this process derives from an economic, political, or social shock that creates a surge in the demand for goods. The shock sets off a series of continuing disequilibria. The surge in demand for goods thus causes a surge in the demand for labor. The surge in demand for labor makes economical its capitalization and increased emoluments. As tangible capital rises, the investment in human capital makes economical a further investment in tangible capital. Capital output ratios increase, first steeply and then tapering off, as the capital stock per capita rises. Income differences between regions narrow. This process is signaled by a sustained rise in per capita product, a complementary growth between rising industrialization and rising agricultural efficiency, and by an overall rise in human capacities.

In a traditional society, social groups have low rates of mobility. As a result, there is little reciprocity between groups, and there are wide differences in values. Most people are very poor. The level of human capital is low.   Excellence is identified with landholdings and idleness. Elites are in positions of authority because of privilege rather than because of contribution to product.

With growth, this closed system breaks down.   Social inequality becomes intolerable.   The capitalization of human beings becomes rewarding.   The proportion of the national income going to education rises.   The awareness of the need for labor organizations increases.   The authoritarian position of traditional elites deteriorates.   Out of the ranks of the poor emerges a new class of managers, able and highly motivated, who obtain social and economic rewards for their performance.   Political and labor leaders who believe in the value of productivity appear, and they are supported by the working classes.   The new elite rejects traditional standards of equity.   It rises to influence through economic and social change.   Its motives are to bring about innovation and to obtain approbation.

The social movement creates conflict.   Out of this conflict issue political and economic institutions of accommodation.   As conflict subsides and value differences narrow, a social system of interrelated groups emerges.   The rise in value sharing brings about a higher degree of mutual trust and reciprocity between groups.   Out of this new reciprocity the working classes receive political and economic representation and the right to take part in decision making.   The pessimistic attitudes of people toward work and toward one another change to optimism, and this affects the outlook in the body politic.

The social structure thus shifts from a closed, quiescent group to conflict, and then to consensus.   The range of choices for the poor widens.   Increasing numbers of workers have developed the habit of improving production techniques and are earning rewards for so doing. New problems respond to the newly structured social system.   Further necessary institutions are appearing spontaneously.

Before economic development begins, labor organizations contribute to the protest movement that energizes it.   Once it has begun, however, they perform no substantial role.   Their leaders have neither the education nor the following to play a policy role.   When organized effectively, their function lies in protecting their members from the impact of change. Organized labor mirrors the enormous human resources problems of the nation, but it is kept at arm's length.

A nation that begins this venture in economic development under an authoritarian government will experience a change in its political structure.   Such a regime must undertake an economic expansion program if it is to maintain its power.   Eventually, however, the price for such expansion will be a decentralization of power.   A rising mass of educated individuals will lead to a controlled pluralism, and a new elite will find authoritarian guidance intolerable.   The authoritarian political group must become more responsive or see its influence taken over by other groups.

The dictates of autonomous growth thus cause an erosion of authoritarianism.

Accordingly, an association exists between emerging democratic institutions and an economic takeoff. The democratic institutions that emerge may differ, however, from those of the West. Moreover, there may be periods in the course of economic change when the government becomes less democratic. Such a political change may have a deterrent effect on economic growth, a fact that, in a negative sense at least, further indicates the interrelationship between political and economic development. In Argentina and Brazil, for example, when political development faltered, so did economic development. Mexico, on the other hand, is an example of the successful evolution of democratic institutions and autonomous economic growth.

These propositions are derived from the postulates stated in the beginning of this section. First, the investment of capital funds alone does not generate a sequence of growth. An ideology adapted to the locality, a close alliance between government and industry, and a total strategy of manpower development are also necessary. Moreover, because of the effects of modern technology, the government must be prepared to support the subsidizing and control of the movement of the people into modern activity. In short, the emergence of autonomous economic growth under contemporary conditions cannot be expected from a free-market economy. Sooner or later, such an economy will falter.

Second, the investment mix of inputs that is required and the strategy of inserting them into the social system are associated with the level of growth already obtained—that is, given that level of growth, it must be determined what new strategies of existing inputs or what new inputs will produce further growth. The same input will have dissimilar effects in different economies. Third, a precise knowledge of the labor markets in agriculture and industry is vital in devising strategy. Fourth, the rise in human capital implies an increase in freedom of choice, without which further growth is impeded. Fifth, it cannot be assumed that the diversified economic structure necessary for a modern economy will issue without supporting local resources. Sixth, concomitant with the tangible and human capital investment must come institutional changes through legislative and administrative means that will have the effect of facilitating the crucial goal of raising labor productivity. These structural changes are required in agriculture, industry, and government. Seventh, the population policy must include control of births. Eighth, the evolution of economic growth must be controlled by an efficient government that obtains the support of all segments of the population.

Finally, a low rate of development implies a social system with the following characteristics: low educational quality and low incentives for learning; closed groups whose leaders attain their positions of authority because of influence rather than ability; leader elites with traditional values and low estimates of rising productivity; low reciprocal relations between functional groups; antagonistic value patterns in the society with a resulting low degree of consensus; and decision-making structures whose ranks are closed to young nonconformists.

Further development possibilities are suggested by these postulates and derived propositions for countries at different stages of economic development. For example, a nation like Argentina is likely to continue to flounder so long as a machinery of consensus is not forthcoming. In Spain, economic development is apt to have recurring crises unless such machinery evolves.

For presently developing areas generally, economic development is a process of forging institutions that permit an extensive and rapid rise of human capacities and that place such abilities in remunerative employment. Favorable changes in tangible capital, human capital, and institutions are not preordained. Developing nations have to work at all three seriously. But an important base for growth, a product that commands highly favorable terms of trade, may require sheer luck.

APPENDIX

PERFORMING RESEARCH IN ECONOMIC DEVELOPMENT

Economic development inputs fall into two general classes: human and material. In measuring human outlays, attention is focused on individuals at the poverty base and the social structure in which they live. Their characteristics fix the potential of growth.

Neither the difference between inputs nor the distinction between inputs and outputs is as neat as desired. Nevertheless, some distinctions must be made to provide a framework for discovering the facts. It is not prudent to develop a rigid model of economic development that lends itself to quantitative analysis and then seek those facts that fit the model. There is a tendency in analyzing economic development to select inputs that are convenient rather than those that are real. Data can be compiled that are the product of statistical technique rather than local development situations.

An investigator has to ask himself: What are individuals in a developing area doing? What aspects of their behavior constitute human resources development? What environmental inputs affect their behavior? Rather than present merely a static summation of their characteristics, he has to maintain a log of their activity over an extended period of time by tracing linked inputs much as the physiology of a biological system is studied.

His purpose is to observe what particular sets of conditions produce outputs within defined geographical areas at different stages of development. From such analysis, a socioeconomic input matrix can be developed that is useful in the formulation and control of policy. The policy problem is to ascertain what tailor-made set of manpower and material inputs will produce a rapid rate of growth.

In assessing the status of manpower, attitudes of the population are easily obtainable. Subjective states are readily measurable even among illiterate people. Such data serve a limited purpose, however. A particular subjective state may not lead to the behavior to which an individual in such a state is disposed. Furthermore, in changing attitudes, one can only provide external stimuli in the hope of encouraging attitudes propitious to growth. For example, people cannot be injected with a dose of optimism. External stimuli have to be provided that may bring about such an outlook.[1] On the whole, an assessment of subjective states is useful in an initial evaluation of problems and in a subsequent study on the impact of policy on them.

Social or external inputs—that is, the factors over which direct control can be exercised by private individuals, groups, and the government—have to be related to the subjective profile to ascertain what combination of both will produce a given result.

Input analysis of a social system raises a threefold problem: to discern the degree of meaningful differences among inputs and to consolidate overlapping variables, to seek proxy variables for those that are not measurable, and to determine relative weights.

An analytical structure has to be devised that is usable in different countries. To do so improves its applicability and validity in any one nation. There is no alternative but to become involved in the complexity of different languages. A comparative study may degenerate into a comparative study of linguistics and interpreters. Intercountry comparisons present an array of different input combinations that provide clues as to the relative importance of each.

Comparisons first have to be made between areas with similar cultural patterns. This first step makes more manageable the attitude survey and the assigning of relative values to variables, and it provides clues as to which outcome differences are due to time lags and which to short-term phenomena of little lasting importance.

Judgments on the relative importance of inputs for a particular site are obtained from the following: (1) employers; (2) government officials involved in economic growth; and (3) university professors in the social sciences. They can be asked to place inputs in order of relative importance for a developing area and to assign numerical values as a percentage of one hundred.

The interview sample consists of three groups: the population base of industrial workers, small farmers, and agricultural laborers; the managerial elite; and an intellectual elite of students and teachers. A statistically

---

[1] J. H. Kunkel, "Values and Behavior In Economic Development," *Economic Development and Cultural Change,* 13 (April 1965), 257–277.

random sample is impractical. It is too costly and too difficult to implement once determined. Randomness of interviewees is achieved instead by improvisation and by not letting the choice be controlled by particular groups and organizations in the developing country. The sample size can be brought to a point where additions do not provide significantly different responses.

The information to be obtained from the population base includes: (1) curriculum vitae; (2) characteristics of family size, life, and housing; (3) extent of sense of marginality and how such marginality becomes manifested in behavior; (4) extent and allocation of income and debt level; (5) education and training; (6) participation in economic and political institutions; (7) extent of coverage in social insurance programs; (8) pessimism-optimism states; (9) characteristics of consumption, including food, beverages, and durable goods; (10) attitudes toward the managerial elite; (11) time orientation; (12) extent of empathy for other social groups; (13) attitudes toward labor organization; (14) general values, norms, and aspirations; (15) extent of change in relation to the past; and (16) attitudes toward economic and social change.

The following individual inputs must be analyzed:

1. *Entrepreneurial drive.* The term is similar to that expressed in the *n* achievement concept of Professor David McClelland.[2] The difficulty in a field investigation is that elaborate measurements of this subjective state are costly, not sufficiently differentiating, and impractical to apply under the conditions that prevail in a developing area. The urge to enter business and to compete for a high income reward is a developed trait. Conditions in Spain suggest that the entrepreneurial drive may perhaps be measured as a proportion of the number of enterprise managers who have risen up the industrial occupation ladder to the number of those who have been selected for top positions on the basis of influence.

2. *Motivation toward self-improvement.* This term refers to the degree to which the labor force is undergoing investment sacrifices to improve its social and economic position. In a field investigation, the number of adults who enroll in occupational training programs is an indication of motivation toward self-improvement.

3. *Production-oriented work attitudes.* This concept is important but difficult to measure. It can exist in different degrees in different geographical areas of the same country such as in northern Spain, where the act of production produces a sense of accomplishment and status, and in the south, where it is merely a requisite of income. A low production-oriented work attitude contributes to a dislike for manual occupations.

4. *High value placed on efficient work.* This trait perhaps has little analytical use because of the difficulty of making a neat distinction from production-oriented work attitudes. Workers who have such a trait tend

2 David McClelland, *The Achieving Society* (Princeton, N.J.: Van Nostrand, 1961).

to identify with their product and express this attitude when they speak of their employment. Sensing this point of view is one matter and tracing it as acts of behavior is another. Its low prevalence is probably an effect of a congeries of social and physical conditions in the environment.

5. *Economizing spirit.* This is measurable in terms of changes in family savings as a proportion of income. The poor are not identical in the matter of the proportion of income they save. In some subsistence households, it is remarkable how much some families manage to save in the course of a year. The willingness to curtail current consumption is tied to a conviction that by so doing the status and income of the children will be greater in their adulthood.

6. *Managerial ability.* The managers in public administration and labor organizations are as important as those in enterprises. Here again, the differences that exist in managerial ability are not revealed readily by simple questionnaires but by a long series of interviews and observations of performance. The ability of a manager may not be reflected by the extent of his formal education and training. Generally the competent manager is intelligent and has a technical approach to problems. In an economy of limited growth, the exercise of influence in acquiring managerial positions has a tendency to inhibit competent types from rising in the management power structure.

7. *Belief in social equality.* This concept involves the extent to which a society finds social inequality intolerable. For example, a considerable number of the more prosperous citizens in Scandinavian societies are interested in raising the social level of their less successful fellow citizens. In Denmark, it has been argued that because the employer gets three weeks' vacation, the employees should get the same. In Latin societies, such a line of reasoning is likely to be considered a non sequitur. This latter attitude is important because its presence makes it difficult to reconcile community goals.

This process of reconciling goals is observable in developing economies because it is preceded by an initial rise in conflict, which later declines. The extent to which the goals of the different groups are made compatible—or coexist without a physical struggle—appears to be a function of the size of the initial differences among the groups themselves. If there is a cultural hiatus between social group A and group B that is characterized by fundamental differences in customs, land tenure systems, technical orientation, and language, it is inconceivable that the economic aspirations of the two groups will be similar. Furthermore, if group A comprises the political elite, decisions are likely to be made within that group's frame of reference. The establishment of communication between the two groups gradually breaks down the hiatus, but the movement is largely in one direction—toward the cultural system of A. The integration of goals, which can be painful, thus takes place as one group absorbs and emulates the values of the other. A major dimension of economic development is the speed with which this detribalization proceeds.

In societies composed of elements with strongly dissimilar cultural systems, the problem of goal integration is formidable. The problem is a common one in Latin America, Asia, and Africa and is implicit in the Black revolution in the United States. Nevertheless, it is always possible to proceed more rapidly. The final result has to be a more integrated system of values such as those of highly industrialized societies.

The external inputs include the following:

1. *Housing.* An appropriate measure is the amount of rural and urban housing for the poverty base as a rate of the total number of its families. In some countries, data are not separated out by different social groups and geographical areas. These nations defend this practice by saying that even in the case of new housing concentrated at higher social levels, the poor profit through a hand-me-down effect. In one developing country visited, a prominent economist referred to this attitude as the philosophy of feeding a horse well in the prospect that good pickings would accrue to the birds. The metaphor is crude, but it captures the moral nuances of economic development policy.

2. *Equal opportunity for education.* This term refers to planned activities of community agencies, schools, and enterprises, entrance to which is based on capacity and interest and which have the effect of raising the social, economic, and political abilities of the person who takes part in these activities. Education does not occur just in schools. A supervised consumption of a nourishing diet is an educational process. A practical measure of the rise in the equality of educational opportunity is the proportion of the appropriate population in school. From the rise in this proportion, if any, should be deducted the increase in the overall population.

Usually, the economic value of education is measured in terms of the number of years of exposure, the total educational budget, or the subsequent economic rewards as measured by income changes. Inquiries in Argentina, Spain, and Mexico suggest, however, that such data do not provide meaningful explanations of the differences among nations. The development value of education depends strongly on the motivation of the students. Motivations in turn mirror the social attitudes in the society. Because the Spanish poor have a strong motivation to learn, the government with modest supporting services succeeds in producing qualified mechanics after only several years of primary education. In Argentina, the high degree of secondary school graduates and graduates of institutions of higher learning is diluted by the low quality of instruction and by the social situation in that country. In Mexico, the relatively low number of years of formal schooling is counterbalanced by the effective training by employers. The deficiencies of the state universities are counterbalanced by the opportunities for special education at home or abroad.

A simple measurement of total years in school can be refined by the type of education offered. The numbers in secondary instruction in the sciences and in technical education are thus more pertinent than the total number in such instruction overall. Similarly, in higher education, the relative number in science, engineering, economics, and agronomy may be more significant than the total enrollment. Nations may be similar in the relative numbers receiving an education on the college level but different in the impact of this fact on economic development.

Accordingly, development areas vary as to the extent of the wealth they produce out of a given amount of education expenditure. Payoffs on educational investment reflect student selection, student activity while in school, quality of instruction, extent of courses offered that assist in the modernizing process, educational materials, and administration. The more time a college student takes in obtaining his degree, the more likely is the payoff to be postponed, and, in all probability, it will be at a lower rate. Upon graduation, employment in low areas of productivity, such as government and other services, will reduce the payoff. The most qualified, as in Argentina, may emigrate and use their training in other nations. Education may also be employed as a symbol of status rather than used as a means of creating wealth.

3. *Health and sanitation.* These are measurable by per capita expenditures for local public health services and by the number of public health services or the number of public health employees to the population. A physician index is misleading; a rise in doctors may not indicate a rise in medical care for the population base.

4. *Job opportunities.* This term refers to a situation of full employment in which anyone who wants to work can find a job, where the society makes available to anyone who is unable to achieve his potential training opportunities to increase his skills, and where available jobs provide opportunities for upgrading. This environment of a rising technological commitment of labor can be assessed through a time series of the occupational distribution of a representative sample of the population and less directly through an index of the skill levels of occupations weighted by the population.

5. *Income distribution proportional to effort.* The acceleration of economic growth shifts the relative income distribution from owners of property to individuals making contributions to production. This shift is occurring at present in Spain in dramatic fashion. The change is observable by the relative shift of income toward wage and salary recipients and by the degree to which overall earnings differences are narrowing.

6. *Economic and political organization.* This term refers to organizations that promote the economic and political interests of their members. They include political parties, labor organizations, and employer associations. These organizations can give development momentum by feeding

knowledge into the population and by gaining agreement among different segments of the population. The degree of participation by the people can be measured by the proportion of the population base in the developing area in such organizations. Miscalculation can occur because of dissimilarities in the institutions of the host country and of the investigator, who, through bias, may underestimate institutions in the host country that are performing roles similar to those of institutions for which he has little esteem in his own country.

7. *Planning institutions.* The concern here is with the actual substance of planning and decision making and with the degree of the population's involvement in fixing objectives and working toward goals. As in the case of political and economic organization, such participation can reduce the lethargy that may obstruct development and provide an esprit de corps not otherwise obtainable. Effective participation in local planning is an educational investment that serves to reduce social deterrents to growth.

With the framework given here and in Chapter 16, as well as the sources of information in the Bibliography, the student can be asked to develop a nation case history of his own interest. He may wish to prepare a report in the form of a briefing. He is likely to find that putting together his study will involve a series of compromises between the sophisticated research methods he would like to use and the available facts. It is a worthwhile exercise in decision making.

BIBLIOGRAPHY

GENERAL SOURCES

Periodicals

American Economic Review
American Journal of Sociology
American Sociological Review
Annals of the American Academy of Political and Social Science
Comparative Education Review
Current Digest of the Soviet Press (Columbia University)
Eastern European Economics
Economic Development and Cultural Change
Free Labour World (International Confederation of Free Trade Unions)
Human Organization
Industrial and Labor Relations Review
International Labour Review
Journal of Human Resources
Journal of Modern African Studies
Labor Developments Abroad (U. S. Bureau of Labor Statistics)
Labor Digest (U. S. Bureau of Labor Statistics)
Monthly Labor Review (U. S. Bureau of Labor Statistics)
Problems of Communism
Quarterly Journal of Indian Studies in Social Sciences
Social Research Journal
Soviet Studies (University of Chicago)

Other Works

Annual reports of labor and economic ministries and annual statistical reports of developing countries

Bibliography on *Labor in Emerging Societies* published by Syracuse
   University
El Trimestre Económico (written by Latin Americans about Latin America)
March 1957 international issue of *The Annals* of the American Academy of
   Political and Social Science
Monographs on different countries and comparative studies of labor legis-
   lation published by the Division of Foreign Labor Conditions of the
   U. S. Bureau of Labor Statistics
Monthly Bulletin of Statistics of the United Nations
"Planning and Economic Development Series" on different countries pub-
   lished by the Johns Hopkins University Press
"Praeger Special Studies" published by Frederick A. Praeger, Inc.
Selected bibliography on *Manpower Problems in Economic Development*
   prepared by the Industrial Relations Section, Princeton University, 1958
Year Book of Labor Statistics of the International Labor Organization

CHAPTER 2

HOW DOES ECONOMIC DEVELOPMENT TAKE PLACE?

Alexander, Robert J. *A Primer of Economic Development.* New York:
   Macmillan, 1962.
Balogh, Thomas. *The Economics of Poverty.* New York: Macmillan,
   1967.
Bauer, P. T., and Basil S. Yamey. *The Economics of Under-developed
   Countries.* Chicago: University of Chicago Press, 1957.
Bhagwati, Jagdish. *The Economics of Underdeveloped Countries.* New
   York: McGraw-Hill, 1966.
*Chenery, Hollis B. "The Role of Industrialization in Development Pro-
   grams." *American Economic Review,* Vol. 45 (May 1955).
*Hagen, Everett E. *On the Theory of Social Change: How Economic
   Growth Begins.* Homewood, Ill.: Dorsey Press, 1962.
Higgins, Benjamin H. *Economic Development: Principles, Problems,
   and Policies.* Rev. ed. New York: Norton, 1968.
Hirschman, Albert O. *The Strategy of Economic Development.* New
   Haven, Conn.: Yale University Press, 1958.
*Hoselitz, Bert F. and others. *Theories of Economic Growth.* Glencoe,
   Ill.: The Free Press, 1960.
Kindleberger, Charles P. *Economic Development.* 2nd ed. New York:
   McGraw-Hill, 1961.
Kuznets, Simon. *Modern Economic Growth: Rate, Structure, and
   Spread.* New Haven, Conn.: Yale University Press, 1966.
————. *Postwar Economic Growth.* Four Lectures. Cambridge, Mass.:
   Harvard University Press, 1964.
Lewis, W. Arthur. *Development Planning.* New York: Harper & Row,
   1966.
Lewis, William A. *The Theory of Economic Growth.* London: Allen &
   Unwin, 1955.
McClelland, David C. *The Achieving Society.* Princeton, N.J.: Van Nos-
   trand, 1961.
Myint, Hla. *The Economics of the Developing Countries.* 3rd ed. New
   York: Praeger, 1967.

* Asterisks indicate basic contributions to the study of economic development.

Ranjan, Suman. *The Strategy for Agricultural Development and Other Essays on Economic Policy and Planning.* New York: Asia Publishing House, 1963.

*Rostow, W. W. *The Stages of Economic Growth: A Non-Communist Manifesto.* Cambridge: Cambridge University Press, 1961.

Scientific American. *Technology and Economic Development.* New York: Alfred A. Knopf, 1963.

Shannon, Lyle W. *Underdeveloped Areas.* New York: Harper & Row, 1957.

*Staley, Eugene. *The Future of Underdeveloped Countries: Political Implications of Economic Development.* Rev. ed. New York: Harper & Row, 1961.

Walinsky, L. J. *The Planning and Execution of Economic Development.* New York: McGraw-Hill, 1963.

CHAPTER 3
THE POPULATION QUESTION

Bird, Richard M. "Crecimiento de la población y desarrollo económico," *Desarrollo Económico* (Buenos Aires), Vol. 1, No. 2 (July–September 1961).

Coale, Ansley J., and Edgar M. Hoover. *Population Growth and Economic Development in Low-Income Countries.* Princeton, N.J.: Princeton University Press, 1958.

*Davis, Kingsley. "The Population Specter: Rapidly Declining Death Rate in Densely Populated Countries. The Amazing Decline of Mortality in Underdeveloped Areas," *American Economic Review,* Vol. 46 (May 1956).

*Dudley, Kirk, and Dorothy Nortman. "Population Policies in Developing Countries," *Economic Development and Cultural Change,* Vol. 15 (January 1967), Part 1.

Hauser, Philip M. (ed.). *The Population Dilemma.* 2nd ed. Englewood Cliffs, N.J.: Prentice-Hall, 1964.

*Kamerschen, David R. "Another Look at the Concept of 'Overpopulation,' " Reply, *Economic Development and Cultural Change,* Vol. 17 (October 1968).

Mayone, Stycos J. *Population Growth and the Alliance for Progress.* Washington, D.C.: Population Reference Bureau, Vol. 18 (October 8, 1962).

Mortara, Giorgio. "Los estudios demográficos y la política de la población en América Latina," *Instituto de La Producción de la Universidad Nacional de La Plata* (La Plata, Argentina), November 1961.

Spengler, Joseph J. "The Economist and the Population Question," *American Economic Review,* Vol. 56 (March 1966).

*————. "The Population Obstacle to Economic Betterment," *American Economic Review,* Vol. 41 (May 1951).

*Strauss, C. B. "Population Growth and Economic Development," *South African Journal of Economics,* Vol. 31 (June 1963).

United Nations. *Demographic Yearbook 1965.* New York: United Nations, 1966.

United Nations, Department of Social Affairs. *Future Population Estimates by Sex and Age,* Report II, *The Population of South America, 1950–1980.* New York: United Nations, 1955.

Vito, Francesco. *Popolazione e sviluppo economico. Problemi dello sviluppo economico con particolare riguardo alle aree arretrate.* Milan: Università Cattolica del Sacro Cuore, 1956.

Walsh, Brendan M. "Another Look at the Concept of 'Overpopulation,' " *Economic Development and Cultural Change,* Vol. 17 (October 1968).

Wigny, Pierre. "Los movimientos migratorios que provocan la industrialización en los países insuficientemente desarrollados," *Revista Internacional del Trabajo,* Vol. 68 (July 1953).

CHAPTER 4
DEVELOPING HUMAN CAPITAL

Abu-Lughod, Ibrahim. *Evaluation in Community Development: Basic Principles and Experiences.* Sirs-el-Layyah, Menoufia, Egypt: Arab States Fundamental Education Centre, 1960.

Ammassari, Gloria P. "Training Problems in Southern Italy," *British Journal of Industrial Relations,* Vol. 3 (July 1965), 182–188.

*Ardant, Gabriel. "A Plan for Full Employment in the Developing Countries," *International Labour Review,* Vol. 88 (July 1963).

Belbin, Eunice. *Training the Adult Worker.* Department of Scientific and Industrial Research. London: H. M. Stationery Office, 1964.

Belbin, R. M. *Training Methods for Older Workers.* Paris: Organization for Economic Cooperation and Development, 1965.

Bolino, August C. *Manpower and the City.* Cambridge, Mass.: Schenkman, 1969. Useful as a basis for making comparisons with United States manpower development problems.

Clay, Hilary M. *How Research Can Help Training.* Department of Scientific and Industrial Research. London: H. M. Stationery Office, 1964.

DeBeauvais, Michel. "La Notion de Capital Humain," *Revue Internationale des Sciences Sociales,* Vol. 14. Paris: UNESCO, 1962.

*————. "Manpower Planning in Developing Countries," *International Labour Review,* Vol. 89 (April 1964).

DiTella, Torcuato S. "Economía y estructura ocupaciónal en un país subdesarrollado," *Desarrollo Económico* (Buenos Aires), Vol. 1 (October–December 1961).

Duncan, Beverly. "Dropouts and the Unemployed," *Journal of Political Economy,* Vol. 73 (April 1965).

Emerson, John P. *Sex, Age, and Level of Skill of the Non-agricultural Labor Force of Mainland China.* U. S. Department of Commerce, Bureau of the Census, Foreign Demographic Analysis Division. Washington, D.C.: Government Printing Office, 1965.

Ferguson, Robert H. *Unemployment: Its Scope, Measurement, and Effect on Poverty.* Bulletin 53–2. Ithaca, N.Y.: Cornell University, State School of Industrial Relations, 1965.

Fischlowitz, Estanislau. "Manpower Problems and Prospects in Latin America," *Monthly Labor Review,* Vol. 83 (September 1960).

*Galenson, Walter, and G. Pyatt. *The Quality of Labour and Economic Development in Certain Countries: A Preliminary Study.* Geneva: International Labor Organization, 1964.

Ginzberg, Eli C., and Herbert A. Smith. *Manpower Strategy for Developing Countries: Lessons from Ethiopia.* New York: Columbia University Press, 1967.

*Harbison, Frederick. "Human Resources Development Planning in Modernising Economies," *International Labour Review,* Vol. 85 (May 1962).

————, and Charles A. Myers (eds.). *Manpower and Education: Country*

Studies in Economic Development. New York: McGraw-Hill, 1965. Covers Communist China, Chile, Argentina, Peru, Puerto Rico, Iran, Indonesia, Senegal, Guinea, Ivory Coast, Nyasaland, and Uganda.

Hollister, R. G. "Manpower Problems and Policies in Sub-Saharan Africa, *International Labour Review,* Vol. 99 (May 1969).

Instituto Nacional de Cooperación Educativa. *Encuesta nacional para capacitación de mano de obra, 1961.* Caracas, Venezuela: Arte, 1962.

International Labor Office. *Problems of Employment in Economic Development.* Reprint Series No. 2. Geneva: International Institute for Labor Studies, 1964.

————. "Vocational Training and the Establishment of Service Workshops in a Poor Rural Area: The Experience of the Andean Indian Programme," *International Labour Review,* Vol. 85 (February 1962).

————. "Employment as an Objective in Economic Development," *International Labour Review,* (November–December 1961).

Jakubasukas, Edward B., and C. Phillip Baumel (eds.). *Human Resources Development.* Ames: Iowa State University Press, 1967. A general work on the order of an advanced economy.

Lester, Richard A. *Manpower Planning in a Free Society.* Princeton, N.J.: Princeton University Press, 1966. An advanced economy interpretation.

*Lewis, W. Arthur. "Economic Development with Unlimited Supplies of Labor," in B. Okun and R. W. Richardson (eds.), *Studies in Economic Development.* New York: Holt, Rinehart & Winston, 1961.

Lutz, Vera. "Some Structural Aspects of the Southern Problem: The Complementarity of Emigration and Industrialization," *Quarterly Review,* Banca Nazionale Italiana, No. 59 (December 1961).

Maunder, W. F. *Employment in an Underdeveloped Area.* New Haven, Conn.: Yale University Press, 1960.

*McVoy, Edgar C. "Relevance of United States Experience in Manpower Programs for Developing Countries," *Industrial Relations Research Association, Twentieth Annual Meeting Proceedings,* December 28–29, 1967. See also comment of Abraham Siegel.

Ministerio de Trabajo, Departamento de Migraciones. *Estudio sobre las necesidades y posibilidades de mano de obra en Venezuela.* Caracas, Venezuela, 1961.

————. Dirección de Previsión. *La mujer venezolana en la educación y en el trabajo.* Caracas, Venezuela, 1961.

Moore, Wilbert E. "Urbanization and Industrialization of the Labor Force in a Developing Economy," *American Economic Review,* Vol. 45 (May 1955).

————. *Industrialization and Labor.* Ithaca, N.Y.: Cornell University Press, 1951.

————, and Arnold S. Feldman (eds.). *Labor Commitment and Social Change in Developing Areas.* New York: Social Science Research Council, 1960.

National Manpower Council. *A Policy for Skilled Manpower.* New York: Columbia University Press, 1954. See Chapter I, "Skill and Economic Development."

Perrella, Vera C., and Forrest A. Bogan. *Out-of-School Youth, February 1963. Part I, A Study of Young People No Longer in School: Their Education, Reasons for Leaving School, and Labor Force Status.* U.S. Bureau of Labor Statistics, Special Labor Force Report No. 46. Washington, D.C.: Government Printing Office, 1964.

*Phillips, Walter. "Technological Levels and Labor Resistance to Change in the Course of Industrialization," *Economic Development and Cultural Change,* Vol. 11 (April 1963).

Rao, K. N. "Skilled Manpower for Continents in a Hurry," *Journal of the American Society of Training Directors,* Vol. 16 (May 1962).

Siguán, Miguel. "Factores humanos y sociales en un plan de desarrollo," *Boletín de Estudios Económicos,* Universidad Comercial de Duesto (Duesto Bibao, Spain), Vol. 17 (September–December 1962).

Sinha, M. R. (ed.). *The Economics of Manpower Planning.* Bombay: Indian Institute of Asian Studies, 1965.

U. S. Bureau of Labor Statistics. *An Assessment of Apprenticeship.* Washington, D.C.: Government Printing Office, 1964.

————. *Counselor's Guide to Occupational and Other Manpower Information.* Bulletin No. 1421. Washington, D.C.: Government Printing Office, 1964.

Weintraub, Leon. *International Manpower Development: A Role for Private Enterprise in Foreign Assistance.* New York: Praeger, 1969.

CHAPTER 5
EDUCATION AND ECONOMIC DEVELOPMENT

Adams, Don, and Robert M. Bjork. *Education in Developing Areas.* New York: McKay, 1969.

*Adams, Donald K. "The Study of Education and Social Development," *Comparative Education Review,* Vol. 9 (October 1965).

Anaya, Ricardo. *Educación y desarrollo.* Revista de la Facultad de Ciencias Económicas, Universidad Mayor de San Simón, No. 3. Cochabamba, Bolivia, 1962.

Anderson, C. Arnold. *The Social Context of Educational Planning.* Paris: UNESCO, International Institute for Educational Planning, 1967.

————, and Mary Jean Bowman (eds.). *Education and Economic Development.* Chicago: Aldine, 1965.

*Becker, Gary S., *et al.* "The Economics of Education," *American Economic Review,* Vol. 56 (May 1966).

Beeby, C. E. *The Quality of Education in Developing Countries.* Cambridge, Mass.: Harvard University Press, 1966.

Bigelow, Karl W., and Philip H. Coombs. *Education and Foreign Aid.* Cambridge, Mass.: Harvard University Press, 1965.

*Blandy, Richard. "Some Questions Concerning Education and Training in the Developing Countries," *International Labour Review,* Vol. 92 (December 1965).

Bravo J., Manuel. "El desarrollo económico y el progreso educativo," *Comercio Exterior,* Banco Nacional de Comercio Exterior S.A. (México), Vol. 12, No. 12 (December 1962).

Cerych, Ladislav. *Problems of Aid to Education in Developing Countries.* New York: Praeger, 1965.

*Chesswas, J. D. *Educational Planning and Development in Uganda.* Paris: UNESCO, International Institute for Educational Planning, 1966.

Committee for Economic Development. *Raising Low Incomes Through Improved Education,* A statement by the Research and Policy Committee. New York: CED, 1965.

Cowan, L. Gray, *et al. Education and National Building in Africa.* New York: Praeger, 1965.

Elliott, W. Y. (ed.). *Education and Training in the Developing Countries, the Role of U.S. Foreign Aid.* New York: Praeger, 1966.

*Gant, George F. "The Institution Building Project." *International Review of Administrative Science,* Vol. 32, No. 3 (1966). An article on the process whereby a developing country with the assistance of a host country establishes an educational, training, or research organization.

García Ordas, Rubén. "Ejecutivos para un país en desarrollo" (Buenos Aires), *Análisis,* Vol. 3, No. 106 (March 2, 1963).

Gay, John, and Michael Cole. *The New Mathematics and an Old Culture: A Study of Learning Among the Kpelle of Liberia.* New York: Holt, Rinehart & Winston, 1967.

Hamuy, Eduardo. *Educación elemental, analfabetismo, y desarrollo económico.* Santiago, Chile: Editorial Universitaria, 1960.

Hanna, Paul R. "Conventional and Unconventional Education in Newly Developed Countries," Reprint from *America's Emerging Role in Overseas Education.* Syracuse, N.Y.: Syracuse University, School of Education, 1962.

Hanson, John W., and Geoffrey W. Gibson. *African Education and Development Since 1960: A Selected and Annotated Bibliography.* East Lansing: Institute for International Studies in Education and African Studies Center, Michigan State University, 1966.

*Harbison, Frederick. *Educational Planning and Human Resource Development.* Paris: UNESCO, Institute for Educational Planning, 1967.

————, and Charles A. Myers (eds.). *Manpower and Education: Country Studies in Economic Development.* New York: McGraw-Hill, 1965.

*Hoselitz, Bert F. "Investment in Education and Its Political Impact," in James S. Coleman (ed.), *Education and Political Development.* Princeton, N.J.: Princeton University Press, 1965.

Levine, H. "Recent Developments in the Soviet Economy," *ASTE Bulletin,* Vol. 7, No. 3 (Winter 1965).

Lewis, Arthur J. *Guidelines for the Planning of External Aid Projects in Education.* New York: Education and World Affairs, 1967.

Lewis, Leonard J. *Society, Schools, and Progress in Nigeria.* London: Pergamon Press, 1965.

*Lewis, W. Arthur. *Education and Economic Development.* Paris: UNESCO, Social and Economic Studies, 1962.

Little, I. M. D. *Aid to Africa.* Oxford: Pergamon Press, 1964.

————. "Educación y desarrollo económico," *Revista de Economía y Estadística* (Córdoba, Argentina), Vol. 6, No. 3 (1962).

*McClelland, David C. "Does Education Accelerate Economic Growth?" *Economic Development and Cultural Change,* Vol. 14 (April 1966).

Moaeira, J. R., *et al.* "La educación y el desarrollo económico y social de América Latina," *La Educación,* Vol. 7 (January–June 1962).

*Mouly, Jean. "Human Resources Planning as Part of Economic Development Planning," *International Labour Review,* Vol. 92 (September 1965).

Organization for Economic Cooperation and Development. *Methods and Statistical Needs for Educational Planning,* Paris, 1967.

Pérez Rodríguez, Jorge. "El desarrollo económico y las inversiones en educación," *Comercio Exterior,* Banco Nacional de Comercio Exterior, S.A. (México), Vol. 12 (March 1962).

Reissig, Luis. *Educación y desarrollo económico.* Buenos Aires: Losada S.A., 1961.

Sanchez, G. I. *Development of Education in Venezuela.* Washington, D.C.: Government Printing Office, 1964.

*Schultz, Theodore W. *Economic Value of Education.* New York: Columbia University Press, 1963.

*Skorov, George. *Integration of Educational and Economic Planning in Tanzania.* Paris: UNESCO, Institute for Educational Planning, 1966.

United Nations Educational, Scientific, and Cultural Organization. *World Survey of Education.* 4 vols. Paris: UNESCO, 1954–1966.

Zook, Paul D. (ed.). "Investment in Human Capital in Poor Countries," Chapter I in *Foreign Trade and Human Capital.* Dallas, Tex.: Southern Methodist University Press, 1962.

CHAPTER 6
LABOR ORGANIZATION DIFFERENCES BETWEEN DEVELOPED AND DEVELOPING NATIONS

Aronson, Robert L., and John P. Windmuller (eds.). *Labor, Management and Economic Growth.* Ithaca, N.Y.: Cornell University, School of Industrial and Labor Relations, 1954.

Barkin, Solomon. "Is the United States the Model for World Labor and Industrial Relations?" *Labor Law Journal,* Vol. 2 (December 1960).

Cassen, Robert. "Desarrollo económico y la minimazación de la coerción. El rol de los sindicatos en el desarrollo económico," *Desarrollo Económico* (Buenos Aires), Vol. 1 (July–September 1961).

Cornell University, School of Industrial and Labor Relations. *American Labor's Role in Less Developed Countries, A Report on a Conference Held at Cornell University,* October 12–17, 1958. Ithaca, N.Y.,1959.

*Deyrup, Felicia J. "Organized Labor and Government in Underdeveloped Countries: Sources of Conflict," *Industrial and Labor Relations Review,* Vol. 12 (October 1958).

Fayerweather, John. *Management of International Operations.* New York: McGraw-Hill, 1960. See Chapter 5, "Labor Relations."

*Fisher, Paul. "The Economic Role of Unions in Less Developed Areas," *Monthly Labor Review,* Vol. 84 (September 1961).

Gamba, Charles. *The Origins of Trade Unionism in Malaya, A Study in Colonial Labour Unrest.* Singapore: Eastern Universities Press, Ltd., 1962.

*Kassalow, Everett M. "Unions in the New and Developing Countries," Chapter 10 in E. M. Kassalow (ed.), *National Labor Movements in the Postwar World.* Evanston, Ill.: Northwestern University Press, 1963.

———. "Union Organization and Training in Emerging Labor Movements," *Monthly Labor Review,* Vol. 85 (September 1962).

Kung, E. "Los sindicatos y la inflación," *Estudios Económicos* (Bahía Blanca, Argentina), Vol. 1 (January–June 1962).

Millen, Bruce H. *The Political Role of Labor in Developing Countries.* Washington, D.C.: Brookings Institution, 1963.

Monthly Labor Review. "Current Structure of African Trade Unionism," Vol. 86 (February 1963).

Ross, Arthur M. (ed.). *Industrial Relations and Economic Development.* London: Macmillan, 1966. A useful work on a variety of industrial relations subjects covering such countries as Malaysia, India, Egypt, Mexico, and the former British and French African colonies.

*Sturmthal, Adolf. "Unions and Economic Development," *Economic Development and Cultural Change,* Vol. 8 (January 1960).
Sufrin, Sidney C. *Unions in Emerging Societies: Frustration and Politics.* Syracuse, N.Y.: Syracuse University Press, 1964.
Van Eerde, K. S. "Problems and Alignments in African Labour," *Social Research,* Vol. 29 (Spring 1962).
Weisz, Morris. "The Structure of Labor Movements in Emerging Areas," *Monthly Labor Review,* Vol. 85 (December 1962).

CHAPTER 7
POLITICAL SYSTEMS IN DEVELOPING COUNTRIES

Aitken, Hugh G. J. (ed.). *The State and Economic Growth.* New York: Social Science Research Council, 1959.
Alderfer, Harold F. *Local Government in Developing Countries.* New York: McGraw-Hill, 1964.
————. *Public Administration in Newer Nations.* New York: Praeger, 1966.
*Almond, Gabriel A., and James S. Coleman (eds.). *The Politics of the Developing Areas.* Princeton, N.J.: Princeton University Press, 1960.
Bueno y Urquidi, Arturo. "El papel del Estado en el desarrollo económico: algunas observaciónes," *Comercio Exterior,* Banco Nacional de Comercio Exterior (Mexico), Vol. 12, No. 6 (June 1962).
Fayerweather, John. *Management of International Operations.* New York: McGraw-Hill, 1960. See Chapter 4, "Community Relationships."
*Horowitz, David. "Economic Development and Democracy," *Journal of International Affairs,* Vol. 16, No. 2 (1962).
Hoselitz, Bert F. "Economic Growth and Development: Non-economic Factors in Economic Development," *American Economic Review,* Vol. 47 (May 1957).
*Mason, Edward S. "The Role of Government in Economic Development," *American Economic Review,* Vol. 50 (May 1960).
*Penrose, Edith. "Economic Development and the State: An Object Lesson from the Past?" *Economic Development and Cultural Change,* Vol. 11 (January 1963).
Sigmund, Paul E. (ed.). *The Ideologies of the Developing Nations.* Rev. ed. New York: Praeger, 1969.
Torres, Gaitán. "La intervención del estado en la vida económica," *Investigación Económica, Revista Trimestral* (Mexico), Vol. 19 (January–March 1958).
Waterston, Albert. *Development Planning: Lessons of Experience.* Baltimore: Johns Hopkins University Press, 1965.

CHAPTER 8
SOCIAL STRUCTURE AND ECONOMIC DEVELOPMENT

DiTella, Torcuato S. "Los procesos políticos y sociales de la industrialización," *Desarrollo Económico* (Buenos Aires), Vol. 2 (October–December 1962).
Doublet, Jacques. Aspectos sociales del desarrollo económico, *Documentación Económica* (Madrid), No. 23 (1961).
Ferrer, Aldo. *Social Factors in Economic Development.* Buenos Aires:

Raigol, 1956.
*Glade, William. "Social Backwardness, Social Reform, and Productivity in Latin America," *Inter-American Economic Affairs,* Vol. 15 (Winter 1961).
International Social Science Council. *Les implications sociales du développement économique.* Paris: Presses Universitaires, 1962.
Kroef, Justus M. van der. "Obstáculos culturales para el desarrollo económico," *Revista de Economía y Estadística* (Córdoba, Argentina), Vol. 6, No. 1 (first trimester, 1962).
Medina Echavarría, José. "Las relaciones entre las instituciones sociales y las económicas. Un modelo para América Latina," *Boletín Económico de América Latina* (Santiago de Chile), Vol. 6, No. 1 (March 1961).
Ortigueira, Roberto. "La desintegración, estado normal de países en desarrollo," *Journal of Inter-American Studies,* Vol. 5 (October 1963).
*Paukert, Felix. "The Distribution of Gains from Economic Development," *International Labour Review,* Vol. 91 (May 1965).
Siguán, Miguel. "Factores humanos y sociales en un plan de desarrollo," *Boletín de Estudios Económicos,* Universidad Comercial de Deusto (Deusto-Bilbao, Spain), Vol. 17, No. 57 (September–December 1962).
United Nations Educational, Scientific, and Cultural Organization. *Social Aspects of Economic Development in Latin America.* New York: United Nations, 1963.
————. *Social Implications of Industrialization and Urbanization in Africa South of the Sahara.* Paris: UNESCO, 1956.
Vera L., José. "Aspectos sociales del desarrollo económico," *Economia, Revista de la Facultad De Ciencias Económicas de la Universidad de Chile* (Santiago, Chile), Vol. 19, No. 63 (April–June 1959).

CHAPTER 9
THE SOVIET UNION

Aleksandrov, G. F. *The Pattern of Soviet Democracy.* Washington, D.C.: Public Affairs Press, 1948.
Ames, Edward. *Soviet Economic Processes.* Homewood, Ill.: Irwin, 1965.
Armstrong, John A. *The Soviet Bureaucratic Elite.* New York: Praeger, 1959.
Balinky, Alexander, et al. *Planning and the Market in the U.S.S.R.: the 1960's.* New Brunswick, N.J.: Rutgers University Press, 1957.
Barton, Paul. "Soviet Labor Conditions under Khrushchev," *AFL-CIO Free Trade Union News* (September 1959).
Bergson, A., and Simon Kuznets (eds.). *Economic Trends in the Soviet Union.* Cambridge, Mass.: Harvard University Press, 1963.
Berliner, Joseph S. *Factory and Manager in the U.S.S.R.* Cambridge, Mass.: Harvard University Press, 1957.
Bienstock, G., et al. *Management in Russian Industry and Agriculture.* New York: Oxford University Press, 1944.
Black, Cyril E. (ed.). *The Transformation of Russian Society.* Cambridge, Mass.: Harvard University Press, 1960.
Boriskin, S. *Trade Unions in the U.S.S.R.: Organizational Structure, Forms, and Methods of Work.* Moscow: Profizdat, 1960.

Bornstein, Morris, and Daniel R. Fusfeld (eds.). *The Soviet Economy.* 3rd ed. Homewood, Ill.: Irwin, 1970.

Borshchenko, I. *The Russian Trade Unions 1907–1917.* Moscow: Profizdat, 1959.

Brodersen, Arvid. *The Soviet Worker: Labor and Government in Soviet Society.* New York: Random House, 1966.

*Brown, Emily Clark. *Soviet Trade Unions and Labor Relations.* Cambridge, Mass.: Harvard University Press, 1966. The most modern and definitive work on Soviet trade unionism and labor relations.

————. "A Note on Employment and Unemployment in the Soviet Union in the Light of Technical Progress," *Soviet Studies,* Vol. 12 (January 1961).

————. "The Local Union in Soviet Industry," *Industrial and Labor Relations Review,* Vol. 13 (January 1960).

————. "Labor Relations in Soviet Factories," *Industrial and Labor Relations Review,* Vol. 11 (January 1958).

Brzezinski, S. K. *The Soviet Bloc: Unity and Conflict.* Cambridge, Mass.: Harvard University Press, 1960.

Campbell, Robert W. *Soviet Economic Power.* 2nd ed. Boston: Houghton Mifflin, 1960.

Chapman, Janet B. "Real Wages in the Soviet Union 1928–1952," *Review of Economics and Statistics,* Vol. 36 (May 1954).

Cohen, Stanley H. *Economic Development in the Soviet Union.* Livingston, Mass.: D. C. Heath, 1970.

Current Digest of the Soviet Press. "Draft of the New Labor Law Principles Is Published," November 18, 1959.

Dallin, David J. *The Real Soviet Russia.* New Haven, Conn.: Yale University Press, 1947.

————. *The New Soviet Empire.* New Haven, Conn.: Yale University Press, 1951.

————, and Norris I. Bicolaevsky. *Forced Labor in Soviet Russia.* New Haven, Conn.: Yale University Press, 1947.

Dementyeva, A. *Labor Protection in the U.S.S.R.* Moscow: Profizdat, 1959.

Deutscher, Isaac. *Soviet Trade Unions.* New York: Macmillan, 1950.

Dodge, Norton T. *Women in the Soviet Economy.* Baltimore: Johns Hopkins University Press, 1966.

Dunlop, John T., and Vasilii P. Diatchenko (eds.). *Labor Productivity.* New York: McGraw-Hill, 1964.

Eason, W. W. "Population Growth and Economic Development in the U.S.S.R.," *American Statistical Association Proceedings of the Social Statistics Section,* 1958.

Economist, The. "Trade Unionism in Russia," April 25, 1959.

Fainsod, Merle. *How Russia is Ruled.* Cambridge, Mass.: Harvard University Press, 1951.

*Fischer-Galati, Stephen (ed.). *Eastern Europe in the Sixties.* Rev. ed. New York: Praeger, 1963.

Galenson, Walter. *Labor Productivity in Soviet and American Industry.* New York: Columbia University Press, 1955.

Granick, David. *Management of the Industrial Firm in the USSR.* Cambridge, Mass.: Harvard University Press, 1954.

————. *The Red Executive.* New York: Doubleday, 1961.

Grishin, V. C. *Report on the Work of the All-Union Central Council of*

Trade Unions and the Tasks of the Soviet Trade Unions Arising out of the Decisions of the 21st Congress of the Communist Party Soviet Union. Moscow: Profizdat, 1959.

*Grossman, Gregory. "Information and Innovation in the Soviet Economy," *American Economic Review,* Vol. 56 (May 1966).

Gsovski, Vladimir (ed.). *Government, Law, and Courts in the Soviet Union and Eastern Europe.* New York: Praeger, 1959.

Hazard, John N. *Settling Disputes in Soviet Society: The Formative Years of Legal Institutions.* New York: Columbia University Press, 1960.

————. *Law and Social Change in the U.S.S.R.* Toronto: Carswell, 1953.

Holzman, Franklyn D. (ed.). *Readings on the Soviet Economy.* Chicago: Rand McNally, 1962.

Inkeles, Alex. *Public Opinion in Soviet Russia.* Cambridge, Mass.: Harvard University Press, 1958.

————, et al. *How the Soviet System Works.* Cambridge, Mass.: Harvard University Press, 1956.

International Labour Office. *Technological Change and Manpower in a Centrally Planned Economy.* Bulletin No. 3. Geneva, 1966. This is a study based on Soviet literature.

*————. *Trade Union Rights in the U.S.S.R.* Geneva, 1959.

*————. *The Trade Union Situation in the U.S.S.R.* Geneva, 1960.

Jasny, Naum. *Soviet Industrialization 1928–1952.* Chicago: University of Chicago Press, 1961.

Kalinin, M. I. *On the Moral Behavior of Our People.* Moscow: Young Guard Publishing House, 1956.

Kostin, Leonid. "Organization of Workers' Education in the Soviet Union," *International Labour Review,* Vol. 79 (February 1959).

Laird, Roy D. "Some Characteristics of the Soviet Leadership System: A Maturing Totalitarian System?" *Midwest Journal of Political Science,* Vol. 10 (February 1966).

*Leontief, Wassily. "The Decline and Rise of Soviet Economic Science," *Foreign Affairs,* Vol. 38 (January 1960).

Manevich, E. "The Principle of the Personal Incentive and Certain Wage Problems in the U.S.S.R.," *Problems of Economics,* Vol. 2 (May 1959).

Mathewson, Rufus W. *The Positive Hero in Russian Literature.* New York: Columbia University Press, 1958.

McCrensky, Edward. "Personnel Management—Soviet Style," *Personnel Administration,* Vol. 23 (September–October 1960).

Moorsteen, Richard, and Raymond P. Powell. *The Soviet Capital Stock.* Homewood, Ill.: Irwin, 1966.

Nash, Edmund. "Purchasing Power of Workers in the U.S.S.R.," *Monthly Labor Review,* Vol. 83 (April 1960).

Novak, Joseph. *The Future Is Ours, Comrade.* New York: Doubleday, 1960.

Nove, A. *The Soviet Economy: An Introduction.* New York: Praeger, 1969.

Nutter, Warren G. "Employment in the Soviet Economy: An Interim Solution to a Puzzle," *Soviet Studies,* Vol. 12 (April 1961).

Petrov, P. *Soviet Trade Unions and Wages.* Moscow: Profizdat, 1959.

Podlyashuk, Pavel. *Factory Trade Union Organization: A Story about the Trade Union Organization of the 2nd Moscow Clock and Watch Factory.* Moscow: Profizdat, 1960.

Roof, Michael K., and Allen Hetmanek. "The Soviet Labor Force: Implications of New Data," *Monthly Labor Review,* Vol. 81 (December 1958).

Rostow, W. W., and Edward J. Rozek. *The Dynamics of Soviet Society.* Rev. ed. New York: Norton, 1967.

Schwartz, Harry. *Russia's Soviet Economy.* 2nd ed. Englewood Cliffs, N.J.: Prentice-Hall, 1954.

Schwarz, Solomon M. "Trade Unions in the Soviet State," *Current History,* Vol. 37 (August 1959).

————. *Labor in the Soviet Union.* New York: Praeger, 1952.

Scott, Derek. *Russian Political Institutions.* 3rd ed. New York: Praeger, 1966.

Sokol, M. "High-Level Manpower Planning: An Analysis of Czechoslovak Experience," *International Labour Review,* Vol. 95 (January–February 1967).

Spulber, Nicolas. *The Soviet Economy.* New York: Norton, 1962.

————. *Foundations of Soviet Strategy for Economic Growth.* Bloomington, Ind.: Indiana University Press, 1964.

Stevens, Leslie. *Russian Assignment.* Boston: Little, Brown, 1953.

*Sukharevskii, B. *Labor Developments in the U.S.S.R.* U. S. Bureau of Labor Statistics, Bulletin No. 311 (September 1966).

————. "The Working Day and Wages in the U.S.S.R.," *Problems of Economics,* Vol. 3 (July 1960).

U. S. Bureau of Labor Statistics. *Principal Current Soviet Labor Legislation.* BLS Report No. 210. Washington, D.C.: Government Printing Office, January 1962.

United States Congress, Joint Economic Committee. *New Directions in the Soviet Economy.* Washington, D.C.: Government Printing Office, 1966.

————. *Economic Office of Mainland China.* Washington, D.C.: Government Printing Office, 1967.

Walsh, Warren B. *Russia and the Soviet Union.* Ann Arbor, Mich.: University of Michigan Press, 1958.

Wilber, C. K. *The Soviet Model and Underdeveloped Countries.* Chapel Hill: University of North Carolina Press, 1969.

*Wiles, Peter J. *The Political Economy of Communism.* Cambridge, Mass.: Harvard University Press, 1962.

World Health Organization. *Health Services in the U.S.S.R.* Public Health Papers, No. 3. Geneva: World Health Organization, 1960.

Yanowitch, Murray. "Trends in Soviet Occupational Wage Differentials," *Industrial and Labor Relations Review,* Vol. 13 (January 1960).

Zelenko, H. "Vocational and Technical Training in the U.S.S.R.," *International Labour Review,* Vol. 80 (December 1959).

CHAPTER 10
ASIA

Benedicto, Roberto S., and José L. Africa. *Philippine Labor Laws.* Manila: Philippine Publishing Company, 1950.

Berton, Peter, and Eugene Wu. *Contemporary China: A Research Guide.* Stanford, Calif.: Stanford University Press, 1967.

Brimmell, J. H. *Communism in South East Asia: A Political Analysis.* New York: Oxford University Press, 1959.

Calderon, Cicero D. "From Compulsory Arbitration to Collective Bargaining in the Philippines," *International Labour Review,* Vol. 82 (January 1960).

Cecena, José Luis. "Desarrollo económico de la China Popular," *Investigación Económica* (Mexico), Vol. 18 (first quarter 1958).

*Chang, John K. "Industrial Development of Mainland China, 1912–1949," *Journal of Economic History,* Vol. 27 (March 1967).

*Chao, Kang. *The Rate and Pattern of Industrial Growth in Communist China.* Ann Arbor: University of Michigan Press, 1965.

*Chen, Nai-Ruenn. *China.* Chicago: Aldine, 1967.

————, and Walter Galenson. *The Chinese Economy under Communism.* Chicago: Aldine, 1969.

Chen, Theodore H. E. (ed.). *The Chinese Communist Regime.* New York: Praeger, 1967.

Donnithorne, Audrey. *China's Economic System.* New York: Praeger, 1967.

*Dufty, N. F. "The Evolution of the Indian Industrial Relations System," *Journal of Industrial Relations,* Vol. 7 (March 1965).

Dwarkadas, Kanji. *Forty-Five Years with Labour.* New York: Asia Publishing House, 1962.

Fonseca, Aloysius J. *Wage Determination and Organized Labour in India.* Bombay: Oxford University Press, 1964.

Francisco, Vincente. *The Law Governing Labor Disputes in the Philippines.* Manila: East Publishing Company, 1954.

*Galenson, Walter. "The Current State of Chinese Economic Studies," in *An Economic Profile of Mainland China.* Joint Economic Committee, U.S. Congress. Washington, D.C.: Government Printing Office, 1967.

———— (ed.). *Labor in Developing Economies.* Berkeley: University of California Press, 1962. Covers Pakistan, Indonesia, and Turkey.

————. *Labor and Economic Development.* New York: Wiley, 1959. Covers India and Japan.

Geertz, Clifford. *Agricultural Involution: The Process of Ecological Change in Indonesia.* Berkeley: University of California Press, 1963.

————. "Religious Belief and Economic Behavior in a Central Javanese Town: Some Preliminary Considerations," *Economic Development and Cultural Change,* Vol. 4 (January 1956).

*Ghosal, S. N. "Developing Human Capital—Indian Study," *Indian Journal of Economics,* Vol. 46 (October 1965).

Giri, V. V. *Labor Problems in Indian Industry.* 2nd ed. London: Asia Publishing House, 1959.

Golay, Frank H. *The Philippines: Public Policy and National Economic Development.* Ithaca, N.Y.: Cornell University Press, 1961.

Harbison, Frederick, and Charles A. Myers. *Manpower and Education: Country Studies in Economic Development.* New York: McGraw-Hill, 1965. Covers Iran, Indonesia, and China.

*Hoffman, Charles. "Work Incentives in Communist China," *Industrial Relations,* Vol. 3 (February 1964).

International Labor Organization. "Labor and Human Resources in the Economic Development of Asia," *Fifth Regional Asiatic Conference of the ILO,* Geneva, April 1963.

Ishikawa, Shigeru. *National Income and Capital Formation in Mainland China, an Examination of Official Statistics.* Tokyo: Institute of Asian Economic Affairs, 1965.

Kannappan, S. "The Ghandhian Model of Unionism in a Developing Economy: The TLA in India," *Industrial and Labor Relations Review,* Vol. 16 (October 1962).

Kapp, Karl William. *Hindu Culture, Economic Development and Economic Planning in India: A Collection of Essays.* New York: Asia Publishing House, 1963.

Klatt, Werner (ed.). *The Chinese Model: A Political, Economic and Social Survey.* New York: Oxford University Press, 1965.

Lambert, Richard D. *Workers, Factories, and Social Change in India.* Princeton, N.J.: Princeton University Press, 1963.

*Lewis, John P. *Quiet Crisis in India: Economic Development and American Policy.* Garden City, N.Y.: Anchor Books, 1964.

Lewis, John W. "The Leadership Doctrine of the Chinese Communist Party," *Asian Survey,* Vol. 1 (October 1963).

Lewis, Stephen R., Jr. *Economic Policy and Industrial Growth in Pakistan.* Cambridge, Mass.: M.I.T. Press, 1969.

Liu, Ta-Chung, and Kung-Chia Yeh. *The Economy of the Chinese Mainland.* Princeton, N.J.: Princeton University Press, 1965.

*Myrdal, Gunnar. *Asian Drama: An Inquiry into the Poverty of Nations.* New York: Pantheon, 1968.

Park, Richard L. *India's Political System.* Englewood Cliffs, N.J.: Prentice-Hall, 1967.

Raza, Mohammed Ali. *The Industrial Relations System of Pakistan.* Karachi: Bureau of Labor Publications, 1963.

Richardson, J. Henry. "Indonesian Labor Relations in their Political Setting," *Industrial and Labor Relations Review,* Vol. 12 (October 1958).

Richman, Barry M. *Industrial Society in Communist China.* New York: Random House, 1969.

Schurmann, Franz. *Ideology and Organization in Communist China.* Berkeley: University of California Press, 1966.

Singh, Baljit. *Next Step in Village India: A Study of Land Reforms and Group Dynamics.* New York: Asia Publishing House, 1961.

Singh, V. B., and A. K. Saran (eds.). *Industrial Labour in India.* New York: Asia Publishing House, 1960.

Social Science Research Council. *Population Trends, Manpower, Employment, and Unemployment, and General Trends in the Economy,* Committee on the Economy of China, meeting of October 21–24, 1965. New York: Social Science Research Council.

Sufrin, Sidney C. *Unions in Emerging Societies: Frustrations and Politics.* Syracuse, N.Y.: Syracuse University Press, 1964.

Sur, Mary. *Collective Bargaining: A Comparative Study of Developments in India and Other Countries.* Bombay: Asia Publishing House, 1965.

Thompson, Virginia. *Labor Problems in Southeast Asia.* New Haven, Conn.: Yale University Press, 1947.

Thorner, Daniel, and Alice Thorner. *Land and Labour in India.* New York: Asia Publishing Company, 1962.

*Tilak, V. R. K. "The Future Manpower Situation in India," *International Labour Review,* Vol. 87 (May 1963).

Vaid, K. N. (ed.). *Labour-Management Relations in India: A Symposium.* Delhi, India: Delhi School of Social Work, 1960.

Waterston, Albert. *Planning in Pakistan.* Baltimore: Johns Hopkins University Press, 1963.

*Wu, Yuan-li. *The Economy of Communist China: An Introduction.* New York: Praeger, 1965.

Yah, Lim Chong. *The Economic Development of Malaya.* New York: Oxford University Press, 1967.

CHAPTER 11
LATIN AMERICA

Alba, Victor. *Politics and the Labor Movement in Latin America.* Stanford, Calif.: Stanford University Press, 1968.

Alexander, Robert J. *Labor Relations in Argentina, Brazil, and Chile.* New York: McGraw-Hill, 1962.

————. *Communism in Latin America.* New Brunswick, N.J.: Rutgers University Press, 1957.

Anaya, Ricardo. "Aspectos político-administrativos del desarrollo nacional," *Revista de la Facultad de Ciencias Económicas de la Universidad Mayor de San Marcos* (Cochabamba, Bolivia), No. 3 (1962).

Baer, Werner. *Industrialization and Economic Development in Brazil.* Homewood, Ill.: Irwin, 1965.

Banco Central de Reserva del Perú. *Plan nacional de desarrollo económico y social del Perú, 1962–71* (Lima), 1962.

Banco Nacional de Comercio Exterior, S.A. "Obstáculos a la planeación económica en América Latina," *Comercio Exterior* (Mexico), March 1963.

————. "Obstáculos al progreso de América Latina," *Comercio Exterior* (Mexico), May 1962.

Bresser Pereira, L. C. "The Rise of Middle Class and Middle Management in Brazil," *Journal of Inter-American Studies,* Vol. 4 (July 1962).

Chapiro, Jorge. "Productividad y desarrollo económico," *Suma* (Buenos Aires), No. 34 (December 1962).

Committee for Economic Development. *Economic Development of Central America.* New York: Committee for Economic Development, 1964.

————. *Economic Development Issues: Latin America.* New York: Praeger, 1967. Countries include Argentina, Colombia, Mexico, Peru, Chile, and Brazil.

Cosío Villegas, Daniel. *American Extremes.* Austin: University of Texas Press, 1964.

Dorfman, Adolfo. "La economía latinoamericana en proceso de evolución," *Revista de desarrollo económico* (La Plata, Argentina), Vol. 2, No. 3 (April–June 1959).

*Dreier, John C. (ed.). *The Alliance for Progress.* Baltimore: Johns Hopkins University Press, 1962.

Duccoff, Louis J. *Los recursos humanos de Centro América, Panamá y Méjico en 1950–1980 y sus relaciones con algunos aspectos del desarrollo económico.* New York: United Nations Economic Commission on Latin America, 1960.

Espinosa Iglesias, Manuel. "Aspectos de la planeación económica en Méjico," *Investigación Económica* (Mexico), Vol. 23, No. 88 (fourth quarter 1962).

Fabian Research Society. *Labour Movements in Latin America.* London: Gollanez, 1957.

*Flores, Edmundo. "The Economics of Land Reform," *International Labour Review,* Vol. 92 (July 1965).

————. "La estrategia del desarrollo económico de América Latina," *Investigación Económica* (Mexico), Vol. 20 (January–March 1960).

*Frankenhoff, Charles A. "The Prebisch Thesis: Theory of Industrialism for Latin America," *Journal of Inter-American Studies,* Vol. 4 (April 1962).

Furtado, Celso. *The Economic Growth of Brazil.* Berkeley: University of California Press, 1963.

Galarza, Ernesto. *Labor in Latin America.* Washington, D.C.: American Council on Public Affairs, 1960.

*Galvin, Miles E. *Unionism in Latin America.* Ithaca, N.Y.: Cornell University, School of Industrial and Labor Relations, 1962.

Gaon, Isaac. "Factores demográficos que retardan el desarrollo económico y social del Uruguay," *Boletín,* publ. del Centro Latinoamericano de Pesquisas em Ciências Sociais (Río de Janeiro), Vol. 3, No. 2 (May 1960).

Garmendia, Beatriz I. de. "El desarrollo de América Latina. Una noción y un esquema de análisis," *Cuadernos Latinoamericanos de Economía Humana* (Montevideo, Uruguay), Vol. 2, No. 5 (1959).

Gibbons, W. J. "Economic and Demographic Factors in Improving Living Levels in the Caribbean Region," *Review of Social Economy,* Vol. 25 (March 1967).

*Gordon, Wendell C. *The Political Economy of Latin America.* New York: Columbia University Press, 1965.

Harbison, Frederick, and Charles A. Myers. *Manpower and Education: Country Studies in Economic Development.* New York: McGraw-Hill, 1965. Countries include Argentina, Peru, and Chile.

*Hirschman, Albert O. "The Political Economy of Import-Substituting Industrialization in Latin America," *Quarterly Journal of Economics,* Vol. 82 (February 1968).

*————. *Journeys Toward Progress: Studies of Economic Policy Making in Latin America.* New York: Twentieth Century Fund, 1963.

Hoselitz, Bert F. "El Desarrollo Económico en América Latina," *Desarrollo Económico* (Buenos Aires), Vol. 2, No. 3 (October–December 1962).

International Bank for Reconstruction and Development. *Economic Development of Venezuela.* Baltimore: Johns Hopkins University Press, 1961.

Johnson, John J. (ed). *Continuity and Change in Latin America.* Palo Alto, Calif.: Stanford University Press, 1964.

Kybal, Elba. "El desarrollo económico de la América Latina," *Revista del Instituto de Investigaciónes Económicas,* Vol. 4, No. 15 (April–September 1961).

Kybal, Milic. "La industrialización de América Latina," *El Trimestre Económico* (México), Vol. 16 (October–December 1949).

Leff, Nathaniel H. *Economic Policy Making and Development in Brazil, 1947–1964.* New York: Wiley, 1968.

Martínez Estrada, Ezekiel. *Diferencias y Semejanzas Entre Los Países de América Latina.* Mexico: Escuela Nacional de Ciencias Políticas y Sociales, 1962.

Morris, James O., and Efrén Córdova. *Bibliography of Industrial Relations in Latin America.* Ithaca, N.Y.: Cornell University, School of Industrial and Labor Relations, 1967.

Naciones Unidas. "El desarrollo económico venezolano en el último decenio," *Boletín Económico de América Latina* (Santiago, Chile), Vol. 5, No. 1 (March 1960).

Owen, Clifford Frank. "United States and Soviet Relations with Underdeveloped Countries: Latin America." *Inter-American Economic Affairs,* Vol. 14 (Winter 1960).

Pan American Union. *Reseña del movimiento obrero en la América Latina.* Washington, D.C.: Pan American Union, 1950.

Pena, Lázaro. "The Trade Union Movement in Latin America," *Political Affairs* (December 1957).

Perdomo, Luis Alfonso. "Basic Problems Facing the Free Trade Unions in Latin America," *Free Labor World* (September 1956).

Porter, Charles O., and Robert J. Alexander. *The Struggle for Democracy in Latin America.* New York: Macmillan, 1961.

Powelson, John P. *Latin America: Today's Economic and Social Revolution.* New York: McGraw-Hill, 1964.

Prebisch, Raul. "El desarrollo económico en América Latina y algunos de sus principales problemas," *Revista de Ciencias Económicas* (Buenos Aires), Vol. 38, Series 3, No. 22 (March–April 1950).

Ribeiro, Darcy. "The Integration of Indigenous Populations in Brazil," *International Labour Review,* Vol. 85 (April–May 1962).

Rippy, J. Fred. "U.S. Postwar Aid to Latin America: An Exhibit of Incomplete Official Accounting," *Inter-American Economic Affairs,* Vol. 14 (Spring 1961).

Sauvy, A. "La population des pays d'Amérique latine. Vue générale sur leur état et leur croissance," *Population,* Vol. 18 (Paris), January–March 1963.

*Schultz, Theodore W. "Latin American Economic Policy Lessons," *American Economic Review,* Vol. 46 (May 1956).

*———. *The Economic Test in Latin America.* Bulletin No. 35. Ithaca, N.Y.: Cornell University, School of Industrial and Labor Relations, 1956.

Shelton, David H. "The Economic Growth of Latin America: Motivations, Prospects and Problems," *Journal of Inter-American Studies,* Vol. 1 (April 1959).

Teichert, Pedro C. M. "Latin America and the Socio-economic Impact of the Cuban Revolution," *Journal of Inter-American Studies,* Vol. 4 (January 1962).

Troncoso, M. P., and Ben G. Burnett. *The Rise of the Latin American Labor Movement.* New York: Brookman Associates, 1960.

United Nations. *Human Resources and Development in Latin America.* New York: United Nations, 1968.

———. *Urbanization in Latin America.* New York: United Nations, 1962.

———. *Economic Survey of Latin America.* New York: United Nations, 1957.

*Urquidi, Victor L. *The Challenge of Development in Latin America.* New York: Praeger, 1964.

Véliz, Claudio (ed.). *Obstacles to Change in Latin America.* New York: Oxford University Press, 1965.

Mexico

American Chamber of Commerce (Mexico), *Mexican-American Review.*

Banco de México. *Encuestos Sobre Ingresos y Gastos en México, 1963.* Mexico City: Banco de México, 1966.

Banco Nacional de México, S.A. *Review of the Economic Situation of Mexico.*

Beals, Carleton. *Mexican Maze.* Philadelphia: Lippincott, 1931.

*Brandenburg, Frank R. *The Making of Modern Mexico.* Englewood Cliffs, N.J.: Prentice-Hall, 1964.

Cline, Howard F. *Mexico: Revolution to Evolution, 1940–1960.* London: Oxford University Press, 1962.

Coe, Michael D. *Mexico.* New York: Praeger, 1962.

Duccoff, Louis J. *Los recursos humanos de Centro América, Panamá y Méjico en 1950–1980 y sus relaciones con algunos aspectos de desarrollo económico.* New York: United Nations Economic Commission on Latin America, 1960.

Espinosa Iglesias, Manuel. "Aspectos de la planeación económica en Méjico," *Investigación Económica* (Mexico), Vol. 23 (1962).

*Flores, Edmundo. "The Significance of Land-Use Changes in the Economic Development of Mexico," *Land Economics,* Vol. 35 (May 1959).

*Glade, William P., Jr., and Charles W. Anderson. *The Political Economy of Mexico.* Madison: University of Wisconsin Press, 1963.

International Bank for Reconstruction and Development. *The Economic Development of Mexico.* Baltimore: Johns Hopkins University Press, 1953.

La Cascia, Joseph S. *Capital Formation and Economic Development in Mexico.* New York: Praeger, 1969.

Lewis, Oscar. *The Children of Sánchez.* New York: Random House, 1961.

———. *Life in a Mexican Village.* Urbana: University of Illinois Press, 1951.

Library of Congress. *Handbook of Latin American Studies.* Annual.

Myers, Charles N. *Education and National Development in Mexico.* Princeton, N.J.: Princeton University, Industrial Relations Section, 1965.

Navarrete, Alfredo. *Mexico's Economic Growth: Prospects and Problems.* Austin: University of Texas Press, 1960.

Navarrete, Ifigenia M. de. *La distribución del Ingreso Nacional y el desarrollo económico de México.* 4 vols. Mexico: Fondo de Cultura, 1960.

Paz, Octavio. *El Laberinto de la Soledad.* México: Cuadernos Americanos, 1969.

Redfield, Robert. *Tepoztlán, A Mexican Village.* Chicago: University of Chicago Press, 1930.

Vasconcelos, José. *La Flama.* México: Compañía editorial, 1960.

*Vernon, Raymond. *The Dilemma of Mexico's Development.* Cambridge, Mass.: Harvard University Press, 1963.

Ward, Mary Jane. *Selected, Classified, and Annotated Bibliography of Books about Mexico, 1932–1952.* Philadelphia: Drexel Institute of Technology, 1954.

Zurita, Alonso de. *Life and Labor in Ancient Mexico.* New Brunswick, N.J.: Rutgers University Press, 1963.

CHAPTER 12
AFRICA

*Aboyade, Ojetunji. *Foundations of an African Economy: A Study of Investment and Growth in Nigeria.* New York: Praeger, 1966.

*Abraham, W. E. *The Mind of Africa.* Chicago: University of Chicago Press, 1962.

"African Trade Unions," *New Republic,* June 26, 1961.

"African Unionism," *New Statesman,* December 26, 1959.

Apter, David E. *Ghana in Transition.* New York: Atheneum, 1963.

Ashby, Eric. *Universities: British, Indian, African: A Study in the Ecology of Higher Education.* Cambridge, Mass.: Harvard University Press, 1966.

Barber, William J. *The Economy of British Central Africa.* Stanford, Calif.: Stanford University Press, 1961.

Barry-Braunthal, Thomas O. "African Unions Fight for Survival," *Times Review of Industry and Technology.* London: Time Publishing Co. (January 1965).

Beling, Willard A. *Modernization and African Labor.* New York: Praeger, 1965.

Benveniste, Guy, and William E. Moran, Jr. *Handbook of African Economic Development.* New York: Praeger, 1962.

*Berg, Elliot. "The Development of a Labor Force in Sub-Saharan Africa," *Economic Development and Cultural Change,* Vol. 13 (July 1965).

————. "Backward Sloping Labor Supply Functions in Dual Economies— The Africa Case," *Quarterly Journal of Economics,* Vol. 75 (August 1961).

*Berg, Elliot, and Jeffrey Butler. "Trade Unions," in James S. Coleman and Carl G. Rosberg, Jr. (eds.), *Political Parties and National Integration in Tropical Africa.* Berkeley: University of California Press, 1964.

————. *Major Issues of Wage Policy in Africa.* Geneva: International Labor Organization, Institute for Labor Studies, 1964.

Bohannan, Paul. *Africa and Africans.* New York: Natural History Press for American Museum of Natural History, 1964.

Brass, William, *et al. The Demography of Tropical Africa.* Princeton, N.J.: Princeton University Press, 1968.

Callaway, Archibald. "Creating Employment for Africa's Youth," *Inter-African Labor Institute Bulletin* (August 1964).

Clark, Paul G. *Development Planning in East Africa.* Nairobi, Kenya: East Africa Publishing House, 1965.

Davidson, R. B. "Labor Relations in Ghana," *The Annals,* 1957.

Davies, Ioan. *African Trade Unions.* Baltimore: Penguin, 1967.

de Wilde, John C. *Experiences with Agricultural Development in Tropical Africa.* 2 vols. Baltimore: Johns Hopkins University Press, 1967.

Eicher, Carl, and Carl Liedholm. *Growth and Development of the Nigerian Economy.* East Lansing: Michigan State University Press, 1969.

El-Kammash, Magdi M. *Economic Development and Planning in Egypt.* New York: Praeger, 1966.

Eshag, E., and P. J. Richards. "A Comparison of Economic Development in Ghana and the Ivory Coast Since 1960," *Bulletin of the Oxford University Institute of Economics and Statistics,* Vol. 29 (November 1967).

*Fearn, Hugh. *An African Economy.* New York: Oxford University Press, 1961.

Friedland, William H. "Unions, Labor and Industrial Relations in Africa." Annotated bibliography. Ithaca, N.Y.: Cornell University Press, 1965.

————, and Carl G. Rosberg, Jr. (eds.). *African Socialism.* Stanford, Calif.: Stanford University Press, 1964.

Gerteiny, Alfred G. *Mauritania.* New York: Praeger, 1967.

Ginzberg, Eli, and Herbert A Smith. *Manpower Strategies for Developing Countries: Lessons from Ethiopia.* New York: Columbia University Press, 1967.

Gonidec, P. F. "The Development of Trade Unionism in Black Africa," *Inter-African Labour Institute Bulletin,* Vol. 10 (1963).

*Greenough, Richard. *African Prospect: Progress in Education.* Paris: UNESCO, 1966.

Grove, A. T. *Africa South of the Sahara.* New York: Oxford University Press, 1967.

Gulliver, Philip H. *Social Control in an African Society.* New York: New York University Press, 1963.

Hance, William A. *African Economic Development.* Rev. ed. New York: Praeger, 1969.

*Hausman, Warren H. (ed.). *Managing Economic Development in Africa.* Cambridge, Mass.: M.I.T. Press, 1963.

Harbison, Frederick, and Charles A. Myers. *Manpower and Education: Country Studies in Economic Development.* New York: McGraw-Hill, 1965. Countries include Senegal, Guinea, the Ivory Coast, Malawi, and Uganda.

*Herskovits, Melville J. "African Economic Development in Cross Cultural Perspective," *American Economic Review,* Vol. 16 (May 1956).

*————, and Mitchell Harwitz (eds.). *Economic Transition in Africa.* Evanston, Ill.: Northwestern University Press, 1964.

Inter-African Labor Institute. "The Development of Trade Unionism in Black Africa," *Inter-African Labor Institute Bulletin,* Vol. 10 (May 1963).

————. *Migrant Labour in Africa South of the Sahara.* London: C.C.T.A., 1961.

International Labour Office. *Industrial Relations in Certain African Countries.* Labour-Management Relations Series, No. 22. Geneva: International Labour Office, 1964.

————. *Record of Proceedings of First African Regional Conference,* Lagos, December 1960. Geneva: International Labour Office, 1961.

————. *African Labour Survey,* Studies and Reports, New Series No. 48. Geneva: International Labour Office, 1958.

International Labour Review. "The Evolution of Labour Disputes: Settlement Procedures in Certain African Countries," Vol. 91 (February 1965), 102–230.

————. "Economic Development, Employment, and Public Works in African Countries," Vol. 93 (January 1965), 14–46.

Jennings, W. I. *Democracy in Africa.* Cambridge, England: Cambridge University Press, 1963.

*Kamarck, Andrew M. *The Economics of African Development.* New York: Praeger, 1967.

Loken, Robert De Long. *Manpower Development in Africa.* New York: Praeger, 1969.

Low, Stephen. "The Role of Trade Unions in the Newly Independent Countries of Africa," Chapter 9 in E. M. Kassalow (ed.), *National Labor Movements in the Postwar World.* Evanston, Ill.: Northwestern University Press, 1963.

Lynd, G. E. *The Politics of African Trade Unionism.* New York: Praeger, 1968.

McLaughlin, Russell U. *Foreign Investment and Development in Liberia.* New York: Praeger, 1966.

Morgan, W. T. W. *Population of Kenya: Density and Distribution.* New

York: Oxford University Press, 1966.

*Nelkin, Dorothy. *Pan African Trade Union Organization.* Reprint Series No. 221. Ithaca, N.Y.: Cornell University, School of Industrial and Labor Relations, 1967.

Roberts, Margaret. "African Trade Unionism in Transition," *The World Today,* Vol. 17 (October 1961).

Robinson, E. A. G. (ed.). *Economic Development for Africa South of the Sahara.* New York: St. Martin's Press, 1964.

Schapera, Isaac (ed.). *Western Civilization and the Natives of South Africa.* New York: Humanities Press, 1967.

Seidman, Ann. *An Economics Textbook for Africa.* London: Methuen and Company, 1969.

Skorov, George. *Integration of Educational and Economic Planning in Tanzania.* New York: UNESCO Publications, 1966.

Thornley, J. F. *The Planning of Primary Education in Northern Nigeria.* New York: UNESCO Publications, 1967.

United Nations Economic Commission for Africa. *Industrial Growth in Africa.* New York: United Nations, 1963.

United Nations Educational, Scientific, and Cultural Organization. *Meetings of Ministers of Education of African Countries.* Final Report. New York: UNESCO Publications, 1961.

U.S. Bureau of Labor Statistics. *Directory of Labor Organizations—Africa.* Washington, D.C.: Government Printing Office, 1962.

U.S. Library of Congress. *Agricultural Development Schemes in Africa.* Washington, D.C.: Government Printing Office, 1963.

Warmington, W. A. *A West African Trade Union.* London: Oxford University Press, 1960.

Whetham, Edith H., and Jean I. Currie (eds.). *Readings in the Applied Economics of Africa.* 2 vols. New York: Cambridge University Press, 1967.

Wraith, Ronald E. *Local Government in West Africa.* New York: Praeger, 1964.

Yesufu, Tijanl M. *Introduction to Industrial Relations in Nigeria.* London: Oxford University Press, 1962.

Zack, Arnold. "The Impact of Western-Trade Unionism on Africa," *Labor Law Journal,* Vol. 13 (July 1962).

CHAPTER 13
THE MEDITERRANEAN BASIN: SICILY

Camera di Commercio Industria ed Agricultura. *L'Area di Sviluppo Industriale di Palermo.* Ufficio Studi, 1961.

Novacco, Domenico. *Inchiesta sulla mafia.* Palermo: Libri Siciliani, 1963.

Renda, F. *L'emigrazione in Sicilia.* Palermo: Libri Siciliani, 1963.

Rivista di Servizio Sociale. *Un lavoro per lo sviluppo in Sicilia Occidentale* (Rome), Vol. 3, No. 3 (1963).

Rochefort, Renée. *Le travail en Sicile.* Paris: Presses Universitaires de France, 1961.

*Schachter, Gustav. *The Italian South: Economic Development in Mediterranean Europe.* New York: Random House, 1965.

Scotto, G. "Uno schema evolutivo per lo sviluppo del Mezzogiorno," *Studi Economici,* Vol. 21 (September–December 1966).

*Singh, B. "Italian Experience in Regional Economic Development and Lessons for Other Countries," *Economic Development and Cultural Change,* Vol. 15 (April 1967).

CHAPTER 14
THE MEDITERRANEAN BASIN: SPAIN

Cachero, Luis Alonso Martinez. *La emigración española antes el desa-rrollo económico y social.* Madrid: Nuevo Horizonte, 1965.
Giminez Mellado, José. "El factor humano en el desarrollo económico español," *Boletín de Estudios Económicos, Universidad Comercial de Deusto* (Deusto-Bilbao, Spain), Vol. 17, No. 57 (September–December 1962).
Green, Otis H. *Spain and the Western Tradition.* 4 vols. Madison: University of Wisconsin Press, 1963–1966.
*International Bank for Reconstruction and Development. *The Economic Development of Spain.* Baltimore: Johns Hopkins University Press, 1963.
*Kellenbenz, H. "The Impact of Growth on Government: The Example of Spain," *Journal of Economic History,* Vol. 27 (September 1967).
Lobo, M. M. "El desarrollo regional en España ante el II Plan," *Revista de Economía Política* (Madrid), May–December, 1966.
Payne, Stanley G. *Politics and the Military in Modern Spain.* Stanford, Calif.: Stanford University Press, 1967.
Tamames, R. "Los movimientos migratorios de la población española durante el período 1951–1960," *Revista de Economía* (Madrid), Sep-tember–December 1962.
U.S. Bureau of Labor Statistics. *Labor Law and Practice in Spain.* BLS Report No. 289. Washington, D.C.: Government Printing Office, 1965.
*Witney, Fred. *Labor Policy and Practices in Spain.* New York: Praeger, 1965.

CHAPTER 15
ROLE OF THE UNITED STATES IN ECONOMIC DEVELOPMENT

Balgooyen, Henry W. "Experience of United States Private Business in Latin America," *American Economic Review,* Vol. 41 (May 1951).
Krause, Walter. *Economic Development: The Underdeveloped World and the American Interest.* San Francisco: Wadsworth, 1961.
Millikan, Max F. *American Foreign Aid: Strategy for the 1970's.* New York: Foreign Policy Association, 1969.
*————, and Donald L. M. Blackner (eds.). *The Emerging Nations: Their Growth and United States Policy.* Boston: Little, Brown, 1961.
Montgomery, John D. *The Politics of Foreign Aid: American Experience in Southeast Asia.* New York: Praeger, 1962.
Radosh, Ronald. *American Labor and United States Foreign Policy.* New York: Random House, 1969.
*Ranis, Gustav (ed.). *The United States and the Developing Economies.* New York: Norton, 1964.
*Shearer, John C. "The Underdeveloped Industrial Relations of U.S. Corporations in Underdeveloped Countries," *Proceedings of the 17th Annual Meeting of the Industrial Relations Research Association,* 1964.

Sturmthal, Adolf, and David Felix. "U.S. Firms as Employers in Latin America," *Monthly Labor Review,* Vol. 83 (May 1960).

Windmuller, J. P. "Labor: A Partner in American Foreign Policy," *The Annals* of the American Academy of Political and Social Science, (November 1963).

INDEX